SANTA FE

The Autobiography of a Southwestern Town

Santa Fe

The Autobiography
of a Southwestern Town

by OLIVER LA FARGE
with the assistance of Arthur N. Morgan

foreword by Paul Horgan

7631

NORMAN : UNIVERSITY OF OKLAHOMA PRESS

By Oliver La Farge

Laughing Boy (Boston, 1929)
The Year Bearer's People (with Douglas Byers) (New Orleans, 1931)
Sparks Fly Upward (Boston, 1931)
Long Pennant (Boston, 1933)
All the Young Men (Boston, 1935)
The Enemy Gods (Boston, 1937)
The Changing Indian (ed.) (Norman, 1941)
As Long as the Grass Shall Grow (New York and Toronto, 1941)
The Copper Pot (Boston, 1942)
Raw Material (Boston, 1945)
Santa Eulalia (Chicago, 1947)
The Eagle in the Egg (Boston, 1949)
Cochise of Arizona (New York, 1953)
The Mother Ditch (Boston, 1954)
Behind the Mountains (Boston, 1956)
A Picture History of the American Indian (New York, 1956)
A Pause in the Desert (Boston, 1957)
Santa Fe: The Autobiography of a Southwestern Town (Norman, 1959)

LIBRARY OF CONGRESS CATALOG CARD NUMBER: 59–7958

Copyright 1959 by the University of Oklahoma Press, Publishing Division of the University. Composed and printed at Norman, Oklahoma, U.S.A., by the University of Oklahoma Press. First edition, June 30, 1959; second printing, August, 1959.

FOREWORD

i.

THE FIRST ISSUE of *The New Mexican* was dated November 28, 1849. In that year companies of United States citizens were proceeding to the gold fields of California by every possible route. One of these was the road west through Santa Fe. A member of an Eastern company kept a diary. His impressions of the Territorial capital of New Mexico bring us vivid reminders of what the city was like when its first local newspaper appeared.

Approaching Santa Fe with his wagon company in May, 1849, he saw a detachment of United States Dragoons coming up from behind. Since the summer of three years before, in 1846, when Santa Fe had been peaceably conquered by United States forces under Brigadier General Stephen Watts Kearny in the War with Mexico, all of New Mexico was United States territory. Garrisons were maintained, including that at Fort Marcy in Santa Fe. The Dragoons presented a gallant spectacle. To keep the strong sunlight off their faces they wore the native sombrero, and their swords and trappings made for the caravanner "a Pleasing noise."[1] The soldiers, who were returning to Santa Fe from Las Vegas, rode on at their fast trot, and the overland party continued at the pace of their work animals.

[1] All diarist references in this section are from William R. Goulding, "Journal of the Expedition of the Knickerbocker Exploring Company of the City of New York from Fort Smith overland to California. March 10 to September 18, 1849." Manuscript in Coe Collection, Yale University Library, New Haven, Connecticut.

They crossed low ridges flanked by grand mountains that lay back against the sky. Color was all about—every blue of air and rock, and the gold of grass, and green of mountain forest all stood forth clear and brilliant and taken by the sun and projected by shadow. Santa Fe was already a famous city at the southward turn of a famous trail which led from Independence, Missouri, to Chihuahua, Mexico. It was a city unlike any other in the nation, as the caravanner saw when he entered it.

He arrived there at nine o'clock at night and called at the United States Hotel on the plaza to engage rooms for his whole company. The landlord, "an American," could put them up. They dined well and had a "comfortable Drink" and went to bed. The diarist slept in the billiard room, where mattresses were laid both on the tables and under them. Gaming went on in another room where twenty or thirty "Americans and Natives" were at play with cards. Heaps of dollars stood on the table. The gaming license cost three thousand dollars a year, and the house took about a hundred dollars a night.

In the early daylight of the next day, the caravanner decided that the city had "a big and Noble name" but was in fact a "miserable looking place." But, like other visitors, the caravanner was to have a glimpse of what lay behind the earthen simplicities of Santa Fe architecture: patios of grace and shade, and rooms strong in traditional style. In the dwellings of several merchants he found that the interiors were "most splendidly fitted up and furnished." Later he dined at the officers' mess of Fort Marcy. The meal was as fine as any he ever ate. The tone was pleasing, too, for one of the officers nominated him, along with other guests—"the cellebrated Kit Carson" and "Cown, the Chief Muleteer of the Government convoy"—as the "Lions of the Day." There was plenty to drink, and later the dinner party moved on to a "Native fandango got up by their ladies."

Two violins, a guitar, and a male singer made music for twenty-five couples—officers and merchants, with their female companions, who were dressed "in as splendid and fashionable style" as the caravanner had ever seen back home, and he delicately noted that there was not "one married couple Present." Nonetheless, he had never seen ladies more genteel, and he gave them marks for their modesty and sedateness, even though he could not help but remark their practice in "the artillery of the eyes." He danced till late—the *cuna*—and relished a cold supper afterward. Santa Fe, for the moment, appealed to him. He retired to his quarters at the house of "Dr Edwards." He believed that the population counted from two to three thousand of the "poorest people in any town." The more fortunate citizens were provided with "excellent beds, but the lower class sleep on untanned skins," he discovered.

When he went to church he shuddered at the decorations—"a great number of the most miserable paintings, and wax figures, and looking glasses trimmed with pieces of tinsel." He heard the musicians from the fandango playing the same tunes in the choir loft, only more slowly, and he saw the same ladies now, if anything, more sedate than ever, and he added, "All appeared to have just left work to come to church." The more proper ladies of the town would, he thought, "appear to be much before the men in refinement, intelligence and knowledge of the useful arts. The higher class dress like the American woman, except instead of the bonnet they wear a scarf over the head, called a *reboso*. This they wear, asleep or awake, in the house or abroad. The dress of the lower class of woman is a single petticoat with arms and shoulders bare, except what may chance to be covered by the *reboso*. The men who have means to do so dress after our fashion, but by far the greater number, when they dress at all, wear leather breeches, tight around the hips and open from the knee down. Shirt and a blanket take the place of our coat and vest, and some sport a cotton or silk sash around the waist, mostly red, but sometimes of yellow, Red or Blue."

Out in the open again, he saw that the city was dependent for its firewood on the wooded foothills to the east and south; and he remarked the "jackasses passing laden with wood" to be sold at two bits the load. These animals—burros—were "the most diminutive" and were "usually mounted from behind, after the fashion of Leaping." He heard that they were the only work animals which could "be subsisted in this barren neighborhood without great expense," and it was true that the garrison mounts had to be driven to pasture twelve miles from the city, where soldiers guarded them at their grazing.

There was much movement on the trails in and out of Santa Fe. "Carravans," he said, "consisting of from twenty to forty waggons escorted by U.S. troops are continually travelling from this City to and fro from Chihuahua in Old Mexico loaded with stores and dry goods of every description." Like others with respect for experience and authority, he asked Kit Carson for advice about routes to the west and travel conditions. Leaving Santa Fe, he took with him a final impression: "The greatest place I ever saw," he wrote sardonically. "The houses . . . when viewed from Fort Marcy . . . presents the appearance of a vast quantity of pig styes." He was not much happier about the population, for it was "composed of scapegoats from every nation of the earth," and he "never heard such profanity or saw so much vice in two days. . . ." In a final shake of his head he said that "the government [of New Mexico] is in the hands of Col. [J.N.] Washington, a very mild and fine man, but he has not the nerve for such a place. . . ."

The caravanner went on past Galisteo to the old Río Grande Road, and through Albuquerque, and on his way.

ii.

In the city of Santa Fe today there are many touches of habit, style, and atmosphere which would be recognized by the California driver of a century ago. Santa Fe has kept her essential character throughout a hundred years of general change. The great landscape is immutable. Its color and shifts of light, its airs and graces of sky, are always different and always the same. Much of what gave offense to the gold-rush diarist and the conquering soldiers before him still survives—and now is admired by the modern devotees of Santa Fe.

For it is the very localism of the character of Santa Fe's style and habit which, scorned as primitive a century ago, now charms observers. Adobe houses, once seen as pig sties, now attract a sophisticated public by their close relation to the earth of which they are made. Blind walls of houses along the streets no longer seem inferior to front porches, but are valued for the patios and the privacy behind them. Works of native religious art which appalled the first Eastern immigrants are now sought for great collections. Santa Fe still brings its piñon wood from the foothills, though not on burros, and the scent of the sweet burning pitch is everywhere over the town. And if the population is not to be described in our day as composed of "scapegoats," it still carries suggestions of "every nation on the earth," for it is cosmopolitan to a high degree.

Santa Fe is a city of junctions and arrivals—many cultures and historical traditions meet there; many roads intersect at its plaza; and every day brings newcomers who, drawn by a reputation diverse and colorful, are at home immediately in a society whose special animation has never flagged in all its history.

iii.

If such is the character of the city, then the same animation must be found in the newspaper which has been its voice since 1849. This book, composed from the columns of the *New Mexican,* is the autobiography of Santa Fe throughout the last hundred years. It is a lively story, and it has the double interest of reflecting both local and national events with the particular vivacity of opinion and temper characteristic of Santa Fe. Through these columns of news and editorial matter, and with the benefit of Mr. La Farge's strong historical sense (illustrated here in his selection of material and in his own connective passages), Santa Fe tells us of her relation to many subjects of enduring interest. They range broadly, covering such topics as Indian affairs old and new, the Lincoln County war, man's accelerated triumph over distance (entry under January 19, 1867—the mail coach arrived from Junction City, Kansas, in six days and nineteen hours), the death of President Lincoln, the activities of Padre Martinez of Taos, the revival of Indian and Spanish arts and crafts, and the usual absorbing stories of local marvels, crimes, and mysteries. The paper frequently went brawling with its opposition, and now its inflamed rhetoric in debate calls up for us the forensics of the frontier.

And, faithful to its mission, the *New Mexican* gave spacious attention to the passions which periodically, as though in obedience to some law of energy baffling in origin, cyclical in nature, and entirely local, engaged the residents. Full accounts are given in this collection of the storms of controversy which arose over an invasion threatened by ladies from Texas who sought to bring to Santa Fe their own cultural colony; what was to be the character of the annual Santa Fe Fiesta; what was to be done with a statue of the Pioneer Woman; and other lively issues. The paper has spoken with a voice that always carried over the city and the state, and occasionally, in latter days, over the nation.

In 1926 the editorial columns made a list of Santa Fe's "special assets." These were, said the editor,

> Antiquity;
> Old landmarks;
> A stirring history;
> A foreign flavor;
> A Spanish atmosphere;
> Pueblo Indians;
> A unique type of architecture;
> Traditional and picturesque customs;
> A group of creative people, artists, writers, sculptors, musicians, architects;
> Individuality, unconventionality and picturesqueness in dress;
> A remarkable array of native talent;
> A cosmopolitan population;
> A democratic social atmosphere founded on individuality and not money.

It is still valid as a catalog of the elements which make up the style of Santa Fe, and the separate "assets" are generously illustrated in the pages which follow.

Paul Horgan

ROSWELL, NEW MEXICO

MAY 15, 1959

x

EDITOR'S PREFACE

THE *New Mexican* first appeared in the little town of Santa Fe, capital of the vast, wild territory of New Mexico, on November 28, 1849, succeeding the earlier *Santa Fe Republican*. Just how often it was published between the time of that initial number and the earliest continuous files, which begin in 1863, is material for endless argument. One number, an extra, for 1850 is preserved in the newspaper's own office; two others for that year, which I have not seen, dated June 18 and July 4, are in the possession of Mr. Thomas W. Streeter, of Morristown, New Jersey. From what we know of the history of the *Republican*, and from the *New Mexican*'s later course, we can pretty safely assume that it appeared irregularly, died at intervals, and was resurrected after lapses of varying length. There probably was enough continuity to justify the modern paper in counting 1849 as the year of its founding. Since Edward T. Davies was a publisher of both the *Republican* and the early *New Mexican*, and since both were printed on the same press and with the same font of type, an argument could be made for pushing the present paper's birthday back to September 10, 1847.

The absence of copies is not conclusive evidence. The newspaper's own establishment was gutted by fire in the 1880's. Early conditions in the Territory were not too favorable for the preserving of such archives, and we should have no files until well into the 1870's, as a matter of fact, were it not that a private individual had saved his copies since 1863 and turned them over to the state museum.

The searching of the files for material for the selections printed here was mainly done under the close direction of Mr. Arthur N. Morgan, a veteran newspaperman who for decades covered the news of Santa Fe. His selections and his comments, informed by long newspaper training and by a great reach of personal memory, have been invaluable.

Historians have searched and used the *New Mexican*'s columns, but, on the whole, its material, uncorrected, is a poor source of history. During most of its life the paper has been violently partisan and has engaged in unstinted controversy, with the result that its news was usually slanted shamelessly until recent times. The aim in this anthology is to narrate social history and to give the feel of the city and, secondarily, the Territory and state as they went changing down the years—an autobiography of a community like none other in the United States, perhaps like none other in the world.

Hence, for example, the news of Lincoln's assassination is of no interest to the purposes of this book; how Santa Fe mourned his death, however, has local color and is of interest. The assassinations of Garfield and McKinley were big news at the time, but they tell us nothing about our hero, and we pass them over.

One aspect of Santa Fe the *New Mexican* consistently ignored. For a long time—from at least the late 1830's on—the town was wide open. In the early issues there are no references to Doña Tules, about whom two novels have been written, her famous gambling establishment, or her equally famous bawdy house. Later continuations of these occupations are not reported, hardly even noted by editorials against them. As late as 1935 there were large and lively sporting houses not far from the plaza, and a lady who studied at Loretto Convent in the twenties has told me of going shopping along with other convent girls and a nun and seeing, shopping in the same store, a group of fancy ladies guarded by a madam—a conjunction not without charm. All that is over, but even the cleaning up passed without mention in the years of the *New Mexican*'s nadir.

I am deeply indebted to the many people who took a turn at the labor of page-by-page reading, an exhausting job, as I can testify. Mr. Jackson E. Towne, librarian of Michigan State University, on his own initiative furnished me with essential bibliographic information all put together and digested for me. I owe thanks for the constant co-operation, the friendliness, and the ready help, during several years of imposing on them, of Miss Gertrude Hill, librarian of the New Mexico State Museum, and her staff, Miss Ruth E. Rambo, Mrs. Elma A. Medearis, and Mrs. Edith G. Manmon.

The idea of this book originated with Hon. Robert McKinney, owner and publisher of today's *New Mexican*, who gave me the fullest help, and I am indebted also to Mr. Emory J. Bahr and Mrs. Anna K. Ormsbee of the paper's staff.

Oliver La Farge

SANTA FE, NEW MEXICO
MAY 15, 1959

CONTENTS

ILLUSTRATIONS

Santa Fe

Will Shuster
Zozobra
Religious procession of Fiesta
Queen of Fiesta
Hysterical Pageant of Fiesta
Indian woman selling goods in open-air mart

SANTA FE

The Autobiography of a Southwestern Town

CHAPTER 1

WEEKLY OF THE WILD FRONTIER

THE New Mexican *first appeared, as a weekly, on November 28, 1849, published by E. T. Davies and W. E. Jones. It is, perhaps, characteristic that it leads off with typographical errors in its heading—one in its motto, which reads* Magna est Veritas es Prevalebit, *and another in the date on the first page, November 24, 1849. On page two it is Wednesday, November 28, and on page three (the first Spanish page), under the masthead, November 28. Since November 28, 1849, did fall on a Wednesday, we can take this as the correct date of publication.*

The paper had other features that were long continued. It consisted of four pages, two in English and two in Spanish. Cut off from the world as Santa Fe was, with one mail a month, the editors made little effort to publish other than local news, which was presented in strongly editorial form. As small as the sheet was, available news did not fill its first issue, the columns of which were padded with humorous and literary material.

NOVEMBER 28, 1849: PROSPECTUS FOR A WEEKLY PUBLICATION, TO BE ENTITLED THE NEW MEXICAN.

The subscribers propose to publish, in this city, a weekly publication, with the above title, to be devoted to the interests of the Territory of New Mexico in general.

THE NEW MEXICAN, in Politics and Religion, will maintain a strict neutrality, regarding partizanship as utterly unnecessary and a barrier to the general good of our Territory.

The views entertained by the people of New Mexico, in Convention assembled, for the purpose of urging upon Congress the immediate formation of a Supreme Civil Government, will also find an able advocacy in the columns of THE NEW MEXICAN. The want of more efficient means to suppress the numerous Indian tribes that surround us, will be promptly laid before our Government.

The advancement of Literature, the Arts and Sciences, and Agriculture, will meet with general attention.

THE NEW MEXICAN will be published on a semi-medium sheet, and issued to subscribers at the low price of Seven Dollars per annum, or Four Dollars for six months, and Two Dollars and Fifty Cents for three months. To those of our friends residing out of the city, we would state, that Agents will be appointed in all parts of the Territory, of whom they will receive their papers regularly.

We learn that the wife of the late Mr. J. M. White has, at last, been deprived of her sufferings, having been shot by the Indians, who had her in possession. Major Greer, to whom was confided the task of treating with the Utahs for her recovery, came within sight of their camp, when she was immediately shot down, almost in the presence of our troops. Upon reaching the camp they found the body perfectly warm, and the savages retreated. Nothing was seen of her infant.

Major Greer captured two young Indians, a number of animals, and all their camp equipage.

THE CONGRESS OF THE UNITED STATES.

The affairs of the Territory demand, and doubtless will receive, the earliest possible consideration of the Congress of the United States....

Without adverting, at this time, to the mooted question of a State or Territorial organization for New Mexico—a question of

4

the greatest consequence to the whole people of this Territory— it is our purpose, briefly, to call the attention of the Government of the United States to a few of the pressing wants of the people, that can be remedied only by the action of the Congress of the United States.

The numerous murders and robberies committed since July last, by the Apaches, Navajoes and Utahs, who encircle this Territory, admonish all concerned, that it is unsafe to attempt to come here, or to go hence, unless travelling parties are sufficiently strong to protect themselves. The recent butchery of Mr. White and the male portion of his party, and the capture of Mrs. White, her daughter and female servant by the Indians, at the "Point of Rocks," call for a terrible and immediate retribution. The destruction and unjust appropriations of property at this same time, is entitled only to this passing allusion . . . .

MURDERS AND CRIMINAL CASES.

The caption of this article shows the unpleasant and melancholy feeling which falls to our lot to record. During the latter part of this month, an affray took place in this city between a Mr. Wheeler, latterly of St. Louis, and Captain Alexander Papin, formerly of the above place. The particulars of this affair run thus: a few days after the arrival of Capt. Papin, Mr. Wheeler wrote several notices and posted them up around town, which bore upon their face the representation of false statements as emanating from Papin. One of these documents were shown to Papin, which he tore down, and entered the store of Messrs. Austin & Daulton, for the purpose of reading it, when Wheeler followed him in. Capt. Papin remarked, that any person using his name in that style was a damn'd rascal, and turned around and asked Wheeler if that was his signature. Wheeler remarked that it was, at which time Captain Papin raised a yard stick, and had scarcely made the blow, when Wheeler drew a pistol and shot him just above the right temple. Captain Papin expired two days afterwards, and was buried with military honors.

Wheeler is now in our prison walls, enfettered with chains.

At the last term of our Court A. J. Sims was convicted of the murder of Johnson Jackson. He is to be executed on the 30th. . . .

We regret to state that Mr. John Adams was murdered at Pena Blanca, a few days since, by a party of Mexicans. The principal murderer has not as yet been arrested.

Charles Wagner, the murderer of Ebstein, whose case was to be tried at Taos last week, was postponed until the next term of the Court, on account of a very important witness.

MAY 5, 1850: NEW MEXICAN—EXTRA.

Ceran St. Vrain   Joab Houghton & T. S. Johnson
Publisher   Editorial Committee
   FOR CONVENTION
   County of Santa Fe
   Ceran St. Vrain
   T. S. J. Johnson
   Francisco Ortiz y Delgado

This is the next surviving issue of the paper. It consists of a single sheet, printed on one side only, in four columns. Two and two-thirds columns are given over to supporting the Territorial party against the new State party and denouncing Major Richard H. Weight of the latter, all relating to a meeting on acquiring statehood, which was held in the courthouse on April 20. New Mexico was then under military rule, and its citizens had been agitating for normal, civil, territorial status. Advice had been received that Congress would not consider that status, but might approve statehood, so the Territorial party moved for that. This part is printed in 10-point type.

A little over one column, in 8 point, gives a formal account in Spanish of the transactions at the April twentieth meeting. The chairman was F. A. Cunningham. The petition to the Governor that resulted was signed by Joab Houghton, Ceran St. Vrain, E. W. Prewitt, Domingo Fernandez, J. W. Folger, José María Abreu, T. S. J. Johnson, Merrill Ashurst, Murray F. Tuley, Donaciano Vigil, and Francisco Ortiz y Delgado.

*The last part of column four carries, in 6 point, the proclama-
tion issued by Military and Civil Governor John Munroe in response to the petition, dated April 23, 1850. It names Monday,
May 6, from sunrise to sunset, for voting "en los respectivos pun-
tos de los condados" for delegates to a constitutional convention,
to meet in Santa Fe on May 15. The allotment of delegates by
counties was: Taos, 3; Río Arriba, 3; Santa Fe, 3; San Miguel,
3; Santa Ana, 2; Bernalillo, 2; and Valencia, 5.*

*The Spanish is printed entirely without accents and is full of
errors. The English is clean.*

*Ceran St. Vrain was a famous mountain man and a close associ-
ate of Kit Carson, who played a considerable part in the history
of New Mexico.*

*After this we have nothing until 1863, as noted in the intro-
duction. It is too bad; Santa Fe seems to have been a lively place,
and one would like to know, at least, what the New Mexican
made of the capture of the capital by Confederates from Texas
and of its subsequent liberation.*

*To give some idea of the kind of material that was available to
an enterprising newspaperman during that period, we reprint here
two stories from the New Mexican of this century. The first, from
1911, needs no comment.*

MAY 18, 1911:

Ex-Governor L. Bradford Prince has dug up an old subscription
list which shows that more than sixty years ago, Santa Fe citizens
were liberal in subscribing for public purposes, and according to
tradition, they did not re-nig on their subscriptions, either. Here
is the start of the list, which is historical as well as instructive:

"We, the undersigned, agree to pay the sums opposite our respective names for the purpose of purchasing a printing establishment to be brought from the United States to Santa Fe, New
Mexico, July 16, 1850:

"Manuel Alvarez, $100.

"Juan Perea, $100.

"W. Z. Auguay, $100.

"Juan C. Armijo, $100.
"J. Manuel Gallegos, $100.
"J. Chavez, $100.
"Messery & Webb, $100.
"Wm. S. McKnight & Co., $100.
"Juan F. Otero, $100. (Vicar General)
"Benito A. Larragoiti, $100."

*The second of our fillers was published in 1902. It was run under the curious headline "*THE DIFFERENCE BETWEEN 1859 AND 1892.*" I have known typesetters and proofreaders who ran a year behind, but one running a decade behind is unusual.*

NOVEMBER 8, 1902:

In the early days of this territory political campaigns were not conducted in as quiet and peaceful a manner as they are now or have been of late years, nor were the majorities obtained very large. The following interesting episode of the delegate campaign in 1859, when Miguel A. Otero, of Albuquerque, father of the present governor [*also Miguel A. Otero*], was the Democratic candidate for that office and John S. Watts, a Santa Fe lawyer, was the Republican candidate, is published to show the difference in times, men and manners between 1859 and 1902.

In an issue of the New York Evening Journal in 1859, under the heading 35th congress, appears the following: "New Mexico has one territorial delegate. It has lately been Democratic, and is represented by Miguel A. Otero of Albuquerque, Bernalillo county. Mr. Otero is a lawyer and has been the delegate in congress from his territory since 1855. He is a Democrat."

In this connection the following from the editorial page of the Missouri Republican of September 27, 1859, will be found of great interest:

FROM ARIZONA.

"Mesilla, Arizona Territory, September 12, 1859.—In a speech made in our plaza on Sunday, the 4th instant, Judge Watts

charged Mr. M. A. Otero with neglect of duty towards his con-
stituents, and stated that on the night of the 2d of March, 1859,
during the pending of a certain appropriation bill before the senate, Mr. Otero was absent at a ball with his family. This Mr.
Otero resented by giving Judge Watts the lie, both in English and
in Spanish, in such a manner that it was impossible for Judge
Watts to overlook it. A challenge ensued, which Mr. Otero,
through his friend, Colonel Samuel J. Jones (Sheriff Jones) late
of Kansas, and now United States customs collector at this place,
promptly accepted; Frank Green of Santa Fe, acting as a friend
of Judge Watts. The weapons selected were Colt's navy 6-shoot-
ers, one barrel loaded, distance 15 paces. The parties met at sunrise on the 7th near the Mexican line. Mr. Green won the choice
of position, also the word. After the first shot, the friends of the
parties endeavored to effect a reconciliation between them, which
failed. The second and third shots were then fired without effect,
when, after a consultation with his principal, and other friends,
Mr. Green declared himself satisfied, and the parties were withdrawn from the field, the difficulty remaining unsettled.

"Both parties were brave and cool, and Mr. Otero won for
himself the golden opinions of all who witnessed the affair. . . .

*The next known number of the paper is Volume I (again),
Number 42, November 7, 1863, the first published by William H.
Manderfield. This and the succeeding issues for some years are
not in the possession of the* New Mexican *but in the library of the
State Museum, deriving from a private collection presented to
the Museum in the 1920's. Many of the issues have been clipped.*

*Manderfield had just bought the paper from C. P. Clever.
Earlier, it had belonged to a Dr. Charles Lieb.*

*The paper was a weekly of four pages—the first two in English,
the next two in Spanish. The Spanish was excellent in vocabulary
and grammar but execrable in spelling, as we might expect of
editors, proofreaders, and typesetters who knew a somewhat archaic Spanish by ear but had almost no contact with the language
in written form. For Volume I, Number 42, the mastheads of the
paper ran,* "THE NEW MEXICAN, SANTA FE, N. M., NOV. 7, 1863"

and "EL NOVO-MEJICANO, SANTA FE, NOVEMBER 6, DE 1863." *Setting aside the discrepancy in dates, we have two gross errors in seven words of Spanish. The motto then was " 'Tell my children to support the Constitution and the laws.'—Douglas."*

In 1863 the telegraph reached to Denver, but not to Santa Fe. "Telegraphic news" consisted of matter from Eastern and Denver papers, which came in the weekly mail. The first page was usually given to such items and advertising; local news appeared on the second page, largely in editorial form. The editors seem to have gone on the basis that there was no point in printing what everyone already knew but that it might deserve comment.

The Confederates, or "Texans," had been driven from New Mexico. Brigadier General James H. Carleton of the California Volunteers was military commandant and was trying to subdue the Navajos and Apaches and concentrate them on a small reservation at Bosque Redondo, under the walls of Fort Sumner, in eastern New Mexico. The state was also under attack from the east by Kiowas and Comanches.

More space was given to Indian troubles than to the Civil War, despite the paper's ardent Republicanism. At times the stock of newsprint ran out, and it was printed on brown paper about halfway between newsprint and butcher paper.

NOVEMBER 7, 1863: ENLISTING IN THE REGIMENTS.

Now is a good time to enlist as a volunteer.

A regiment is being raised, by authority of the government. Many a poor, healthy man, is now working as a peon, for scarcely anything, worthy to be called wages, and for equally scanty food and clothing. When a soldier, and is sick, a physician attends him. His officers are bound to treat him, with care and justice. He receives thirteen dollars a month, as pay, with good and abundant food and clothing. When mustered into service, he receives some portion of his pay in advance. He becomes entitled to a bounty of one hundred dollars. He will stand his chances, for the future favors, liberality and justice of the government. When discharged, there will be no danger, of his having to pay a portion due him, to some person not entitled to anything, under pretense that such person procures his pay from government. The laboring man can find no mode so easy, creditable and profitable, to discharge himself from poverty and servitude, as enlisting as a volunteer. The duties of the service promote patriotism, punctuality, courage and manliness.

The whole number of votes, including those of the volunteers and Embudo, cast at the September election for Delegate, exceeds 14,000. This shows a much larger population in New Mexico, than is found in either of the other Territories.

A few weeks since, the body of Frederick Smith was found dead upon the street leading from the Exchange Hotel to the church of San Francisco. He had kept a drinking saloon, on the west side of the Plaza. He was seen, the night of his death, to drink an almost incredible quantity of whiskey at one time. He went from his house, and doubtless died from apoplexy, caused by excessive drinking. So sure it is, that "John" will carry off his victims in the end, if they will remain, keeping up the "wrestle" with him. How many and how striking are the examples in New Mexico! Yet, who takes warning?

*In the Spanish portion of this issue is a story headed "*BRU-JERIA.*" A resident of Las Vegas was tried for killing a witch who was supposed to have given him tuberculosis. The jury found him guilty "en el querito grado," meaning "en el cuarto grado" or "in the fourth degree," and the judge gave him a light sentence. The story also mentions two youths of Mora who atrociously assaulted a woman who was a healer* (curandera), *apparently for suspected witchcraft, but makes no mention of any arrest or punishment.*

NOVEMBER 14, 1863:   THE NAVAJOES

Are on their walks for plunder. Look out, rancheros, for your herds and flocks. On Thursday of last week, about nine miles below Santa Fe, by the road over the mesa, to Pena Blanca, a deep

trail was made, by Indians crossing eastwardly, towards the Pecos.
They were on foot, and from the deep, permanent trail they made
upon the earth, are supposed to have been some two or three
hundred. Such a movement bodeth no good. A detachment of
soldiers were sent from here to scout for the Navajoes, but returned "without tidings." The Navajo is for plunder and escape
again, and may succeed. "Can such things be, and overcome us
like" a winter cloud, pestilence and tempest, "without our special wonder?"

*This story refers specifically to the Navajos, a tribe of Apaches
who had developed a special culture and grown to number somewhere between nine and twelve thousand, hence being one of the
strongest tribes in North America. Below will come other stories
dealing with "Indians." Note that, with rare, specific exceptions,
the term* Indian *was not used in reference to the farming Pueblo
Indians who were, in those times, the white men's dearly needed
allies. The Navajos were also farmers, but they were always ready
to drop the hoe and join a committee to steal sheep or whatever
else might offer.*

A. M. HUNT.

Our post master, has opened, adjoining the post office, a reading room, in which he has a choice selection of books, Spanish,
and English, scientifical, historical and miscellaneous. He receives, weekly, from the states, by mail and express, a full supply
of magazines and newspapers. His rooms are very pleasant and
elegantly fitted up. His enterprise is a new one in Santa Fe. It is
very different from the fandangos, and much less expensive. The
one occupies the feet and lower sentiments, the other the intel-
lect and the higher nature. The one brings a person in contact
with "all sorts" of the living, the other with the thoughts, knowledge and reasonings of the "mighty dead."—Dissipation of the
passions and time, leads to weakness and ruin. The discipline of
the mind and the virtues, to strength, usefulness, honor, influence
and prosperity. Persons known by the distinction of the "New

Style Turkies," may be kings, princes, almost any kind of "bugs" at the fandangoes and bailes. In the reading room and library, the intellectual princes, great thinkers and wise men, discourse through their works, to the mental, proud and immortal being of man's nature.

DECEMBER 12, 1863: THE GOVERNOR'S MESSAGE.

Gentlemen of the Council and House of Representatives . . .

INDIANS.

It is my disagreeable duty to again repeat that our Territory still suffers from the hostility of the Indian tribes which surround us. During the last three years our losses in life and property by these tribes have been greater than ever before suffered in the same numbers of years. Some progress however is being made towards reducing them to subjection and obedience to the Government authorities. Since your honorable bodies assembled last year, one very troublesome tribe—the Mescalero Apaches—have been reduced to comparative state of peace, and placed in such a situation on the Pecos river as will not only secure us against all further danger from that tribe, but according to present appearances they will soon cease to entertain a desire for their nomadic pursuits and become one of our industrious and thrifty Pueblos.

There are of this tribe about four hundred souls located at the Bosque Redondo, who, during the past summer cultivated about two hundred acres of land, raising thereon fair crops and in sufficient quantities to go far towards supporting them during the cold months of the winter. The industry which they have exhibited, and the aptness with which they apply themselves to the work of agriculture, evince a spirit in existence among them that will eventually lead them into the adoption of civilized modes of life should they for a few years more be properly treated, instructed and cared for.

The Utahs are observing their usual good conduct and it is to be hoped that by the kindness and liberality of the Government they will be induced to refrain from any hostile feelings or demonstrations against the people.

The Navajoes are still hostile and are at this time waging a relentless warfare against our citizens which renders insecure every highway and has left scarcely stock enough in the country for the ordinary purposes of domestic use.

These Indians occupy the finest grazing districts within our limits, and in their wanderings infest a mining region extending two hundred miles north by about the same extent east and west. By their hostile presence in that region of country, from which they obtain but a precarious subsistence by robbery and depredations upon our citizens, an immense pastoral and mining population is excluded from its occupation and the treasures of mineral wealth that are known to exist within the limits mentioned have remained untouched. The public interest demands that this condition of things should cease to exist. Brig. Gen. Carleton has taken the first step in the right direction and is pursuing the only policy by which the Indian problem can be solved, and the savages made to yield to the demands of advancing civilization. What is that policy? It is by force of arms and persuasion to compel them to leave the mountain districts where by instinct bandits and robbers always seek refuge to conceal their stolen plunder and elude pursuit and punishment. In the plains, Indians can always be reached and despoiled of the fruits of their robberies, and more than this, they can then be civilized and reduced to agricultural pursuits. Not so in the mountains, where the places and means of concealment are so abundant, and where contact with civilization is almost entirely excluded by the nature of the country.

In pursuance of this policy the Department Commander proposes to withdraw the whole Navajo tribe from their present locality of mountain recesses, and place them upon the Pecos river where there is an abundance of the finest land for agriculture and immense plains bordering upon the river for their flocks and herds to graze upon. There they can be taught the arts of civilized life whilst they are receiving the protection of Government arms against all enemies. What a change will this policy, successfully carried out, produce upon the future of New Mexico! . . .

The indications now are that the Department Commander will be successful in the prosecution of this policy. Already a large number of the tribe has been removed to the Bosque Redondo. Some of these are prisoners of war, captured by the troops in the campaign in the Navajo country and others are of those who have become tired of the war, and in order to obtain the advantages of peace, have willingly surrendered themselves and expressed a readiness to comply with the wishes of the authorities. Should these gradual diminutions continue, and they doubtless will, the tribe will shortly be reduced to a state of numerical weakness that will render its further opposition to our arms futile, and the last remnant will be forced from necessity to abandon their ancient homes and seek companionship with their fellows in the valleys of the Pecos.

It is well known that the Navajoes are somewhat acquainted with the arts of husbandry. During the campaign of the past summer the troops are reported to have seen many fields of fine corn and wheat. The peaches which they grow are said to excel those grown in any other part of the Territory and their melons have for years been celebrated for their good qualities. There is therefore much to hope from them after they shall have been thoroughly reduced to peace, and become contented to live in their new homes and cultivate the soil there given them.

This policy of locating the Indians should not stop with the Navajoes and Mescalero Apaches. It should be applied to all the tribes of New Mexico and Arizona. Peaceably if possible, forcibly if necessary. Too long have they roamed lords of the soil over this extensive and valuable tract of country. They are entitled to a portion of it for their maintenance, but to no more. The white man has an urgent necessity for the lands which have heretofore been thus dedicated to the unprofitable use of the savages and the white man must see to it that the savages are displaced to make room for him. In doing this there is no necessity for violating any of the rights which properly pertain to the Indians. The condition of the latter will be greatly improved, and if in making this improvement a savage custom or prejudice should have to be overthrown let the custom or prejudice go. If, in placing them in reservations, we put it beyond their power to scalp the white man and prevent them from celebrating a war dance over that scalp after it has been obtained, no great damage will have been done to the cause of Christianity nor will either of the races have suffered any detriment from the change.

During this period the paper regularly recorded the visits of businessmen from Leavenworth, then the eastern end of the Santa Fe Trail. It also ran editorial notices calling attention to the advertisements of important firms or supplementing the advertisements with a puff.

JANUARY 16, 1864:   SECOND VOLUME.

This week's paper concludes one year of THE NEW MEXICAN. We now commence a new year, and we solicit subscriptions of the old friends who desire to patronize us, and such new ones as desire to read THE NEW MEXICAN. It will continue steadily and permanently. Our subscribers may be sure of receiving their papers during the year.—It will in no respect fall short in style, matter and interest. We shall depend upon our friends to sustain it. We do not expect any patronage from the public printing. We shall defend and preserve our self-respect. We trust our friends, everywhere, will send in the cash for their subscriptions.

The following item is the first mention of Bishop (later Archbishop) Jean B. Lamy, who was the first bishop of New Mexico and the original for the hero of Willa Cather's Death Comes for the Archbishop.

JANUARY 23, 1864:   BISHOP LAMY.

This Prelate has arrived at the Arizona gold mines, with Major Willis and his military command. A letter has been received, at this place from him, by Vicario Quillon, dated the 19th of December. The party reached the mines on the 10th of that month. Between that time and the 19th, the Bishop with Major Willis, had visited and examined much [*sic*], the mines and surrounding locations. The Major had selected a site for his Post near the mines. It is in the midst of abundant pasture. Wood for fuel was plenty, between three and six miles. Building timber within fifteen miles. The number of persons at the mines, was not large. The miners could not work and obtain much gold, for want of water, with which to wash the dirt. They expect water and corresponding success in the spring. Provisions were scarce and prices high, so much so, that many had gone to winter elsewhere. Major Willis' command arrived safely, and in good condition. The Bishop had found travelling in his ambulance so difficult, that he had parted with it, and taken solely to the saddle. He was in the midst of the finest kind of trout fishing. He had delivered to the persons at the mines, the letters placed in his hands at Santa Fe, for that purpose. He had some idea of going as far as Los Angeles in California. He probably will not. In case he does not, his return may be expected early in March.

SHAMEFUL.

We have heard of what we hope never will again occur in Santa Fe. It is, that at a fandango, a few evenings since, two of the females became insulted and enraged at each other, and that American men present endeavored to inflame the ill will and violence of the two women, the one against the other, and that a ring was formed and knives placed in the hands of each, for a desperate fight.

We hope no American will so far forget the dignity of human nature—his name and race, as to be found encouraging, again, such an exhibition of passion and violence between two females who, but for being animated and excited by spectators, would restrain within decent bounds their personal animosities.

JANUARY 31, 1864:

Reliable information has been received in town, that Col. Carson, with a portion of his command, has passed through the Cañon de Chelle, making war upon the Navajoes, in the places of their safest residences, retreats and fastnesses. In his route, his command killed twenty three Indians and took one hundred and fifty prisoners. The passing of the Cañon, with a military body, has been several times, as we are informed, attempted by other commanders, such as Gen. Sumner and Col. Miles, and perhaps Gen. Canby. It may be that some command succeeded, but we are not now, so informed. The success of Col. Carson, will distinguish him and those with him. They deserve, and will receive the gratitude of the people, for every Indian they have killed or made captive. Go on gallant Kit, says New Mexico, and "wipe out" the hostile Indians.

This is one of the very few references in the New Mexican *to the remarkable campaign by which Kit Carson, then a colonel of U. S. Volunteers, broke the Navajos. He was in fact the first to pass through Canyon de Chelly (as it is now written), a great natural fortress.*

FEBRUARY 6, 1864: MEXICAN SOLDIERS.

We have often, and with much pleasure, received warm recommendations from officers of the regular army, in favor of the patience, good order and discipline of volunteer Mexican soldiers. We have ever thought, since we have contemplated upon the matter, that they ought to possess excellent elements, to form good and reliable soldiers.—Their country is high, mountainous and healthy. No part of the United States surpasses this country in climate and health. The people are raised abstemiously. Their diet is simple and frugal. They are always surrounded by dangers. The Indians are their natural enemies. If they, in spirit and action are not equal to physical circumstances where they are born and raised, there must be some defects in the opinion, instruction or the direction of pride and ambition. Army life will correct these defects, if they exist. Motives will become higher and more intense. Pride will grow warmer and more honorable. We know how patiently this people will bear hunger, fatigue and various privations. Travel and campaigns seem natural to them. The soldiers of the first regiment are said to have improved, since the first day they were mustered into service. They have recently done excellent service, in the Navajo country, under Carson's command. These men deserve high credit and consideration. We trust they will receive such from the government and country. As the government and politics of the world now are, and especially in North America, the true military spirit and merit, should be carefully cultivated and rewarded. Great events are still ahead.

FEBRUARY 13, 1864:   THE CONVENT SCHOOL.

We have observed with anxious solicitude the progress of this school. It is managed and taught by a branch of the Sisters of Charity, as we understand. It is under the patronage and supervision of the Bishop. It was commenced by Sisters from the United States. They now manage it. There have been additions to their numbers, from native women of New Mexico. The Sisters endured many privations and sore trials, at their commencement in this country.—They have by patience, endurance, christian hope and merit, overcome the most of their difficulties. They have the complete confidence of the community at large. None but females, of course, are admitted to their school. Their school is of two parts. One is composed of scholars who board in the convent, are educated there, are subject to all the regulations, and enjoy all the rights and privileges, of scholars *within* the convent. The other part consists of a school within the convent buildings, but of scholars who attend from the city during the day, and who are not subject to the discipline of those who board within the convent.

THE BROTHER'S SCHOOL.

Like the Sister's, has two apartments. One is occupied by scholars, who board within the school, and submit to all the discipline by day and by night, and share all the benefits and privileges of the chief school. The other is where the boys of town, go and are taught during the day, and from where they return to their parents, friends and families during the night. This school is very prosperous. The teachers are Frenchmen from France.

They belong to the Brotherhood, and are devoted to it, we believe for life. They attend to no other business or interests. They are not priests, they are governed by an universal head. They teach English, Spanish and French, and we presume the ancient languages. The price of board and tuition per annum, is two hundred dollars. They have over forty, permanent boarding pupils.—In their exterior school, they have a multitude of the boys of the town. We take pleasure, daily, in seeing the cleanly, joyous little fellows, going and coming from the place, where they receive the seeds of instruction, from which shall grow the future rulers, teachers and business men of New Mexico.

These two schools are now Loretto Academy and St. Michael's High School and College and are still served, respectively, by the Sisters of Loretto and the Christian Brothers. Like the bringing of the Sisters of Charity to found a hospital the following year, they exemplified Archbishop Lamy's energy and progressivism. At this time, no public schools or other regular, properly equipped schools existed in New Mexico.

FEBRUARY 27, 1864:

The mail came in very good time on Thursday. Our paper was so filled with matter, already set up, that we cannot devote space this week upon the news. It, however, does not disclose, any very important army news.—The political and Congressional increase in interest. When space will permit, we will give some of these matters to our readers.

APRIL 2, 1864:   MORE THAN TWO HUNDRED YEARS OF INDIAN MURDERS AND ROBBERIES DRAWING TO A CLOSE.

An event is upon New Mexico, which would not fail to attract marked attention were it not for the mighty national drama displayed in the states. [*There follows a flowery passage on Indian troubles from the arrival of the first Spaniards until recent times.*]

. . . Commanders seemed to think that if they could get through with their temporary duties here without positive censure, or with some slight commendation, it mattered not what became of the country or its inhabitants. To this were some exceptions. Colonel Bonneville commanded an expedition against the Apaches, in the south-west, which . . . was creditable. Gen. Garland sent a campaign against the Utes and Jicarillas, in which was the present Gen. Carleton, Col. Carson and Col. St. Vrain, now a citizen. When Gen. Carleton took command of this department, in August, 1862, the Indians were devastating the Rio Abajo and other portions of the territory. . . . The Texans [*Confederates*] had just left. From the then general condition of affairs, there was no security they would not return. Carleton had to provide against such a contingency. So soon as he felt he could use his forces against the Indians, he arranged them and put them in motion, and the results disclose a new epoch in New Mexico. For the first time, for generations following generations, have permanent peace and safety with the Indians been brought within sure grasp. . . . Carleton has caused the reduction of the Mescalero Apaches, and a portion of them have joined the colony at Ft. Sumner. The Navajoes have been so reduced, that 6,000, as we are informed, have gone and are going to the colony. Such are some of the events passing here. Carleton has arrived at the point that ages have so long desired in this land. . . . While the great rebellion is being driven to extremities, it is a matter of pride and great satisfaction that the government has supplied the commander, officers, men and means, whose joint action with the New Mexican volunteers, have brought within power and control the savages who have been the blight and ruin of New Mexico for more than two centuries.

THE MERCHANTS AND FREIGHTERS.

Have started or are preparing soon to start to the States to prosecute their business. In former years, it would have been considered as a very serious and dangerous enterprise, but now it has become a matter of business, so now crossing the plains from two to four times a year with the "big wagons," and long trains of oxen or mules, make the spring, summer and fall employments of owners and laborers. A correct statement of the number of wagons, oxen and mules employed in this business, would surprise the quiet, house farmer of the States. From Santa Fe to Kansas city or Leavenworth, is over 800 miles. The road, however, is the best natural road, of anything like similar extent, upon the face of the earth. It runs, until it reaches Las Vegas, coming this way, one dry vast plain. The Laboring Mexicans, generally, like to go trips as teamsters and in other service across the plains. The procuring of such men, this year, is more difficult than usual. This is much owing to so many peons and laborers, having entered the volunteer service. The United States soldier's pay, much exceeds the former prices for Mexican labor, in New Mexico. A large number of peons, have extricated themselves from their thraldom as servants, by going into the United States volunteer regiments. Owners and masters of freight trains, now have to pay a fair price, to obtain Mexican teamsters and herders.

Formerly the sheep in this country were never sheared, except a few had some wool "jerked" away for domestic uses. Now the shearing for wool has become a matter of profit. The wool is taken to the States, in the wagons that are sent for goods. Some trains will not leave until the shearing time shall be over, so they can carry the wool at a low freight. Thus the traffic of this country continues to enlarge, and the comforts and property of the people to increase.

It is impossible to avoid remarking that the statement that the Santa Fe Trail ran over "one dry vast plain" from Leavenworth all the way to Las Vegas, a town lying seventy-five miles east of Santa Fe, is a classic example of the booster in operation. Among other items, this statement happily ignores the Raton Pass, over which the road climbed to better than ten thousand feet. At this period there was not only competition between various major routes to California, but men were also beginning to think of spanning the continent by rail; the choice of routes for the principal railroads could make or break cities and whole territories.

MAY 15, 1864: THE GOVERNMENT AND THE NAVAJOES.

We understand that something over 600 more of these savages have surrendered to take their fate with others of their tribe now colonizing at Bosque Redondo. We think over 7,000 are now gathered. The Secretary of the Interior has recommended that an appropriation of one hundred thousand dollars be made by Congress, for the present maintainance of the colony, and the furnishing of those Indians with implements of civilization and labor, so they may soon become self-sustaining by husbandry, with their pastoral resources. The New York *Times* seems to doubt its being a better policy to feed and take care of them, than to fight them. It fears their treachery, and quotes the repeated treaties they have made, and as often broken.—That they are perfidious, as a tribe, we believe. That if left to live at large in their cañons and fastnesses, where they have so long lived and roamed, they would soon again break treaties, rob, murder and kidnap, we do not doubt. To maintain the usual military force in New Mexico, the costs to the government are enormous. . . .

Another thing: The *Times* does not seem to consider the enormous losses the people of this country endure whenever the Indians are in hostility. They sweep the sheep from the plains, and the herds from the ranches. It has not been uncommon for an owner to be robbed of five, ten and twenty thousand sheep in a day, and each sheep of the value of two dollars to the owner. While the government has its outlays, in fulfilling its obligations to this people, the people themselves suffer immensely whenever the Indians are abroad upon plunder. This can be prevented by carrying out, wisely, the plan the government is now adopting. Let the plan be executed in stern, good faith, with high intelligence and integrity, and the benefits will soon be "clearly seen."

The damage claimed in this article to have been done by Indians is fantastic. Few ranchers ever owned as many as 20,000 sheep, and seldom were as many as 5,000 bunched in a single flock, for obvious reasons of enabling the animals to graze. Exaggerations of this kind were common to frontier newspapers from early times until westward expansion and expropriation of Indian lands had ended.

On May 27, 1864, the New Mexican announced that it was then owned by the partnership of Wm. H. Manderfield and Tho. S. Tucker. Mr. Tucker seems to have brought with him a better command of written Spanish, since the Spanish masthead was changed to read "El Nuevo-Mejicano." Shortly the partners reversed Manderfield's previous views of General Carleton and his policies, to become his leading opponent. In the "Salutatory" that announces the partnership, the paper expresses the usual lack of animosity towards anyone, loyalty to the Union without partisanship, and intent to serve all. In the last two paragraphs, the owners get down to some of the brass tacks of the frontier newspaper business:

MAY 27, 1864:

. . . Owing to the advanced prices of labor and all kinds of printing material, the publication of the paper will incur a considerable expense: we therefore require that all our business transactions be on the cash system.

Being as we are practical printers, and in as much as the paper alone will hardly pay expenses, we would respectfully solicit a portion of public patronage in job printing, as well as subscriptions, and hope in all cases to give entire satisfaction, feeling confident that we will be able to execute printing in as good style and as promptly as can be done in the Territory.

JUNE 3, 1864:   THE UNITED STATES AND MEXICO.

The national representatives have unanimously declared that no foreign government should be recognized by the United States while the Mexicans continue to struggle for the maintenance of their own. This, though galling to every true American, is perhaps all that can be done in the present unfortunate condition of our domestic affairs, and we must be satisfied with it for the present.

France has seized Mexico to secure the payment of bonds, held by her citizens, amounting in the aggregate to about seventy million dollars. This is the pretence; but the facts stare us in the face that Mexico is a conquered country, and will soon be under the sceptre of the Austrian, Maximilian, who assumes the title of Emperor, and is to be sustained by French bayonets and French gold until he becomes able to sustain himself.

In the Spanish half of the paper a full column was devoted to this topic. Maximilian's career thereafter, including his overthrow, was hardly mentioned, and his execution was ignored. The paper did, however, reprint, in the Spanish section only, a long account from a Spanish newspaper of his final burial in Austria, from which readers could reasonably infer that he was dead.

AUGUST 12, 1864:   INDIAN OUTRAGES.

Are becoming of frequent occurrence. An express arrived in town on Tuesday last, bringing information that the train of Charles G. Parker, which left here about two weeks ago for Chihuahua, had been attacked by Indians, and the mules taken. We are indebted to Mr. Stevens, who had the letter from the wagon master in his possession, for the following particulars: The train was camped about twenty miles below the Gallinas Mountains, and while driving the mules to water, the Indians (supposed to be Mescalero Apaches,) made their attack and run off all the animals but five. The wagon master, Lovell, with some of his men, mounted the remaining animals and pursued the Indians for about a mile, when the latter dismounted, drove their horses and mules into the timber, and formed for a fight. The encounter was of the most desperate nature, the combatants being at times within a few yards of each other, and lasted until Lovell received two severe wounds in the hip, and one of his men had his leg broke by a ball above the ancle, when they returned to the train. The letter states that they are twenty miles from permanent water, and that unless it rains or assistance arrives they will be compelled to abandon the train.

About the 1st of August, twenty-three animals were stolen from Ramon Vigil and others near the town of Santa Clara, by Navajoe Indians.

On the 4th of August, three Indians, supposed to be Navajoes, stole some stock near the town of Abiquiu, drove it as they supposed to a secure place, and returning to the herd killed a beef. While absent, the herders found the stock tied with Navajoe ropes, and raising an alarm, the Indians were frightened off.

On the night of the 5th inst., nine animals were stolen from the same place. The thieves were followed, and one of the horses retaken, together with three others that had been stolen from Tierra Amarilla about two months ago.

Nine men, it is said, were killed last week at Chaparito by the Mescalero Apaches, and the same Indians run off all the sheep belonging to Don Tomas Baca, of Las Vegas.

It is of interest that this article does not identify the "town of Santa Clara" as a Pueblo Indian settlement. During this period the inhabitants of the nineteen pueblos of New Mexico were evidently regarded as being almost of another race than those who were called "Indians." The Pueblo of Santa Clara is about twenty-five miles west and north of Santa Fe, on the west bank of the Río Grande. In the first half of the nineteenth century it was much harassed by Navajos.

AUGUST 19, 1864:   ANOTHER TRAIN GOBBLED UP.

The train of Mr. Peter Allison was taken by Comanche Indians at the lower Cimarone Springs, and all the Americans with it butchered. The circumstance of this melancholy affair as related by the Mexican teamsters who arrived here on Sunday evening last, are substantially as follows: The train had encamped to prepare their dinner, and some were playing cards.—While thus engaged, entirely unsuspicious of danger, a party of about two hundred Comanches came over the brow of a hill and immediately charged upon the camp. The wagon master, who was the only man in the party armed, fired four shots into them, when he was lanced and an arrow shot through him. The Indians then butchered the remaining Americans, scalped three of them, and horribly mutilated their bodies. The Mexicans were given a wagon with two yoke of oxen, and were allowed to return unmolested. The Comanches were very proud and defiant, and boasted that if Gen. Carleton came out they would kill him too, as he had taken their lands and given them to the Navajoes. They threatened to take all the trains and kill every American they could find.

One of the Indians told the Mexicans that on the previous day they had killed forty men belonging to a train that had preceded them a few days.

At about this time, the paper made an important change in its policies and politics when, while remaining firmly Republican, it turned against Territorial Governor Connelly and General Carleton and, above all, against the plan of confining the Navajos at Bosque Redondo, near Fort Sumner. The first signs of this change may be the appearance of the notices of "Indian Outrages" quoted just above. On September 16, the New Mexican *berates its rival,* The Gazette, *for having printed the full text of Governor Connelly's proclamation announcing the subjugation of the Navajos. On May 15, the* New Mexican *had summarized a proclamation to that effect with approval; whether its new attack refers to that, or to another, is not clear.*

It then goes on to say of the Navajos:

SEPTEMBER 16, 1864:

. . . Those that have surrendered are known to be the poor and defenseless, who, after having their crops destroyed were willing to surrender under the promise of being fed. But the rights, power and pride of the nation is [*sic*] scarcely touched; send back the prisoners, we would say then, to their own country, and there compell the whole tribe to maintain themselves, as they were compelled to do for years at a time under the Mexican Government, instead of taxing the treasury annually for an indefinite number of years for their support under circumstances that gives [*sic*] us no hope of a permanent success.

The statement that these warriors had been "compelled" to maintain themselves is a way of saying that they were totally free and raided at will that is really remarkable.

The New Mexican's *opposition to the existing Navajo policy led the paper into a surprising attitude of sympathy towards those Indians. The suddenness and violence of the shift suggests that its motivation was political, but in the end the newspaper turned out to be right. The policy aimed to confine not less than ten thousand people on forty square miles of semiarid land lacking in irrigation, with the idea that in a few years they would become peaceful farmers like the Pueblos. The Navajos were already good farmers, but they were free men and devoted to their wild homeland. It proved impossible to raise a crop at Bosque Redondo. The Comanches looked on the area as their preserve and raided it constantly. There was not even enough firewood.*

The next two extracts are fair samples of the New Mexican's *treatment of this subject.*

DECEMBER 23, 1864:   STARVED TO DEATH.

Near the Pecos Church, the bodies of some fifteen Navajoe Indians were observed a week or two since, exposed to the view of the traveller and the instincts of the wolf. The Superintendent of Indian Affairs, we are happy to learn, has made arrangements for their burial. These poor creatures were prisoners of war on their way to Fort Sumner, and perished with starvation during the severe weather which occurred the beginning of the past month, and were permitted to go without burial for five or six weeks. Possibly photography might have drawn from their sightless orbs the paradise of the Bosque Redondo; and the Translator, had he been there, could have caught from their dying lips, it may be, the sweet expression, "Content, content!" as in delirium they dreamed of the Pecos Reservation.

JANUARY 20, 1865: MORE THIEVING AND MURDER.

It is our unpleasant task to chronicle more robberies and a murder, undoubtedly the work of the escaped Navajoes from the Bosque Redondo. . . . [*There follows an uncritical retailing of every recent report or rumor concerning the presence of hostile Indians, possibly Navajos.*]

The question is simply this: Is it better for the people of New Mexico to be liable to Indian depredations with the right to pursue and kill them, or, is it more satisfactory to have them located on a Reservation near our settlements, under the protection of the Commanding General, where they can sally out and commit their outrages at will, and the people prohibited from chasing them? The latter proposition (Carleton's policy) adds insult to injury.

Yet, strange to say, there are in our midst a few who advocate the latter plan in order to uphold the vain and empty theory of a single man. But, thanks, the people are beginning to investigate the project of locating fifteen thousand Arizona Indians in our center, and when they have an opportunity they will render a verdict that will, to some extent, blast the star-ry aspirations of a certain individual.

JANUARY 6, 1865: THE NEW BUILDING.

Of Messrs. Elsberg & Amberg, referred to in our article on the Masonic Dedication, requires more than a passing notice. It is by far the most commodious and elegant building in New Mexico, and we doubt if it has its equal west of the Missouri River. It is situated on the northwest corner of the Plaza, is two stories high, 90 feet front, 130 feet in depth, with a portal[1] around the entire front and side. In its construction was consumed the enor-

---

[1] A *portal* (accent on the last syllable) is a sort of veranda, usually without outer rail and with the floor flush with the street or patio on which it fronts, the roof of which is carried on heavy posts. The term (plural *portales*), with its Spanish pronunciation, has passed into New Mexican English. In the sixties and seventies almost all commercial buildings had *portales* that entirely sheltered the adjacent sidewalks.

mous amount of 300,000 feet of lumber, 150,000 adobes, and 90 kegs of nails. All the articles used in its construction were of the best material and quality; the lumber being brought from their own mill, where it had been prepared especially for the purpose. The house contains twenty-six rooms. The lower story is divided into store rooms and occupied by the Messrs. Zeckendorf, James Hunter, Esq., and Messrs. Elsberg & Amberg. The corner store occupied by the latter firm is 28 feet by 31, with a wareroom attached 33 feet wide and 80 feet deep, and has a commodious and spacious cellar. The upper story, leading to which are five winding staircases, elegant specimens of workmanship, is laid out for private apartments and warerooms, and contains two magnificent halls occupied respectively by the Masonic and Odd Fellows' Lodges. The entire building is well lighted with large windows, which with the judicious arrangement of the rooms, give it a peculiarly light and tasteful appearance for a building of its strength and solidity. Altogether, it is a fine specimen of architecture, a credit to Santa Fe, and an enduring testimony of the enterprise, liberality and public spirit of those sterling business men and gentlemen, Messrs. Elsberg & Amberg.

On February 3, 1865, the New Mexican *ran its first article on the projected railroad "from Atchison via Topeka and the Neosho Valley in the direction of Santa Fe" with great hopes that the road would soon be built to that city. The railroad reached Lamy, New Mexico, its nearest point to Santa Fe, in 1878.*

At this time the New Mexican *was furiously at war with* The Santa Fe Gazette. *Much of the matter of the disputes was absurdly trivial, and an essential part of the argument was attempting to show that the rival paper, or someone it supported, had at some time during the Civil War wavered in support of the Union. The following sample is included to show the general style. The whole article, which is four times as long, is too dull and confused to be worth reprinting.*

MARCH 10, 1865:

We would not condescend to notice the malignant and abusive articles in the GAZETTE of last week, under the head of "Another witness on the stand"—if it were not for a desire on our part to do justice to a high civil officer of this Territory.

Like the fish that naturalists inform us, in order to shield itself from its enemy, possesses the faculty of emitting a dark fluid, sufficient to color the water, and there by effect its escape, so too, the GAZETTE, when called upon to make the issue, and make a manly reply, to a provoked attack, seeks to shield itself and escape by indulging in low truculent abuse against some of our Territorial officers, and no one has been more the recipient of this wholesale abuse, than Chief Justice [*Kirby*] Benedict.

But we propose briefly to notice this article, although it will be well remembered, that every statement therein made is an assertion without any proof, save the *ipsi* [*sic*] *dixit* of the Editor himself.

APRIL 28, 1865:

The southern stage arrived on Wednesday last. We learn from the New Mexico Press that they had a grand celebration in Albuquerque over the fall of Richmond. Speeches were made, cannons fired, toasts drank and a good time had generally. Among those most prominent getting up the celebration were marshal Cutler, Wm. J. Strachan, W. H. Henrie and our old friend Ben Stevens. The whole proceedings were worthy the patriotic citizens of Albuquerque.

MAY 5, 1865:

The last mail from the east, brought to our citizens the unwelcome and appalling intelligence of the assassination of Abraham Lincoln, the late President of the United States. The sad tidings flew through the city with electric speed, and never in the history of Santa Fe was there such a sudden and general depression and gloom cast over her citizens.

When the news was first made known; it was universally hoped that it wanted confirmation, that it was too horrible, too strange to be believed, but alas, after a glance at the telegraphic despatches, it was found to be too true, that Abraham Lincoln was no more, that one of the mighty of the nation had, at an untimely hour, unfortunately, both for the friends and foes of the Government, fallen a victim to a blow of a cowardly assassin. As if by general consent after the unhappy and awful conviction had forced itself upon the minds of our inhabitants, that the late intelligence was true; the business houses were all closed.

An informal meeting was held at the Hall of the House of Representatives, preparatory to a more general meeting of the citizens to give expression to their feelings.

After the adjournment of the meeting, all the quarters occupied by officers, soldiers or persons connected with the military service, were hung with heavy drapery, and soon the palace of the Governor, and the houses of the civil officers, and the citizens in general living on and contiguous to the Public Plaza, displayed from their fronts the dark emblems of death.

Truly the Sunday following was a sad and mournful day with the citizens of Santa Fe, there was scarce any sound save every half an hour the deep roar of cannon from Fort Marcy, which together with the intervening stillness, and the dark drapery on every house, betokened too plainly, that some awful and terrible calamity had befallen our nation.

According to the direction of the committee of arrangements, public notice was given to the citizens that a general meeting, would be held in front of the Palace at 3 p. m., Monday, at which place, a neat platform was erected, and highly embellished appropriate to the occasion. At the hour appointed all the military and civil officers of this city, and the largest assemblage of citizens ever known in the Territory of New Mexico, collected in the public plaza, in front of the Palace. The officers elect took their seats, an appropriate air from the military band of this place, indicated that everything was ready for the occasion.

His Excellency Governor Connelly, the President of the meeting, was the first to break the deep silence that pervaded the assembly, by explaining in both English and Spanish in the shortest, strongest and most appropriate terms, the object of the meeting, and paying a high but just tribute of respect to the memory of our late and lamented President, after which Chief Justice Benedict, as Chairman of the Committee on Resolutions, offered a series of resolutions, very appropriate, and we think expressing exactly the sentiment of our entire population, after the resolutions together with those of Captain Quintana were read they were unanimously adopted. After which at the solicitation of many, Major Jose D. Sena addressed the meeting in Spanish, in a brief, but very appropriate and impressive manner. He was followed by Col. Oscar M. Brown, our present able post commander, who delivered a short but effective and stirring address, adverting in terms most pertinent to the solemnity of the occasion, and referring with effect to the many excellent qualities, magnanimity and patriotism of him, the untimely death of whom, was the subject of the occasion, closing with a sublime apostrophe to our glorious flag, the emblem of our nationality. After which Chief Justice Benedict was called upon, whose speech upon that solemn occasion, to be properly appreciated, should have been heard, he more than all others could speak of the character and virtues of the late President, for they had been intimate friends for near a quarter of a century. . . .

Rev. J. Kermott being called upon did justice to the occasion in a short, elegant and appropriate address, which was delivered in impressive manner, and seemed to touch every heart present. Capt. Quintana also spoke in Spanish, in the strongest terms of the wickedness of the act and the great calamity, that had befallen the nation. Miguel E. Pino, one of the vice presidents of the meeting entertained the assembly with a few appropriate and affecting remarks and assured the people that the wise measures as adopted by our late President would be adhered to by his successor. . . .

Erostratos is said to have set fire to the temple of Diana in order to perpetuate his fame. Empedocles to have leaped into a burning volcano for a similar purpose; but the dark fiend in human shape, who at one blow struck off the great head of the American

Republic, will have greater notoriety than either of them. He will go down to posterity the cursed of the accursed, with his name enshrouded in the darkest infamy and disgrace, and unborn millions of freemen, as long as time shall last will remember him and read of him, as the meanest of his race.

JUNE 2, 1865: OUR TERRITORIAL CAPITOL.

We are happy to learn that work upon our capitol buildings is again to be resumed.

[*An appropriation for the buildings, made in "1860 or 1861," had been lost through a mistaken agreement between the Territory's representatives and the Treasury.*]

We are pleased, however, to announce to the friends of the Territory, to the mechanics and laborers of Santa Fe, that although their interests had been bartered off by one delegate and grossly neglected by another, through the activity and energy of their worthy Secretary [*i.e., Secretary of the Territory*], Hon. W. F. M. Arny, the appropriation has been secured, and that a commissioner to appoint the work will be appointed; that the rattle of the hammer, saw, plane and crowbar will soon be heard upon the capital grounds to be followed by the softer rustle of greenbacks to make glad the hearts of your families.

JUNE 15, 1865:

In the last coach from the east arrived four Sisters of Charity, who, we are informed, design establishing a hospital in this city under the auspices of Bishop Lamy.

This was the first small step towards the founding of Saint Vincent's, long the only hospital in northern New Mexico. Today it is a multimillion-dollar institution, with an attached training school for practical nurses, and is still the only considerable hospital in the city, and still run by the Sisters of Charity.

34

OCTOBER 13, 1865:

By rcfcrcnce to an advertisement in another column, it will be seen that the Sisters of Charity are about opening a hospital in this city for the needy and infirm. The undertaking is praiseworthy and deserves the encouragement of our citizens. We understand that they will shortly visit our citizens for the purpose of soliciting and in the way of subscriptions, and it is to be hoped that our people will contribute liberally, knowing the benevolent purpose for which it is intended.

The year ended with more notices of Indian depredations, mostly ascribed to Navajos, and corresponding attacks upon General Carleton.

The new year opened with fresh hope of obtaining statehood. The legislature passed an act on January 31, 1866, authorizing a state constitutional convention, the election of delegates for which was duly called by Governor Connelly in a proclamation dated February 2, 1866. As usual, this development caused great excitement and proved to be a waste of effort.

FEBRUARY 16, 1866:   THE REPLIES OF THE LEGISLATURE TO THE INTERROGATORIES OF MR. J. K. GRAVES.

Santa Fe, New Mexico,
January 30th, 1866
Julius K. Graves, Esq., Special Indian Agent for New Mexico:

Sir—The following answers to the questions you proposed in your communication of January 9th, 1866, were adopted by the Legislature, and are respectfully submitted to you as follows, to wit:

In relation to the Navajos

Ans. to question 1.—We approve of the Reservation system, and believe it to be the only means by which the interests of the Territory can be permanently secured; but we *disapprove* of the establishment of the Navajoes upon the Bosque Redondo Reservation.

Ans. to question 3d.—We do not approve of the Navajos being permanently established upon the Bosque Redondo Reservation on account of its proximity to the settlements of our territory. But would recommend that said Indians be removed to the confluence of the Rio Bonito with the Pecos river, or to a point on the Colorado river about eighty miles below Fort Bascom, on reservations, ranches or pueblos, with the limits of said establishments well defined;—which, in our opinion, would secure the territory from further molestation from these savages, whose depredations have been so frequent during many years past, in consequence of their wandering propensities; there to be guarded by regular troops. We will, however, accept with pleasure such disposition as the government in its wisdom, may make of these Indians. We would recommend that Indian agents have the supervision of said Indians on their respective reservations; said military force should be sufficient to prevent the Indians from leaving the Reservation, and when the reservation is permanently established, and the limits thereof well defined, should any of the Indians leave the same, they should be punished therefore as fugitives, and in case of resistance, be considered in open hostility against the whites, and be killed.

Ans. to question 4th.—We believe the military department (except in but a few cases,) has done but very little towards the subjugation of the hostile Indians in New Mexico; and we believe, that with special reference to the Navajos, its acts have not been characterized by efficiency or humanity, and it is not entitled to praise therefore; and we are satisfied that their efforts, efficiency and humanity have not contributed to elevate or improve the condition of said tribe, and their policy has caused the contrary.

APRIL 6, 1866: LINCOLN AVENUE.

The military are improving their grounds between the plaza and the quarters by the planting of trees and building of walls and fences which will give quite an improved appearance to the grounds belonging to Fort Marcy, and be a great advantage to our city. We see that Secretary Arny, who is also Superintendent of public buildings, has united with our military officers in opening the street to the new state house by removing the dilapidated hall of the house of representatives, which will open an avenue between the civil and military grounds, and which the parties having authority so to do have named Lincoln Avenue, in honor of our much lamented president. The execution of the work has been under the direction of Lieut. Ayres, who we have no doubt will make it an attractive avenue.

The appropriations for the public buildings are before Congress, and with the fifty-eight thousand dollars already appropriated, will in a short time be available for the completion of the state house and the improvement of the grounds belonging to it, and we have no doubt but that our efficient Superintendent of public buildings will so use the appropriated sums as to make the edifices a credit to the Government and an ornament to the capital of our Territory.

Reports of Indian troubles ran all through 1866, involving Navajos, Apaches, "Utahs" or Utes, Comanches, and "Indians." Complaints continued that, with Navajos both at Bosque Redondo in the east and in their own country in the west, the settlements were between two fires. At the same time, Comanche raids on the helpless Navajos at the Bosque were reported. The Indian stories became repetitious and dull; a single example will suffice. The raid on Camp Mimbres reported in it was probably made by the Mimbreño band of Chiricahua Apaches under Mangas Coloradas.

JUNE 29, 1866: INDIAN NEWS.

From Mesilla we have advices that the Indians have dismounted another cavalry company. If this is allowed to go on much longer, there will not be horses enough left in the territory to mount an escort. In the affair at Camp Mimbres, according to our correspondent, the Indians stole the horses of Captain Nichol's command, in open day, as was the case at Fort Craig where over eighty head were run off. Our people are beginning to see

exactly how "the Indians lie prostrate at the feet of the military."
We would advise that another day be appointed for thanksgiving
in view of our signal deliverance (?) from Indian depredations.

AUGUST 4, 1866:

Otto Bachman will accept the thanks of the "New Mexican"
employees for the supply of beer left at our office on Thursday.

On the eastern mail route the time has been reduced to ten
days for eight months of the year and twelve days for four months.
It is almost certain that the mail service on the southern route
will be increased to three trips per week so as to make regular
connection with the eastern mail.

SEPTEMBER 1, 1866:

Notwithstanding the murmurs of the opposition who are opposed to any public improvements being made by the county
authorities, we suppose but few of our citizens will deny and
refuse to see the necessity of bridging the river. For almost two
weeks communication between the two sides of the river has been
impossible, unless persons chose to risk life and limb and waded
the stream, and this in a town two hundred years old! The stone
abutments that were partially completed when the rise commenced have been partially damaged by the torrent, but the Prefect is busily engaged in repairing the damages and will place the
piers in better condition than when first built, by enclosing them
with cedar piles and the interstices filled with large rocks. The
woodwork is all completed and only waits the completion of the
piers. In a few weeks at furthest we will have a fine and permanent
structure that will be a credit to our city. Although this bridge will
take some money out of the county treasury, we do not doubt but
that our worthy prefect, Don Antonio Ortiz y Salazar, will receive
due credit for using it for such a purpose.

*Ninety-one years later, in the summer of 1957, as work was
going forward to replace the then successor to the bridge described*

above with one competent to handle heavy automobile traffic, the Santa Fe River again rose up and wiped out the construction, partially cutting the town in half. The new bridge was completed almost on time, however, and will probably not be obsolete for several years.

OCTOBER 27, 1866:

A meeting of citizens was held at Knapp's Hall on Saturday evening last to consult as to the best means to be adopted to suppress violence in our midst. Hon. W. F. M. Arny was chosen President, and John Anderson, Esq., and Sheriff Sena Secretaries. After addresses from various gentlemen, a subscription was made for the support of a police to be selected by an executive committee, after which the meeting adjourned. The police have already been appointed and are on duty.

With the police force in operation, the New Mexican *republished the "rules" issued on June 2, 1860, by Judge of Probate Anastacio Sandoval with the approval of the then governor, Abraham Rencher. Since the American occupation, Santa Fe had had no city government. In 1860, Judge Sandoval set up his court, along with the county Justice of the Peace courts, to handle misdemeanors. A few extracts from these rules follow:*

NOVEMBER 10, 1866:   POLICE RULES.

RULE 2.   It shall be prohibited to any person or persons to make excavations in the public squares, roads, streets or lanes, within the limits of the city of Santa Fe. . . .

RULE 4.   Every house-owner or head of a family within the limits of the city of Santa Fe shall specially take care, that his servants or attendants do not throw dirty water, rubbish, ashes or kitchen offal in the public squares, roads, streets or lanes of the City. . . .

RULE 5.   If any animal or animals shall die within the limits of the City of Santa Fe, the person or persons to whom such animal or animals belong, shall be required, within twenty-four hours after the death of said animal or animals, to remove the carcass or carcasses out of said city to a distant place, where they cannot incommode by their appearance and offensive smell. . . .

RULE 8.   It shall be prohibited to any person or persons, who shall enter or go with any animal or animals in the public squares, roads or streets within the City of Santa Fe, to tie the same to any post or pillar of any portal, and also to drive the same under the portales or on the sidewalk. . . .

RULE 9.   Any person or persons who shall keep a disorderly house within the limits of the City of Santa Fe, or shall permit riots or other disorderly conduct within the limits or upon the premises occupied by him, her or them shall . . . be fined in any sum not less than one dollar nor more than fifty dollars, or shall be sentenced to imprisonment and hard labor in the county jail for a term of not less than one day, nor more than ten days.

NOVEMBER 3, 1866:

As the coach due here on last Tuesday was passing the Arroyo Hondo early on Wednesday morning, an attempt was made to stop it, no doubt with intention to rob the mail and passengers but without success. Five men sprang from the bushes by the roadside and tried to catch the mules, but the leaders being mettlesome animals they sprang forward and soon left the would be robbers in the rear. It is believed that the deserters who returned and gave themselves up the same morning were the men who made the attempt.

DECEMBER 8, 1866:

The United States mail for the Rio Abajo, is now carried by the way of La Bajada, being a saving of five or six miles as compared with the old road to Algodones. The objection to travel this road heretofore has been that it was too rough, but by the labor of about one hundred men under the direction of Samuel Ellison, Esq., this has been entirely obviated, and it is now a most excellent road both for carriages and wagons. All who have passed over it, speak of it in the highest terms.

The mail company has established a station at La Bajada, where they will hereafter change stock. The new road will be of incalculable benefit to the county of Santa Ana, which has hitherto been without the advantges of a main road traversing it.

Río Abajo, "Down River," meant the territory south of Santa Fe. U. S. 85 still goes by La Bajada, but somewhat farther south than the original descent.

This anthology makes no attempt to follow elections and appointments to office. However, an exception is made for the list following, since so many of the names on it are still strong in New Mexico.

DECEMBER 22, 1866:   APPOINTMENTS.

Within the past week Acting Governor Arny has made the following appointments, and the appointees have been unanimously confirmed by the Council:

S. B. Elkins as Attorney General, vice C. P. Clever.

Theodore S. Greiner as District Attorney for the 2nd Judicial District.

Thomas B. Catron as District Attorney for the 3d Judicial District, vice Frank Higgins.

Anastacio Sandoval as Territorial Auditor, vice Epifanio Vigil.

Simon Delgado reappointed as Territorial Treasurer.

Trinidad Alarid as Territorial Librarian, vice Ed. Thompson.

The above are excellent appointments, and will meet with the approbation of our citizens.

JANUARY 12, 1867:   THE HANGING OF COL. THOS. MEANS.

We learn from parties arrived from Taos, that Col. Means was hanged in the court house in Taos, on the night of the 2d inst. by a party of men unknown.

The circumstances as narrated to us are as follows: Means who was a desperate character, has for a long time been a terror to his family and the town, and the community at last became so enraged at his actions that his presence was no longer to be tolerated. A few days previous to his death, he attempted to murder Judge Blackwood, and cut him across the face and on the head, and would have killed him but for the timely interference of other citizens.—On the day of the evening he was so summarily executed he attempted to take the life of his wife, and was arrested about six o'clock in the evening for his act, and as he was too drunk to be examined, was placed by the Alcalde in the court house, under a guard of two men to be held till morning.

About twelve o'clock that night a party of some twenty men, masked, broke open the door and demanded him. His guard could not resist the posse, and Means seeming to see at a glance his fate, said "I suppose you have come to kill me." These were his last words, as he was immediately strung up, to the rafters in the center of the court house, where his body was left dangling until the next day.

CHURCH ORGANIZED IN SANTA FE.—On last Sabbath morning after religious services in the Council chamber, a church was organized in the Presbyterian form, consisting of twelve members, by the election of M. L. Byers and W. W. Carothers ruling Elders, who are to be ordained to that office next Sabbath, after sermon at the usual hour of service, also, a board of trustees was elected, consisting of Gov. R. B. Mitchell, Judge John P. Slough, Col. James L. Collins, M. L. Byers and S. B. Elkins.

JANUARY 19, 1867:

The Eastern mail is now making the best time ever made on the route. The coach that came in on Monday last made the trip from Junction City through in six days and nineteen hours. Quinby was the conductor. We are told that this is the quickest trip ever made on the route, and when it is taken into consideration that it was made in the most inclement season of the year, Mr. Quinby may well be proud of his triumph over space.

JANUARY 26, 1867: INDIANS.

During the past week, delegations from six Pueblos have been here, three of which complain of outrages by the whites and Utes. This should not be. If the charges made are substantiated, the guilty parties ought to be punished. The Moquis send one delegation of seven persons, who state that the whites, while ostensibly hunting Apaches, stole seven hundred sheep and goats, murdered seven men and carried off to Abiquiu eleven children and one woman. The Governor of *Jemes* reports the Utes as having (by the advice of parties at or near Abiquiu) stolen seven horses from his people, besides committing other outrages.

It is high time something was done to protect these Indians from these outrages. They are peaceable, friendly to a fault, and as affairs are now arranged they are at the mercy of their enemies. Col. Henderson, their agent, has worked beyond the means at his disposal, and has now on foot parties endeavoring to secure the return of the captives and restitution of the stolen property; but he has to do this out of his private purse, no money being here to defray any expenses for these Indians. The delegation from the Moquis are still at Col. Henderson's house, and will remain until the arrival of Maj. John Ward, who was sent by Col. H. to endeavor to get the children.

"Moquis" were Hopis, non-Christian Pueblo Indians living in Arizona, who were as severely plagued by the Navajos and Apaches as any white men. They suffered several times at the hands of parties of white trappers. On another occasion some of these came upon Hopi cornfields and began helping themselves. When some Hopis protested, they were shot.

The Jemez were not quite such innocent victims. Their pueblo lay on the western edge of the Jemez Mountains, facing towards Navajo country, and their alliance with the Navajos went back to the late 1600's. They seem to have bought stolen goods from them and were accused by other Pueblo Indians of having sometimes joined them in their raids.

AUGUST 3, 1867:   DEATH OF PADRE MARTINES.

The painful intelligence of the death of Padre Antonio Jose Martines of Taos, was received by Wednesday's mail. He departed this life on the evening of the 27ult at 9 o'clock P. M. and was buried the following day at 10 o'clock A. M. The deceased had lived many years in Taos, and was universally beloved by all who knew him. Taos county has lost one of her most worthy citizens and will sadly lament his loss.

Padre Martinez (the spelling Martines is eccentric) was an interesting and controversial figure. He may or may not have had a hand in fomenting the Taos Rebellion of 1847. In his later years, he was in constant controversy with Archbishop Lamy. In the 1830's he maintained at Taos a college and seminary that trained twenty men for the priesthood, as well as educating a number of laymen—and this at the darkest depths of New Mexico's illiteracy. In 1835 he obtained a printing press that had been brought into Santa Fe, probably by the Abreu family, and published El Crepusculo de la Libertad *(The Dawn of Liberty; the present newspaper at Taos is published under that name), the first newspaper west of the Mississippi.[2] Under American rule, he served with some distinction in the Territorial legislature.*

On December 3, 1881, the paper reported the acquisition, by the Historical Society, of "a valuable collection of a dozen volumes of theological and scientific works" from Padre Martinez' library, including a Latin edition of Saint Thomas Aquinas, "in bellum" (!), printed in 1750. The story remarked, "Among the graduates of his institute, so long a feature of the Villa de Taos, are nearly all of the most intelligent of those who figured prominently in New Mexican affairs prior to the American," and noted that at that time his birthday was still being celebrated by the people of the northern counties.

It has become usual for popular writers to describe this notable

2 W. A. Kelleher, a distinguished New Mexico historian, says that *El Crepusculo* was probably first published in Santa Fe in 1834 by Antonio Barrero, then "briefly" in Taos by Martinez.

priest as a villain of the deepest dye, a characterization definitely not warranted by the record.

NOVEMBER 5, 1867: LAYING OF THE CORNER STONE OF THE MONUMENT.

We this week present to our readers a condensed account of the ceremonies attending the laying of the corner stone of the monument in commemoration of the gallant soldiers who fell at Valverde and Apache Cañon in 1862.

At 2 p. m. the procession of citizens formed in the middle of the Plaza, headed by the band and marched to the front of the Cathedral where it halted, and was joined by the committee from Colorado, G. W. Griffey, Gov. Evans and C. A. Chever, Gen'l Getty and Staff and the Masons and Odd Fellows of the city. Thence the procession marched through the principal streets of the city and returned to the Plaza where the formal ceremonies took place, as follows: . . .

Chief Justice Slough whilst the box was being sealed read the list of articles contained in it as follows:

List of relics deposited in Corner Stone of the Monument:

Constitution of the United States; Declaration of Independence; Organic Act of New Mexico; compiled laws of New Mexico.

1866–7 Laws of the Territory of New Mexico English.

1866–7 Laws of the Territory of New Mexico Spanish.

1866–7 Journals of the Legislative Council, English.

1866–7 Journals of the Legislative Council Spanish.

1866–7 Journals of the House of Representatives, English.

1866–7 Journals of the House of Representatives, Spanish.

List of Civil officers of the Territory.

List of Military officers on duty in Santa Fe.

Specimens of coins of the United States as follows:

One half dollar, coined A. D. 1855, silver; one quarter dollar, coined A. D. 1858, silver; one dime, coined A. D. 1854, silver; one half dime, coined A. D. 1855, silver; one dollar, coined, A. D. 1860, California Gold; one cent, coined A. D. 1843, copper; one

45

half dime, coined A. D. 1867, nickel; one cent, coined A. D. 1859, nickel, one union medal, coined A. D. 1863, nickel.

Names of Monument Commission and Architects.

Copy of oration delivered on occasion of laying corner stone, October 24th, A. D. 1867.

Copy of programme of said occasion.

Copies of the "Gazette," "New Mexican," and "Albuquerque Press," newspapers published in this Territory.

List of military officers in battle of "Valverde," "Apache Canon" and "La Glorieta."

Masonic Relics.

Executive seal of New Mexico; seal of Secretary of New Mexico; seal of Supreme Court of New Mexico; seal of the First Judicial District Court of the United States for the Territory of New Mexico; specimens of United States fractional currency as follows:

One half dollar issue of 1863; one quarter dollar, Issue of 1863; one dime, issue of 1863; one half dime, issue of 1863.

The stone was then lowered and declared by the Deputy Grand Master to have been properly laid in conformity with the usages of the Ancient order of Masons.

Some comment on the laying of the cornerstone of the monument must be made. The monument still stands in the plaza of Santa Fe and is beloved because of the misspelling of February in one panel. The entire ceremony was long and included vast quantities of oratory. The monument, as finally inscribed, was a memorial not only to those who fell in the two battles against the Confederates mentioned but also against the "savages." In short, a majority of those commemorated were native Roman Catholics; yet the ceremonies were flatly Masonic, even though the procession formed in front of the cathedral, and the prayers offered were by a Protestant minister only.

Anglo-Americans, as we call them now, were a small minority in the Territory, but they were too secure in their strength to make concessions to a sect in which they disbelieved.

46

La Fonda, or the Exchange Hotel, built at the end of the Santa Fe Trail, has always been the town's leading hotel. This drawing, which also shows Seligman's general store, was made about 1868–70.

The beginning of a century of social history: Volume I, Number 1, of the *New Mexican*, November 28, 1849.

Photograph by the U. S. Army Signal Corps

Flat-roofed adobes flanked San Francisco Street, one of the two principal streets of the city, leading eastward to St. Francis Cathedral, about 1875.

Photograph by W. H. Jackson; Courtesy the State Historical Society of Colorado

Gold's Old Curiosity Shop was an early tourist attraction.

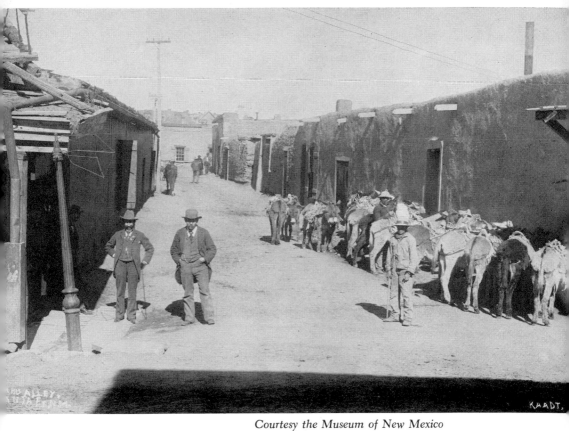

In the early days Burro Alley was a gathering place for firewood venders, who tethered their burros there; hence, its name.

The bandstand was the center of activity in the Santa Fe plaza around 1880.

Photograph by the U. S. Army Signal Corps

The Bishop Building shows two-story construction in the early Santa Fe style. This photo was taken between 1875 and 1885.

The parade ground at old Fort Marcy. Much of the soldiers' time was spent in Indian-fighting in those days.

On December 15, 1867, Chief Justice John P. Slough was shot and killed in La Fonda bar by "Captain" W. L. Rynerson, a former sergeant in the California Volunteers and at that time a member of the Territorial House of Representatives, who shortly before had introduced a resolution censuring the Justice. The affair is so beautiful an example of a high-class killing that we reprint here a fairly extensive extract from the testimony at the preliminary hearing.

JANUARY 14, 1868: FOR THE PROSECUTION.

Daniel Tappan, sworn, says: He is acquainted with defendant; was acquainted with J. P. Slough; believes he is dead. First thing he saw, was when gong rang; he started for dinner; saw Rynerson with pistol and heard him say "will you take it back." Judge didn't make direct answer, but advanced one step towards Rynerson with right hand in his pocket, and raised his left, saying "take care, take care, don't shoot." Mr. Rynerson said again, "take it back." Slough turned a little and said: "I don't propose to take anything back," at that moment Rynerson fired. Judge Slough fell on the floor; I heard something fall on the floor and saw it was a Derringer—advanced to pick it up, but, McDonald was ahead of me and picked it up first; I then asked Judge Slough where was he hit, he said "in the side—send for a doctor"—I said I thought he was hit in the hip, and that he was not badly hurt. He said "yes I am, send for a doctor." That is all.

R. M. Stephens, sworn: Know prisoner at bar; saw him on Sunday, 15th of Dec.; I was on my way into dinner and had got two or three steps into billiard-room, when I heard loud talking and turned. The first word I heard was, Capt. Rynerson said "I want you to take it back," Judge Slough said "What did I say?" Rynerson replied, "you called me a son of a bitch and a thief," Slough answered either "I won't take it back," or "I don't take it back." I don't know which. Rynerson then drew his pistol and said "If you don't take it back I will shoot you." Slough then turned around and seemed as if he were going to put his hand in his pocket and said "shoot and be damned" or "shoot damn you." Then I found myself back of the door, so that both were thrown out of my sight for a moment, and while I was standing in the door I saw Judge Slough; I heard Rynerson say "take it back" or "do you take it back"; Slough replied, "I don't propose to take anything back," and the pistol fired immediately, and Slough dropped.

I had not drank a single drop on that day; that was boarding place of Rynerson, he told me himself he boarded there; I understood he was a member of Senate and saw him officiating in that capacity; he had come here some time previous to first of month; it was usual hour of taking dinner. He had his coat on cloak fashion, without his arms in sleeves; have frequently seen him wear his coat so. At time I came saw Rynerson holding skirt of coat in his hands; he had no pistol in his hands; heard Rynerson say, "take it back." I saw Slough move his hand toward his pocket, at time Rynerson drew his pistol; when Slough said "shoot and be damned," I was near Van Smith and I think McDonald was there also. Did not hear Slough mention Rynerson's name; saw Slough fall after shot; saw no Deringer then; saw one after I went in and came out again. Rynerson spoke very calmly; seemed to be very cool. (Question—Do you know the general character of Slough as to violence in attacking persons?—objected to; objection sustained by the court.) I was not present the evening before in billiard room, when Slough and Rynerson were present— nor was I in Slough's room; Slough was not in my room. Slough weight about 200 pounds; about 38 or 40 years of age, a hale, hearty man. Had no conversation the evening before; neither Slough nor Rynerson were in my room the evening before that I am aware of; did not help convey Slough away at the time he fell; saw them carry him out. Persons present were Hubbell, Smith, McDonald, and a Mr. Johnson who lives at or near Wagon Mound. Saw Slough and Hill sitting near him in bar room evening before. (Question by court—Did you ever hear Slough use words that Rynerson asked him to retract? No. Rynerson said "you called me a thief and a son of a bitch"; Slough said "I don't" or "I won't take it back."

Santiago L. Hubbell, sworn; Know parties—was present at difficulty, on Sunday; don't remember date; as I was going to dinner I met Rynerson half-way between outer room door and billiard room door, and met Judge Slough right close to billiard room door. I passed on into billiard room, and was about opening placita door, when I heard loud voices in angry tone, when I returned to door leading to office; I saw Slough and Rynerson approaching each other using angry words. I heard Rynerson say to Judge Slough, "you have called me a lying son of a bitch, and a thief, and I want you to take it back." Slough said "If I have said so, I don't propose to take it back I will shoot you," and with that I saw a pistol. Don't know if he had it in his hand or drew it from under his coat. As Capt. Rynerson pointed his pistol Judge Slough changed his position, turning himself more towards the fire place, or counter of the office. Capt. Rynerson changed his position so that he stood nearer to the door going into billiard room; says he, "take it back or I'll shoot you." Judge Slough answered, "shoot and be damned," or "shoot damn you," and at that the pistol went off and Judge Slough fell upon his side. I then, from the appearance, thought from the manner in which Rynerson held the pistol that he was trying to shoot again. I then gathered Rynerson and tried to get his pistol; he resisted to give it up to me; how we got into bar-room I do not know. Right at the stove I said "Captain give me your pistol" says he "I won't do it." Mr. Van Smith was standing right by the stove when I first saw him; he said, "Captain give me the pistol"; Captain said "take it" and handed it to him; he received it; I then let go of Rynerson and went back to Slough; what became of Rynerson I don't know. After the shot, Rynerson had one hand on muzzel of pistol and the other on lock, and approached about one step; I think he was trying to cock pistol; cannot state positively. At report of Rynerson's pistol, Slough drew from his pocket his right hand as from a spasmodic efforts and therefrom dropped a Deringer.

As I came back from bar-room, to pick up Slough, my attention was not drawn to any but the two persons; after Slough fell then I remember to have seen McDonald and Tappan; I saw six or eight persons there; cannot remember their names. I had seen Rynerson before that time during the day; I saw him about one o'clock that day; he was passing up and down in front of his room in Sena's building; Rynerson was boarding at the Fonda; Afterwards I went from the Assessor's office in company with Mr. Everett around to hotel and went in to take a drink; as we passed into bar-room I said to Capt. Rynerson, "come in and take a drink"; he said "no I thank you." Everett and I went in, and afterwards stood a few minutes under portal. I observed nothing particular about Rynerson, more than that I thought he had a little political ill feeling, on account of remarks I had made about Legislative action; but observed no excitement; don't know if my remarks reached him; never spoke of him bitterly that I remember. When I went into billiard-room to dinner, I left Rynerson walking back and forth in bar-room; had not seen him previous on the same day; boarders generally assembled in that room or billiard-room to wait for dinner. I met Judge Slough right at the door as I went in to dinner; I had seen Slough in the room where Rynerson was previous to this on the same day; I never saw Rynerson in the hotel; never saw Rynerson pass to billiard-room, nor to door of billiard-room. Before church Slough came to bar-room, and billiard-room and was talking with me; said "I didn't go to church to day and my wife was scolding me about it." I do not know whether there was any anticipated meeting between them on that day; never heard any threats made by Slough against Rynerson on that day; was not in billiard-room on evening previous while Rynerson and Col. Kinzie were playing billiard, and while Slough and Rynerson were in there together. I observed nothing more than common in Slough on that day, nothing more than his usual mode of talking; I told Rynerson "give me that pistol"; my impression is that I lifted him and carried him into billiard-room; Rynerson had not turned to billiard-room when I spoke to him; when I heard loud words I returned; don't remember that I heard Rynerson say "stand back"; both were advancing when I came in sight; there were no pistols in sight; when Rynerson said "take it back" second time, he had pistol in his hands; Slough had hands in his pockets; saw no pistol in his hands; saw no pistol in Rynerson's hands first time; words that Rynerson wished Slough to take back were "you called me a damned son of a bitch and a thief"; do not know when those words were used; do not know if Slough used the words.

After obtaining change of venue to Las Vegas, Rynerson was acquitted on grounds of self-defense.

FEBRUARY 25, 1868:   GRANT COUNTY CREATED.

By an act of the last Legislature the new county of Grant was created out of all that portion of the Territory lying west of a line running near Fort Cummings from south to north across the Sierra Miembres to the former line between the counties of Socorro and Dona Ana. Fort Cummings is included in the limits of the new county, which is composed of four precincts—one at Pinos Altos, one at Eureka (mouth of Rich Gulch), and one at the town of Rio Miembres. The new county contains within its limits some of the finest agricultural and pastoral lands in the Territory, and from all accounts mineral wealth almost beyond conception or calculation.

MAY 26, 1868:   PEONAGE IN NEW MEXICO.

The GAZETTE has been for some time past, greatly troubled about "Peonage and Indian slavery" in this Territory.—In its issue of last Saturday it ventilates itself on that subject, but it is very careful not to say that it is opposed to that system of slavery; and it is equally cautious in its endeavors to show that the CHAVES party as a party, only hold or continue to permit former peons to remain in their old homes. But its assumptions on this head are all false. Peonage had, before the passage by Congress, and the Legislature of this Territory, of laws abolishing that species of servitude, permeated every class of society; it existed among all parties, and there are as many such persons, now held, or remaining with their former masters, of the CLEVER party as of the CHAVES party.

The GAZETTE parades the names of certain persons belonging to the CHAVES party who still have persons about them who were once held as peons. But it forgets to name any of the prominent men in its own party, like the Roivals, and Archuletas, and Garcias, and Jaramillos, of Rio Arriba, and others, whose houses are still filled with them, whom we might name.

We deny, and we say it is false, as the GAZETTE alleges, that in New Mexico, the Republican party "is the peon and slavery party." That sheet knows this to be false. Who was the delegate from New Mexico when the law passed inhibiting peonage in this Territory? Colonel Chaves. Who has always fought for the pro-slavery side here in New Mexico? The GAZETTE and its friends. It is the GAZETTE that is today, as it has been in the past, that is pro-slavery—it and its friends.

We understand the object of such articles as the GAZETTE now and then publishes on this subject of peonage; we understand the object of the one published by it last week. It was not intended for home, but for foreign consumption. Does it, in its innocence, suppose that the members of Congress who will vote next month to turn Clever out of the seat in Congress to which he has no just right, are to be misled—fooled—by such articles as that published by it last week? By no means. There is a record of this matter already in Washington, which shows how much Clever has been opposed to peonage in New Mexico, and how he is indirectly connected with it now. Does the GAZETTE wish that record published here? If it does, it has only to continue its perverse misrepresentations of this question, as it has been doing for some time past, and we assure it of an ample ventilation not long hence.

Two types of bondage existed in New Mexico—true peonage based on debt, as in the old Mexican system, and outright slavery of captives taken from the hostile Indians, especially Navajos and Apaches. In earlier days the Comanches used to take prisoners from other Plains tribes and sell them to the Spanish. Pueblo Indians also held some slaves of this type. The Apacheans (Navajos and Apaches) took Mexican, Spanish-American, and Pueblo slaves. There is some reason to believe that the practice of slave-taking began with the Spanish.

The slavery was not rigid. Children of slaves were accepted in their various communities, and many captives in time merged into the general, free population, aided in this by the strong Indian racial element among the Spanish-Americans. A number of important Navajo clans derive from captives.

This seems the best spot at which to mention the little-known role Abraham Lincoln played among the Pueblo Indians. In the midst of all the pressures of the Civil War, he found time to confirm them in their grants of land and to recognize their traditional governments by sending them silver-headed canes, similar to those originally given by the Spanish, which they still treasure. In the minds of older Indians who told me of these matters twenty or so years ago, Lincoln was responsible for freeing the captives, even though much of the actual freeing occurred after his death, and for ending the generations of war with the Navajos.

The contest referred to in this story was over election as delegate to Congress between Charles P. Clever and Colonel José Francisco Chaves (not Chávez). Clever has already appeared in these pages as former owner of the New Mexican *and former Territorial attorney general. He was an associate of General Carleton's, hence an enemy to the* New Mexican. *Colonel Chaves was the head of one of the most powerful landed families of the Spanish aristocracy, a man of influence in the Territory. His title derived from his service in the Civil War, which was distinguished. He was finally seated by Congress.*

For further light on the question of peons and slaves, see the entries of June 16 and August 6, 1868.

JUNE 9, 1868:   LT. GEN. SHERMAN AND THE NAVAJOS.

Lieut. General [*William Tecumseh*] SHERMAN of the Indian Commission, arrived in this city on Friday evening last, from the Bosque Redondo, in company with Major General Getty, where he had been to investigate the condition of the Navajos. From a gentleman of this city who has seen and conversed with the Lieut. General on the subject we learn that it has been determined to remove those Indians at once back to their native country. General SHERMAN has made an arrangement with them to go upon a reservation in their country, the boundaries of which are clearly defined; they to remain thereon, and pursue their pastoral and agricultural avocations; the government agreeing to give annually to each member of the tribe a sum, in wool, or other articles necessary, equal to five dollars, and secure them against the intrusion of whites. If the Navajos act in good faith, the government is to assist them in their efforts to sustain themselves; if they do not, then the United States is to withdraw its material aid and enforce obedience to the agreement entered into.

Troops, in sufficient numbers, will of course be stationed near the Indians to protect them and the settlements; Fort Wingate being one of the posts prominent south of the reservation. The agents of the Navajos to live with, or at some military post near them.

Gen. SHERMAN proposed to the Navajos that they remove to the Wichita country, east, but the tribe was averse to going to any location save to their own country. Convinced that the welfare of the Indians depended upon their immediate removal from the Bosque Redondo, where at an annual expense of half a million a year they were fast becoming extinct, with a humanity and regard for the interests of both government and Indians, General SHERMAN promptly determined upon their immediate removal to their own country, under the stipulations named, and the business of exchanging the graveyard of the Bosque for their native mountains and valleys is already being executed. Major CHAS. T. WHITING, 3d, U. S. Cavalry, is the officer to whom has been committed the important business of superintending the removal of the Navajos.

General Sherman's decision was wise as well as humane. The sufferings, not only of those Navajos who went into exile but of those who remained at liberty, have never been forgotten. They are vivid tribal memories to this day. Once returned to a portion of their homeland, the tribe set itself to making a peaceful living and did extremely well at it. Three-quarters of a century later, however, their population had grown to such a size that all the land available could not support it. The Treaty of 1868 provided, among other things, that the government would provide a teacher and schoolroom for every thirty pupils, for all of school age who could be "persuaded or forced" to attend school. Until very recently, the Navajos themselves largely opposed education, and the government made no serious attempt to live up to this promise. This resulted in a state of ignorance from which has come much sorrow.

The reader will have noticed some variety in the spelling of Navajo. *This name has an interesting history. It derives from the Tewa name for a tract of land in the Jemez Mountains, meaning "Large Cornfields," which the Spanish rendered, not inaccurately, as* "Nabajú." *The tribe of Apaches cultivating those fields was called "Los Apaches de Nabajú" in the seventeenth century. By the end of the eighteenth century, having moved farther west, this tribe had become so large and its culture so distinct that the generic "Apaches" was dropped. Also, for euphony, "Nabajú" was altered into "Navajó." The plural of this latter form in Spanish is "Navajoes," the stress remaining on the* o *and the* e *being pronounced.*

When the name was adopted into English, the stress was shifted to the first syllable. Probably, when the plural "Navajoes" was written in English in the 1860's, it was read with the e *silent, as in "hoes." From this, in turn, came back a singular, "Navajoe," which occurs occasionally in the* New Mexican, *while phonetics led to the modern plural spelling "Navajos," as in the passage last quoted.*

Annoyed by the great number of people who pronounced the j *as in English or in French, Washington Matthews, the great ethnographer, put forth the spellings "Navaho" and "Navahos" in the 1890's, and these are now accepted by most anthropologists. The word also passed into the Navajo language, with the pronunciation "Naweho," stressed on the last syllable.*

In the late 1940's, the Chairman of the Navajo Tribal Council asked that the spelling with h *be adopted generally, but the Tribal Council itself was forced to revert to "Navajo" since that form had become established in federal law. Thus, in 1959, the correct spelling of the name of the largest tribe in the United States remains uncertain.*

"KIT CARSON IS DEAD!"

This announcement has now become familiar to the public ear. Yet, sorrow has not ceased to shroud the public mind. The announcement of Colonel Carson's death did not take us by surprise. For years he has been subject to an affection of the heart which he himself has told us he expected would "carry him off!" And so the great King, whom KIT CARSON had often braved, and in so many forms, has at last triumphed, and borne his victim down the narrow valley of gloom.

KIT CARSON, a citizen of New Mexico, was a remarkable man. Possessed of no education whatever, he was the possessor of a vast fund of common sense. He was an honest and kind hearted man, and we have often wondered at this softness of a nature inured to so much turmoil, strife and wild life. We part with the great KIT with sorrow; but he has been a faithful citizen, a true soldier, a sound patriot and we trust in a great reward for him hereafter.

JUNE 16, 1868: PROCLAMATION BY ACTING GOVERNOR HEATH ON THE SUBJECT OF PEONAGE.

In another column of this week's issue we publish a Proclamation by acting Gov. HEATH, relative to Peonage in New Mexico. Two laws were passed in 1867, one by our Territorial Legislature, and another by Congress, abolishing and forever prohibiting slavery or peonage in New Mexico. These laws have been but indifferently observed, and the acting Executive in view of these facts has very properly taken this method to inform the people that the law must be obeyed.

To hold peons now, is unlawful, not in New Mexico alone, but throughout the United States. The statutes, both territorial and federal, inhibit the holding of peons, and Gov. HEATH'S proclamation is designed to more thoroughly inform the people of these facts.

JUNE 23, 1868:   THE INDIANS OF GOV. ARNY'S AGENCY.

The head Chiefs of the Capote Utahs and the Jicarilla Apaches, who are at the Abiquiu Indian Agency under the charge of Gov. ARNY arrived in town last week to have an interview with the peace commissioners and with the Navajoe Indians with whom they have been at war for many years.

The Indians of the Abiquiu Agency contributed largely in the conquest of the Navajoes when they were put upon the reservation at Fort Sumner, and owing to the constant depredations of the Navajoes upon them, and the loss of many lives and horses, has made the Utes and Apaches indisposed to make a peace with them.

We are informed that Mr. ARNY has succeeded in getting from the Indians in the San Juan country the horses they stole some time since, and restored them, and that a peace has been made so that all the Utah bands are now again friendly, and have promised him to continue so.

Gov. ARNY the indefatigable agent of the Indians, now here, we understand intends to visit in a short time the San Juan river and its tributaries, which is the country claimed by his Indians, and a considerable portion of which has never been explored. He will be escorted by his Indians who desire him to go with them.

Mr. ARNY and his two interpreters, TOMAS CHACON, and his son W. E. ARNY have for a month past been engaged night and day in the mountains settling the discontents amongst the Indians, which was very imprudently caused by the meddling with them, by some of our citizens, and he proposes to be with them during the summer in their own country, and outside of the settlements, so as to prevent if possible any hostilities on their part.

It is known that the two tribes under his charge are as warlike as any of the Rocky Mountain Indians, and their appearance and behavior while in Santa Fe is a credit to them, and although designing persons have endeavored to stir them up to mischief, they say they have full confidence in their agent and will do as he directs and will keep the peace, unless assailed.

A proper disposition of these Indians upon a reservation in their own country would be a great blessing to our people and also to them.

Arny was successful in negotiating agreements with these tribes. The Utes received as reservations the greater part of their traditional home in western Colorado. But this was too much good land for white frontiersmen to tolerate leaving in Indian possession; eventually, after the Meeker Massacre in 1879, they were stripped of most of it.

The Jicarilla Apaches were shunted about. For a time they were placed in traditional Navajo country just east of the then Navajo Reservation. There was constant fighting between the two tribes. Then they were put on the Mescalero Apache Reservation, with the same result. Finally, in 1888, they were moved to their present reservation, which consists of a portion of their homeland in northern New Mexico and has turned out to be rich in oil and gas.

On or about July 7, 1868, the telegraph line came to Santa Fe, and on that date the New Mexican *took the great step and became a daily. It celebrated the double event with the editorial reprinted below.*

JULY 7, 1868:   STEPS FORWARD.

Twenty years ago, New Mexico was an entirely isolated country. The nearest towns east were but small villages on the banks of the Missouri river, and the time required to traverse the dreary distance between, say, Santa Fe and Kansas City, was long, weary and sometimes dangerous. Then, no railroad penetrated even to St. Louis, nor was there a telegraphic line in operation to the Mississippi from the Atlantic slope.

Twenty years ago, all that vast area of country lying between the Rocky Mountains and the Missouri river was known on the maps as the "Great American Desert," a land fit only for the bison and Indian to inhabit. The idea that all this vast central half of the American continent was then or was ever to be valuable to man, had not gained much if any ground, and all west of the "Big Muddy," to most people, was a *terra incognita*.

But these twenty years past have wrought wonderful revolutions in the mysteries of the "Great American Desert." New Mexico was certainly known as *existing* twenty years ago,—that is all. Kansas, Nebraska, Colorado, Minnesota, Dakota, Arizona, Montana, Idaho, Nevada, California, Oregon, Washington Territory, aye, *Alaska,* who knew about these?

How is it *now*, after the lapse of these twenty past years. California, Kansas, Nebraska, Oregon, Minnesota, Nevada—these are now states. Colorado is a state, and requires only the last finishing touch of Congress. Montana, Utah, Idaho and New Mexico have already populations nearly or quite sufficient to become states in the Union. This is the progress of population, and the advance of civilization, where but a short time since was wilderness and savage life.

But, moving with the line of civilization through the wilderness, and over the "Great American Desert," that stretches itself across twenty degrees of longitude, are the wonderful developments of the grand handiworks of man and the energies of capital, invigorated by enterprise. The railroad has reached, on the east, from the waters of the Atlantic to the peaks of the Sierra Madre, of the Rocky Mountains, in Colorado, and the summit of the Sierra Nevada, on the Pacific side of the continent. A line of telegraph from the Atlantic to the Pacific brings those two great oceans within a moments time of each other, and the moment of sunrise on the western rim of the former may be known by the subtle agent that speaks through the telegraph wire, upon the eastern rim of the latter, whilst darkness still envelops the sleepers upon it.

Santa Fe, that twenty years ago was seventy or eighty days travel from the Missouri river, is now within three days of the western terminus of the iron track and the railroad car, and before most of our readers peruse these lines, the telegraph will be established here in our midst, to give us intelligence of all that is going forward daily in every part of the civilized, and in many portions of the uncivilized world.

Twenty years ago, a mail from the States once in each thirty days, was all that could be hoped or that was expected. On the first of the present month we leaped, at a single bound, through the munificence of a great and good government, from a tri-weekly to a daily mail, and this daily mail does not pause here, in Santa Fe, but passes us westward and southward to bless the population beyond us, to El Paso in old Mexico.

Twenty years ago it is probable that there were not two thousand Americans in New Mexico. To-day, there are not less than from twelve to fifteen thousand. The condition of the people native in New Mexico is greatly improved since that day. Life to them is, for the most part, of a more cultivated and more elevated character. Education struggles to break the bonds of ignorance, and religion moves onward with its wondrous softening and christianizing influences.

The spirit of enterprise has commenced a significant development of the internal and material wealth of our mountains, which must move onward to the music of the genius that gives to America her peculiar characteristic, and makes her equally the wonder and delight of men throughout the world.

"Westward the star of empire" has taken "her course," and New Mexico is within the range of its glorious influences. Under these she will one day, not long hence, we trust, shine as brightly and potently in the national galaxy, as any of her now more favored sisters.

We have thus shown that everything is tending to the grand development of the sentiment expressed in the two words that head this article—"Steps Forward."

AUGUST 5, 1868:   MUD ROOFED HOUSES.

It is deemed a proper occasion to make some suggestions to the public on the subject of house roofing, and this subject is suggested by the recurrence of the "rainy season" just passed; a portion of the year never to be avoided, in its consequences at least.

During the past two days the outpouring of rain from the skies has been nearly incessant. The consequence is nearly every roof in the town has considered it a special privilege to leak like a sieve, to the utter disgust of all who have been affected thereby. Health is injured, furniture destroyed, homes are made uncomfortable, housewives are without good humor, and all because our people persist in the antiquated custom of piling *dirt* upon their roofs instead of building good shingle or board roofs to their houses.

Modern Santa Feans are inclined to rail at their predecessors, who insisted on destroying the native architecture by adding pitched roofs; they forget, or never knew, the inadequacy of mud roofing in really wet weather. The preferred roof today is, once again, flat and has on it from two to four inches of mud (adobe) which provides an unbeatable insulation. Over that is a waterproof covering of tar and roofing paper, which is what makes the whole arrangement tolerable.

New Mexico stood with the Union during the Civil War, and it is quite clear that the great majority of her citizens heartily supported the Northern cause. It seems, however, that it did not occur to these good people that the liberation of slaves would be interpreted to apply to the Indian captives in their homes. As we have already seen, even after the passage of federal and Territorial laws on the subject, peonage and slavery continued. When a serious attempt was made to enforce full emancipation, even some of the most vociferous Unionists began to howl, including the editors of the New Mexican, *as in the editorial below.*

AUGUST 5, 1868: "NAVAJO CAPTIVES."

Some two or three hundred people from Taos and Rio Arriba [*counties*] were summoned to appear at the present term of the U. S. District court, to answer to the charge of holding Navajoe captives and others in bondage, but we understand that the Grand Jury failed to find a solitary indictment.

We apprehend that there are few subjects upon which there is greater misunderstanding and ignorance, than this one question of what is termed "Navajoe captives." And this very misunderstanding, particularly on the part of Congress, causes this territory, and our people great injustice in the public estimation.

It should be known, first, that most of the Navajoes, men, women and children, scattered over our territory, are those who, during past years of war between their tribes and the whites, and Indians hostile to them were captured, and by one means and another, passed into the families of our citizens. At first these people may have been regarded in the light of peons, perhaps of slaves, but, it is certain, that, as soon as Congress and the Legislature of this Territory passed laws abolishing both peonage and every other class of slavery in the Territories, these people became free, and there are few, if any of them, who do not know that they are, and have been, since the passage of those laws, at liberty to go when, and wheresoever they may have pleased.

The Navajoes are a savage and barbarous people. These captives from this tribe have now for years, lived among civilized people; have learned the language of the country, have become christianized—all being catholics; their habits have become those of the civilized race among whom they dwell, and not one in fifty of them desire to leave their civilized for a renewal of their barbarous and uncivilized life with their tribes. They prefer a life among our people to one among their own. They are free—they may hire to any person whom they may please to serve; but it is certain, that, constituted as they are, with large organs of inhabitiveness, most, if not all of those who come under the classification of "Navajo captives," prefer to remain in homes where they have so long been domesticated, and where they possess the advantages of not only religion, but of civilized life. These they cannot possess if returned to their nation.

This condition then, is not one of bondage to these people. It is not involuntary servitude. It is rather, and it is in fact, an abandonment, voluntarily, of a savage, barbarous life for one of civilization and religion.

It becomes then, a serious question of humanity, whether those Navajos who now voluntarily live amongst our people, upon the terms, and in the manner named, shall be forced back upon savage life against their will, and only, because their tribe desire their

62

return, or whether, by their voluntary action they shall remain as they are, the objects of care by the church, and civil protection by the Territory.

Surely no Southerner ever drew a more touching picture of the benefits of happy, voluntary slavery.

OCTOBER 20, 1868: AN OUTRAGE.

For some time past the working of the telegraph line has been occasionally interrupted by being torn down or cut in the vicinity of the Arroyo Hondo, five miles from this city. Though this trouble has been quite frequently experienced lately, it has been hitherto attributed to accident; and the distance from this place was so small that the damage has been usually repaired in two or three hours without causing much delay in the operation of the line.

On Sunday night the line was working well, and we received our usual night dispatches. On Monday morning the line was ascertained to be broken, and a man coming from that direction reported seeing two men and two boys engaged in the pastime of destroying the line near the crossing of the Arroya Honda [*sic*]. An employee was immediately dispatched to make repairs; and upon returning last evening he reported that he had made partial repairs, but that the damage was so extensive that he had been unable to put the line in working order. For a distance of nearly two miles the wire was torn from the poles, the glass insulators removed and broken upon the rocks, and the wire cut in several place.

In some cases the insulators had been ground to atoms between two stones. The repairer returned to his work this morning, and we hope to receive dispatches yet before we go to press.

This is one of those instances of purely malicious destruction which is almost enough to cause belief in the doctrine of total depravity. No benefit could possibly result to the perpetrators, while to the stockholders of the line and the public generally serious loss and annoyance ensues. If this occurrence is repeated, steps will be taken to ascertain and punish the guilty scoundrels.

Similar notices of damage to the telegraph line were fairly frequent for some years. The motive seems to have been mere vandalism, unless it could have been some feeling among rural Spanish-Americans that the line somehow served, or would serve, to oppress them. On some occasions, wire was taken for purely practical purposes, such as repairing wagons.

NOVEMBER 11, 1868:   [*Advertisement.*]

U. S. MAIL ROUTE.
Denver and Santa Fe
Stage Line,
consisting of
4 HORSE
CONCORD COACHES,
Leaving Trinidad upon the arrival of the
southern mail coaches, every
MONDAY,
WEDNESDAY
and FRIDAY
Time from Santa Fe to Denver
three days and a half.

DECEMBER 24, 1868:

We have to express our thanks and acknowledgements for the "Christmas presents" with which the New Mexican outfit has been honored and regaled up to this present writing, and it's not yet very late in the day this Christmas Eve either. First came the jovial Dr. W. T. Strachan with a bottle of fourth-proof Pennsylvania brandy. We'll give it the fifth proof tomorrow in proof of our remembrance and good opinion of the amiable donor. Then came along a note from our Abiquiu friend Major J. Carey French officially suggesting that the accompanying big fat *cocono de campo* wouldn't be a bad thing for our Christmas dinner table: we'll see how it will look there tomorrow. And last but not least our friend Colonel M. de LaFayette Cotton the Taoseño has just handed in a brace of fat and plump and tender "dead ducks," just captured in the Taos sporting fields. Thanks, gentlemen—thanks!

JANUARY 14, 1869:

Hon. Thomas B. Catron, of Doña Ana county, having been appointed Attorney General by Gov. Mitchell, was confirmed by the Legislative Council on Tuesday last. Mr. Catron is a young lawyer of much promise, and we have every confidence that his appointment will give universal satisfaction.

This item is included for two reasons. The first is the pleasure of being able to note, ninety years later, that Thomas B. Catron, of Santa Fe County, is a young lawyer of much promise. The second is that the present Mr. Catron informs me that his grandfather, mentioned with such approval in the item, was an officer in the Confederate Army (not the Missouri guerrillas) who moved to New Mexico because, after the Civil War, he was proscribed from practicing law in his native state of Missouri. This sheds an interesting little light on the anti-Confederate ardor of Messrs. Manderfield and Tucker.

JANUARY 25, 1869:   TO OUR SUBSCRIBERS.

Many of our subscribers to the weekly New Mexican, are now in arrears two, three, and even four years. It should be manifest to them, constantly, as they peruse our sheet, that as publishers it is impossible to print a paper year after year, and receive no compensation therefore. Every sheet of paper that we print for the benefit of our subscribers costs us cash in advance out of our pockets, and it is neither profitable to us, nor just toward us on the part of our subscribers that we should remain subject to this constant drain upon our resources for their benefit without return. We therefore earnestly call upon our delinquent subscribers to liquidate their indebtedness to us as nearly without delay as possible.

One word more: we publish the largest sheet in New Mexico.

Both our daily and weekly are ornaments to the Territory; our party has the advantage of both, and yet there are hundreds of prominent and wealthy men in the Republican party who are patrons of neither the Daily or Weekly. We put this question to them, whether they feel under no obligation to aid in the support of their party organ? We leave this question with them.

OCTOBER 28, 1869:   ACQUISITION OF MEXICAN STATES.

The readers of the New Mexican need not to be told that we have for years been in favor of the acquisition of the two Mexican States lying immediately on our southern borders, Chihuahua and Sonora. We have advocated it, and shall continue to do so, until they become, as we believe they will, at no far off day, integral parts of the American Union. The splendid port of Guaymas, on the Gulf of California, must, at some time, perhaps not distant, become a great commercial point on the western slope of the continent, and such, it can only become, through the vitalizing energies of the American people.

This is the last item of interest before the beginning of 1870. The end of the sixties provides a convenient stopping place for the "Weekly of the Wild Frontier," which had been a daily, by then, for eighteen months. The days of serious trouble with Navajos, Jicarilla or Mescalero Apaches, or Utes, were ended. Times were changing, so were weapons—the Colt revolver with metallic cartridges was becoming common, and its great partner, the Winchester 30-30, was soon due.

CHAPTER 2

GUNS AND LAWS

THIS next period is markedly different from the one that preceded it. Navajos, Utes, and the New Mexico Apaches no longer caused concern, but from time to time the Territory was harassed by Comanches raiding out of the Oklahoma-Texas Panhandle country and by those dwindling bands of Arizona Apaches who still held to independence. White men had peace and were increasing in numbers, so they turned to warring on each other. Shootings, holdups, and lynchings bulked large in the news; what we include here are only the choice samples.

The city and Territory were growing and evolving. For all the gunplay, we can see the advance of material civilization. The railroad arrived. Reports of gold fields were frequent and usually proved to amount to little or nothing. There was a flurry over diamonds, and, more prosaically and more practically, coal mining began.

New Mexico had by no means become tame by the end of the 1880's; it is not entirely tame now, in the 1950's. Nonetheless, it had become far more than before a land of laws—less fabulous, less starkly primitive, and more closely tied to the rest of the nation.

67

Santa Fe

Thomas D. Burns, Esq., of Tierra Amarilla, is in the city on a visit. He reports a number of miners congregated at that place waiting for the snow to clear off so they can enter the San Juan country to prospect. Rich mines are reported to have been discovered, and many parties are on their way thither from Prescott and White Pine.

This was one of the many gold reports that failed to pan out. Thomas D. Burns, founder of the town of Park View, was one of a handful of remarkable Anglo-Americans who settled in the high, remote, northern part of Río Arriba County, land of Jicarilla Apaches and of "Mexicans" too independent to remain under the dominion of the great families farther south, in milder country. These Anglos were northerners and brought with them a northern, ultimately New England, architectural tradition, including the captain's walk and the lantern, which they superimposed upon the native adobe architecture with most striking results. The Burns family continues in the region to this day.

If the New Mexican *was hostile toward Democratic publications, its rage became volcanic when faced with a newspaper that challenged its position as the state Republican organ. Such a challenger now appeared in the* Post, *and the injury was made all the greater by the fact that its editor and publisher was also appointed postmaster, a sure sign of party status.*

JULY 7, 1870:

A. P. Sullivan, "editor and publisher" of the Santa Fe *Post*, has gone to Washington, in the interest of the anti-administration party of New Mexico, composed of Copperheads and self-styled-for-the-sake-of-office republicans and sore heads, who affiliate with and use what influence they have for the interest and benefit of the democratic party of the Territory. Mr. Sullivan is, and has been ever since he came to New Mexico, the active enemy

of the republican party and of all working administration republicans in the Territory. He has no standing in the community, and
the republican party does not recognize him as one of its members. His stock in trade is brass, impudence and brag. He is not
authorized to speak for the republicans of New Mexico, and has
neither the confidence or sympathy of any republican in the Territory who is in accord with the party. Mr. Sullivan came to New
Mexico ten months since and was well received by our people,
and especially by republicans. But their confidence was betrayed,
and Mr. Sullivan and his paper have been hurtful to the party to
the full extent of their ability and influence. He is rather plausible,
but we trust that no republican friend of New Mexico will suffer
Mr. Sullivan to impose upon him. He only lacks ability and discretion to be dangerous. He will, doubtless, represent at Washington and elsewhere that he is editor of the republican organ of
the Territory. He is the editor of the organ of some half dozen
individuals claiming to be republicans, but always found in opposition to that party; and his paper is supported by democrats, and
is antagonistic to republicanism and their party. The resolutions
which we publish to-day, show that the NEW MEXICAN is the
only recognized organ of the party in this city.

Mr. Sullivan is entirely harmless where he is known, as he is in
New Mexico; his reputation here is that of a conceited braggart,
a shallow pretender with much brass and little brains, and much
pretension but no principle.

*The first apparent extra we know of in the series beginning in
1863 is found bound between July 18 and July 19, 1870, giving
bulletins of the Franco-Prussian War. It is undated. The war was
covered in considerable detail, sometimes by means of bulletins
inserted in the regular paper; this may have been the first such
insert. The city was strongly pro-German. A story of July 19 tells
how the German colony, led by the Hon. C. P. Clever, thanked
both the New Mexican and the Post for their support. They also
thanked the Governor, who delivered a strong, pro-Prussian
address.*

69

AUGUST 30, 1870: "LET US HAVE PEACE."

For several days this community has been kept in continuous excitement by the recounters occurring between Gen. H. H. Heath and Mr. A. P. Sullivan, editor of the *Post*. It is due to the public that we make an unvarnished statement of the facts, and express what we believe to be the almost unanimous feeling in this community in reference to the matter.

General Heath recently returned to New Mexico and, as we learn, was temporarily employed in the office of the U. S. Assessor. At once upon his return, there appeared in the columns of the *Post* several paragraphs of a more or less offensive character in reference to him, and finally, in Saturday's issue, a very abusive article, calling him a "liar," "scoundrel," "coward," "thief," and various other epithets, not usually found in a "high-toned reform journal." About half past twelve the parties met in the store of Z. Staab & Bro., and Heath at once attacked Sullivan with a cane. Sullivan ran out of the store and down the street, making good time, to the south-west corner of the plaza, Heath firing shots at him as he ran without effect.

About two o'clock in the afternoon, Mr. Sullivan walked up the street, in the direction of Gen. Heath's residence, and when about ten feet north of the adobe fence, opened fire on Heath with his revolver, as he was standing on his porch, about four rods distant. Heath replied with a carbine, and three shots each were exchanged without any other effect than scarring the paling fence and puncturing the adobe wall to the right and rear of Sullivan. After the firing of three shots each, Sullivan turned and walked down the street, where he was met and arrested by Marshal Pratt, who also immediately arrested Gen. Heath. The parties were taken before his Honor Judge Johnson and put under bonds to keep the peace.

. . . Is there no other field of usefulness open in this country for a young man and ambitious journalist with evident talents than that of personal abuse? Are there no important events transpiring worthy his pen and talents? Must he attempt to purify the public service by the use of the vilest epithets and grossest personal abuse toward everyone employed in the most subordinate position, whose person or character is distasteful to him, or whom he may deem disreputable? And are we to have the lives of peacable citizens endangered by such reckless use of firearms as does not endanger the person shot at, but everybody else, because a newspaper has insulted Gen. Heath, and made charges against him, be they true or false? Is there no remedy for wounded honor but in shooting holes through unoffending signboards and disturbing the peace of an entire community?

Out upon this whole business! In the name of common decency let us have done with it. *"Let us have peace."*

MAY 18, 1871:

At the reorganization of the First National Bank yesterday, the following named directors were elected:

Jose Leandro Perea, S. B. Elkins, Manuel A. Otero, James L. Johnson, Frank A. Manzanares, Thomas B. Catron, W. W. Griffin, John Pratt, and S. B. Wheelock. At a subsequent meeting of the board of directors, the following named persons were elected and appointed officers of the bank:

President, S. B. Elkins; vice-President, Jose L. Perea; Cashier, W. W. Griffin; Ass't Cashier, S. B. Wheelock.

The bank is now fully organized under its new stockholders and officers, all of whom are well and favorably known in our community, and some of them are among the wealthiest and most substantial citizens of our Territory. All persons having dealings with the bank may rest assured that their business will be promptly attended to, and that the affairs of the institution will be managed upon a sound basis.

JULY 3, 1871:

We again call attention to the reckless disregard of the regulations prohibiting fast driving in the streets. If parties wish to test the speed of their nags, the proper place to do so is outside of the city limits, and not around the public plaza, where there are

71

always more or less children and infirm people, especially in the afternoon when the band is playing in the pagoda. It may be fun for some people to dash through a drove of burros and scatter them, but it is no amusement for parents to see their children served in the same manner.

SEPTEMBER 1, 1871: GREAT RIOT IN MESILLA. Hon. John Lemon, Republican Candidate for Probate Judge, Killed by the Mob.

La Mesilla, New Mexico,
August 28th, 1871.
Editors of the New Mexican:
   On yesterday evening a great riot occurred, in which eight men were killed and about fifteen wounded in this place. Over five hundred shots were fired. The plaza was full of excited people, and it is a miracle that more were not killed. The row was commenced by the killing of Hon. John Lemon, who was struck over the head with a heavy club by a man named Kelly; Lemon's skull was fractured and he died in a few hours; Kelly was instantly shot and killed. The people are very much excited. A detachment of troops from Fort Selden is now here to aid the authorities to maintain order. Gallegos addressed a meeting of democrats, and at the same time the republicans held a meeting in a different part of town. No disturbance of any consequence occurred until after the adjournment of both meetings. The republicans organized a procession and marched around the town. The democrats organized a procession also, and proceeded around town. The two processions were passing each other, when the disturbance commenced as before stated.

Verdad.

SEPTEMBER 9, 1871:

   —The Democrats had their customary display of torch-lights and fireworks last night in celebrating their recent victory in this Territory. Such things are harmless, and are a source of pleasant amusement for children. Speeches were made by Mr. Rencher, Judge Benedict and others.

In this election, J. Manuel Gallegos, Democrat, defeated the New Mexican's candidate, Colonel J. Francisco Chaves, for Territorial delegate.

SEPTEMBER 25, 1871:

—The completion of the improvements in the Exchange Hotel or "Fonda" of this city, to which we have frequently called the attention of our readers as they rapidly progressed, was celebrated yesterday morning by a "house-warming" banquet in which a multitude of the genial and popular proprietor's friends participated *con mucho gusto*. A sumptuous collation provided by the hospitable host was discussed with great spirit and manifest relish, and the liquid treasures of the bar, embracing every variety of beverage, simple and compound, to be procured at a first-class dispensary of the "rosy" were imbibed with a vigor that indicated a just appreciation of their excellence. The Exchange has been thoroughly reconstructed; it is now unquestionably one of the most commodious and comfortable hotels in the West, and its "presiding genius" has no superior as a landlord on this side of the "Father of Waters." "Here's to his good health and his family's and may they all live long and prosper."

OCTOBER 16, 1871:   HIGHWAYMEN ROB THE STAGE.

As the Elizabethtown U. S. Mail and Express Coach was on its down trip last Monday morning, 9th inst., and while the driver was watering his horses at clear Creek, three men—Taylor, Jones and Jas. Buckley, *alias* "Coal Oil Jimmy"—stepped out of the brush, and presenting their revolvers demanded the Express box, which they took and opened, and obtained from it about $500 in cash. Several passengers were aboard, but, we understand, were not molested.

On October 20 a stage was held up near Vermejo, and another on October 21 near Trinidad, Colorado. Members of the same gang, especially Taylor, were believed to have been involved.

73

While these and the following news items were being published, and for weeks before and after, the lead stories on page one dealt with raising hogs, under former Governor W. F. M. Arny's by-line, and with scientific agriculture.

The date line on the following story is as shown here. It may be an error for October 21.

NOVEMBER 6, 1871: THE HIGHWAYMEN KILLED.

Cimarron, New Mexico
November 21, 1871
Editors of the New Mexican:

This community now breathes free. The notorious highwaymen who for the past month have kept our people in constant apprehension, were this morning brought into town stiff and stark, with ghastly bullet holes through their heads. The manner of their "taking off" was as follows: Two men from Ute Creek determined upon securing the reward of twelve hundred dollars offered for the apprehension of the robbers, and the better to accomplish their object, sought an alliance with Taylor and Burns, with whom they were previously acquainted. The men from the Ute Creek, M'Curdy and Stewart, had an appointment with the highwaymen near Loma Chiquita, where they met and agreed to act together. As Taylor and Burns had only one horse between them, and that a poor one, the party agreed to start for Collier's station, about six miles from Fort Union, and there steal a good mount. They arrived in the mountains near Collier's early in the evening, and made camp in the mountains close by, calculating to stay there until it was late enough to make the attempt on Collier's horses; a fire was started and Burns laid down to rest, Taylor standing by the fire; this was the wished for opportunity; M'Curdy drew his pistol suddenly and shot Taylor through the forehead, and Stewart at the same time shot Burns dead. This took place on the night of the 31st instant. M'Curdy and Stewart then started for Mr. Ame's ranch on the Ocate, where they procured a wagon in the morning, and brought the bodies of the highwaymen to this place, arriving this morning. As they laid in the wagon, the bodies presented a horrible sight—Taylor was lying on his back, booted and spurred, with one gloved hand raised and his double barreled shot gun by his side, resting in the hollow of his arm; Burns was on his side with his legs drawn up and hands clenched as if he had died in terrible agony. As the bodies had been left in the mountains all night, just as they fell, of course they were stiff and stark when placed in the wagon to be brought here, and arrived as related above. It is sincerely to be hoped that other evil disposed parties in our community will take warning from the terrible end of these two men, and seek some honest mode of gaining a livelihood.

By the end of 1871 the Spanish section of the paper was confined to page four, about half of which was taken up by advertising. The greater parts of the ads in Spanish did not duplicate those in the English section.

On January 27, 1872, the New Mexican *reprinted verbatim an article from the* Post *asserting, with convincing details, that William H. Manderfield had been an officer in the "rebel" army—a charge that was totally without foundation. After denying the allegation, the* New Mexican's *editors expressed their feelings in terms too rich to be lost to posterity.*

JANUARY 27, 1872:

. . . The slanderous charge is not now made for the first time. It was made to do duty in the interest of parties whose rascalities we exposed, more than once before the forger of telegrams, publisher of false affidavits and cowardly would-be assassin who has again preferred it, ever entered the Territory, and we dare say that every creature of the same sort who may hereafter feel our lash will, while bleeding and writhing in the pain most justly inflicted, hurl the harmless lie at us and hope therewith to stay our hand. We care no more for the falsehoods fabricated by the ring of democratic corruptionists whose appropriate organ is the Santa Fe *Post*, than we do for the braying of a herd of asses or the barking of Tray, Blanche and Sweetheart—fit representatives of its leading spirits—when they assail us in the streets, and we cannot be diverted by them, nor by any other means, from our purpose to lay bare the rascalities of the graceless crew and hold them up to the contempt and detestation of the people. The *Post* will find that it will require something more than old lies revamped, about one of the editors of this paper, to avert the blows we intend to give it in the performance of our duty as public journalists and the organ of the party it has shamefully betrayed, and wounded nearly to its death.

MARCH 21, 1872:

We very earnestly urge upon persons who come in contact with the poor of the city to press upon them the necessity of vaccination. The small pox has been declared epidemical in nearly every large city in North America. The very least mortality has been twenty five per centum. There has been no such scourge since the time of Jenner.[1] Some odd day it will drop down upon us, and when this pest does strike us here—unless the ignorant are urged to vaccination—it will be simply horrible. If this plague shall come among us relatively as virulent as it is in Germany, England and the United States, the poor, ill conditioned and badly fed will be killed outright, and other people suffer accordingly. There is little use in sweeping before your own door where no one else does.

AUGUST 8, 1872:

If some men about the plaza, would go to the trifling expense of constructing a suitable place to receive and conceal their offal and swill, it would be a move towards decency, and give less offense to the feet and nostrils of those who are compelled sometimes to pass by their doors. If they are without shame they will not object to have us mention their names in this connection.

[1] Edward Jenner, the discoverer of vaccination against smallpox.

AUGUST 13, 1872:

Gen. Smith, U. S. Collector, has added another attraction to our streets in the form of a delightful little buggy and a beautiful pair of white ponies, geared in silver mounted harness. The buggy is called an "Umbrella Top." It was made by Mr. Walter Taylor, Decatur, Illinois. It is the General's own design, made to order, for his use about the Territory as collector. It is one of the neatest and prettiest things of the kind that we ever saw. The workmanship and finish are perfect. Instead of a clumsy top, it has a large umbrella that can be veered round to suit the direction of the wind, sun or storm; or may be taken down entirely and stowed under the seat. Behind the glossy little bed, which is fine enough for a jewelry casket, is a convenient little boot for carrying a trunk or other baggage. The bed which accommodates two passengers, sits on high easy springs. It is very light and runs like a dream; on a level road the noise of its motion is soft as the "low murmur of the Indian shell ta'en from its coral bed beneath the wave." Altogether it is the "dearest duck" of a rig in the territory. We congratulate the General on his good taste and wish him many happy and pleasant trips in it.

AUGUST 22, 1872:

The diamond excitement is increasing among us, and reports favorable to the existence of great quantities of precious stones in western New Mexico and Arizona, are constantly coming in. Parties in search of fortunes en route to the gem fields, are passing through Santa Fe every day. It is becoming well known that Santa Fe is the most convenient road to the mines, and offers the best road and facilities for getting there. Come by way of Santa Fe.

Once again we depart from strict chronological order, to run as a unit the principal stories on a long-forgotten swindle. In regard to the later mentions of garnets, it should be explained that these stones are fairly common in northeastern Arizona, although most are of rather small size.

77

AUGUST 29, 1872:

Santa Fe has slumbered for centuries in the midst of the most superior natural advantages of soil, climate, etc., and in the face of some of the most astounding discoveries of rich mines of the precious metals, but at last she is waked up; the flash of sparkling gems before her eyes has "murdered sleep," and her boasted stoicism has become intent concern and restless inquiry. The gem excitement is too much for her. Everybody are bringing out from among their "curiosities" the pretty bright pebbles and exhibiting them as evidence incontestable, of the existence of "fortunes in the sands and glory in the stones." Scarcely a pocket in town without its stones and little else forms the burden of street talk. Several parties are already talking of "going" and scores of men and Indians are waiting to lead them, or anyone else "to the very spot." No better proof of the existence of these gem fields is needed, than that Santa Fe which not even war could excite before, is aroused to the "magnitude and importance of the occasion."

NOVEMBER 30, 1872: THE DIAMOND EXPOSURE.

Our readers will remember that a company of twenty men, headed by Mike Gray, was sent out by Harpending, Roberts & Co., to search for gold and silver, diamonds, &c. They were piloted by a man named Jones, who claimed to know the whereabouts of vast stores of the precious metals. After outfitting at Pueblo [*Colorado*] they then proceeded down the San Juan, making a laborious and fruitless trip to the Colorado river. When about one hundred and fifty miles from Fort Defiance, becoming exasperated by failure and privation, their supplies of food began to grow small, and they turned their attention to the cause of their misfortune. Hanging, shooting and all kinds of punishment were proposed, but Jones was finally set adrift with only one day's rations which he managed to eke out into three—to find his way alone and unarmed, as best he could to Fort Defiance. The party now split up. Jones came into Fort Defiance first; the same day two of the company; the next eight, and two or three days later the remaining ten. They were all so disgusted, having found ncither gold or silver, not even a garnet or diamond, that seventeen out of twenty, were for lynching Jones, but milder counsels prevailed. When last heard from Jones and two others were in Santa Fe, and the rest in parties of eight and twelve, were on the way overland to San Francisco.

We have heard often of a Mr. Buckley, an agent of the "Pacific Ruby and Diamond Company." This gentleman bought stones of a jeweler in Denver, as he went to Santa Fe, and when he returned here he brought back one or more of them and represented them as coming from the "diamond fields" of Arizona. He also stated that he had no diamonds, and found none. He showed stones which he called sapphires and rubies, to the lapidaries, who declared them simply garnets. Still this man is reported in San Francisco as having found a "large number of diamonds and rubies which he consigned to the company." One stone was shown to a gentleman in this town, which Mr. Buckley called a sapphire of eight carats weight. The following extract of a letter was published in the *Tribune*, October 10th: "Among the lot is a ruby found by himself (T. Keams) not far from Fort Defiance, for which he has refused one thousand dollars cash." This stone is the eight carat ruby, and Mr. Buckley the man who offered the $1000. Mr. Keams refused the offer but let Mr. Buckley have the stone with the understanding that whatever it might prove to be worth, should be sent him. Mr. Keams stated to parties now in this city that it was only a garnet, and gave the parties another which he said was like the first, only smaller. This smaller one is a garnet. Mr. Keams, contrary to another sentence in the same letter, said "all he knew about diamonds in Arizona was what others said, and that he never found any."

A Mr. Arnold has made his appearance here, claiming to have in his possession $600,000 worth of precious stone from Arizona, and also "that he had twenty-five negroes at work in the fields," which were "only two days ride from the railroad." A portion of these diamonds he gave to another party in town, who has exhibited them about and represented them as from Arizona, when he was privately given to understand by the said Arnold that they never came from or saw, the reputed diamond fields.

Neither Mr. J. L. Crosland nor the stone which he exhibited here, and which was afterward declared by A. Brookman of Chicago, genuine diamond of the value, in the rough of $8,000, have been heard of lately. Mr. Crosland has not made "his solemn affidavit that this stone came from Arizona," and no reliable person has (as we are aware) certified that Mr. Crosland is a person of integrity."

We have further "rebutting" testimony to give, but conclude this to be sufficient for the day.

DECEMBER 4, 1872:   THE DIAMOND SWINDLE.

Speaking of the *expose* made by Clarence King of the reputed diamond fields of Arizona, the San Francisco papers now declare that the swindle was one of the most remarkable ever perpetrated, and was near being one of the most disastrous. In thirty days more, but for the complete and timely exposure by Clarence King, no less than twelve million dollars of the stock would have been put upon the market, a large proportion on the Atlantic side of this continent and in Europe, where, it is reported, the great house of Rothschild was ready to place some of it. In San Francisco three leading banking houses were interested in the stock, through their managers. The influences backing the diamond company were powerful enough to procure necessary legislation by congress for the location of diamondiferous territory under the placer mining act. So confident were some of the leading parties there of the value of the alleged discoveries that extraordinary precautions were used to prevent the locality being known, and the sum of their own expenditures to secure the ground is probably not under $600,000 in gold. The directors of the "San Francisco and New York Co." denounce the fraud perpetrated on their company by the pretended discoveries. They say their certificates of stock shall be speedily canceled and the company dissolved. It is said that Arnold and Slack, who were the originators of the "discoveries," were paid upwards of half a million.

SEPTEMBER 3, 1872:

—The police of Santa Fe have resigned. They asked for "protection," but were not protected. They have resigned for the very good reason, that the city refuses to do anything for them, more than to pay the miserable pittance of a policeman's wages. They must uniform and equip themselves out of this starving allowance; pay their own doctor bills, if in the execution of their duties they get injured, and in fact, run at their own expense and on their own responsibility, the whole machinery! Santa Fe should hide her face in shame! No city requires police vigilance and supervision more than she does, and yet in the face of all her necessities for such an organization, to save a dollar or a little trouble, she gives the loose reins to lawlessness, drunkenness, and every shade of nuisance and debauchery! If the police are not protected, the citizens cannot expect to be. What does this sluggish community propose to do? force every official in it to resign or run the city out of his own pocket?

SEPTEMBER 9, 1872:

We are glad to see that our merchants about the plaza, are displaying more taste and evincing more pride in their windows than formerly. It is the best advertisement that can be put out, and gives a business like, city air to the place. The day for crawling through dark holes in a mud wall have passed, and *show* and advertising have taken place. Look for instance at the superb show windows, crowning the front entrance to Staab & Co's, Johnson & Koch's, E. Andrews, Spiegelberg and others. The firm of Seligman & Co. do not do justice to their large and elegant stock, because of the old fashioned construction of their building. This firm has one of the best and largest stock of goods in the Territory, and yet, from the outside they make but a poor show. We hope soon to see that Seligman & Co. are as anxious to have a bazar window as other merchants of less note about the plaza. Our Mexican friends are too careless in this respect, and we would suggest that they take more pains in rendering the fronts of their stores more attractive to customers and passers. We like to see elegant show windows and the business houses well lighted. At night much of the buying is done, and nothing so much as a cheerful store front invites the customer. We are glad to notice this growing pride among our merchants, and hope it will be general about the plaza before the year is out.

OCTOBER 18, 1872:

The streets of Santa Fe were never so dirty as now. Hay wagons, bull trains, etc., have been camping about the plaza for more than a week, adding all their filth to the already abundant dust, until the public square presents a shameful appearance. Hay and produce trains should be compelled to camp beyond the limits of the plaza, where their debris will not annoy the most frequented promenades and the most central business parts of the city. Cleanliness is health as well as comfort. Trains must unload about the plaza, but we object to their camping or waiting for sales, about it. Let us see some measures taken, to prevent making a barnyard of the heart of the city.

OCTOBER 24, 1872:

At last we have a police force. The Probate Judge, Don Felipe Delgado, never deaf to the requirements of the time when fulfillment of his duties can meet them, has listened to the cry for protection from rowdies and cut throats, made by the victims of the late frequent outrages, and appointed an efficient corps of reliable men to patrol the city and guard the peace. We have needed this long, and hope it will accomplish the desired reform.

JANUARY 20, 1873:   THE EPIZOOTIC IN NEW MEXICO.

The states with their railroads and steamboats, and their water travel, and engines, can laugh at the epizootic with a grim smile, such as a man with another resource may sometimes be supposed to manifest; but New Mexico without any of these advantages of the 19th century, must take the deal as it is made. The only communication which we have with the east is by mules and horses. Our railroad train is a coach and six mules, our mail carriers are a horse or mule and a pair of saddle bags; and the great body of our transportation is done on the backs of animals. Our wood, our grain, and in fact, our produce are brought to market on the backs of animals. The stage communication is already interrupted, and we stand now in the same relation to the civilized world that we did years ago. Instead of having a daily mail, we are entirely without mails, and the indications are, that no mails will come for weeks yet. Some enterprising citizens, on their own private risk, have undertaken to run to the railroad and back, but the very least time in which they can accomplish the trip, is twenty-four days. We are thus cut off from all communication with the east and are now what we once were—a mountain town in the wilderness, isolated and alone. All the rest of the world is nothing more to us. To us the epizootic means this and much more. If it breaks out among our burros then we will be in a sad condition indeed. Most of our citizens depend on the labor of that industrious little animal alone, for the support of themselves and their families. The burro is the stay and the staff of their living; and if he fails, then misery and suffering must follow. For the sake of the poor people in our Territory, we sincerely hope that this dreadful disease will touch us lightly. Its effects are already severe enough upon us. No mails, no arrivals, nothing that once contributed to the life and excitement of the city. Cut off from everything we walk and gape like a man in search of something. Business is almost stopped, and the very hearts of the people are stagnated. Whether the disease is amongst us as is reported, we do not know —for the good of the people we sincerely hope it is not. The epizootic has visited no part of the country with such direful consequences as in New Mexico, and we sincerely hope that its stay will be of short duration.

Epizootic is a vague term, meaning an epidemic among animals, usually of the nature of an influenza or distemper. Perhaps it is also needful to explain that burro, *absorbed into Western English from the Spanish, means "donkey."*

83

MARCH 17, 1873:

—Peter Knapp, the popular saloon keeper on the east side of the plaza knows how to feed a printing office, and has wisely done it in the form of a "big bellied bottle" of the finest brand in the city. Let this example be liberally followed and this office will have no bones to pick.

MARCH 18, 1873:

Going up: Another stairway on the plaza in the Don Simon Delgado building. Such stairways are obstructions to the sidewalks, but as long as our old adobe structures stand, we may expect to see them. The increasing business of the city demands two story buildings about the plaza to furnish offices and halls for the professions and public entertainments. Entrances to such places should be constructed as in the states, by hallways entering the buildings from the plaza. But at present, in consequence of the primitive construction of our buildings, we must suffer temporary inconveniences until we can do better. We would suggest that most of the structures about the public square, be raised to two stories, both to give greater beauty and dignity to the appearance of the city and to furnish the much needed office room for officials, professionals and other enterprises. All such rooms could be readily rented and would give a more business like look to the center of the city. But entrances must be furnished, so that the upper and lower parts of the building will be distinct and independent.

MAY 7, 1873:

The sprinkler is doing a good work; but until we get rid of our dirt roofs, it wouldn't be a bad idea to run another one over the tops of the houses, as on a windy day the greatest clouds of dust come from above.

JUNE 20, 1873: THE CONDITION OF OUR ROADS.

The frequent rains and the wear and tear of years, without repairs, have made sad havoc of our roads. There is not a road leading out of the city, that is passable or safe to travelers in the daylight let alone in the darkness. Even horsemen, not to speak of
vehicles, are in constant danger of running over some great "jump
off." The Taos road on the north traversing sands and orgillaceous
earths, is cut and washed by the waters from the mountains, most
frightfully. In some places along this road travelers are compelled to "go around" several miles in order to escape some steep
sided channel that a few hours work would bridge or fill up. The
La Bajada road going south, is absolutely unfit to travel. Passengers do not know at what moment the coach will upset and dash
their brains out against the ragged rocks below. So great is the
dread on this road, that the usual custom is to get out of the coach
and walk down the frightful hills. The expense of putting this
route in a safe and decent condition would probably be great and
more than we could afford at present, but by a slight expenditure,
it could be so far improved as to rob it of some of its terrors. As
a road for freighters it is almost impassable. The eastern road, the
one most used and the one upon which we depend for all our
goods and supplies, our daily mail and expressage, and for visitors
and intercourse with the states, is in a most shameful condition.
Cut by arroyos and streams; washed by freshets from the mountains; crossed by hills and gullies, and literally paved with boulders, it is as much as a man's life is worth to travel it in a coach
drawn by four or six wild mules; and if it were not for skilful and
wary drivers, many a passenger would go to his doom, or have
broken bones to mend. Heavy laden trains can scarcely travel it
at all, and the route is strewn with the wreck of many a "prairie
schooner." A little bridging, a little blasting of rocks, and a little
rolling away of boulders would insure life and save many a broken
wagon. The roads and streets in the city are in a like disgraceful
condition and should be looked to at once. We therefore call the
attention of the county authorities to this important matter, and
hope that some steps will be taken to remedy the defect as far as

possible. Good roads are next to good houses, and they should be built with an eye to comfort, safety and utility.

OCTOBER 13, 1873:

A noticable difference among the dwellings put up by our Mexican citizens during the last year, is in the style of windows and doors. Instead of the narrow low doors that squeezed a man both endways and sideways when entering them, we see now full-grown entrances; and instead of the little barred manger-like windows, we see the more comely cottage window. In fact, the natives seem to have quite a pride in large windows and doors; and why should they not? A house looks more cheerful, is more convenient and decidedly more healthful with large, light air openings. Another thing too, they are getting over—the old practice of putting all the doors and windows within the placita.[2] Nearly every house put up within the last few years, has both doors and windows opening into the street as well as into the placita, thus giving a healthy circulation of air from one side of the building to the other. This prison-like architecture originated in the stormy and bloody past, when the inhabitants to protect themselves from Indians, mobs, armies and lawless desperadoes, were compelled to make each house a fort of itself. In many of the old buildings the loopholes and other means of defense are yet to be seen. Those times, however, are gone by, and in their place we have the more welcome days of peace and quiet, and all of civilization that they bring. These improvements are more noticeable on the outskirts of the town among the poorer classes. We are glad to see and note these things as being indicative of the growth of the city, and the improved condition of the people. There is yet much of the rude and primitive to erase in Santa Fe, but the work has already commenced, and we believe will steadily go on. There is material enough in this subject to fill a volume, but we will leave it at present with the single allusion we have made, until some other time when something else shall strike our observation.

[2] A New Mexico localism for what is usually called a "patio" in Spanish, and in English, a "patio" or "courtyard."

JANUARY 9, 1874: PROCLAMATION BY THE GOVERNOR. $500 REWARD.

Whereas it appears from satisfactory evidence presented to the undersigned, that Zachariah Crompton, E. Scott and three other persons, brothers by the name of Harrold, whose first names are unknown, late of Lincoln, in the Territory of New Mexico, did on the night of the 20th day of December A. D. 1873, at the county of Lincoln aforesaid, aided and assisted by other persons, unlawfully kill and murder Isidro Patron, Isidro Padilla, Dario Balazan and Jose Candelario, and whereas the said Zachariah Crompton, E. Scott and the three brothers have not been arrested but are still at large, now therefore, I, Marsh Giddings, Governor of the Territory of New Mexico, by virtue of the power and authority in me vested by the laws of said Territory, do hereby offer and declare a reward of five hundred dollars for the apprehension of the said Zachariah Crompton, E. Scott and the three persons, brothers, by the name of Harrold, and their delivery to the said sheriff of the county of Lincoln; the sum of one hundred dollars for the apprehension of each or either of them as aforesaid—such reward to be paid out of the Territorial Treasury to the person or persons entitled to the same, upon the presentation of satisfactory evidence of the arrest and delivery of said persons or either of them aforesaid.

Done at Santa Fe, this 7th day of January, A. D. one thousand eight hundred and seventy-four. In testimony whereof I have hereunto set my hand and caused the Great Seal of the Territory to be affixed.

Marsh Giddings,
Governor.

W. G. Ritch,
Secretary of the Territory.

What became known as "the Lincoln County war," and is so called in the next story, is usually taken as beginning in 1876 and ending in 1878. But, as this proclamation shows, it started earlier. It was a bitter feud between cattlemen and sheepmen, and be-

tween immigrant Texans and the native Spanish-Americans (the two divisions coincided), fortified by party affiliations. Although the New Mexican was probably the first publication to call it a war, the paper did not cover it as such but was mostly content with publishing such accounts of individual fights and killings as were reported to it.

The Lincoln County war had two contrasting by-products. It led to the appointment of General Lew Wallace as Territorial governor, which in turn led to his writing Ben Hur in Santa Fe— thus making him the first recorded member of the town's art colony—and it provided the first adequate opening for the exercise of the peculiar talents of William Bonney, better known as "Billy the Kid."

JANUARY 27, 1874: THE LINCOLN COUNTY WAR.

A private letter of the 21st instant which has been shown us from Placita, county seat of Lincoln county, gives the following concerning the unfortunate war, in that section between the Texans and Mexicans: "All here is war and rumors of war. The sheriff left here yesterday with sixty men to arrest the Harrolds and from a courier just returned we learn a fight was going on last night. A general distrust prevails throughout the whole section. Every man met is armed to the teeth. Up and down the Rio Hondo a number of ranches have been deserted, and now many fine places could be purchased for a song, their owners and occupants being determined and anxious to depart from a place where the reign of peace and order will not apparently, be re-established for a long time to come, and to where peace and quiet prevail now."

MAY 9, 1874:

The public schools in Santa Fe county, with the exception of the two in this city, will be closed on the 17th instant. The reason for this step on the part of the school board is that in the precincts outside of Santa Fe nearly all the children have been withdrawn to aid their parents in planting, and it would be a waste of the funds to keep schools open for one or two scholars only. Arrangements have been made, however, so that children from any of the precincts will be admitted to the schools open here.

AUGUST 26, 1874: THE INDIAN QUESTION.

They have come and gone. The Indians of this territory are perfectly peaceful and quiet. The settlers have no trouble with them whatever and indeed, they volunteer to assist the troops in endeavoring to defend us against invasion, and as scouts they are of great use. Having no trouble from our Indians, we must needs suffer invasion and have our people murdered and scalped, and our stock run off by breech clouted whelps, robbers and vaga-bonds, who come five hundred miles or more to do it.

SEPTEMBER 28, 1874: A NEW INDUSTRY.

A new wagon shop recently started by Ritter, Harrison & Co. at the foot of San Francisco street in this city, have just turned out a heavy farm wagon, said to be the first ever built in Santa Fe, if not in the territory of New Mexico, and have others under way. The wagon is made from selected material, and, it is safe to say, is much better than the usual sale work brought to this country from the large manufactories of the States.

. . . There is no good reason whatever, why a great varicty of industries should not be established on a paying basis in Santa Fe. Among leading industries, which might be named, there is a need to-day of a good furniture and chair factory; a manufacture of doors, sashes and blinds; a foundry and machine shop. These are industries, the products of which are either manufactured by hand at great expense or imported from the States at greater ex-pense. Their customers would be the territory at large. Capital and a little tact and push is all that is needed to make a first class business, out of either of these branches of manufactories.

FEBRUARY 19, 1875: IS IT OR IS IT NOT? THAT'S THE QUESTION!

Santa Fe is the seat of the Catholic diocese of New Mexico and is about to become an Arch-Episcopal diocese of the same denomination.

It is also the seat of the Protestant Episcopal diocese of New Mexico and Arizona. Santa Fe is thus, residence of two bishops and will soon become the residence of an Arch Bishop. There are three Catholic churches and one Protestant Episcopal and one Presbyterian, in each of which regular services are held every Sunday and on certain week days.

Santa Fe is the capital of the Territory, the commercial centre and the centre of intelligence, education and social refinement. And notwithstanding all this, the stores of Santa Fe, both jobbing and retail, are kept open for trade;—and the pursuit of mammon goes on quite as lively while church bells summon their several congregations, as on any other day of the week. Is Santa Fe a civilized community or is it not? Is not the public morals, the public opinion, that rests beneath these high teachers of morals and religion, and still tolerates this work of the money changers in the sight of the temples, if not in them, sadly obtuse or demoralized?

JULY 12, 1875: SATURDAY'S SOUTHERN MAIL LOST.

The Southern mail which left Santa Fe at 9 o'clock Saturday morning, together with Henry Ferry, mail carrier, team and vehicle may be regarded as virtually among the things that were.

It appears that on crossing an arroyo near the Galisteo creek, twenty five miles south of this city, usually dry at the crossing, which was well up from rain in the mountains, the whole outfit was carried down stream. The mail, on Saturday was taken out on a single buckboard and consisted of three mail sacks; one for Bernalillo, one for Las Cruces and the way mail. All the sacks have been found, but most of the mail matter, is in virtually obliterated condition; indeed, we may say much of the contents of the sacks, especially single letters and small packages, are completely worked up into a pulp mixed with sand; or, in other words, as mail matters, utterly, annihilated. It is difficult to appreciate the condition of the three sacks as we saw them in the post office this morning. With the exception of the larger packages it was a pile of sand with small scraps of paper mixed. Those posting letters by Saturday's Southern mail would do well to duplicate their letters as very few of them can be sufficiently recognized to be forwarded.

The body of Ferry had not been found up to last night. We shall give fuller particulars to-morrow.

DECEMBER 3, 1875:   POLITICAL BARNACLES.

In the NEW MEXICAN of the 1st of November, in the Spanish column, we took occasion to call attention to the gross inefficiency in the past, of most of the employees of the Legislative Assembly, as illustrated in the unintelligible reports of its doings as they appear in the printed journals; of the illiteracy and disgrace thus liable to be unjustly charged upon the Territory, upon the Legislative Assembly and upon its members.

Looking over the records and files of the Legislative Assembly, of late years, at least, among bills considered or enacted, the same disgraceful evidence is equally apparent, showing unmistakably that members or at least the engrossing and enrolling committee, more particularly the latter, have either been very derelict in duty or that they have been supplied with Engrossing or Enrolling clerks who knew little or nothing about their official duties.

The Legislative Assembly which convenes next Monday is composed of a class of men, believed to be above the average; and hence we believe we speak nearly or quite the universal sentiment of the members, in calling attention to a most flagrant abuse; and which is so manifest, not only in the records referred to, but to every intelligent observer of the proceedings of our law makers.

To a New Mexican, the complaint above has a singularly contemporary sound. The biennial sessions of the legislature are occasions for employing an extensive staff, positions on which are regarded as the victor's spoils. As a result, many procedural oddities occur, over and above those emanating from the legislators themselves.

91

JUNE 23, 1876:   REMINISCENCES.

The recent covering of the roof of the NEW MEXICAN printing establishment with tin, by our enterprising landlord, Mr. J. L. Johnson, makes its inmates feel safe from wind and weather and brings to the minds of the publishers remembrances of the times as far back as 1868, when the Daily was commenced in another building, during the Summer showers of that year, when a wagon-sheet had to be stretched over the press from day to day so as to print off the daily editions. The rains that season were so continuous and heavy that every dirt-covered roof in the city was in a leaky condition and the roofs saturated with water, so that it was impossible to make repairs, and when they were over, there was no necessity for it.

As a rule, we have not included reports of national political news in these selections. The following item, however, regarding the famous Hayes-Tilden electoral contest, seems worthwhile for the extremity of the point of view expressed. The language is of another period, but the sentiments suggest those that were common when That Man was in the White House.

MARCH 3, 1877:   FINISHED! THE ANXIETY OVER—PEACE!

Our telegrams to-day announce that the Electoral Tribunal and both Houses of the Congress have declared in favor of HAYES AND WHEELER as President and Vice President of the United States of America. Mr. Hayes is on his way to Washington and will be peacably inaugurated. Let us feel thankful that the vexed question has been so amicably settled, and that we are again a nation of free people.

The New Mexican *did altogether better than it imagined in its efforts to have the Sabbath properly observed (see February 19, 1875). On Monday, April 23, 1877, it ran a long lead editorial plugging the baseball game that had been played the previous day. This led to a communication from the Attorney General, reported as follows:*

APRIL 26, 1877: BALL PLAYING ON SUNDAY. OFFICE OF ATTORNEY
GENERAL, TERRITORY OF NEW MEXICO, SANTA FE, N. M., APRIL
25TH, 1877.

Editors New Mexican:

Please publish this notice for the purpose of informing all persons concerned that the parties engaged in playing base ball or any other game on Sunday last were guilty of a violation of the law known as the "Sunday Law," which denounces a penalty against all persons who engage in "game or sports" on that day. The persons who engaged in the game on Sunday last, doubtless were not aware that they were by so doing rendering themselves liable to prosecution and punishment. And I give this notice in order that they may hereafter act advisedly, as if it is reported it will be my duty to prosecute the offenders.

Respectfully
WM. BREEDEN
Attorney General

For some time after this, the paper devoted Monday's page one leads to Sunday's services.

The Palacio Real or Palace of the Governors was completed, probably, in the winter of 1609–10. It was the governor's residence and office under Spain; center of a sort of government of Pueblo Indians during the success of the Pueblo Rebellion, 1680–93; seat of Mexican and American governors in their turns, until after the Civil War; and must have been used as a capitol by the Confederate forces during their brief occupation of Santa Fe. After 1870 the building underwent many vicissitudes and at one time narrowly missed being torn down in the name of that "progress" that has always threatened, and still does threaten, Santa Fe. The following editorial gives a good idea of the state of the Palace in the latter part of the nineteenth century. Established finally as a state museum, it was carefully restored under competent archaeological direction in the early 1900's and today presents a fair approximation of its original appearance.

JUNE 28, 1877: THE "PALACE."

If there ever was a misnomer applied to anything on earth, from what we are led to infer from the word as used in other lands, it is in the name as applied to the long, one-story adobe building which fronts the north side of the plaza. Since the year 1600 it has stood there through calm and storm; has seen nations rise and disappear, and if its old walls could only speak they could a tale unfold that would make a fortune for almost any sprightly historian. With the changes which have taken place in the last few years, and yet going on in the frontage of the "Palace," it now looks as speckled and spotted as Joseph's coat or Dave Montgomery's statuary.

U. S. Marshal, John E. Sherman is just having completed his fine office on the western corner, formerly the U. S. Depository. He has had a low stone wall run along the end of the building to protect the foundation; a plank sidewalk has been placed in front; the wooden pillars supporting the portal roof have been faced, capped with heavy moulding and stone bases placed under them; this with the ornate cornice on the front, adds very much to the appearance of that end of the "Palace." With Marshal Sherman is lawyer E. A. Fiske; next is Governor S. B. Axtell's office and rooms, and Hon. W. F. M. Arny's residence, looking every inch their age, and as if they hadn't been repaired during the ages which have rolled over them. Then comes Attorney General Breeden's office, with granite finish and in good shape; then the Territorial Library and Senate Chamber, with their frontage in its original condition—naked adobes—on both streets. It will be seen from this cursory glance at the "Palace" that it is occupied by several prominent United States and Territorial officials, and is all that is allowed them. With the exceptions named above, this building as it stands is a disgrace to any civilized and enlightened nationality and ought to be so represented to the authorities at Washington. A small appropriation will finish the "Palace" in the same style as Marshal Sherman's portion, render its three fronts neat and uniform and make the whole a respectable place to dwell in.

The "Palace" building has a frontage of 277 feet and a depth of 45 feet. Mr. Simon Filger, contractor and builder, did the carpenter work on Marshal Sherman's office, and Mr. F. Donoghue the stone work; both of which are very creditable jobs.

JULY 20, 1877: THE SMALL-POX IN SANTA FE AND SOME FACTS ABOUT IT.

As there have been many and various reports in circulation about the prevalence of small-pox in this city and vicinity, we took the trouble yesterday to make inquiry to those whose business it was to know, so as to get the plain facts and figures. We first accosted Dr. R. H. Longwill, who has been employed by the board of County Commissioners since the disease first made its appearance in April last to attend on and vaccinate the poor at the expense of the county. Since that time he has had about ninety cases of small-pox on his hands in what is known as the "city limits"—not having been privileged to go into the villages beyond—and has vaccinated some 300 persons. His labors have been arduous and disagreeable in the extreme, but as yet he has lost no flesh in prosecuting his humane work. As we stated a day or two ago the Doctor has lost seven of his patients by death. Doctors McParlin, Symington, Aljovin and Woodin have had a small number of small-pox patients among a class of persons who were able to call in the services of a physician.

Along in the cool of the evening we repaired to the study of the Rev. Father J. A. Truchard, Parish Priest for the parish of Santa Fe, who has his residence immediately adjoining the Cathedral at the East end of San Francisco street. Passing the front of the Cathedral we found the Reverend gentleman engaged in administering the last rites of the Church over a small-pox corpse tightly enclosed in a wooden coffin painted black, the body being that of a Navajo Indian girl who had died in the southern part of the city on the night previous. Besides the officiating Priest there were two men who had charge of the coffin, and two acolytes who composed all of the funeral procession to the cemetery, immediately south of the Cathedral, across the river. It has been the custom heretofore among the native population in all cases of death to leave the coffin open, exposing the corpse, going from the residence to the church and from thence to the grave. In small-pox cases particularly, Rev. Truchard has requested that the coffin shall be closed and attended to the vestibule of the church and thence to the grave by as few persons as are absolutely necessary to perform the rite of burial. The Catholic Church, it is well known, is no respecter of persons in its membership. Its priesthood administer the last rites of the Church to any of its members in case of death, when requested, whether they be rich or poor. Rev. Truchard has been quite busy during June and so far in July ministering to the sick, dying and dead, but we found him genial and very willing to comply with our request.

Messrs. Manderfield and Tucker may have been a bit over-optimistic in issuing their newspaper as a daily when they did. After managing to keep it going for nearly ten years, they suspended publication on December 31, 1877. In 1878 the Atchison, Topeka, and Santa Fe Railway came to Santa Fe—or rather, did not come. Annoyed by the attempts of certain Santa Feans to detain the railway by buying part of the pass along which the Santa Fe Trail ran from Glorieta to Santa Fe and demanding a high price therefor, the Santa Fe Railway simply turned aside, brought into being the settlement of Lamy, seventeen miles from the city, and went on to Albuquerque, where it established its shops and went about the procedures by which, in those days, railroads created towns.

This by-passing was one of the most fortunate things that ever happened to the Ancient City, but at the time its inhabitants did not think so. It is a shame not to have our old friends' editorial comments on the matter.

The railway then ran a spur from Lamy to the city. Santa Fe could be by-passed, but it was still the capitol. On February 27, 1880, the New Mexican was revived under ownership of a stock company controlled by the A. T. & S. F., officially headed by Charles W. Greene and Colonel J. L. Bartew. Its masthead lists

Wm. Breeden as president, Wm. H. Manderfield as vice-president and manager, and Wm. W. Griffin as secretary-treasurer.

One important change in the content of the paper was made, with the dropping of the Spanish section. Instead, the New Mexican *resumed publication, also, of the* Weekly New Mexican, *to which it added the Spanish-language* El Nuevo Mejicano. *In the spelling* Mejicano *the publishers retained a somewhat archaic form of the word; later it was changed to* Mexicano *in accordance with general Spanish usage (it should, of course, be* Méxicano). *The English-language weekly was continued until about 1900.* El Nuevo Mexicano *lasted until May 5, 1958, when it was discontinued. By then, although Spanish of sorts was still the daily speech of several hundred thousand New Mexicans, only a small minority of these could read the language with any ease. Those who could were among the best educated and naturally preferred the much fuller coverage of the various English-language dailies.*

The fact of the matter is that at the present time New Mexico's school system does not give the masses of Spanish-Americans a competent command of English, yet at the same time it is allowing the common Spanish to degenerate into an illiterate patois which is daily more inadequate for communication with the Spanish-speaking world.

FEBRUARY 27, 1880: OUR GREETING.

With this issue the DAILY NEW MEXICAN makes its bow to the public.

With the advent of railroad, and the consequent rapid increase in the population, both floating and settled, of Santa Fe, has come the imperative need of a good daily paper; a paper which besides giving fully the local news of our city, would also worthily represent to the outside world our mining, business, stock and agricultural interests, and thus form an important factor in the attracting of immigration and the developing of our Territory. Such a paper Santa Fe demands, and such a paper the NEW MEXICAN purposes to be. Being the only newspaper in New Mexico publishing the Associated Press dispatches, and having special correspondents in every mining camp and town of importance throughout the Territory the NEW MEXICAN assures its patrons that through its columns they will be kept well informed upon all events of interest at home or abroad.

New Mexico has hitherto been little known in the east, but this is now changed. With easy rapid communication assured, her wonderful advantages can now be heralded to the world with a certainty that attention will be attracted. Invalids will come to recuperate, and build up exhausted constitutions, capitalists will be drawn here by the great mineral wealth of the Territory, and the pleasure seeker and tourist will come to revel in the delights of our mountain scenery.

Our Territory is advancing with rapid strides, her fame is spreading day by day and it will not be long before she takes her place in the Union as the peer of any of her sister states. To every effort to advance the interests of the Territory and its people, the NEW MEXICAN will lend its hearty co-operation and support.

After the Chiricahuas under Cochise made peace, no Apache tribe as such remained actively hostile, but various bands and small groups continued their raiding. Of these the most powerful and effective was a sizable band of Chiricahua irreconcilables under Geronimo, who attacked their own tribesmen as willingly as they did whites. They operated out of bases in the high mountain country of northern Mexico. A spectacular raid was conducted in 1880 by Geronimo's lieutenant, Victorio.

MAY 20, 1880: THE RED REPEATERS. THE MOGOLLON MASSACRE FOLLOWED BY ANOTHER DAY OF BLOOD. LUNA'S RANCH THE SCENE; SEVEN PERSONS THE VICTIMS. A REPORTED FIGHT WITH MORMONS.

Special Dispatch to the NEW MEXICAN.

Los Lunas, May 19th, 1880.—The Indians have attacked the ranch of the Luna Brothers at Las Lunitas, about one hundred and eighty miles from here, and killed several persons, three of the men there, three women and several children. They have also captured several children, whom they have taken away with them.

All the men left in the place are closed up in a house surrounded by the Indians, and the band has possession of all the ranches in the vicinity. A company of men is being collected here who will start Friday morning for Las Lunitas.

AS STRONG IN FORCE AS POSSIBLE.

A telegram has been sent Sheriff Sena, stating that we want the Governor to furnish us with as many rifles and as much ammunition as possible, with which to arm the party. We are insufficiently provided with arms, and if those are not sent us, we cannot start out with as many men as we should have.

Special Dispatch to the NEW MEXICAN. MORE DETAILS—A FIGHT WITH MORMONS.

Los Lunas, May 19th, 1880.—On the twelfth of this month, the Indians, numbering about one hundred in the band, attacked Luna's ranch, about seventy-five miles from Rito Quemado, and killed seven people, two men, three women and two children. They also carried away as captives two girls. On the same day the band killed three herders of Placido Romero. On the eleventh instant the Indians are said to have had a fight with a party of Mormons at a place twelve miles from Luna's ranch in the Sierra Las Escudrillas in Arizona, but the result . . . is not yet known.

NOVEMBER 24, 1880: A HISTORICAL SOCIETY TO NEW MEXICO.

The NEW MEXICAN has understood that a movement is underfoot in Santa Fe among gentlemen of well known interest in all matters appertaining to the scientific, antiquarian and general history of this Territory to found in Santa Fe an organization for the collecting and preservation of all papers, personal reminiscences, historical facts and traditions bearing upon the history of New Mexico from the earliest period at which it began to have a distinct and characteristic existence.

DECEMBER 4, 1880: GAS BEGOSH! LET YOUR LIGHTS SHINE BEFORE MEN. Santa Fe's First Great Improvement Stands Complete and

Ready for Work. What the Gas Company and Mr. Ireland Have Accomplished in a Few Months. The Enterprise from Incipiency to Accomplishment—Something about Those Who Have Placed Us under the Gas Light.

At last Santa Fe has light, good solid light, which shall hereafter gleam from innumerable gas burners, bring joy to the hearts of midnight workers, and consign to obscurity these troublesome, unsatisfactory, dangerous and greasy lamps and candles which through three centuries have dimly shone upon the labors of past generations in the ancient city. The completion of the works which are to supply the city with gas—one of the greatest comforts and conveniences of metropolitan cities—affords occasion for general rejoicing, and many will be the benedictions pronounced upon the heads of those who have brought about this great blessing.

Santa Fe, the oldest city of the country, having enjoyed undisturbed its Rip Van Winkle sleep has within the past year shaken off its lethargy, and as if refreshed by its long indulgence in "tired nature's sweet restorer," now takes up the burden of life with renewed vigor. By well directed energy its inhabitants are supplying themselves with the comforts of existence, and within the last six months have inaugurated a number of schemes looking toward the improvement of the city. Probably the most important of these schemes was that which the NEW MEXICAN to day has had the pleasure of announcing as an accomplished fact. Certainly it is as full of importance as any other, and no other excuse is therefore necessary for the prominence which is here given it. The prime movers in this gas matter, then, were a number of the city's most prominent men, who first conceived the idea and then put it into execution.

DECEMBER 14, 1880:   ROUNDABOUT.

Governor Lew Wallace has issued a proclamation offering $500 reward for the capture and delivery to the sheriff of Lincoln county of Wm. Bonny, alias "The Kid." This is a good step and will make it too hot in New Mexico for the prominent young man whose presence is so much desired by the executive.

DECEMBER 22, 1880:

The first edition of *Ben Hur* has been exhausted, the entire five thousand copies composing the edition having been sold. The publishers, Harper Brothers, will begin to issue the second edition of five thousand copies immediately, having many orders in advance for the second series. And the author smiles.

DECEMBER 28, 1880: BEHIND THE BARS. "The Kid" and Two of His Gang in Limbo—They Now Roost in Santa Fe Jail.

The most important arrivals on last night's train were Billy, "The Kid," Rudabaugh and Billy Wilson, whom it is unnecessary to introduce to readers of the NEW MEXICAN. Everybody in the Territory has probably heard of the famous outlaws, who have for so long infested the country and filled the papers with accounts of crime, and every law-abiding man will be delighted to hear that last night they were safely lodged in Santa Fe jail. For this great boon Sheriff Pat Garrett and his posse of brave men are to be thanked. The outlaws were captured three days ago at Stinking Springs, about 16 miles east of Fort Sumner. According to the accounts of the men the capture was easily effected, which was as great a surprise to them as to the public generally. They say that at Sumner during the latter part of the week they were informed that "The Kid" and his gang were at Stinking Springs and having collected a posse of 16 men they set out after them. "The Kid's" party consisted of Dave Rudabaugh, the murderer of Lopez, the Las Vegas jailer; Billy Wilson, Tom Pickett and Chas. Bowdre making with himself five men in all. The posse under Sheriff Garrett reached Stinking Springs just before day break and surrounded the house in which "The Kid" and his men were quartered. They satisfied themselves that the outlaws were in the house and then waited quietly for them to come out. Soon after it had become light enough to see perfectly one of the doors of the house opened and a man stepped out.—The besiegers thought it was "The Kid" and fired. The man went back into the house, then came out again and fell dead. It was then ascertained that Chas. Bowdre had been shot. The posse continued to guard the house until nearly dark when the outlaws surrendered although "The Kid" was violently opposed to it, and were made secure by their captors. They were then taken to Las Vegas and brought from there here. At Vegas there was a strong disposition to lynch the men and it was deemed safer to bring them through to Santa Fe. It is said that the Vegas people were for taking the prisoners away from the guard. Pickett was the only one of the four captives who was left at the Vegas jail. The arrival of the prisoners here created a good deal of excitement and Sheriff Garrett is the hero of the hour.

FEBRUARY 4, 1881:   THE ALBUQUERQUE LYNCHING. An Eye-Witness Account of the Affair.

A gentleman just arrived in town from Albuquerque gives a graphic account of the lynching of the prisoners concerned in the murder of Colonel Potter.

He in company with several friends chanced to be in the streets when the vigilance committee were on their way to the jail, and on being seen both himself and companions were seized and securely guarded till the lynching was over.

The body of men who took upon themselves the duty of anticipating justice, numbered some two hundred men, the majority of which were Mexican citizens. Each man had his face concealed by a handkerchief, and a spirit, not of exasperated rage such as so often animates a mob administering lynch law, but one of cool determination pervaded the whole assembly. On arriving at the jail no demonstration was made, everything was conducted quietly and in order. No resistance was met with at the hands of the officials, they doubtless knowing full well that the calm exterior of these men resembled a volcano at rest, the fire within liable to burst forth in fury at any instant, and on slight provocation. One prisoner on being seized struggled, or rather tried to struggle and escape what he saw was his certain fate, but his feeble efforts were as the dashing of waves on a rock-bound shore; the avengers were there and they were pitiless. The three men were brought outside of the jail and under the condemning eyes of this little multitude were without any delay launched into eternity. The self appointed executioners then, with many regrets expressed to the gentleman who gave this narration to the NEW MEXICAN, and his friends, for the inconvenience which had been imposed upon them, quietly dispersed, and no token was left save the three ghastly bodies swinging in the cold night air, to tell of the weird scene that had been enacted under the jail walls.

Though lynching in general is to be condemned yet to every case there is an exception which simply proves the rule, and in cases such as the cowardly and dastardly murder of Colonel Potter, it is very doubtful whether justice can be too swiftly meted out.

There is a band of outlaws in the neighborhood of Albuquerque which to a man, fully deserves the fate which has overtaken their three companions, and while having every respect for law and order, the NEW MEXICAN refrains from saying that the sooner such a fate does overtake them the better will it be for that section of the country and New Mexico at large.

On February 17, 1881, the New Mexican *announced that Chas. W. Greene, one of the controllers of the company, "took charge of the business office of the NEW MEXICAN yesterday afternoon, and tomorrow will assume the editorial conduct of the paper."*

Telegraphic news, with a main headline, began to be concentrated on page one. This was a period of departments under fixed headlines: HUMOR, MERRY THOUGHTS, TOWN AND COUNTRY, FLOTSAM AND JETSAM, CONCERNING WOMEN, WHAT THE WITS SAY, *and* GENERAL NEWS.

Shortly alliterative headlines became usual, such as COURT CULLINGS, DEATH'S DOINGS *(obituaries),* CULPRITS CAUGHT, SEDATE SOLONS, DEADLY DUEL, *and* VINCENT VAMOSED.

MARCH 20, 1881: COFFINS.

The best and most complete assortment of coffins and burial
caskets in the Southwest is at A. O. Robbins. He now manufactures all the goods he sells in this line, and offers to the public as
handsome burial cases for as little money as any house in the
Territory. Elegant caskets in imitation of rosewood can be had at
low figures. Coffins of more ordinary material can be bought very
much cheaper.

MAY 1, 1881:

If a shell had hit in Santa Fe yesterday it could scarcely have
created more astonishment, or at least more talk, than did the
receipt of the news of the Kid's escape from the Lincoln county
jail. Not that any desperate deed by the young cut throat was surprising, but because the Kid has made so many narrow escapes,
and was consequently placed in the keeping of such good and reliable men, that people while apprehending some unfortunate
occurence that would interfere with his execution, could not help
believing that the halter was around his neck in earnest this time.
The death of Bob Ollinger and Bell added force to the shock also,
and news of all three calamities coming at once in a three line
dispatch was very well calculated to startle persons acquainted
with the three men and their careers. Bob Ollinger and Bell were
well and favorably known in Santa Fe, and the former had hosts
of friends here. He was a noble fellow in many respects, being
brave, generous and true as steel. His services as an officer of
the law were conspicuous, and time and time again did he pass
through the most trying ordeals without shrinking once from the
personal danger to which he was subjected. Bob took a hand in the
Lincoln county war, where his steady nerve and ready hand made
their impression. During that time he killed one or two men, but
was so clearly justified that he was never indicted. He was willing
at any time to stand his trial, and offered to give himself up, but
the authorities did not want him. He was one of the quickest,
coolest men in the country, and was withal as fine a specimen of

the human race physically as could be found anywhere, standing six feet two inches in his stockings and pulling the scales at a figure far above two hundred pounds. He was quiet and well behaved and was never in any trouble on his own account. J. W. Bell was also a courageous man and a good fellow. He served as deputy sheriff of Lincoln county for a long time and was reliable and ready. The Kid could not well have committed a crime which would have created such a feeling against him as the killing of these two men has done, and New Mexico will be a bad place to linger in hereafter.

It is painful to have to record that copies of the New Mexican *for much of July and August, 1881, are lacking, depriving us of its handling of Billy the Kid's death on July 14. The first mention we have of it is a week later.*

JULY 21, 1881:

Early yesterday morning Mr. James Donan, one of the Lincoln county men with reason for congratulation upon the death of the Kid, started out with a subscription list in search of donations to the fund to be presented to Pat F. Garrett, sheriff of Lincoln county, and the slayer of the worst man the Territory has known. Two men who are interested in property in the South headed the list with subscriptions of one hundred dollars each. These were followed by donations ranging from twenty-five dollars down, and before night the sum had reached five hundred and sixty dollars. The list was carried around in the afternoon and was also successful in securing subscriptions. It is hoped by those who have the matter in hand that the sum will be raised to at least six hundred dollars. Garrett deserves every cent of this and even more, but if the other towns do as well he will receive a good round sum.

GARRETT EXONERATES MAXWELL.

There is a disposition on the part of a good many people to censure Pete Maxwell for harboring Billy the Kid, the finding and killing of the desperado in Maxwell's house having given rise to much talk on the subject. In view of this state of affairs a reporter of the NEW MEXICAN had a talk with Sheriff Garrett yesterday afternoon knowing that he would be more likely to know and more likely to tell the true state of things than almost anyone who could be found. Garrett does not think that Maxwell was in with the Kid at all or that he deserves to be held responsible for the presence of the cut throat in his house on the night upon which Billy met his death. He says that Pete was intimidated and was afraid to speak above a whisper when the Kid was around, otherwise he would have given notice of his whereabouts. Garrett knows Maxwell well and knows that this is in keeping with his disposition. He says that Pete acknowledged that fear kept him from informing on the Kid, and told him that if he could have found any safe way of letting Garrett know that his man was there he would have done so.

"How did the Kid happen to stop at Maxwell's house?" asked the reporter.

"He didn't stop there," replied Garrett. "He had only made three visits to Sumner since his escape and just came in unexpectedly while I was there. You see I went in to see Maxwell and ask him where the Kid was. I asked him as soon as I got in whether Kid was in the country and he became very much agitated, but answered that he was. Just then a man came in at the door and spoke to my men outside in Spanish, supposing them to be Mexicans. I didn't recognize him. He then came in and approached the bed, and after speaking to Maxwell, asked who were those outside. I had not had time to fix my revolver, and had not expected to see him there. I therefore reached around and adjusted it, and Maxwell started in the bed. The Kid pulled down on me, and asked, "Who is it?" He must have then recognized me, as I had him, for he went backward with a cat-like movement, and I jerked my gun and fired. The flash of the pistol blinded me, and I fired in the same direction again; and I was ready to shoot the third time, but I heard him groan and knew that he was struck. All this, however, has been told. What I want you to say, is, that Maxwell is not guilty of harboring the Kid."

"I shall do that but I also want to ask you a few questions first.

How do you account for the Kid not shooting when he first recognized you?"

"I think he was surprised and thrown off his guard. Almost any man would have been. Kid was as cool under trying circumstances as any man I ever saw. But he was so surprised and startled, that for a second he could not collect himself. Some men cannot recover their faculties for some time after such a shock. I think Kid would have done so in a second more, if he had had time."

"It is said by some people that Kid was cowardly, and never gave a man a chance?"

"No, he was game. I saw him give a man one once. I have seen him tried. He would fight any way. I've known him to turn loose in a crowd of Mexicans, and get away with them. He would lick Mexicans that would weigh twenty-five or fifty pounds more than he did. He was quick as a flash."

"Was he a good shot?"

"Yes, but he was no better than the majority of men who are constantly handling and using six-shooters. He shot well, though, and he shot well under all circumstances, whether in danger or not."

"Why do you suppose he hung around Lincoln county, instead of leaving the country?"

"Oh, he thought that was his safest plan. In fact, he said so. He said he was safer out on the plains, and could always get something to eat among the sheep herders. So he decided to take his chances out there where he was hard to get at."

After some more conversation, into which Mr. Garrett entered more freely than is his wont, and another reference to the Maxwell affair, the reporter left.

From the statements of all who know Pete Maxwell, it would appear that Garrett's idea is the correct one, and that he is guilty of nothing except of being abjectly afraid of the Kid.

SEPTEMBER 21, 1881: AN ELOPEMENT.

. . . This new piece of news comes under the head of elopements, showing that while Mars has been busy Cupid has not been idle. The individual figuring most prominently in this affair is Miss Rosa Seitman, a young Jewess, whose pretty face and figure has played sad havoc with the hearts of several Santa Fe swains.

Miss Rosa is the daughter of Mrs. Seitman, who keeps a small fruit store on San Francisco street, and worked in her mother's store. Her pretty eyes fell into the heart of a young man whose name is not given for the reason it is not ascertained, he having managed his love affair with discretion and skillfully enough to fool not only outsiders and rivals but also the mother of his sweetheart. How long the courtship had been going on it is a matter of no consequence. Certum est the artful young man took time enough to convince Miss Rosa that life with him was sweeter even than life in a fruit and candy store, and having done this he took the train for Las Vegas Monday morning and yesterday morning Miss Rosa followed suit, leaving her mother and lovers disconsolate. Besides the mischief which the young lady created among her friends she got the hack driver who took her over to the depot in trouble, the irate mother having had him arrested for complicity in the theft of her daughter. The driver gave bond and will be tried to-day. Where the lovers went is a question for the young men and the mother to solve. They got off very cleverly and if they conduct all their affairs as well it is safe to predict for them a happy future.

SEPTEMBER 24, 1881:   THE RECENT ELOPEMENT.

The recent elopement has been cause of no end of trouble to all parties concerned. First of all came the trouble of the two lovers in succeeding in getting the connubial knot tied, despite the parental opposition encountered, then came the arrest of the hack driver, who hauled the bride to the depot, followed by the arrest of Cohn, the groom at Las Vegas, and lastly the arrest of the infuriated mother of the bride. It will be remembered that on the day of the bride's departure, Mr. Crosson, who drives the hack, was placed under arrest and his trial set for the next day, the charge being complicity in the spiriting away of the girl. When the time arrived for the examination of Crosson, who had given bond for his appearance, he was on hand but his accuser did not show up. Why this was, does not appear, unless, indeed, it was because Mrs. Seitman was in such a hurry to get to Vegas, that she did not want to carry out her threats against Crosson. However this may have been, her failure to appear at the appointed hour resulted in the dismissal of the accused. This, however, did not satisfy Crosson, who, on yesterday had Mrs. Seitman, who had arrived from Vegas the night before, arrested for carrying concealed weapons and threatening to take his life. The accused was taken before Justice Ortiz yesterday and requested to give bond in the sum of five hundred dollars for her good behavior. Altogether the marriage of Miss Rosa has been attended by a series of events which it has been interesting to follow. The affair is at an end now, however, so far as the old lady is concerned, and the lovers of sensations will have to look elsewhere for matter to satisfy their relish for such things.

OCTOBER 8, 1881: DANCING ON THE AIR. Justice Meted Out at Socorro Yesterday. How Socorro Treats Horse Thieves and Foot-Pads. SOCORRO JUSTICE. A Double Lynching—Two Members of the Stockton Gang Hung.

Special Dispatch to the NEW MEXICAN.

Socorro, Oct. 7.—The citizens of this quiet city were surprised this morning in finding the stiffs of Clark and Frenchy, two members of the Ike Stockton gang, the robbers of Browne & Manzanares store at Lamy, a few days ago, and horse thieves on general principles, hanging chained together in a narrow street just off the plaza called "death's alley," with a plackard on their backs saying: "This is the way Socorro treats horse thieves and footpads." They were arrested on October 5th and were placed under a strong guard, but last night about one hundred armed men held up the guards, took the prisoners and hung them. This seems to be an unhealthy part of New Mexico for bad men. It is said they died game.

Santa Fe

A man who sends a son to school at one of the public schools took occasion to say that it was his opinion that the county commissioners could afford to furnish fuel to keep the scholars warm while the teachers are endeavoring to teach the young ideas to shoot. As it is now the boys are required to pack wood on their backs to school in the morning, and those who fail to do so have to take a back seat and suffer. This is rather a novel idea and an ingenious plan for making the parents of scholars bear personally an expense which the county is supposed to assume. A sufferer suggests that the boys be required to carry to their teachers their daily bread. This would be as light an expense and would not be attended by the labor and suffering which the little ones have to undergo when required to do burro work at the expense of the home wood pile. If the commissioners are going to run the schools they might as well do it properly. No tax payer would begrudge the children his share of the expense of buying a stove or two and a few loads of wood for precinct No. 4, or any other precinct that may be in a similar fix. The attention of the commissioners is called to the matter with the belief that the evil will be remedied.

DECEMBER 14, 1881:

NO MORE LEAKING ROOFS!

NO MORE WET BEDS.

THE SANTA FE ROOFING CO.

W. M. Berger.   East Side Plaza.

DECEMBER 31, 1881:

THE rumors that Mr. E. B. Purcell of Manhattan, Kansas, has become proprietor of the Santa Fe NEW MEXICAN are quite correct, that gentleman having purchased the stock of Messrs. Manderfield & Tucker several days ago, and having since secured the balance, Mr. Purcell is now sole proprietor of the property, which he has purchased simply as a good business investment. The large increase of business done by the NEW MEXICAN Printing and Publishing Company during the last year and the rapidly increasing circulation and influence of the paper have made it a very desirable property, which will prove lucrative to its new owner. The management of the NEW MEXICAN, as well as its political course and general policy, will remain unchanged.

Despite this announcement, the masthead remained unchanged until July 1, when E. B. Purcell's name appeared as president, with Greene remaining as editor. The Spanish section was restored. On the whole, under this management the paper had less color than it did under Manderfield and Tucker.

JANUARY 4, 1882:

FORTUNATELY strikes among employes are getting less frequent as the relative positions of capital and labor are getting to be better understood. Yesterday the typos of the NEW MEXICAN, not content with the best wages paid anywhere, struck for a higher rate of pay, presuming on the pressure of work now in the office to be able to enforce their demands. They could not be acceded to without involving the office in a heavy loss upon its contracts. They were given ample time to consider the matter and return to their work at the old terms if they saw fit. This they refused to do and their discharge was made final. The occurrence is much to be regretted, as some of the men who have been drawn into the strike by the roaming "ne'er do wells" have families who will necessarily suffer from the course they have taken. The matter will cause only a temporary embarrassment to the paper, as a new force of men have been telegraphed for, some of whom are already on the way here.

FEBRUARY 1, 1882:   ENLARGED.

We present the NEW MEXICAN to-day an eight-column paper, not filled with advertisements—indeed, not quite so full as we intend to fill it—but furnishing to the readers of New Mexico the local news of the Territory, general news, and able editorial discussion and review of the events transpiring in all parts of the world. In making the enlargement, which was intended to have been made some weeks sooner, but was delayed by the "strike" of our printers, we make no promise to publish a larger paper than the people of the Territory will furnish support. While we need thirty-two columns we shall publish it; when twenty-eight will accommodate our advertising patronage and the usual reading matter we shall make but a seven column paper. It will, in the words of our greenback friends, be adapted to the demands of trade. It may be eight columns to-day and seven to-morrow, or vice versa. The paper speaks for itself as to its typography and mechanical excellence; its wonderfully rapid increase of circulation and the favor it is meeting attests the satisfaction it affords to its patrons. With increased facilities for news-gathering and with an exceptionally strong editorial force, it is but reasonable to anticipate that its growth in the future will not be less rapid than in the past.

In February, 1882, the first notices began to appear of coal as one of New Mexico's assets. Eventually, coal mining became an important industry in several parts of the state, notably at Raton in the northeast, in the Cerrillos Mountains south of Santa Fe, and at Gallup in the west. Both anthracite and bituminous coal were found, of a poor grade, and today, with the conversion of the railroads to oil, coal mining in the state has all but ceased.

On September 12, 1882, J. L. Scott replaced Charles W. Greene as editor and publisher of the New Mexican.

OCTOBER 2, 1882:   WHIPPED FOR WITCHCRAFT. Rio Arriba County Furnishes a Startling Case, and One Which Happily Is As Unusual As Atrocious.

Persons just returned from Tierra Amarilla, where the Rio Arriba county court was in session last week, report a trial before Chief Justice Axtell, which recalls the dark deeds of centuries ago, when torture and even the stake were resorted to as persuasives in cases where confessions were wanted, renunciations of faith were desired, or withheld information was sought to be extorted. This modern barbarity occurred in Tierra Amarilla in the year of our Lord, 1882. The offender is Felipe Madrid, and his victim was a woman with whom years ago he was intimate. Felipe had broken off relations with his sometime associate, and after years of promiscuous distribution of attention to other females was seized by a loathsome disease. After some months of suffering he conceived that he had been bewitched by the woman alluded to, and whose name, the writer could not learn. He was encouraged in this by Cipriano Medino, and other associates, and finally determined to free himself of the spell by adopting the only course known to the believers in witchcraft, which course is to make the offending witch cure the patient, and if she refuses, to whip her to death. Accordingly he sent three men from Tierra Amarilla to Abiquiu with instructions to bring the woman to his house. They obeyed, and when they had brought her to him Madrid tied her up by the hands in his house, and told her if she did not cure him he would whip her to death. She protested her innocence and declared her inability to effect the cure, whereupon Madrid whipped her with a "black snake" whip until she was very nearly dead. She at last promised to cure him, being willing to promise anything in order to be released.

Madrid let her down promising to renew the whipping if she failed to make her promise good. The woman, to gain time, called for ointments and medicines and finally succeeded in escaping from the house, whence she made her way back to Abiquiu.

The matter was brought to the attention of the grand jury and an indictment for assault and battery was the result. The cause being tried the prisoner was fined $150 and costs, that being the extent of the law in the case, as the prisoner was in a state of health which would not admit of his being imprisoned.

Hon. T. B. Catron, acting as attorney-general, filed complaint against Madrid and his associates for riot, and the matter will come up before the next grand jury and court. Altogether the case is an exhibition of ignorance and brutality such as is rarely encountered in this age and in this land.

This was the golden age of patent medicines. While enlight-

ened readers of the New Mexican *shook their heads over the medieval superstition displayed in the story just above, they could read—and many of them could believe—advertisements such as the following samples, culled from the issue of December 15, 1882:*

JANUARY 12, 1883: "IF IT TAKES BLOOD." Governor Sheldon Declares That Crime in New Mexico Must Be Suppressed. A Case in Point—A Den of Desperadoes—Old Criminals—An Important Law.

A representative of the NEW MEXICAN dropped into his

excellency, Governor Sheldon's office yesterday afternoon, and found that gentleman in a most excellent humor to talk about crime in New Mexico. He had just opened and perused a letter which occasioned him no little annoyance and surprise. "I seldom have to complain of a disinclination on the part of officers to make arrests," said the governor, "but in the case at hand it does seem to me that the criminal should have been captured even if it had taken blood to do it." The letter referred to contained the appended facts: Three days ago Sheriff Jos. Smith, of Conejos county, Colorado, and Under Sheriff Spear, of Rio Arriba county, New Mexico, started for Coyote, a small town in Rio Arriba county, to arrest Ignacio Chacon, who had murdered two men in 1876, and for whom Governor Sheldon a few months ago offered a reward of $500. Smith and posse surrounded Chacon's house, when the criminal rushed out with a pistol in each hand and arrayed only in his night clothes. They did not fire on him, desiring to take him alive. Chacon managed to reach the Chama river, which is skirted by heavy timber. As soon as Chacon reached that timber, he began firing, shooting one of the posse, Antonio Baldonado, hitting him twice. Baldonado is expected to die. Sheriff Smith's clothing was pierced twice with the bullets. Chacon then escaped into the town of Coyote, which is the rendezvous of the worst characters of Mora, Taos and Rio Arriba counties. Francisco Nolan, who killed two men at Sapello, two months ago, is an unmolested resident of this town, besides several well known desperadoes. Sheriff Smith and party were not strong enough to attack the town, and therefore left for Ballicito [*Vallecito*], a small Mexican settlement, hoping to arrest Deonicio [*Dionisio*] Lopez, an alleged cattle thief, who has driven away some 300 head of cattle during the past year.

Governor Sheldon intends to offer rewards for these desperadoes, and organize a strong posse to oust them. His excellency is determined to break up the nest of criminals at Coyote.

Ignacio Chacon must have been a criminal of some distinction; the usual reward for the apprehension of desperadoes in this period was only $250.

FEBRUARY 8, 1883:

THE NEW MEXICAN's list of subscribers is just double what it was when the "tenderfoot management" came in. How is that for progress? And how is it for an explanation of the bitterness of the Vegas and Albuquerque papers towards it? Eh?

The item immediately above should be compared with the one for May 27, 1883, reproduced a few pages below.

FEBRUARY 17, 1883:   A PENITENTIARY.

The first thing the legislature should do when it assembles again, should be the passage of an act providing for the erection of a penitentiary at once. It could authorize the issuance of bonds to run, say thirty years. These could be predicated, or sold outright and a sufficient sum realized at once to put the enterprise on its legs. It is now costing the territory over thirty thousand per year to support her convicts in outside prisons. Four years' savings would alone build the required institution. If it were properly and wisely handled, it would very soon become self-sustaining. It might be located at or near Cerrillos and the convicts could be worked in the mines there, and instead of being a great charge and a bill of expense to the territory, a profit could be realized from their employment in this way.

The New Mexican *for August 9, 1884, reported the letting of the contract for the penitentiary. The columns of this newspaper did not reflect what is the accepted belief in New Mexico, that the leaders of Santa Fe, offered the choice between securing the state penitentiary and the state university and unable to obtain both because of the demands of the growing city of Albuquerque, chose the jail. It appears that the commercial advantages of a penitentiary, which was bound to have a considerable number of inmates at all times, seemed more immediate and more secure than those of a university of uncertain future and unpredictable enrollment. In the 1950's, however, the University of New Mex-*

116

ico has consistently had a much larger enrollment than the state penitentiary.

MARCH 8, 1883: CRUMBLING CHAPEL. The Old San Miguel Church Likely to Fall—Prospects of Tearing It Down. An Historical Feature Which Santa Fe Cannot Afford to Lose.

San Miguel chapel, the oldest house of worship on the American continent, located on the bluff on the left of the old Santa Fe trail and north of the Christian Brothers college, is likely to fall and become a mass of ruins at any moment. Unless something is done at once to prevent it the walls of this ancient and honored structure will soon be razed to the earth and Santa Fe will have lost one of its chiefest features of historic interest. However odd it may seem, the christian brothers are actually considering the feasibility of tearing it down.

A representative of this paper called on the brothers at the college yesterday and asked many questions regarding the matter. It seems that when Brother Paulian, Provincial of the brothers' Christian Schools, St. Louis district, visited Santa Fe the other day, this old chapel was subjected to a critical examination and the conclusion was at once reached that it was unsafe and likely to fall at any time. The question of tearing it down was thereupon considered, but no definite conclusion was reached. The brothers say they have not the necessary funds to expend in bracing it in such a manner as to secure its safety, but express a desire to lend their hearty co-operation to any plan the citizens might see fit to adopt, by which the ancient edifice may be kept from utter ruin and made secure, and it does seem that some action in the premises is demanded without delay.

The move to rescue San Miguel Church was successful. In 1957 a further, excellent job of restoration was done by the archaeologists of the State Museum. As to San Miguel's age, detailed archaeological studies have revealed no positive evidence that a structure existed on that site before 1710. There is a powerful tradition, however, that the church had been built well before the

Pueblo Rebellion of 1680, was partly destroyed in the rebellion, and was rebuilt in 1710.

It stands at the intersection of two ancient trails, now College and De Vargas Streets, and was the church and center for the Barrio Analco, the section of Santa Fe that was settled by the Tlascalan auxiliaries who came to Santa Fe with De Vargas' army when he reconquered New Mexico in 1693.

APRIL 21, 1883: OLD SPANISH SHAFT. Discovery of Old Workings, Stone Hammers and Chisels.

Messrs. Blonger and Whalen, who have the contract of sinking a shaft in the Bottom Dollar mine, near Cerrillos, made an interesting discovery on Monday last. While working at a depth of 110 feet they dropped into an old tunnel made by the Spaniards no less than 200 years ago and out of the debris they took a number of stone hammers, chisels and picks and found every evidence that this mine belongs to the same class of silver producing mines as does the Mina del Tiro property, which is the most perfect Spanish mine yet discovered in this part of the country. These stone tools were left in the mine by the Pueblo Indians, and have lain there since the revolt of 1680, at which time the Indians filled up the mines with rubbish to hide them and prevent the Spaniards from discovering and working them. The owners of this mine, who are in Santa Fe, are very much gratified of this evidence of the former value of the Bottom Dollar property. Messrs. Blonger and Whalen will resume work to-day and will bring these old chisels and hammers to Santa Fe to-morrow or the day following.

MAY 27, 1883: TO OUR PATRONS.

The NEW MEXICAN Printing and Publishing company having concluded some time since to withdraw the paper, they announce the present as their last edition. The causes which have led to this conclusion need not be stated now. It is sufficient to say that the amount of revenue derived from the community was insufficient to sustain the paper on a respectable basis, and they could not consent to run a paper which was not superior to any other in the territory. They feel it to be due their generous patrons to say that the company regrets as sincerely as any one can the necessity for this suspension.

The subscribers who paid in advance will have their balances adjusted at the Second National Bank of New Mexico in this city. They will be duly notified as to the amount of such balance. . . .

I desire to say that the presses, type, fixtures and appurtenances, together with the press franchise of the NEW MEXICAN are for sale.

E. B. Purcell.

JUNE 6, 1883: TO THE PUBLIC.

The New Mexican Printing and Publishing company has withdrawn from the field and suspended their daily and weekly issues. This left Santa Fe without a newspaper, and at the solicitation of the business men and citizens we have removed the Albuquerque Review to this city. It will hereafter be published as a morning paper under the name of the Santa Fe New Mexican and Review, with full associated press dispatches and local and general news. For the information of new readers it may be stated that while the paper will be firmly republican in sentiment, the opinions of the opposition will be duly respected. Its chief aim will be to advance the interests of Santa Fe and Santa Fe county in particular and the territory in general—and we confidently expect that all persons in sympathy with these objects will accord it a liberal support. The office is located in the building recently occupied by the New Mexican company, northeast corner of the plaza. A complete job printing office is attached to the establishment.

W. H. Bailhache & Co.
Publishers and Proprietors.

JUNE 30, 1883:

The Mormon settlements in the western part of Valencia county, Savsia and others, are growing rapidly, and will contain a considerable population in a short time. The statutes of this territory forbid polygamy, and if this plague spot exists in these settlements the full force of the law should be applied to break it up and the sooner the better.

Arbitrarily selecting 1550, a year in which there were no white men whatever in New Mexico, as a starting date, in 1883 the enthusiasts of Santa Fe (meaning most of the population) decided that the city was 333 years, or a third of a millennium, old. Accordingly, a celebration called "Tertio-Millennial" was staged, extending over several days. The success of the affair led the Daily New Mexican Review, *as it then called itself, to one of its congratulatory editorials.*

JULY 3, 1883:   OUR CELEBRATION.

The Ancient city yesterday donned its holiday attire in honor of the inaugural ceremonies at the Tertio-Millennial celebration. It was a success in every detail. The arrangements for the procession through the city were admirably carried out, and within the grounds everything went smooth and pleasant; even the weather was on its good behavior. During the proceedings a bright sun and almost cloudless sky greeted the thousands of visitors who assembled to do honor to the earliest seat of western civilization. There have been many expositions in various countries, international, national and local, since Paxton built his fairy palace of glass in 1851. Some of them have been gigantic undertakings by the side of which as far as regards extent and cost the Tertio-Millennial exposition must modestly hide its head, but in originality of design and in the unique character of the exhibition it presents features that no other public enterprise of the kind has ventured upon. Expositions usually consist of collections of articles showing the growth of arts, sciences, inventions, manufactures and specimens of what skilled handicraft can accomplish. The Tertio-Millennial exhibit is a collection illustrative of the growth of New Mexico from its earliest day, showing this historic land as it is today and as it was when Cabeza de Baca crossed its borders. This is the characteristic of our celebration which makes it such a novel and interesting sight and one which will be unusually attractive to eastern visitors.

The speeches by Governor Sheldon and Hon. Tranquilino Luna, which are reported in full elsewhere, were both masterly efforts, and will abundantly repay a careful perusal by those who were not fortunate enough to listen to them.

The president, board of directors, secretary, manager and the various committees, under whose supervision the work has been brought to successful issue, are entitled to great credit and have the thanks of the whole community for their untiring efforts in accomplishing this result. The celebration now so auspiciously begun will excite great interest in New Mexican affairs throughout the country, and it will be a benefit not only to Santa Fe, but to the interests of the whole territory.

JULY 7, 1883:   WESTERN WANDERINGS. Fifteen Hundred and One Miles on Horseback by Professor Bandelier.

Mr. Adolph Bandelier, of the American Archeological Institute, after an arduous journey covering a period of over six months, has at last returned to enjoy a few days rest in Santa Fe.

Bandelier, a Swiss, best known to the general public (to the extent that he is known at all) as the author of The Delight Makers, *was the first real field ethnographer and archaeologist to visit the Southwest and one of the first true ethnographers anywhere. His work is outdated, but he blazed many trails that the moderns have followed. Bandelier National Monument, containing the famous Frijoles cliff dwellings, was named for him.*

MAY 5, 1883:   A NEW DEPARTURE.

The DAILY NEW MEXICAN REVIEW, formerly owned by W. H. Bailhache & Co. has been organized and incorporated as a joint stock company, and at a meeting of the board of directors Mr. C. B. Hayward was elected president of the company and its general manager.

121

The NEW MEXICAN REVIEW will be changed from a morning to an evening paper.

MARCH 27, 1884: A HIGH OLD TIME. Five Thousand People Indulge in Booming Bon Fires, Pyrotechnics, Music, Etc., Etc. Speeches by the Legislators on the Passage of the Capital Bill Yesterday.

At 4 o'clock yesterday afternoon the bill appropriating $200,000 for the erection of capitol buildings in Santa Fe went to the governor, receiving his approving signature and became a law. When this became known on the streets a dozen enthusiastic citizens determined upon celebrating the event, and in less than an hour $200 had been subscribed by the business community to help the boom along. At 7 o'clock the 22nd United States infantry band and the St. Francis band opened the festivities in the plaza. The streets were black with the participants and spectators, a dozen huge bon-fires climbed high about the square, and San Francisco street away to the foot and on Sandoval clear around to Water street was a blaze of brilliant glory.

MAY 20, 1885: AN HISTORIC WAIF. Le Garita de Santa Fe—The Old Spanish Watch-House on Washington Avenue. A Structure As Ancient As the Adobe Palace—Some Readable Facts Connected Therewith.

But little is known among the American population of this territory about "La Garita," or guard-house, and the ancient governmental magazine situated at the western lap of Fort Marcy and south of the Santa Fe Academy.

From the best information ascertainable the garita is a little house, situated on the frontier lines of Spanish countries and kept by the government for the prevention of smuggling, and where guards are stationed whose duty it is to search all incomers and out-goers and keep always on the alert for any invasion by the enemy or any other danger whatsoever and apprise the government thereof. With us it is a simple guard-house or sentry box.

122

The garita here spoken of is a little adobe situated near the head of Washington avenue, and in which a guard, years ago, could be seen day and night, patrolling about it with the same duties as all the other garita officers around the then "Reino de la Nuevo Mexico." But in connection with this garita, located some thirty-six feet distant, is a venerable and historic building, which like the garita, is quite as ancient as the governor's adobe palace.

This building originally consisted of the fortresses of the northwest and southeast corners of the square and a torreon, or rondel, in the center of the placita twenty-four feet in diameter and about twenty-four feet high. At the top of this rondel stood a guard, day and night, ever on the watch, and giving the results of his observation to the guard at "la garita," just below, who communicated them to another officer who in turn communicated with the governor. This larger house was also used as a dungeon, a magazine, and as a depository for all the valuables then belonging to the Spanish and afterward the Mexican governments.

At the southwest corner of this crumbling structure is the identical place where the Montoyitas, two brothers, were shot to death by order of Governor Armijo in January of 1838. They were the very first revolutionists who caused the Chimayo revolution in that year.

La Garita remained a waif. Nothing remains today of it or its related buildings, nor is there any fragment of the wall that once enclosed the city. Although citizens could be rallied, on occasion, to the rescue of such a building as San Miguel, on the whole this was a time of "progress" and of breaking away from the past and its cumbersome relics.

MAY 22, 1885: "HEAD 'EM OFF!" Geronimo and Party Cross the New Mexico Line and Slay Several Settlers. Cavalry Concentrating in Front of Them and a Battle Confidently Expected.

Trustworthy advices from Fort Bayard and Silver City, received at 9 a. m. to-day, state that old Chief Geronimo with thirty-four

123

Chiricahua warriors and nearly 100 women and children have crossed the line from Arizona into New Mexico and were last heard from near old Fort Tularosa, in the northwestern portion of the Black Range mountains. The military authorities at Fort Bayard have reports that they are raiding settlements on the San Francisco river and moving toward Hillsboro, Sierra county. Gen. L. P. Bradley, commander of the military district of New Mexico, is at Fort Bayard directing the movement of troops in the field, and should the Indians remain in New Mexico Gen. Crook will proceed from Fort Apache, Arizona, concentrate his cavalry at Fort Bayard and use that post as a base for operating against them. Three troops of the 6th cavalry are now scouting on the upper Gila and San Francisco rivers, and one troop is near Hillsboro, moving northward. Two troops of cavalry were ordered out from Fort Wingate this morning and were conveyed to San Marcial by lightning special on the A. T. & S. F. These will take the field and operate in a western and southwesterly direction. Thus it will be seen that at this time the chances for the Indians making a dash into old Mexico are most unlikely. There are troops following them in the rear, and five troops are in the field to head them off should they move east or south from the Tularosa range.

As usual, the Apaches got away, taking booty with them. Not until fellow-Apaches were enlisted in considerable numbers to support the troops was Geronimo caught. By and large, the white man's record in combat with Chiricahua Apaches is pathetic.

In the beginning of July, 1885, the word Review *was dropped, and the name of the paper became the* Santa Fe Daily New Mexican.

AUGUST 7, 1885:   THE FIRST PUBLIC BUILDING. New Mexico's New Penitentiary Completed and Ready for Occupancy. Some Reports of the Gala House Warming which Took Place Therein Last Night.

Fifty public and as many private conveyances charged about the streets of the ancient capital city last evening all loaded with guests, and heading for New Mexico's first public building, the newly completed territorial penitentiary. From 8 to 10 o'clock the crowd poured into that magnificent structure until every chair in the building was held at a premium and the grand chapel hall was filled with gay promenaders. The second and third floors were devoted to the entertainment of the guests. On the second landing as one passed up the broad stairway was encountered a score or more of white-aproned waiters rushing to and fro like mad and arranging the four long tables at which the visitors were to feast later on in the evening. At one end of the spacious chapel hall, on the third floor, on a high platform, sat the 13th U. S. infantry band discoursing good music, while from the gallery of the chapel the crowd below, the ladies with their rich, bright colored toilets, the gentlemen in full dress, with a profusion of flowers everywhere visible, presented an ever changing variety of kaleidoscopic views, as the gay revelers promenaded about the hall, tripped merrily the jolly waltz or stepped through the figures of the more dignified quadrille.

OCTOBER 3, 1885:   CONSECRATED GROUND. Description of an Interesting Spot a Few Miles out of Santa Fe.

Perhaps it is not generally known that there is a spot of consecrated ground within a day's drive of Santa Fe, where there is not a day in the year but that some distressed one visits the place, has the "Novena" read, applies the consecrated dust to his or her body on the five points representing the five wounds our Savior received at the time he was crucified, and goes away firmly believing that they will get well. The writer was told by the devout layman that has officiated in the chapel for thirty years that not a case that has visited the holy place, in good faith, but has recovered.

This note refers to the Santuario, *a chapel on the outskirts of the village of Chimayó. The village was settled by Hispanicized southern Mexican-Indian weavers, brought to New Mexico at the end of the eighteenth century. It is still a weaving center. The*

settlers brought with them the cult of the Black Christ of Esquipulas, which is maintained at the Santuario to this day. The chapel
remains an important center of pilgrimage.

NOVEMBER 10, 1885:   ANNOUNCEMENT.

The New Mexican Printing Company has this day sold the
DAILY and WEEKLY NEW MEXICAN and its job office
and bindery to Mr. G. W. Collier, formerly of Ohio. Mr. Collier
has had long experience in the newspaper business, and will make
the DAILY and WEEKLY NEW MEXICAN a power for good
for the people of New Mexico.

We thank the people of Santa Fe and the territory for their
kindness in the past, and trust they will give to the new management their hearty support.

C. B. Hayward,
President and Manager.

APRIL 1, 1886:

The trouble between the cattle and sheep men in Valencia
county, which threatens to lead to more bloodshed, should receive prompt judicial attention.—Albuquerque Journal.

The trouble should be stopped and that at once. Last summer
two sheep herders were wantonly and brutally murdered by cowboys in the Zuni mountains. That was the commencement. The
murderers escaped. Latterly a cowboy was shot and killed by
sheepherders in the same locality. We understand that some of
the cattle owners in that locality are to blame. Let the matter be
thoroughly investigated and the guilty parties punished.

GERONIMO'S KID. A Little White Boy Who Was Captured on
the Mimbres.

A dispatch to the Pacific coast papers from Wilcox, A. T., relates that Geronimo's band of Chiricahua Apaches had in camp
with them on San Bernardino creek an American boy 10 years old,
who was afraid to talk while the late peace conference was in

progress. However, what little the lad did say may furnish a clue to his identity. He stated that his name was Santiago McKinn, and when asked if his father was an Irishman he glibly answered "si." He said also that his mother was a Mexican woman and that he was captured by Geronimo's band during their raid along the Mimbres river in New Mexico last fall. The boy is light complexioned and his face is badly freckled. He said the Indians had treated him kindly.

APRIL 3, 1886: LATEST FROM THE APACHES.

Special to the New Mexican.

Tucson, A. T., April 2.—Chiefs Nana, Clothia and Josamie of Geronimo's band of Apaches, together with nine bucks and sixty women and children, all of whom surrendered to Gen. Crook at San Bernardino ranch on the 27th ultimo, arrived at Fort Bowie this morning under military escort. Geronimo, Nachez and Chihuahua, who fled the camp after the surrender, are being pursued by Lieut. M. P. Maus and a company of scouts. Geronimo and the other two chiefs, together with twenty warriors and eleven women, constitute the remnant of the band now out. They are now in the Sierra Madre mountains, in Mexico, and are evidently trying to reach Mangus' camp some 300 miles toward the interior of Mexico.

APRIL 16, 1886: BAKER'S EXPERIENCE. A Santa Fe Convict's Story of How It Feels To Be Hanged.

Theodore Baker, now in the penitentiary awaiting trial for murder in Colfax county, relates a rather interesting experience which Deputy Warden Burnett has written up for an eastern journal. Baker and Mrs. Unruth are charged with having murdered Frank Unruth, the woman's husband. A gang of Colfax citizens lynched Baker, hanging him to a telegraph pole, and left him for dead. In seven hours he was restored to life. He says:

"I went with them, and at the jail door I began to curse them, when one of them put the muzzle of his pistol to my ear and said:

'Keep still or I'll put a bullet through you.' I knew him by his voice and knew he would do it, and I kept still. A little further on we came to a telegraph pole. From the crossbar swung a new rope. On the end was a big slip-noose. They led me under the rope. I tried to stoop down and pull my boots off, as I had promised my folks not to die with my boots on, but before I could do it the noose was thrown over my head and I was jerked off my feet. My senses left me a moment and then I waked up in what seemed to be another world. As I recollect now, the sensation was that everything about me had been multiplied a great many times. My five executioners had grown in number until there were thousands of them. I saw what seemed to be a multitude of animals of all shapes and sizes.

"These things changed and I was in great pain. I became conscious that I was hanging by the neck, and that the knot of the rope had slipped around under my chin. My hands were loosely tied, and I jerked them loose and tried to catch the rope above me. Somebody caught me by the feet just then and gave me a jerk. It seemed like a bright flash of lightning passed in front of my eyes. It was the brightest thing I ever saw. It was followed by a terrible pain up and down and across my back and I could feel my legs jerk and draw up. Then there was a blank, and I knew nothing more until 11 o'clock the next day.

"My first recollection was being in the court room and saying: 'Who cut me down?' There was a terrific ringing in my ears like the beating of gongs. I recognized no one. The pain in my back continued. Moments of unconsciousness followed during several days, and I have very little recollection of the journey here. Even after I had been locked up in this prison for safe keeping, for a long time I saw double. Dr. Symington, the prison physician, looked like two persons. I was still troubled with spells of total forgetfulness. Sometimes it seemed I didn't know who I was."

Baker was hanged a second time, legally and successfully, at Las Vegas, on May 6.

During these years the paper followed a practice that today

*seems amazing: page one was used as a "slop page," on which
stories that began on pages three or four were continued.*

JULY 26, 1886:

It has been rumored that the editor of this paper is to be indicted. We would mildly but emphatically inform the thieving
villains who seek to intimidate the press of New Mexico by such
contemptible and cowardly threats, that the NEW MEXICAN
will continue to defend the rights of the people as against the
corruption schemes of imported bulldozers. The grand jury has
no more to do with the editor of this paper than it has with any
other citizen. If we transgress law we are ready to answer. But the
suggestion of common curs that we ought to be and probably will
be indicted don't carry any weight at this office.

JANUARY 10, 1887: CROWDED TO A FINISH. The Last Spike
Driven That Unites the Capital Cities of Colorado and New
Mexico. A Flying Trip of Inspection—On to Cerrillos and Salt
Lake City.

With four steady strokes Gen. L. M. Meily, president of the
Texas, Santa Fe & Northern Railroad Company, "sent home" the
last spike that connects this road with the Denver & Rio Grande
system at Espanola, about 10 o'clock on Saturday night last. Some
300 people of the southern portion of the San Luis valley, in
Colorado, and from Rio Arriba, Santa Fe and Taos counties, were
there to witness the event, and such a shout as went up from that
beautiful spot in the Rio Grande valley and echoed and re-echoed
from mountain and peak was a happy augury of the new life that
thus dawns upon northern New Mexico and southern Colorado.

The first passenger train over the new road left Santa Fe for
Espanola at 11 a. m. yesterday carrying some 200 citizens in the
happiest mood imaginable. The train consisted of the passenger
engine, "Gen. Meily," a baggage and mail car and two passenger coaches.

... About half way out the wheels on the rear trucks of the baggage car slipped the tracks and caused a short delay, but this was

soon adjusted and the crowd went on its way rejoicing. The track, its easy grade and solidity, elicited very general comment. The line strikes the river about twenty miles out and thence hugs the mountain side for five miles, crossing the Rio Grande on a 700 foot bridge at the southern entrance of the Santa Clara valley. Thence an easy grade leads on to the village of Espanola. Arriving here at 4 o'clock a splendid dinner was served at the railroad hotel, and after an hour spent in sight seeing, the visitors boarded the train on the return trip. Twenty minutes after leaving the station the moon crawled up over the mountains a little to the east of Sierra Blanca's snow covered crest, which, by the way, can easily be seen from Espanola, and cast a refulgent hue over the view that greatly enhanced its cheerfulness and picturesque beauty. The run from Espanola to Santa Fe was made in two hours, which is a rate of speed seldom made on even the older mountain roads. The trip throughout was most enjoyable.

The sonorously named Texas, Santa Fe, and Northern never did cover much more ground than the thirty-five miles from Santa Fe to Española. Later it was absorbed into the Denver and Río Grande Western. This new link was a narrow-gauge spur, connecting, at Chama, New Mexico, with the narrow-gauge line that ran from Alamosa, Colorado, to Durango and Ouray in that state. The spur was known as "the Chile Line Branch," because of the considerable business it did hauling chile in the fall. It was discontinued, and the rails torn up and sold to Japan, shortly before Pearl Harbor. Two years later the Manhattan Project was established at Los Alamos, only a few miles from where the Chile Line had crossed the Río Grande. Had the line still been in existence, from then on it would have done a thriving business.

The failure of any railroad to run its main line through the capital of New Mexico led to a number of abortive local ventures in railroad building. The president of one of these, proprietor of perhaps fifty miles of standard gauge used mainly for carrying lumber from the Jemez Mountains, sent out impressive-looking passes to the presidents of major railroads and received passes from them in return. When one line investigated, and protested

*against the unequal exchange, he answered, "My railroad may not
be as long as yours, but it's just as wide."*

MAY 28, 1887:   A UNIQUE PROCESSION. The Jicarilla Apaches Pass
through the City To-day.

The Jicarilla Apache tribe that passed the plaza this forenoon
en route to their new reserve in Rio Arriba county, found the
streets crowded with people, all anxious to see the unique and
motley out-fit. The ladies and children especially enjoyed the
scene. The tribe numbered 502, mostly women and children, and
travelled in true Apache fashion, most of the women being
mounted on ponies or burros with a child in front of her and a
little one either hanging on behind or bound to her back in a
blanket. Of loose ponies, burros and dogs, pack animals, raw-hide
bundles, tepee-poles, etc., there seemed to be no end. Capt. Welton led the procession and three U. S. cavalrymen brought up the
rear, while the direction of the band, the route of march, etc., was
in the hands of ten stalwart bucks who "marshalled" the tribe
through town and obeyed Agent Welton's orders to the letter.

In front of the district headquarters building forty-one Jicarilla
boys and girls from Ramon Indian school were drawn up in line
and exchanged grins of recognition with the members of the tribe
as they passed. Many of the women checked their horses for a
moment and called out to a son or daughter who walked solemnly
forward to the street curb and shook hands with them, and there
were tears in the eyes of the smaller girls when they shook hands
for the good-bye and resumed their place among the pupils. The
bucks in the party wore an expression of general satisfaction, as in
fact, did the women also, for they are delighted at the idea of once
more getting back to their former home in northern New Mexico.

JULY 12, 1887:

Gov. [*Edmund G.*] Ross has gone to Las Vegas, where he is
appreciated as a boom prophet. According to the governor, Las
Vegas will soon be a city of 30,000 inhabitants, while Albuquerque is not to stop short of 100,000. As for Santa Fe, well, "Santa

131

Fe is a healthy resort and a good place for schools, but it can never be a commercial city." "Why," he says, "Albuquerque is an American city." We are sorry to hear it if there is any truth in the accounts of lawlessness daily telegraphed from that point and vouched for by its morning paper. But we don't believe that our neighbor is as utterly given over to lawlessness and the banditti as these alleged news gatherers would have us believe. What the governor means by an "American city" is, evidently that there are fewer people of Mexican descent in Albuquerque than there are in Santa Fe, and the governor refuses to class these as American citizens. These people probably form a majority of the population of Santa Fe, and the enterprise, peaceableness and good order of the city amply attests their qualities as American citizens. The governor doesn't seem to like our Mexican fellow citizens. Pity.

JULY 14, 1887:

WE don't accuse the Albuquerque morning paper of stealing all of its telegraphic news from the columns of the NEW MEXI-CAN, and even if it did we wouldn't kick, for the NEW MEXI-CAN daily furnishes its less fortunate neighbors with their latest and best news; but what we object to is the habit our morning contemporary has fallen into of waiting until the NEW MEXI-CAN's publication of a dispatch is forgotten before it is allowed to appear in the Democrat. That paper printed yesterday morning an alleged Washington dispatch headed "Blaine and Allison" which was published verbatim and literatim in the NEW MEXICAN more than two weeks ago.

FEBRUARY 13, 1888:   HE IS AT REST.

The most Rev. John Baptist Lamy, for nearly forty years the beloved archbishop of Santa Fe, fell asleep in death at 7:45 o'clock this morning. He passed away as he had lived, calmly and beautifully, a smile of Christian contentment encircling his noble face like a halo of glory.

Just four weeks ago Archbishop Lamy was taken ill at his home farm a few miles north of the city. Immediately he was removed with great care to his arch-episcopal residence near the cathedral, and there Drs. Longwill and Symington and a multitude of kindly friends have ministered to his wants both day and night. It soon developed that the good man was suffering from his second attack of pneumonia; he was very weak, and could take but little nourishment, still, after the fateful ninth day had come and gone he began to rally and great hopes were entertained for his recovery.

AUGUST 20, 1888: TO OUR SUBSCRIBERS.

Subscribers to the NEW MEXICAN are reminded that our subscription books and mailing lists were all destroyed by the great fire of July 21. We are endeavoring by every means available to obtain our full list of names again, which, as will readily be understood, is a very difficult undertaking. From various sources of information we have succeeded in making up a list containing a majority of our subscribers, but it will necessarily take considerable time to complete it. Those who fail to get their papers can do us a great favor by notifying us of the fact, so that their names can be put on the list.

We earnestly desire to fulfill every subscription and will see in each case that subscribers lose nothing by our temporary suspension. . . .

The NEW MEXICAN upon this fine afternoon again puts in an appearance. The NEW MEXICAN extends its thanks to many papers throughout the territory for kind remarks. But one paper, and that a disgrace to journalism in New Mexico, has taken advantage of the situation and used unbecoming language and made lying and dirty remarks about the misfortune which befell the NEW MEXICAN and the people of Santa Fe. The Albuquerque Democrat, that Judas Iscariot of New Mexico and professional blackmailer, was that paper. Of course nothing else could be expected from that source. The NEW MEXICAN has only been helped by the falsehoods and the meanness of the Albuquerque Democrat, and therefore can well afford to dismiss the subject with this short remark.

Santa Fe

When the NEW MEXICAN says that the teaching of English in our public schools should be made compulsory by legislative enactment it does not mean that the Spanish language should be excluded. It would be better, perhaps, owing to the peculiar composition of our population, to have the teaching of both English and Spanish made compulsory, as suggested by Judge Axtell and others. The trouble now is that the latter language is taught exclusively in most of our public schools and the teachers employed are not educated in English. This is the evil that the NEW MEXICAN would remedy.

OCTOBER 8, 1889:   SANTA FE.

Santa Fe has more advantages for a residence city than any other town in the southwest. We have an unequaled diversity of views here. Eight mountain ranges clothed with foliage of the richest hues encircle our beautiful plain. There are nearer hills, canons, bluffs and table lands, and a mountain stream winding through these and down a broadening valley. From the hill sides we look upon stately public buildings, a massive cathedral and hospital, elegant chapels, churches, colleges, academies and industrial schools, a spacious sanitarium and a graceful and capacious hotel prominent among other structures. Here are ancient buildings and modern in curious contrast for the sight seer. Our mercantile houses are piled with goods daily distributed by two railroads over the territory. The narrow business streets are often crowded with queer looking Mexican teams, through which the great American transfer wagons find difficult passage. At this season and in spring are seen cavalcades of well painted and gayly dressed Navajoes with a score or two of horses, or the poorer but wiser Apaches, bringing their children to school. Always the somber looking Pueblo stands dreamily looking upon American activities as dumb as the ever present burro under his loads of wood, fruit and grain. For a little while well dressed school children thread their way among rough looking workmen standing at the street corners, or the devout worshipers going or returning from feast day services, or the easy going miner in dun colored garments. The blue coated soldiers are moving about Fort Marcy, their gentlemanly officers mingling with the bystanders. Handsome carriages with graceful riders halt under the plaza shade trees to listen to the evening military concerts. On the hillsides are cottages with green lawns and thrifty fruit trees; on the avenues more stately mansions. Everywhere the thick foliage of fruit gardens rises above adobe walls. Occasionally, groves of cottonwoods with darker hues, and shade trees on the streets more completely each year hide the shapeless adobe houses that must give way gradually to modern buildings. Above all these a clear sky and inspiriting and beautiful air. These products of many years, with a history full of incidents the most tragic and romantic, and older than any other American town, are rare encouragements to our citizens for the exercise of energy and enterprise with modern inventions to make by a rapid development under better conditions the most beautiful and interesting city west of the Missouri river.

JANUARY 12, 1889:   DIRECTED TO DEPART. "Will give you thirty-six hours to leave town." Signed, "ONE OF THE DEATH COMMITTEE."

Col. J. Frank Chavez and Col. Albert J. Fountain, president and speaker of the senate and house, each received epistles as above through the mail this morning. The notice was well written, though, evidently, in a disguised hand. It is understood that the writer of the above is well known, and that the evidence is being worked up to bring him to justice and send him to the penitentiary.

In the mean time, it is timely to remark that Cols. Chavez and Fountain saw four years active service during the war and participated in several bloody Indian campaigns, and are not easily scared.

APRIL 2, 1889:   GOV. L. BRADFORD PRINCE.

At last President Harrison has filled the very important office of governor of New Mexico. THE NEW MEXICAN gallantly and to the last supported for that position Col. J. W. Dwyer, of Colfax county, but is well satisfied now since the choice has been made.

The appointment of governor became of special importance at this juncture, as we have every reason to believe that New Mexico, with proper work and proper efforts of its wide awake and leading citizens, will be admitted as a state during the sessions of the 51st congress.

We are of the opinion that the appointment will prove an excellent one, and we know of no one who possesses more qualifications for the office.

Governor Prince was the founder of a family that remains active in New Mexico affairs to this day.

CHAPTER 3

THE BRICK HOUSES

A FEW PAGES back, I remarked that the 1880's were a time of "progress." This was equally or more true of the following decades. In the rather charming account of Santa Fe in 1889, near the end of the last section, is the significant remark that ". . . shade trees on the streets more completely each year hide the shapeless adobe houses that must give way gradually to modern buildings."

There are few greater follies than dedication without reservation to current concepts of "progress" and "modernity." Decade by decade the concept of progress changes. In 1957, Santa Fe hailed as its most important act of progress the passage of an ordinance to preserve historic architectural styles. In 1890 it was to get rid of every trace of "Mexican" culture. "Modern" meant brick or stone, bay windows, turrets, jigsaw work, and, if possible, some fairly conspicuous stained glass. In the 1920's and 1930's competent architects could, if they wished, make a good living in Santa Fe at nothing but the remodeling and conversion of such structures to the appearance of native adobe construction. In the 1890's, Santa Fe was struggling hard to become banal and calling it progress, as it has done at intervals since and probably will do again.

The following extract from 1889, printed here out of its order, perfectly sets the tone of the period now beginning.

APRIL 19, 1889:   ADOBE TOWN.

"Our new governor is welcomed to adobe town," is the language used by an Albuquerque sheet in announcing the reception of Gov. Prince in Santa Fe, and on the same day this item is printed in an Albuquerque paper:

"The large two story adobe residence of Jacob Yrisarri still remains unfinished."

Now let us see about this.

Not to mention a number of brick dwellings and store houses already completed this spring, it may be well to figure a little on the brick and building industry in the capital city at this time.

To-morrow, according to the advertisement, Mr. Kahn will let a contract for the construction of a business house that will require 200,000 brick.

Yesterday the contract was made for 101,000 brick to go into a new Presbyterian parsonage.

McKenzie has been awarded the contract for erecting Santa Fe's second brick Indian school, which will consume three quarters of a million brick.

Hon. S. B. Axtell is now clearing the ground on Hillside avenue preparatory to the erection of four neat brick cottages and thus far he has contracted for 80,000 brick.

The foundation walls are in for the new Missions boarding school, and the contractors say it will take 200,000 brick to do the job.

Hon. T. B. Catron has contracted for 500,000 brick for a new business block on the old post office corner.

Berardinelli has paid the cost for 125,000 brick for enlarging the K of P hall, and has ordered 175,000 more to go into two new dwellings.

Messrs. Donoghue & Monier said to-day that the 1st of May would find their yards in full blast, as they expected to manufacture 1,500,000 brick this spring.

The above figures represent a total of over 3,500,000 new brick already contracted for in Santa Fe this spring, and which will loom up in the shape of fine modern buildings before midsummer rolls around. No account is here taken of the many small dwellings in contemplation of erection, requiring from 20,000 to 40,000 brick.

A conservative estimate would bring the number of brick to go into capital city improvements this year at about 6,000,000!

The following, copied from the issue of January 2, 1890, is part of a column that was repeated at intervals through that year.

THE CITY OF SANTA FE

is making a steady modern growth; has now a population of 8,000, and has every assurance of becoming a beautiful modern city. Her people are liberal and enterprising, and stand ready to foster and encourage any legitimate undertaking having for its object the building up and improvement of the place. Among the present needs of Santa Fe, and for which liberal bonuses in cash or lands could undoubtedly be secured, may be mentioned a canning factory; a wool scouring plant and a tannery. Skilled labor of all kinds is in demand at good wages. The cost of living is reasonable, and real property, both inside and suburban, is steadily advancing in value.

Once again the paper was printed in English only. Patent medicine advertisements were shamelessly printed as news, in a column of news items and jokes called, at first, "Territorial Topics," and later, "Among the Jokers."

JANUARY 6, 1890:   ROUND ABOUT TOWN.

. . . The university opened this morning with an attendance of sixty-one scholars and a full corps of competent teachers, who are very much elated over the excellent start they have made. . . .

The bill establishing a Territorial university at Albuquerque was passed by the legislature in 1889. Most sources state that the University of New Mexico did not open its doors until 1892, but if this item is correct—and it can hardly have been fiction—it must have started informally two years earlier, in Santa Fe.

JANUARY 16, 1890: ROUND ABOUT TOWN.

Surveyor General Hobart to-day addressed a letter to Chief John Gray, of the fire department, thanking the fire-men for their excellent services in saving his residence from destruction yesterday, and inclosed was a check for $50 to be equally divided between the hose and hook companies. Capt. Gray wrote a neat letter in response in which he said: "While we do not expect donations for our services, having organized ourselves for the protection of life and property, and hold ourselves always in readiness in time of need, still we nevertheless extend you our heartfelt thanks for this liberal gift." It was stated yesterday that there was no insurance on the building which burned, but this was incorrect, Mr. Berger's agency having $500 on the building and $500 on the furniture, all of which was destroyed.

This is the first mention of the volunteer fire department which is still, nearly seventy years later, serving Santa Fe with notable efficiency and is still a source of pride to the people of the city.

JANUARY 20, 1890:

To-morrow, on Tuesday, the 21st day of January, in the year of our Lord 1890, will be opened the first territorial educational institution, namely the agricultural college of New Mexico, at Las Cruces. Truly this territory is advancing in the right direction. The NEW MEXICAN wishes the new institution the fullest measure of success.

New Mexico was really going places. The penitentiary was in operation, a university and an agricultural and mechanical college had been started, and shortly after this, work was begun on an insane asylum at Las Vegas.

JANUARY 23, 1890:   FLYING NELLIE BLY. One of the Round-the-World Travelers Passes Lamy—Rapid Time by Rail Her Competitor.

Nellie Bly, the plucky young woman reporter whom the New York World sent out to beat the record of Jules Vernes' creation, Phineas Fogg, in his mythical voyage of eighty days around the world, passed Lamy junction on a special train at 11:25 o'clock last night. The little woman was fast asleep, as were also Messrs. Hobson and Jennings, editorial writers on the World, who met her at San Francisco, on Tuesday. A special train over the A. & P. was in waiting for the fair junketer when her steamer reached San Francisco, and she was soon speeding eastward. This train ran through to Albuquerque in a little over thirty-six hours, distance 1,135 miles. The distance from Mohave to Albuquerque, 815 miles, was run in twenty-five hours. Over about 100 miles of this line Miss Bly rode in the engine cab and took lessons in mechanics from the throttle pullers. At Albuquerque a special A. T. & S. F. train of a day coach, a Pullman sleeper and an engine awaited Miss Bly, and it left there at 9:45 p. m. A stop at Wallace was made to change engines, and a second halt at Cerrillos to get water, and the sixty-seven miles to Lamy was made in ninety-eight minutes. The A. T. & S. F. is taking special pride in running this globe-trotter over its line in the quickest time possible, with the view to making the run from the Pacific coast to Chicago the quickest on record. Over two-thirds of the way it is expected the special will show a speed of sixty miles an hour. The train left Las Vegas at 12:45 this morning, and according to schedule time was due at Raton, 111 miles, two hours and twenty three minutes later. The fact that the northern transcontinental lines are all snow bound makes this a big card for the Santa Fe route.

JANUARY 25, 1890:   GOVERNMENT INJUSTICE TO NEW MEXICO.

For the past forty years the government of this country has been chargeable with almost criminal neglect and imbecility in administration of official affairs in New Mexico.

The United States took this territory as an integral part of the union and endowed the people thereof with full citizenship. Instead of living up to the obligations assumed by it toward New Mexico the federal government and congress have shamefully neglected them. The administrations have often made this territory the dumping ground of political dead beats, judges and other officials who were not wanted elsewhere, and set them to rule over our people in the name of enlightened justice, civilization and republican principles. During the past democratic administration especially, it sent corrupt and incompetent officials here to make havoc of titles and surveys, to persecute our citizens and retard development and progress generally.

The German empire has made Alsace and Lorraine the test of what the best teachers and officials of the highest qualities and self control could do to break the power of language and natural sympathies, and make loyal citizens of their peoples.

The United States has given to thinly populated states and territories other than New Mexico, sections 16 and 36 in every surveyed township, to each state university 90,000 acres of public land, and special donations of many thousand acres for state agricultural, normal and mining schools and institutions for the insane and helpless. The swamp lands in the Mississippi basin and on the coast as in Florida have been given by millions of acres, and these gifts have stimulated immigration, educated the people, encouraged enterprises, developed resources, and multiplied industries till they have become populous and enlightened and prosperous states.

To New Mexico during forty years not one acre has been donated. On the contrary, by official decisions the people have been robbed of much land in their rightful possession. Subject to invasions and savage raids, they have repeatedly risen to defend themselves, uphold the government and rescue the southwest from rebel possession in volunteer service, for which they are still unpaid.

Now congress men frown on our third or fourth petition for statehood, though we present an exceptionably good constitution for our state. Asking for the privileges promised us forty years ago, we are stung with reproaches of total ignorance. We have helped ourselves so much under paternal neglect that our illiteracy is not so great as that of several southern states, where two senators and six representatives are sent to congress on a less vote than our one delegate who has no power to vote there.

We are called a foreign population, though there are 3,000,000 foreigners in the states and we have a less foreign population than Louisiana.

If congress would do us even justice, let us have statehood. If less than justice, let us have public lands such as have been given to the states, with which to remove our quite unmerited reproach of excessive illiteracy. Let us have some legislation that will give us titles to land, concerning which there are interminable disputes.

Give us, most honorable congressmen, a tithe to the encouragement you have bestowed so freely on the new states, and we will soon show you, with our magnificent resources, one of the fairest jewels in the crown of federal sovereignty.

In addition to running a column boosting Santa Fe at intervals, the paper at this time had several rabid editorials against the Democrats, which it repeated verbatim from time to time, of which a sample follows.

JULY 21, 1890:

The people of New Mexico must not forget that under the Ross boodle administration, from 1885 to 1889, when this territory was cursed with corrupt judges and dishonest federal and territorial court officials, the cost of running the courts was $160,-000 per year; the people must not forget that, owing to wise and beneficial legislation passed by a Republican legislature over the veto of that boodle governor, put into office by Grover Cleveland, and owing to just and honest administration of the courts, the entire expense of their administration for the first twelve months of the present Republican regime, amounted to only $60,000, in which sum there is included an estimate of a deficiency in the pay of jurors, etc., of about $10,000; this means that under the

Democratic administration the people of New Mexico were systematically and constantly robbed by corrupt judges and dishonest court officials.

OCTOBER 1, 1890: THE ANTI-STATEHOOD COMMITTEE, THROUGH ITS CREATURES VIOLATES THE LAW.

We call attention to the following communication, sent us by responsible parties from Mora county:

"It has just come to light that the board of county commissioners of Mora county (advised thereto by a member of the Democratic executive committee), have openly and defiantly violated the law in using the ballot boxes just sent out by them to the several precincts by filling these self same ballot boxes with printed circulars, directed against the constitution and sending only ballots printed "against the constitution" in the self same boxes, to be used in the coming election. Addresses and circulars abusing prominent and good citizens and containing most fearful lies and slanders have been sent out with and in these ballot boxes. How is this for fair play? The law expressly prohibits the use of ballot boxes for any such purpose. It behooves all good citizens, Republicans as well as Democrats, to take the matter up and have these faithless officials prosecuted.

We have complete and full testimony to prove what we say in the above. Please give this the fullest publicity."

OCTOBER 8, 1890: DEFEAT OF STATEHOOD. Latest Obtainable Figures—The Influences That Brought about Such a Result—"Not a Political Question."

Meagre returns from yesterday's special election for the adoption or rejection of the state constitution show that the statehood movement has been pretty effectually downed. The best estimate gives some 3,000 majority against the constitution throughout the territory. On the whole, however, and considering the influences at work and the methods adopted by the opposition, the vote is sufficient to make a very cheerful showing for the cause of progress.

As for the part taken in this defeat by a good many members of the Roman Catholic clergy, the NEW MEXICAN is informed that they say they took an entirely non-political view of it, working against it simply because they considered it best for the people as a whole that New Mexico should not become a state. They in the same connection disclaim any attempt to interfere in political matters and say they took the part they did in this matter for the reason that they deemed it in no wise a political question.

From early times right up to the present, the liberties taken with ballots and ballot boxes and the quite open devices for changing the results of elections in New Mexico have been of a raw frankness that is astonishing. This situation is slowly improving, and the gradual introduction of voting machines since 1950 has helped greatly. The report above, of the abuse of ballot boxes in Mora County, is partisan and may or may not have been accurate. It is significant that it could be made and published as entirely credible. The following story gives what seems to be a pretty circumstantial account of an almost hilarious attempt to upset an election. It is a juicier-than-average sample of New Mexico politics of the time.

DECEMBER 6, 1890:   THE ACTION OF ACTING GOVERNOR THOMAS.

On November 4 last an election was held in this county. The entire election machinery was in the hands of the Democratic leaders and candidates for office. Every county official then and there was a Democrat and an intimate friend of the candidates on the Democratic ticket.

The election passed off, and lo and behold, much to the astonishment of the Democratic leaders and candidates, the Republicans made very large gains and elected their entire ticket, with the exception of sheriff, treasurer, clerk and coroner. This was a bombshell in the camp of the gang; they were lost should Republican county commissioners take over the county affairs and examine in to the mismanagement and corruption that have characterized this county government during the past few years; besides, it appears, that the legislature was very close and if the legally and honestly elected Republicans from Santa Fe county to that body could be swindled out of their certificates, that the legislature could be made Democratic.

Secret meetings were held by the leaders and bosses and the first result was the stealing of a ballot box and returns from a precinct that gave an honest and large Republican majority; these were stolen from the custody of the Democratic clerk, Marcelino Garcia, from the vault under his charge in the court house and from the custody of the Democratic board of county commissioners; it must be remembered that every employe in the court house was a Democrat and that no one else but members of the clique have free access to the building.

Thereupon the Democratic board of county canvassers commenced the canvass of the returns; the Republican candidates upon being informed of the theft proceeded to obtain from the judges and clerks of election of Galisteo precinct official certificates as to the result of the election in that precinct, in accordance with the statute and obtained a mandamus from the district court for the count of these certificates and of three of the regular returns, that the Democratic board of county commissioners attempted to throw out illegally, unlawfully and unjustly and for no other reason, than because the precincts in question gave Republican majorities.

A little game of defiance of law and obstruction and disobedience to the orders of the court then commenced and was carried on by the Democratic lawyers here and the board of county commissioners for some time; money was raised and the board of county commissioners one by one was spirited away; the law and the dignity of the court were openly and defiantly and with malice aforethought insulted, violated and broken.

A peremptory writ of mandamus from the district court had been issued for the canvass of the vote in question and all the returns; two of the county commissioners endeavored to evade this writ by absenting themselves; the sheriff of this county in making return on the attachment for one of these commissioners reported that Martinez could not be found, and it was believed that he had gone to the state of Chihuahua in the republic of Mexico. The other county commissioner, it was notorious, had gone according to all reports to the state of Virginia. The terms of office of these two men expire on the last of this month.

Prior to that date the legislature would meet and the honestly and legally elected members of that body from this county would have no certificates and therefore, in the opinion of the men who put up the whole job, would have no standing in the organization of that body; besides the honestly and lawfully elected candidates for county offices on the Republican ticket would have to contest and be made to incur great expense and annoyance.

This being the situation, several of the candidates who received a lawful and honest majority at the recent election and who would not stand being swindled out of their just rights, appeared before acting Governor Thomas with affidavits giving the situation fully and honestly and requesting the action of the executive in this most important case.

Acting Gov. Thomas consulted with the proper law officer, Solicitor General Bartlett, and after having become thoroughly and fully acquainted with the law, the precedents, the public necessity for prompt and vigorous action and the demand of the people for justice and right, acted immediately. Seeing the great importance for a proper compliance with the law, he held that the two absent commissioners had willfully and unlawfully abandoned their offices; that vacancies existed in them, that the best interests of the commonwealth and the requirements of the law demanded speedy filling of these vacancies and appointed on yesterday morning two honest and well known citizens, G. W. North, of Cerrillos, and Frederick Grace, of this city, to the vacancies. In accordance with law these two gentlemen qualified at once and in accordance with an order from the district court met and canvassed the vote and declared the result as the returns showed and the vote actually cast at the last election showed and issued certificates accordingly.

147

APRIL 23, 1891:   ELECTRIC LIGHTS TURNED ON. A Great Throng on the Streets Last Night To See the New "Glims" Set off.

The electric light plant was set in motion yesterday afternoon, and when the lamps were turned on at 8 o'clock last night the streets were thronged with people, all anxious to see and examine into the workings of the new enterprise. There were 320 lamps in operation, including about thirty street lamps. The principal mercantile houses started in with from twelve to thirty lights each, and these establishments were in a flood of light all night. The street lamps, too, worked admirably. During the evening at least a thousand people visited the power house and there took note of the magnificent plant that supplies the power for this latest improvement.

JUNE 2, 1891:   EIGHT TO ONE! [*Cut of Rooster.*] This Is the Song the Santa Fe Cock Sings in Favor of Incorporation. An Easy Victory for Progress Won amidst the Greatest Good Feeling. NOTES BY THE WAY.

By a vote of about eight to one the citizens of Santa Fe arrayed themselves on the side of progress to-day and in favor of city incorporation. The victory was an easy one, made so by the splendid energy of the citizens' committee of forty who had charge of the details, and the perfect system with which everything was carried out. The opposition had scarcely a leg to stand on.

JUNE 22, 1891:

Our friend, the ex-Apache chief, Geronimo, is dead; he is a good Indian now and hence our friend; all good Indians are our friends.

OCTOBER 24, 1891:   FORT MARCY NO MORE. The President Orders Its Transfer to the Interior Department and It Will Be Sold. Is the American Health Resort in it? Good News That Will Add $100,000 to the City's Taxable Property.

The Fort Marcy military reservation, comprising between sixteen and seventeen acres of land in the very heart of the city, and which has stood as a menace and an eye sore to the modern progress of the city since the post was abandoned last spring, has been ordered transferred from the custody of the war department to the interior department and the same will be sold at public auction. The papers in the case received the approval of the president on the 7th inst., and came to hand this morning addressed to the register and receiver of the local land office.

There are few more controversial matters in New Mexico than the religious order or society known as Penitentes *or* Hermanos de la Luz, *"Brothers of the Light." In part it is a society dedicated to special observances, rites, and penances leading up to Good Friday, in part a brotherhood that practices mutual aid and works for community harmony. It may or may not be a peculiar outgrowth from the Third Order of Saint Francis, developed in the mountain country of northern New Mexico during the centuries when that region was all but cut off from contact with the organized Roman Catholic church.*

From the time of Archbishop Lamy on, the church made vigorous efforts to suppress the society because of the extremity of the penances and incorrectness of many of the observances. These efforts, including imposition of interdicts, were unsuccessful. The present archbishop, the Most Reverend Edwin Byrne, after careful study, tried a different tactic, offering the society acceptance and church approval if it would bring its observances into line with church requirements. This move has met with real success.

Popular newspaper accounts often state that the Penitentes *are Indians. It should be noted that this is absolutely incorrect. The society is entirely Spanish-American.*

MARCH 11, 1892: THE PENITENTES.

As already announced in the columns of the NEW MEXI-CAN, the head of the Catholic church in this arch diocese, the Most Rev. Archbishop J. B. Salpointe, is taking strong and effective measures for the suppression of the order known as the Penitentes.

The NEW MEXICAN is informed that recently in the county of Rio Arriba where the order is strong and where the San Miguel county White Cap leaders are endeavoring to use it for political purposes, in one day nearly 300 Penitentes recanted and promised to leave the order and abstain from further intercourse with it.

The action of the Catholic church authorities must meet with the hearty approval of all right minded people, no matter what their religious opinion.

In the late nineteenth century the rate of growth of Santa Fe did not compare with that of other towns, such as Albuquerque in the center of the state, which was destined to become its chief metropolis, or Clovis and Roswell in the eastern part. Las Vegas, on the A. T. & S.F.'s main line seventy-five miles east of Santa Fe, also enjoyed something of a boom. It was natural enough that these expanding settlements, and especially Albuquerque, should make attempts to become the capital of New Mexico, although none seriously threatened the old city's position.

MAY 24, 1892: LET THE FIGHT GO ON.

Our esteemed contemporaries have more or less to say upon the capitol removal question; the NEW MEXICAN gives full publicity to their sayings for two reasons: First, let the people know what our esteemed contemporaries would like to have, and secondly, to show that the people as a whole are "not in it" when it comes to having anything to say about the capitol question; but the NEW MEXICAN will make the good fight on the side of the vast majority of people who desire the capitol retained in Santa Fe, and the NEW MEXICAN will make a winning fight.

The New Mexican's *direct reporting remained one of the wonders of the world. On May 13, 1892, a disastrous fire occurred in the new Territorial capitol. In the excitement, the paper's news and editorial coverage leave a later reader sadly confused. The follow-up story below gives the only whole account of the fire.*

MAY 28, 1892: THE OFFICIAL FINDINGS. What the Capitol Commission Concludes Relative to the Recent Fire.

The New Mexico capitol custodian committee yesterday drew up and signed the following:

We, the capitol custodian committee, having fully considered the testimony of fifty-one witnesses taken before us, from the 14th to the 21st of May, 1892, inclusive, under the direction of the solicitor general of the territory, in an investigation into the origin of and a failure to extinguish the fire which destroyed the capitol on the evening of May 12, 1892, have reached the following conclusions:

First. That there were two distinct fires, one in each dome, appearing very near the same time, but first in the south dome; from which fact, in the absence of accidental or spontaneous origin of the fire, we conclude that it was the deliberate and well planned work of a fiendish incendiary, of whose identity there is so far no evidence.

Second. That the city fire company was at the scene of action with the utmost promptness, and had their hose directed upon the fire in time to have extinguished it but for the failure of the water service; and the evidence clearly shows that the hose connected with the several water pipes in the building and promptly brought into requisition by the janitor and others, would alone have been adequate if the pressure in the pipes had been sufficient to force the water to the top of the building; that the valve of the service pipe at the main in the street was partially turned off and the key to the same was in possession of said company, and that the Santa Fe Water company, which was under contract to furnish water to the building and grounds, is responsible for the failure to maintain sufficient pressure of water in its pipes leading to the capitol.

B. M. Thomas,
Sol Spiegelberg,
Capitol Custodian Committee.

MAY 31, 1892:   ASSASSINS' WORK. Frank Chavez Shot to Death
in the Dark. A Dastardly Deed Effectively Executed.

Francisco Chavez, ex-sheriff and collector for Santa Fe county,
was assassinated while returning to his home near Guadalupe
church, at a few minutes past 10 o'clock on Sunday night. He was
shot down within a hundred yards of his own door-step and the
perpetrators of the cruel, cowardly outrage skulked beneath the
very shadow of the church to make good their escape. For a time
the wildest excitement prevailed and Sunday night and all day
yesterday the terrible deed was the chief topic in all circles. All
the sad circumstances, the possible motive, the details of the killing and every feature were gone over again and again, repeated
and enlarged upon. Of course, there were numerous wild theories,
many of them as absurd as they were vicious, but the rank and file
were for the most part silent and thoughtful, feeling keenly a sorrow that found no vent in words, reflecting upon the fact that this
is another sad blow to Santa Fe and her good name, and grieving
over the loss of a popular and widely known resident, who, whatever his faults may have been, was a faithful friend to the poor
and far too generous toward his friends for his own good.

DETAILS OF THE TRAGEDY.

Frank Chavez was about the plaza on Sunday evening till near
10 o'clock, when he went into Dixon's saloon, and, meeting there
Atilano Gold, suggested that they go home together. Accordingly
they walked down the street, being accompanied part way by
Marshal Gray. The latter left them at Cartwright's corner. Passing Joseph's saloon Chavez suggested going in and taking a drink.
He was perfectly sober, Gold says, but upon approaching the side-
door they observed that the saloon was crowded with people, and
Chavez then said, "no, let's go straight home; it will cost me a
dollar or two to go in there," meaning that he would be compelled to treat the crowd, so he and Gold passed on to Water
street, passed the planing mill and started over the Guadalupe
street bridge. The moon had gone down; the wind was blowing a

stiff breeze, and the night was dark. Chavez walked at the right hand of Gold and was nearest the narrow gauge railroad track. As they proceeded they talked of commonplace topics. When within twenty feet of the south end of the bridge and nearly opposite a telegraph pole that stands just across the railroad track in Guadalupe church yard, a volley was fired at them from behind the telegraph pole, scarcely ten feet away. Chavez stopped, turned toward the right and exclaimed as he reached out for Gold with his right hand, "The brutes have murdered me." As he said this he fell and at the same instant two or three more shots were fired. Gold ran off the bridge to the center of the street fronting Chavez house, and as he stopped he heard two men running through the church yard. They came diagonally from the vicinity of the telegraph pole, passed through the side gate and entered the street, whereupon they fired once or twice at Gold, who was yet standing there, completely paralyzed by fear. Prior to the last two shots Gold, however, had called to Chavez but received no response. When fired upon he ran back over the bridge, jumping over Chavez' body, yet calling him. Again there was no response, and Gold then ran rapidly across the bridge to Soehnchen & Co's. planing mill. Near there he met A. P. Hogle and another man who had heard the shooting and were hesitating about crossing the bridge.

SEPTEMBER 2, 1893:   ARTIST LUNGREN'S LUCK. He Sees and Tells of the Famous Snake Dance of the Pagan Ho-pi Indians. Real Live Rattlers Harmless As Doves—A Barbaric Ceremony and Its Whys and Wherefores.

Mr. F. H. Lungren, the brilliant artist who prefers New Mexico to Europe as affording opportunity for studying effect and picturesqueness, has just returned from a novel experience among the Moqui, or, as he terms them, the Ho-pi Indians, which means peaceful men. Moqui is a term of reproach applied to them by the Piutes and the Navajos, and means dead men, and refers to the fact that their enemies thought them inert and listless in self-defense or revenge.

During his stay among the Ho-pis Mr. Lungren witnessed the

famous snake dance, and he gives many quaint descriptions of the
ceremonial incident to it. He is one of four white men who have
been initiated into the priesthood of the Antelopes and he has
therefore been admitted into the kiva, or underground chamber,
corresponding to the estufa of Spanish speaking Pueblos.

*This is one of the earliest popular mentions of the now famous
Hopi Snake Dance. The headlines stress the sensational element
of the use of live rattlesnakes, the element which nowadays draws
such enormous crowds of curiosity-seekers to see the dances that
it has become exceedingly difficult for the devout members of the
Snake and Antelope Societies to carry out their ritual.*

DECEMBER 27, 1893:   THE COCHITI FIND. A Few Facts Touching
the Discovery of Rich Mineral in a New District.

Some two weeks ago the NEW MEXICAN announced the
discovery by a German prospector of a well defined mineral lead
over west of Cochiti that yielded under assay by Burlingame, of
Denver, 2,900 ounces in silver and two ounces in gold per ton.

Cerrillos parties were known to have an interest in the discovery and they have managed to keep all news quiet touching the
progress of work or the real value of the find.

To-day, however, a Santa Fe business man is in receipt of a
letter from friends at Pena Blanca which speaks cheerfully of the
new discovery. Last week several wagon loads of ore, carefully
packed in sacks, sealed up and well guarded, passed through Pena
Blanca for Wallace station, whence it was shipped to Denver over
the A., T. & S. F. What the returns have been is, of course, known
only to the parties directly interested, but from the fact that some
fifteen men have been put to work on the find it would indicate
that returns have been highly satisfactory.

*For once a gold strike in the Santa Fe area turned out to have
some solidity. "The Cochiti Find" contained excellent gold-
bearing ore, with silver to boot. The location developed into the
mining town of Bland, which flourished over the following twenty*

years. Slowly the diggings petered out, although a few determined individuals still worked them until 1941. By then Bland was a ghost town, with only a few buildings occupied, the heavy machinery stilled. There is still metal there, but it is doubtful that it would justify commercial operations. What remains is a singularly thrilling ghost town, of houses, mine shafts, and mills, hidden away in a wildly beautiful, deep, narrow high mountain canyon.

DECEMBER 30, 1893:   THE SALE OF THE NEW MEXICAN.

The capital stock of the NEW MEXICAN Printing Company has been sold and a new management with a new policy assumes control on January 1, 1894.

The undersigned, as representative of the stockholders has had editorial and business control of the different publications of the company, namely the Daily NEW MEXICAN, the Weekly NEW MEXICAN REVIEW and EL NUEVO MEXICANO, for the past seven years. With this issue he ceases to have any further connection with the papers named. . . .

The sale is brought about entirely by circumstances over which the undersigned has no control and in retiring he thanks the many readers of this journal and the people generally for their kind support during the years that have gone. Wishing the readers and patrons of the NEW MEXICAN and indeed all the citizens of the Sunshine state a happy New Year, the undersigned remains their obedient servant.

Max Frost.

The president of the new corporation was W. T. Thornton. The editor was George H. Cross.

MAY 15, 1894:   "HELLO, CENTRAL!" Inauguration of Santa Fe's New Telephone System—A Great Convenience to the Business Public.

The capital city at last has a telephone system that citizens may feel proud of. Last July Messrs. H. B. Cartwright and

I. Sparks started in upon the task of supplying a "long-felt want" by constructing here a telephone system, and after overcoming many obstacles they to-day have the satisfaction of knowing that they are now on the winning side.

No longer will the housewife, in whose home is a telephone, tire herself out by a long walk down town to order her groceries. The inauguration of the "hello" system marks an era in the advancement of Santa Fe and the completion of it is a cause of satisfaction to every business man.

The New Mexican's *telephone number was 31, which was continued until the installation of the dial system.*

MAY 18, 1894: THE TELEPHONE SYSTEM. In Perfect Running Order—A Great Convenience—Send News Items to No. 31.

Santa Fe's new telephone system is now in full operation and subscribers generally pronounce it a success. Supt. Sparks says that the service is being improved every hour and will soon approximate perfection. This afternoon elaborate cards of instructions will be placed in the hands of all subscribers and tomorrow a complete printed directory of patrons will be circulated. The sixty-five instruments ordered will be in position before this is printed and there is a demand for more.

OCTOBER 2, 1895:

Young men, ye who dally with the innocent-looking cigarette, stand up. Do you know what scientific research has taught the people of this enlightened age about the cigarette? No? Well, here it is as revealed by a chemical analysis recently made: The tobacco was found to be strongly impregnated with opium, while the wrapper, which was warranted to be rice paper, was proved to be the most ordinary quality of paper whitened with arsenic. The two poisons combined were present in sufficient quantities to create in the smoker a habit of using opium without his being aware of it, his craving for which can only be satisfied by an incessant consumption of cigarettes.

OCTOBER 31, 1895: WORLD'S RECORD BEATEN. Fastest Train Service in the World for the Distance Inaugurated by the A. T. & S. F. Co. 2,265 Miles in Seventy-Four Hours. Some Readable Facts about the New Schedule—Improved Mail Facilities—Splendid Equipment.

The fastest regular train ever run in the world, taking distance into consideration, is passing through New Mexico today over the A., T. & S. F. route. It is the first train of the Santa Fe's new transcontinental service, and passed Lamy junction at 9:35 this morning en route from Chicago to Los Angeles. It left Chicago at 6 P.M. night before last and will reach Los Angeles at 6 P.M. tomorrow, making the run of 2,265 miles in seventy-four hours, allowing for the difference in time.

NOVEMBER 2, 1895: THE MEEK-EYED BURRO. Story of Guileless Innocence, Savage Litigation and Justice as Is Justice.

The docility, meekness and patience of the Rocky Mountain burro are proverbial. He is under all ordinary circumstances as much of a non combatant as a jack-rabbit. He never defiantly carries a chip around on his shoulder with a view to picking quarrels. He is distinctly a lover of peace and never would consciously stir up strife or excite the angry passions of any living thing.

Yet two meek-eyed and uncomplaining burros, heretofore and at this critical moment the undivided personal property of Judge W. J. Eaton, caused litigation in Santa Fe yesterday alongside of which the trial of Catron and Spiess pales into a matter of minor moment. In order that the burros may be acquitted of all intentional wrong in the premises without being forced to prove an alibi a brief recital of the circumstances leading up to and surrounding this memorable case is necessary.

Happily it is not needful to establish the fact that the ownership of the burros was vested in Judge Eaton. It is conceded by all that they were "hisen." And realizing that his property needed sustenance, and noticing a rank growth of weeds in the grounds surrounding the quarters of Col. Lawton, the judge persuasively lured the colonel's messenger to grant permission for the burros to fatten themselves on the weeds aforesaid.

The burros proceeded patiently to the task assigned to them, and, in the course of their explorations, discovered and devoured some corn that, by special permission of ex-Custodian James L. Johnson, Diego Abeyta had artistically concealed amid the weeds.

Right here trouble began. Unmistakable spots of gore appeared on the moon. Diego removed the obnoxious and ravenous burros, passed them over to the tender custody of City Marshal Gold, charged with the heinous crime of trespass, and in due season the innocent corn patch ravagers were sold to Juan Sisneros for $3 cash in hand paid to the marshal.

Judge Eaton then brought an action to replevin his property in the mighty court of Chief Justice Jose Maria Garcia; a jury consisting of Messrs. Marcos Eldodt and Fritz Muller, respected members of the board of education, was impaneled to pass upon the knotty problems of fact while Chancellor Garcia "adjudicated the law;" after a legal battle of two days' duration the burros were adjudged and decreed to be the property of Judge Eaton; the costs were assessed against Sisneros; Sisneros was advised to recover his $3 of the marshal, and the marshal was recommended to institute proceedings for breach of promise, alienation of affections or something else against Diego Abeyta.

Anyway Judge Eaton is now the proud possessor of probably the most costly pair of burros in New Mexico. They stand somebody in about $40 apiece. Yet they manifest no signs of vaulting ambition.

The disappearance of Colonel A. J. Fountain and his son is one of New Mexico's best-loved mysteries. It was unquestionably part of the inspiration of Conrad Richter's fine short novel, The Lady.

We include here three of the news stories on the subject, which pretty well cover what is known of the affair.

FEBRUARY 4, 1896: IS COL. A. J. FOUNTAIN DEAD? Disappearance of Albert J. Fountain of Dona Ana under Singular Circumstances. His Fondness for the Sensational. Searching Parties Leave Las Cruces—A Notable Stock Thief Prosecutor—May Have Been Murdered.

A Las Cruces telegram announces that Col. Albert J. Fountain is missing and is supposed to have been murdered on the public highway between Tularosa and Las Cruces.

Up to this writing, 11 a.m., only meager details are obtainable. It appears that on Friday last Col. Fountain started alone from Tularosa to drive a double team to his home at Las Cruces, a distance of some sixty-five miles. Some parties passed him on the road after he left Tularosa on Friday. On Saturday his wagon was found in the mountains about five miles off the road, but no trace of Col. Fountain could be discovered. His team was also missing and a search instituted by friends was without result. Then a messenger was sent to Las Cruces to give the alarm and yesterday a large posse was organized to go out and scour the country. Fears are expressed that Col. Fountain has been murdered and his body buried in the soft sand of one of the numerous arroyos which abound in that locality.

On the other hand, many who well and personally know Col. Fountain and appreciate his inordinate weakness for the sensational, are inclined, in the absence of more definite information, to believe he will turn up all right. He drove a team that had a will of its own and was in the habit of straying off when given an opportunity. Those who hold to this view argue that Col. Fountain may have had a run-away and been thrown out in the mesquite brush; or he may have intentionally left the road to stay over night at some country house from whence his team strayed to the point where it was found.

FEBRUARY 5, 1896: NO TRACE OF COL. FOUNTAIN. All the Circumstances Surrounding His Disappearance Point to Murder Most Foul. His Bright Little Boy with Him. A Special from El Paso This Afternoon Says Searching Party Is on Trail of the Rustlers—The Colonel and His Boy Doubtless Dead.

Judge S. B. Newcomb, of Las Cruces, arrived in the Capital city on the early morning train from the south and soon after breakfast was sought by a NEW MEXICAN scribe for the very latest particulars touching the sudden disappearance of Col. Albert J. Fountain, on Saturday.

Judge Newcomb adds deeply interesting and thrilling details to the story printed in these columns yesterday. It appears that Col. Fountain was met by the mail carrier, about 3 o'clock on Saturday afternoon, on the lonely road between Tularosa and Las Cruces. This meeting occurred about forty miles out from Las Cruces, and soon after the mail carrier rode on toward Tularosa and Col. Fountain, accompanied by his bright 7-year-old son, Henry, drove away in the direction of Las Cruces. That was the last seen of either the colonel or his son by friendly eyes.

The mail carrier reports that when he met and talked with Col. Fountain, the latter expressed some anxiety and alarm respecting the purposes of three horsemen whom he had several times noticed suspiciously riding at a distance from him, sometimes on one side of the road and sometimes on the other, and asked the carrier if he had seen them and knew who they were or what was their probable design.

The carrier replied that he had observed the three horsemen at a distance, that they had seemed to avoid him and had also apparently avoided a ranch near the road. He urged Col. Fountain to turn back with him and suggested that they return to Las Cruces together in the morning. But Col. Fountain, who was well armed and had a good team, answered that urgent business required his presence at home and that he must move on.

The next day, as he was returning to Las Cruces, the mail carrier saw apparently the same three horsemen he had noticed the day before riding toward Tularosa, but they again avoided him, riding across the plains toward the mountains. Further down the road he was surprised to observe that Col. Fountain's buggy had abruptly turned out of the road and moved out on the plains toward the Sacramento mountains. He alighted and followed the tracks for some distance. He distinctly recognized the foot-prints of three horses, apparently ridden by men on either side of the buggy and one following the vehicle. There were no signs of a struggle at that point, except that in one place he noted that the colonel's team seemed to have given a sudden jump, as if under somebody's lash, and the buggy had lurched to one side.

The carrier, filled with alarm for the safety of Col. Fountain and his little boy, rode as swiftly as possible to Las Cruces, where, on hearing that the colonel had not arrived at home, he related his startling story and a searching party of about thirty resolute and well armed men was quickly made up and started back to the place described by the carrier.

This posse left Las Cruces on Sunday night and returned the next evening, bringing reports that greatly intensified the general alarm and excitement prevailing among the people of all classes.

FEBRUARY 17, 1896:   HOPE YIELDS TO DESPAIR. Discovery of Clews that Unmistakably Point to Murder of Col. Fountain and His Son. A Pool of Blood—Part of Boy's Shirt. Belief That an Important Witness at Las Vegas Has Been Murdered—A 12-Year Old Boy Killed at Alma—Probably Accidental.

Gen. E. L. Bartlett returned from a visit of a week or so at Las Cruces yesterday morning. In a conversation with a NEW MEXICAN scribe this forenoon he fully confirmed the reports that the searchers have found the spot where Col. Fountain and his son Henry were undoubtedly murdered.

A pool of blood, part of what is supposed to be Col. Fountain's brains, a button from his coat, a napkin in which sandwiches were wrapped, a blood-stained sleeve from the little boy's shirt, and 15 cents in change scattered on the ground mark the place where the awful tragedy occurred. The bodies were believed to be buried near by in the white sands, but it is feared that the winds have obliterated all signs.

JUNE 16, 1896:   DESTRUCTION OF ST. VINCENT SANITARIUM.

The burning of St. Vincent sanitarium in this city, on Sunday evening, is not only a serious loss to the noble order of Sisters of Charity, but it is a loss of no slight magnitude to the city of Santa Fe. It is the pioneer institution of the kind in the far west. Through its wisely directed efforts national attention was first attracted to the superior climatic advantages of New Mexico and the entire Rocky mountain region for the cure of pulmonary troubles, and among the substantial fruits of its initial and successful experiments are similar institutions at El Paso, Colorado Springs and Denver, and still more important and beneficial to the human family—incontestable proof that the pure, dry, tonic air of the Rockies will cure consumption if taken in time. St. Vincent led the way to this beneficent discovery; others followed and shared in it. Under these circumstances, if the good Sisters of Charity find themselves financially unable at once to restore their almost ideal home for invalids, we are confident that there are plenty of philanthropists in the country who are familiar with their good works and will gladly assist them to rebuild on broader and more enduring foundations than before. In common with every well-wisher of Santa Fe, the NEW MEXICAN sincerely sympathizes with the Sisters in their loss and hopes that they may soon be able to rear a finer and more substantial structure on the site now disfigured by the ruins of the one destroyed by fire.

JANUARY 23, 1897:   ADIOS.

The undersigned this day retires from the editorial management of the NEW MEXICAN, the stockholders of the company have sold their interests to Max Frost, Republican.

In thus severing his connection with the paper, with which he has been identified for nearly fifteen years, first as news reporter and later—since 1894—as managing editor under Democratic control, the subscriber feels that he is but doing his duty to offer his sincere thanks to the public generally for its loyal support and patronage.

A clean, earnest and honest newspaper has been given the people. There are no apologies to be made to anybody; everything the editor has written is hereby re-stated and those who do not like it may make the most of it.

No man will dare say that under the editorial management now about to retire the NEW MEXICAN has not labored in season and out of season for the best interests and the general advancement of New Mexico, and the editor severs his connection with the paper feeling that his course has been approved by the masses, and that the paper while under his care will long be referred to as the livest and best public journal New Mexico has ever had.

Geo. H. Cross.

The announcement above was followed, on January 25, by a statement from the new management, which promised a return to the Republican ranks and contained the charming understatement that, "Mr. Frost, who assumes control, is tolerably well known throughout the territory as a staunch Republican." (We may note, incidentally, that the names of the two major parties were now printed with initial capitals.)

APRIL 3, 1897:

THE BORREGOS EXECUTED.
Francisco Gonzales y Borrego, Antonio
Gonzales y Borrego, Lauriano Alarid
and Patricio Valencia Hanged this
Morning.

———

Final Act in the Chavez Tragedy.

———

In the Old Jail Yard, Guarded by Uniformed Sentries, the Four Men Convicted of the Murder of Frank Chavez
Paid the Penalty of Their Crime.

The paper ran on at great length over the details of the hang-

ing, in sharp contrast to the offhand way in which such affairs were treated a decade or so earlier. The long story adds nothing of any real interest to what is succinctly told in the headlines quoted.

JUNE 2, 1897: THE NEW EXECUTIVE. President McKinley Appoints M. A. Otero as Governor and Geo. H. Wallace as Secretary of New Mexico. The Nominations Not Unexpected and Satisfactory to Friends of the Other Candidates for the Positions Named.

Washington, June 2.—The president today sent the following nominations to the senate:

Interior—Miguel A. Otero, to be governor of New Mexico.

Geo. H. Wallace, to be secretary of New Mexico.

William M. Jenkins, to be secretary of Oklahoma.

Miguel A. Otero, a Republican, having served for some time as Territorial delegate to Congress, served as governor for nine years. He was the son of the Democratic Miguel A. Otero who fought the duel in 1859. The change in political affiliation was probably the result of the Civil War. He was the father of the present Miguel A. Otero, an active Republican and onetime district judge.

JULY 26, 1897: DEVILISH DANCES. Indian Cruelty and Persecution Led by Them—They Should Be Stopped.

Captain Charles E. Nordstrom, of the Tenth United States cavalry, acting Indian agent at the Pueblo and Jicarilla agency, in New Mexico, has written an interesting letter to the commissioner of Indian affairs with regard to the Indian dances. The letter treats of the subject in a manner novel of official communications, and throws new light on a matter that has long given great concern to everybody interested in the Indian question. The letter is dated June 25. Captain Nordstrom says:

"During my recent inspection of the day schools attached to and lying south of this agency, many of the teachers complained that on the occasion of a 'dance' in the Pueblo they were either locked in their rooms and compelled to remain there until the festivities were over or were driven out of the village entirely, and ordered not to come back under a given time—the teacher at San Felipe being ejected and driven across the Rio Grande.

"The Indians pretend that it would be sacrilege to admit an outsider to participation in them, or even to be present as a spectator, but this is only a pretext, an excuse to allow them to assert their prerogative, the traders at Jemez and Zuni inform me that neither of them are molested when the dancers are going on, and they have both been invited to and have witnessed even the most secret of them. If these dances, like the meeting revivals of the southern negro, resulted only in a harmless enthusiasm or religious fervor, no exception could be taken to them, but they are often the origin of great outrages. The trader at Zuni related the circumstances of one case which took place in that village not long ago, which does not speak very well for the advancement of those engaged in it.

"A young man, just from Carlisle, was ordered to dance, and declined, representing that he had graduated at school, had learned a trade, and was now an American, and Americans did not dance that way. Thereupon the governor arrested him, tied him up to a tree, and ordered him beaten, and beaten he was—nearly to death. He danced after that.

"Zuni, it will be recalled, was the scene of the recent hanging of a poor old creature as a witch. While I was there Miss DeSette, the estimable principal of the school, sent for the victim of this revival of the days when our New England forefathers piously devoted their neighbors to the stake, and bared her poor, old arms to my inspection. There was no difficulty in discerning the scars made by the cruel cords, which had cut the flesh through to the bone. This poor old woman is at least 75 or 80 years old. At the imminent risk of her life, and the forfeiture of her popularity with the medicine men, Miss DeSette went to the old woman's house, and by nursing her night and day revived the flickering flame of life which had so nearly been extinguished. As this lady, her voice trembling with indignant emotion, described the circumstances of this unspeakable horror, my own cheek blushed that 36 years of my life had been spent in the service of a government under which such things could be done.

"The trader's cook, an Indian youth about 20, unfortunately incurring the displeasure of the medicine men, was arrested as a witch, and, but for the firmness of his employer, would have been put to death, and even now he dares not venture outside the premises after dark for fear of being kidnapped by the emissaries of these fiends in human shape, who will never rest satisfied until he is immolated upon the altar of their beastly superstition.

"It may be asked, 'What has this got to do with dances?' Everything, because all the outrages committed originate in a dance. Is rain wanted? They dance. If there is a flood? They dance. Should the doctors have made a mistake in their estimate of the amount of humidity the clouds contain, and precipitation fail to ensue, or if the rain continues, and the floods fail to subside, they immediately cast about them for a scapegoat, who is arrested and threatened as a witch, for making medicine against their medicine; and they invariably hit upon some poor old woman who has neither money nor friends, or other poor devil (no profanity intended) without connections or influence, whom they devote to torture, often to death, and thus save their reputations as augurs and soothsayers.

"This whole question in all its damnable ramifications, will, of necessity, have to be settled sooner or later. The government cannot go on appropriating millions year after year for the civilization of the Indian while these plague spots exist, and thrive on its bounty. But this letter is principally concerned for the protection of the teachers. What shall I do to secure them from insult in the future? I respectfully ask for instructions. It is no use to turn the matter over to the territorial authorities. That has been tried and failed. The general government has got to take hold of it, through the strong arm of its arbitrary powers. Force, by which these people govern themselves, is the only argument which appeals to their obedience and the state of things I have described will continue to go on until, by a show of force, they become convinced the government is in earnest."—St. Louis Globe Democrat.

Captain Nordstrom's report is not entirely incorrect. A sincere belief in witchcraft led to many abuses among both the Pueblos and the Navajos of this period. The belief was particularly strong, and its results particularly ugly, at Zuñi. Also, the Pueblos still used brutal corporal punishment to enforce obedience to their rules, and participation in appropriate ceremonies was included in the rules. The captain's chain of reasoning leading from these two points to requiring the suppression of dances, however, is poor if not plain false. The dances were, and are, innocuous and often beautiful expressions of living religious belief.

That the traders were allowed to remain in the pueblo during a dance at Jemez and Zuñi while the teachers were made to leave is easily explained. Indian Service personnel then and later were inclined to be hostile to Indian culture, and especially Indian religions, and to express this hostility freely. A trader had to be friendly to those same things or go out of business. All non-Indians, nowadays including traders, are excluded from many pueblos to this day when certain ceremonies are going on, and even visiting Indians from other pueblos often have to answer a number of questions to prove that they have been properly initiated before they are admitted.

Simple political evolution in contact with white Americans has brought about the ending of physical punishments to enforce conformity in most pueblos. Where it survives, it survives because the overwhelming majority, including young people, almost all of whom have a high school education and many of whom are veterans, approve of it. Such punishments could exist in these small, thoroughly democratic communities only because they were approved by the people.

Captain Nordstrom's attitude was symptomatic of his times, the spirit of which was actively hostile to the idea that any culture other than our own was acceptable, even permissible. This led, from the 1880's on into the 1920's, to a constant series of attacks on Indian religions and religious practices, which, of course, had to be justified on grounds other than opposition to the religions as such.

JANUARY 15, 1898:   NEW MEXICO'S GOLDEN ERA.

Active, systematic, continuous and productive development
work is in progress on the great bodies of gold bearing quartz at
Amizett, La Belle, Red River, Elizabethtown, Cochiti, Dolores,
Golden, San Pedro, Hillsboro, Pinos Altos, Mogollon, White
Oaks and numerous other promising mining districts in New
Mexico, and the results of this diligent work are certain to add
immensely to the future gold output of this territory. In several
of the districts named the surface indications of yellow riches are
much more marked and inviting than were the grass-root indications at Cripple Creek, and, since most of the land grant clouds
have been dissipated by the courts and perfect titles can be secured, capital is eagerly seeking investment in the mines of the
territory and there are substantial reasons for confidence that
among the fruits thereof will be the early disclosure of several
rivals of the great Colorado gold camp in New Mexico. All that
is required to accomplish this is money for development purposes
and the erection of adequate reduction plants, and this desidera-
tum is being rapidly and plentifully provided by men possessing
the requisite nerve, energy, experience and sagacity to employ it
to the best possible advantage. During the past year the NEW
MEXICAN has published columns of cheering details concerning operations in the numerous mining districts of this territory
and hence need not here enter into a specific statement of the
reasons why it has unbounded faith that a golden era is about to
dawn upon the magnificent territorial empire known on the map
as New Mexico.

*This anthology includes only a sampling of the many articles
and editorials that appeared from the 1860's to the 1920's, to pro-
claim that "a golden era is about to dawn upon the magnificent
territorial empire known on the map as New Mexico." That New
Mexico was full of gold and silver, or both, was an article of faith,
if not a fixation. In the long run, it has turned out to be tolerably
well supplied with oil, helium, uranium, and vanadium, as well as
potash, pumice, low-grade coal, mica, and other humble resources.*

For all the mineral development of the 1950's, the state would be hard put to it to get along without its stock-raising, its farming, or its tourist industry.

FEBRUARY 16, 1898:

THE MAINE IS SUNK.
Near 300 Souls Hurled into Eternity
without Shrift—Monster Battle-
ship a Total Wreck and at the
Bottom of the Sea in Havana
Harbor.

———

Death on the Ocean Wave.

———

Many Lucky Officers and Many Unlucky
Sailors—Conflicting Accounts of
the Horrible Disaster—Details
and Particulars, Harrowing in
the Extreme—Still a Fearful
Mystery.

APRIL 26, 1898:   LOYALTY OF THE NATIVE NEW MEXICANS.

Rumors have been gaining circulation in this city and elsewhere in the territory for the last few days to the effect that several prominent men, some of them government officials, have sent telegrams to Washington to the president and to other officials informing them that the native people of New Mexico are openly sympathizing with the cause of Spain and that they are disloyal to the government of the United States, and requesting that regular troops be sent here to avoid an open revolt. These rumors are not only false but infamous. The native people of New Mexico have repeatedly proved their loyalty to the American flag and their patriotism is unquestioned. At the breaking out of the war of the rebellion almost every man, who was old enough to carry a musket, enlisted in the Union army and served during the most trying time of the war. Few people know what temptation the leading men of this territory had for joining the southern instead of the northern armies.

The New Mexican was entirely correct. The record of the Spanish-American or "Mexican" people of New Mexico in defense of their country in all conflicts since the Civil War has been magnificent. As the following story shows, a disproportionately large part of the Rough Riders came from New Mexico. Many of these volunteers were Spanish-American.

JUNE 25, 1898:

Colonel Wood's 1st U. S. volunteer cavalry, the "rough riders," received its baptism of blood in a fight yesterday a few miles from Santiago de Cuba. The United States forces, consisting of eight dismounted troops of that regiment and a battalion of regulars, numbering about 1,000 men, attacked double that number of Spaniards who were in a strongly fortified position and routed them. One officer and seven troopers were killed and three officers and 17 troopers were wounded. Among the wounded is Sergeant G. W. Armijo, of troop F, a grandson of Colonel J. Frank Chaves, of Valencia county. In its first fight the regiment distinguished itself and fought bravely and successfully and the NEW MEXI-CAN fully believes such will be its record during the entire war. The regiment will do its duty gallantly and fearlessly wherever placed. Five of the troops of the regiment consist of New Mexico volunteers. All honor to them.

JULY 15, 1898:   CHAMITA CELEBRATION. 3,500 People Attend the Festivities—Gorgeous Indian Costumes—Elegantly Entertained by Hon. Samuel Eldodt. Addresses by Well Known Citizens— Affair a Great Success.

The most magnificent pageant ever seen in New Mexico, with

the possible exception of the day of historical tableaux at the "Tercio" in 1883, was presented on Wednesday at the tri-centennial celebration at Chamita. The whole affair from first to last was a grand success.

The special train from Santa Fe took up about 200 passengers to the celebration. As it approached Chamita, two long lines of Indians from the Pueblo of San Juan, on horseback and gorgeously appareled for the occasion, were formed, one on each side of the track. The whole vicinity and the surrounding heights were covered with a crowd of visitors, in carriages and wagons, on horseback, on foot, all awaiting the arrival of the train. The long lines of Indians referred to made a most effective picture, as the costumes were very brilliant and a number had large ornaments of eagle feathers on their heads. A special bodyguard of six Indians was provided for the governor, and as Secretary Wallace represented that office, he was carefully attended by this guard of honor throughout the day.

Chamita is a settlement immediately adjacent to the Pueblo of San Juan, on the Río Grande about thirty miles north and west of Santa Fe; it approximates the site of San Juan de los Caballeros, the first capital of New Mexico, founded by the Spanish under Oñate in 1598.

AUGUST 26, 1898:   THE FAMOUS "ROUGH RIDERS." About to Be Mustered out of the Volunteer Army. Four Troops Are from New Mexico—Will Be Accorded an Enthusiastic Welcome Home.

The NEW MEXICAN contained the positive announcement from Washington yesterday that the famous "Rough Riders," otherwise known as "Teddy's Terrors," would be mustered out of the United States volunteer army and given transportation to their respective homes in the course of a few more days.

Since over 500 of the brave men are residents of New Mexico, nearly one entire troop belonging in Santa Fe, the mustering out and home coming of the "Rough Riders" will of course be an event of much more than ordinary moment in this territory.

The people of this territory feel a keen sense of personal pride in the valor and prowess of these intrepid men and will accord them a welcome home that will only be surpassed in patriotic enthusiasm by its heartfelt sincerity. Troops E, F, G, H and I, of this regiment, commanded respectively by Captains Muller, Luna, Llewellyn, Curry and Lieutenant Wientge, of New Mexico, were all mustered in at Santa Fe last April, and the people of New Mexico would be very much gratified if the War department should decide to have these troops finally mustered out at the historic capital. It would be a graceful act.

In any event Santa Fe will cordially and enthusiastically join the rest of the territory in tendering a grand ovation to the boys of the troops mentioned when they reach home and the comfortable positions they left to defend the country's flag will be promptly restored to them.

The people of Santa Fe will take particular delight in bestowing honors upon the gallant men of Troop E, commanded by Captain Muller, with W. E. Griffin and Sherrard Coleman as lieutenants, nearly all of whom are residents of this city, six being attaches of the NEW MEXICAN, and all of whom saw perilous service before Santiago. Preparations for the fitting reception of this troop in Santa Fe should immediately be made.

The paper nowhere mentions it, but the six "attaches" who joined the Rough Riders included the entire composing room, who joined up in a body, causing the paper to miss an edition.

NOVEMBER 15, 1898: THE RACE ISSUE IN NEW MEXICO.

The returns of the recent election in this territory show that in many precincts of the so-called "American" counties, and in many of the towns, Mr. Fergusson ran ahead of his ticket and Mr. Perea consequently behind. In the so-called "Mexican" precincts Mr. Perea secured his party strength only, and in the counties of Taos and Mora he ran behind the Republican ticket. This shows conclusively how the natives of New Mexico, of Mexican descent, cast their votes. The truth is, that they, of either party, are mostly loyal to the principles of their party, and have not raised the race issue in any part of the territory. The question of race was only raised by friends of Mr. Fergusson along the line of the railroads, in the mining districts and in the so-called American districts.

There were probably not 20 cases out of 33,000 votes in the territory where a New Mexican citizen of native birth and Mexican descent voted against Mr. Fergusson because he is what is termed in New Mexico, an "American," whereas, there are doubtless hundreds and hundreds of so-called "Americans" who voted against Mr. Perea because of his name and blood.

As far as the NEW MEXICAN is concerned, it trusts that the question of race will enter into no future campaigns; this for the benefit of the entire territory.

It is doubtful that the situation in regard to the so-called "race issue" in New Mexico in 1898 was quite as rosy as the New Mexican makes out, although it is quite credible that what are now called the Anglo-Americans took the lead in exploiting it. In any case, more recently the issue has been a serious detriment to New Mexico politics, exploited by certain politicians of both races. In the 1950's there are some indications that it may be fading.

FEBRUARY 27, 1900:   LOOK TO THE MORMONS.

The Mormon colony at Ramah, Valencia county, seems to be a blot upon New Mexico that should be obliterated. Despite efforts of Mormon missionaries who have poured into New Mexico, Mormonism has been spurned by the people of the territory more generally. Valencia county is an exception. The world does not hear much of Ramah, but what it does suspect is that polygamy is secretly or openly practiced there. A murder which happened last week seems to confirm that suspicion, for its motive is said to be a Mormon's jealousy of one of his plural wives. New Mexico cannot let this imputation of allowing polygamy within its borders rest upon it, and the officers are called upon to investigate and sift the matter thoroughly. If the Mormons at Ramah are a peaceful, law-abiding people the world should be assured of it, but if they practice polygamy and other crimes against the law of the land the sooner the colony is transplanted to the penitentiary the better for the reputation of New Mexico.

The Mormons at Ramah were, and are, entirely law-abiding citizens. Ramah, in west central New Mexico south of Gallup, has become an anthropologists' paradise, since in that vicinity rather primitive Navajos, Spanish-Americans, Texas Panhandle migrants, and Mormons live in close proximity. Mormons also settled the Farmington–Bloomfield–Blanco area along the San Juan River, producing a string of stable, pleasant, prosperous little towns which in the mid-1950's were ruined by the boom population brought in by rich finds of oil and uranium.

APRIL 7, 1900:   LITERATURE FOR CHILDREN.

Parents should know what their children are reading. It will be news to many parents in Santa Fe that considerable literature of the blood and thunder kind is being read in this city. This is undoubtedly true in every other town of the territory. There is plenty of good literature interesting to children published nowadays at low prices, and there can be no excuse for children being allowed to read dime novels and wild, woolly west stories. The trouble lies in the home training and the scarcity of standard and periodical literature in many homes. A boy who has Cooper's and Scott's novels, Robinson Crusoe, a good juvenile magazine and his local daily paper to read at home will not go out and filch money to buy himself a blood and thunder story. A girl who has access to the standard novels of the day, to several volumes of fairly [*sic*] tales, to a good woman's journal and the daily paper will not pine for the Saturday Evening Gazette or the Family Story Paper with their perverse and silly love stories. Give children good literature to choose from, and their minds will stand in no danger of being poisoned by the flashy literature which finds too great a circulation in an enlightened country like the United States.

Brigadier General James H. Carleton, commander of the Department of New Mexico (1862–66), was one of the Territory's most controversial figures.

Archbishop Jean B. Lamy, first bishop of Santa Fe, was the inspiration for Willa Cather's *Death Comes for the Archbishop.*

Billy the Kid, one of the many desperadoes who terrorized New Mexico in the 1870's, was killed by Pat Garrett, sheriff of Lincoln County, at a surprise meeting in the home of Pete Maxwell.

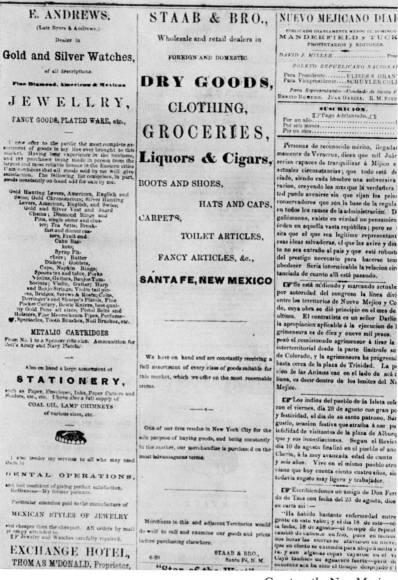

Courtesy the New Mexican

E. Andrews, dealer in articles and services of all descriptions, advertised in the *New Mexican* of September 1, 1868.

Delegates at the Constitutional Convention held at Santa Fe in 1910 tried once again to draft an acceptable constitution. The Territory finally became a state in 1912.

A view of San Miguel Church about 1883, when the Christian Brothers wanted to tear it down. According to local tradition, it is the oldest church in the United States, but tangible evidence goes back only to 1710.

Courtesy the New Mexico State Tourist Bureau

The same church after careful restoration by archaeologists in 1957.

U. S. Buildings, Santa Fe, N. M. 830

Hook Photo

Courtesy the Museum of New Mexico

Which looks older? *Above* is the Palace of the Governors in 1900;
below, the building in its present condition shows the return of modern
Santa Fe to the ancient Spanish architectural style.

Courtesy the New Mexico State Tourist Bureau

APRIL 17, 1900:   INDIAN CURIO FAD. It Has Reached the East and Creates a Demand for Indian Ware. Rarity of Curios Compared. The Indian Arts Will Soon Be Lost Arts—An Indian Collection to Be of Scientific Value Is Very Expensive.

Now it's the Indian. Awhile ago it was the Oriental, then it was the Japanese—now it is the Indian.

The paper was now in some conflict with itself as it began to appear that Indians and their products were a tourist attraction and source of trade, while the standard frontier desire to break up Indian reservations and turn the land over to white men, who alone were believed capable of using it properly, remained strong. This conflict ran through the decade and will be illustrated by a selection of samples.

APRIL 27, 1900:   JEFFRIES-FITZSIMMONS FIGHT.

The management of the opera house has secured an entertainment for this evening that will without a doubt pack the house. The entertainment will consist of an exhibition of the first genuine Edison cimeograph machine ever shown in the city. Every film as shown by this company is guaranteed to be as advertised. Although the cimeograph company have been showing throughout the west at regular prices, the acting manager will show them here at popular prices. The curtain will not be rung down before 8:30 o'clock.

MAY 8, 1900:

The large Indian reservations in the west are a hindrance to the growth of the sections in which they are located. Generally they are a hundred times larger than necessary for giving homes to a few hundred Indians. They assist in keeping the Indians out of touch with civilization, and have made the education of the children of the Indian tribes much more difficult than it would be otherwise. The government could do nothing better for the Indians and for the western commonwealths than to throw open all Indian reservations to settlement. Those Indians who could not be reconciled to more civilized modes of living might be taken to Yellowstone Park, which will remain national domain anyway, and which would make a good reservation for Indians and buffalo.

The passage above is typical of the anti-Indian attitude which was standard in great parts of the West and which menaces the Indians to this day. Usually to the arguments stated was added the one that Indians did not use their land but let vast quantities lie idle. Editorials along this line appeared frequently in the New Mexican during this decade. Actually, the Pueblo grants and reservations of northern New Mexico were farmed and grazed to and beyond the limits of their capacity, and the total amount of land reserved for Indians in the United States, had they been allowed to keep all of it, would be no more than just about enough for the present population. Here prejudice has been the servant of greed, and ignorance has fortified both.

SEPTEMBER 6, 1901:

NEW MEXICAN BULLETIN!

PRESIDENT MCKINLEY SHOT!

PRESIDENT MCKINLEY WAS SHOT THIS AFTERNOON AT THE PAN-AMERICAN EXPOSITION, BUFFALO.

NEW MEXICAN BULLETIN!

NO. 2.

PRESIDENT MCKINLEY SHOT!

PRESIDENT MCKINLEY'S WOUNDS ARE FATAL; HAVING BEEN SHOT THROUGH THE LEFT BREAST AND IN THE STOMACH. THE ASSASSIN ARRESTED.

NEW MEXICAN BULLETIN!

NO. 3.

PRESIDENT MCKINLEY SHOT!

PRESIDENT MCKINLEY'S WOUNDS ARE FATAL; HAVING BEEN SHOT THROUGH THE LEFT BREAST AND IN THE STOMACH.

LATER.

PRESIDENT WAS SHOT BY WELL-DRESSED MAN WHO WORE HIGH HAT, AND WHO WHILE SHAKING HANDS WITH HIM FIRED THE SHOTS WITH HIS LEFT HAND.

MAN IS UNDER ARREST BUT IS UNIDENTIFIED.

———

NEW MEXICAN BULLETIN!

NO. 4.

PRESIDENT MCKINLEY SHOT!

A BULLET WHICH LODGED AGAINST THE BREAST BONE HAS BEEN EXTRACTED. THE PRESIDENT IS RESTING EASIER.

APRIL 1, 1902:

A great deal of interest is being taken in the proposed change of name for New Mexico. It is gratifying to know that the people from all parts of New Mexico consider the NEW MEXICAN as the representative newspaper of the territory through whose columns it is best to give their opinions on the question. Thus far nearly every communication has been in favor of a change of name although at the same time condemning some of the names proposed. The NEW MEXICAN however, is of the opinion that the objections given against the name of New Mexico are mostly theoretical or imaginary and founded upon the expressions of ignorant persons in the east who have vague ideas about New Mexico just as they probably have about Oregon or Montana. When a commonwealth once gets to be as old as New Mexico, it is very unusual for it to change its name and generally very foolish.

The name of New Mexico has always caused some confusion, and to this day it is a sourish joke among us that so many North Americans think we are part of a foreign country. Nonetheless, most New Mexicans are proud of the state's name and the history behind it. There were several proposals to change it to such curiosities as "Montezuma," which came to nothing.

177

MAY 10, 1902:   AMERICANS AND MEXICANS.

It is rather indefinite to call the residents of the United States Americans to distinguish them from other nationalities of the western continent and when it is used as a term of distinction between the descendants of the original Caucasian settlers and the later arrivals from other parts of the United States in New Mexico, it is not only an indefinite but a vicious term. It is to be regretted that quite a number of New Mexico newspapers and many citizens still, unwittingly perhaps, use the terms Mexican and American as terms of disparagement to the former. There is some difference in race and blood between the descendants of the Spanish settlers of New Mexico and the later immigrants who represent scattered nationalities from Europe, Asia and Africa, but if anybody is entitled to the appellation of American it certainly is the people who are descendants of men and women who lived in New Mexico when the ancestors of the later comers were probably living in the squalor of some European hamlet or Asiatic village. But aside from that, the word American is not at all distinctive, for the United States occupies but one-fifth of the area of the Americas, has but one-half of their population and its population is about as mongrel as that of any nation on the face of the earth. The filthy Eskimo of Labrador, the ignorant half-breed of Yucatan, the superstitious negro of the West Indies, the dishonest coolie of Suriname and the naked savage of Tierra del Fuego are all American and why should that name be used by any one in New Mexico as a badge of superiority over a people who have been American, and good Americans at that, longer than any son or daughter of the Revolution or than any family that can trace its ancestry back to the Mayflower? It is certain that this unjust and invidious distinction is at the bottom of all the existing prejudice against this territory and has kept many thousands of dollars of much needed capital and many good settlers out of the territory. Now that statehood is almost assured and that the public schools are teaching the rising generation without distinction of nationality to speak, read and write English and to love the nation and its history, isn't it time for every one, especially in New Mexico, to use the terms American and Mexican only where and as they should be used?

This editorial is the first demonstration of tenderness concerning the term Mexican, *which became opprobrious because of the way it was applied by the large numbers of Texans settling in the state. By the 1930's it had become definitely insulting to refer to a Spanish-American in English as "a Mexican," or, conversely, to an Anglo-American as "an American." An Anglo-American is pretty nearly anybody not Spanish, although Texans or Texians may be separately classed. In speaking Spanish, Spanish-Americans may refer to themselves as* Mexicanos, *but even in Spanish it is better for an Anglo not to use the term.*

JUNE 28, 1902: KEEP UP THE FIGHT.

Of course, New Mexico will not pull down its flag and surrender in its fight for statehood because the senate has postponed action on the omnibus statehood bill for six months. But it should do more than merely holding the fort. A Fabian policy will win no laurels in this instance. An aggressive fight must be waged from now until December so that the whole nation may be convinced of the righteousness of the demand of New Mexico to be admitted to statehood. Says the Denver Republican:

The fact that the senate has agreed to make the consideration of the bill to admit New Mexico, Oklahoma and Arizona the unfinished business for the tenth day of the winter session of congress resulted in a compromise whereby Senator Quay withdrew his resolution to take the bill away from the committee on territories.

To this course the friends of statehood have no objection apart from the fact that they still think the bill should have been passed at the present session.

From this time until it was achieved in 1911, New Mexico seemed forever on the very brink of statehood. This collection will omit most of the editorials and news stories jubilantly announcing

179

that the Territory is about to become a state, of which this is a fair example.

The New Mexican now displayed new names on its masthead. Paul A. F. Walter later became president of the First National Bank and was important in such cultural developments as the State Museum.

SEPTEMBER 1, 1903:

SANTA FE NEW MEXICAN

Max Frost . . . . Editor

Paul A. F. Walter . . . . Asst. Editor

Charles M. Stauffer . . . . Manager

OCTOBER 14, 1903:

"Saloons and gambling houses will be thrown wide open to ladies who are in masque," says the Albuquerque Journal in mentioning one of the attractions at the Albuquerque fair this week. The NEW MEXICAN is not prudish, but if the above sentence were read in the United States Senate during the statehood debate, the coming winter and telegraphed all over the country, it might give more than one outsider the impression that Albuquerque really is a wild and woolly western town in a wild and woolly western commonwealth.

OCTOBER 19, 1903:   BONANZA NEAR CAPITAL CITY. Gold and Silver Vein Seven Feet Wide and Six Thousand Feet Long Struck Four Miles Northeast of the Plaza. Gold Runs Ninety-Nine Per Cent to One of Silver.

A gold and silver bonanza has been struck four miles northeast of Santa Fe.

The bonanza consists of a vein seven feet wide, which runs across ten claims, and is 6,000 feet in length. Specimens of the ore taken from five different points, approximately 600 feet apart, shows from $20.90 to $41.10 to the ton, in both gold and silver, the gold running 99 per cent and the silver one per cent.

The property is located in the Santa Fe mining district which was laid out four years ago by D. C. Allard, which commences two miles northeast of the plaza, and runs a distance of six miles due north. The district now has 110 claims, doing regular assessment work, the lowest value in any claim being $2 in gold, and the highest $12 in gold, at a depth of 12 feet.

No less than four companies are now operating in the district. They are the United Gold and Copper company, of Chicago; the Gibson Development company of New Haven, Conn., the American Consolidated Copper company, of New York City, and the Santa Fe Mining and Reduction company, recently organized.

Professor E. J. Hutchinson, of Chicago, was recently sent here by Chicago capitalists who are interested in the Santa Fe Mining and Reduction company. As a result of his investigating, he pronounced it one of the best properties he had ever seen, and predicted that handsome dividends would be returned from the very first day's work.

The mining and reduction work in this district is to be carried on with power furnished by the Capital Light and Power company. An eight pound specimen of the ore that assays $20.90 to the ton is on exhibition in one of the show windows of Ireland's pharmacy.

Finds of any gold at all seem to produce hallucinations. This bonanza amounted to so little that a generation later hardly anybody remembered that there had been a gold strike so close to the city.

APRIL 7, 1904: UNIQUE PUEBLO INDIAN CONGRESS. Held Yesterday in This City—Sixty-Four Delegates from Seventeen Communities Participated—Protests against Recent Decision of Territorial Supreme Court.

Seventeen of the nineteen communities of the Pueblo Indians of New Mexico were represented in a meeting here yesterday by delegates, 64 in number. The delegates being the governors, assistant governors and minor officers and principal merchants of such Pueblos. They represented about 8,000 Pueblo Indians, and were in council for the purpose of protesting against the operation of the recent decision of the territorial supreme court, which decided that the lands of the Pueblo Indians of New Mexico are taxable, and that the Indians themselves are citizens. This congress was exceedingly unique and interesting. The meeting was held in the chapel of the United States Indian Industrial School, was held upon the request of the Indians, was witnessed by Superintendent C. J. Crandall and Judge A. J. Abbott, as United States special attorney for the Pueblo Indians of New Mexico. The congress on behalf of all the Pueblos of the Territory signed a protest addressed to the President of the United States, the department of the interior and Congress against the taxation of their lands and other properties, and expressed their disinclination to assume the rights, duties and responsibilities of citizenship, and their wish to keep themselves entirely free from participation in political affairs of the Territory and county governments. They expressed a consciousness of their unfitness to participate in governmental matters for want of both education and experience. They claim they were the original owners of the lands, that their ancestors owned it before the advent of the Spaniards in New Mexico before the organization of the Mexican government, that of right the government of the United States should not impose any burdens upon them, nor any restrictions so long as they do not violate the laws, nor in any way interfere with their neighbors, the white people. It is entirely proper to say that much credit is due Pablo Abeita, the assistant governor of the Pueblo of Isleta for his intelligent interpretation from the English into the Indian and Spanish languages and for the discreet direction of his people in the matters connected with their council, and in putting into form and intelligent expression the ideas of his people, who are so deeply interested in this, a matter of such vital importance to them. Much credit is also due to Ulysses Grant Paisano of the Pueblo of Laguna, who interpreted from the English into the Indian language, spoken by a number of the southern Pueblos, being a different language from that spoken by the larger number of the representatives present from the central and northern Pueblos. The congress was orderly and the proceedings were conducted with gravity and dignity. The Indians treated Superintendent Crandall and Attorney Abbott with phenomenal respect and courtesy and seemed to appreciate all efforts put forth by them to facilitate their labors and to promote the objects and purposes for which the congress was called. Just before the close of the afternoon session there were a number of addresses made by prominent Indians from several of the Pueblos expressing their good will to all their people wherever located and to whatever Pueblo they might belong and sending greetings to the various Pueblos through their representatives present. The council was addressed by Superintendent Crandall and Judge Abbott upon the subjects of vital importance to them and to deliberate upon which this meeting was called. The history of the way in which this matter of taxation of their lands came into court, and finally resulted in the decision before referred to, was first taken into court [*sic*], was given to them in as comprehensive a manner as could well be done in a brief address. It is hoped that this congress will result in much good to the Indians. [*There follows a long list of the representatives from Acoma, Cochiti, Isleta, Laguna, Nambe, Picuris, Pojoaque, San Juan, Santa Clara, San Ildefonso, Santo Domingo, San Felipe, Santa Ana, Sandia, Tesuque, and Taos, with the notation that the only two pueblos not represented were Jemez and Zuñi.*]

Much credit is due to Harvey Townsend of the Pueblo of San Felipe for his efficient services as interpreter and for other valuable services to the Indians and to the agent and attorney.

This story was run as a double-column spread on page one, with large display headlines. The finding of the Territorial court was overthrown in due course by the U. S. Supreme Court, to the surprise and somewhat to the disappointment of the New Mexican. Had the original finding been upheld, it would have resulted in the progressive acquisition of Pueblo Indian lands by white men, since the Indians failed to pay their taxes (in a later story the New

Mexican *estimated that the average Indian would be liable to from $500 to $1000 in taxes, which would be ruinous).*

Pressure upon Pueblo land, much of which was choice farming land under irrigation, was becoming heavy at this time, leading to the Pueblo land controversy of the early 1920's.

This is one of the earliest, if not the earliest, account of a council of all the Pueblo tribes, although undoubtedly the Pueblo superintendent—or, in earlier days, "agent"—must on occasion have called together representatives of many or all the Pueblos for matters of business common to all. The question is of interest because, beginning about 1922, the All-Pueblo Council became a distinct entity, functioning independently of the Indian Bureau. Some of the white people who encouraged it claimed that this institution could be traced back with full continuity at least to 1680, when the Pueblos united to drive out the Spanish. This claim strikes this writer as bosh.

OCTOBER 1, 1904: DESTRUCTION IN WAKE OF POWERFUL FLOOD. Staunchness of Reservoir of Santa Fe Water Company Prevents Great Disaster and Inundation of Lower Part of City—Much Damage by Storm King Elsewhere.

Residents of the Capital City fail to realize how fortunate they were on last Thursday night in the breaking up of the first immense volume of flood waters of the Santa Fe River by the reservoir of the Santa Fe Water & Light Company in the cañon. If the crest of the flood had struck Santa Fe the entire lower portion of the town would undoubtedly have been inundated and many buildings washed out. When the waters, unheralded, reached the protecting dam of the large reservoir the crest was eight feet high and the torrent was racing down the cañon at an estimated velocity of twenty miles an hour.

Santa Fe was fortunate in having a reservoir just above the city to break the first impetus of the waters and to gather into its basin 200,000,000 gallons of water, which would otherwise have been thrown in one great mass against the frail structures that would have opposed it and which would have reached the city from the site of the reservoir in about four minutes. With such great rapidity did the waters rush onto the reservoir that a helper narrowly escaped with his life. He describes the flood as a huge black animal running after him and says that if he had been standing a few feet farther in the cañon he could not have made his escape.

NOVEMBER 28, 1904: BY THE BULLET OF A DASTARDLY ASSASSIN. Colonel J. Francisco Chaves Shot through the Heart while at Supper at Pinos Wells— Death Instantaneous—Posse in Pursuit.

The community was greatly shocked and grieved when early yesterday morning the fearful news of the assassination of Colonel J. Franco Chaves, superintendent of public instruction and member-elect of the legislative council from Valencia and Torrance Counties, was flashed over the wires and was given out. The awful deed was unexpected and so black and cowardly in details that citizens generally were greatly aroused and nothing was talked of all day except the grewsome particulars and the desire expressed by all alike that no possible efforts should or must be spared to bring the inhuman wretches who perpetrated the murder and that as speedily as possible, to well deserved and condign punishment. The particulars of the awful crime are about as follows:

Colonel J. Franco Chaves went to Pinos Wells Saturday afternoon with Louis Trauer, the sheep and wool dealer of Albuquerque, and after transacting some business went to the home of Juan Dios de Salas, in the rear of the post office, for supper. Mr. Trauer remained in the store of Mr. Salas talking with several ranchmen. Seated at the table with Colonel Chaves were Mr. Salas and Donaciano Chaves, the mail carrier. The Colonel was seated a few feet from and alongside of the window when the shot was fired. He raised himself out of his chair, took two steps toward the window, and fell dead with a bullet piercing his lungs just over the heart and passing out of the body under the right arm and imbedding itself several inches in the wall. The bullet did not even shatter the window glass, only making a small hole in the pane.

The others at the table were too dazed for a few moments to take any steps toward pursuing the assassin and there was sufficient time for escape. On investigation, however, tracks of one man were found leading from the window. The bullet is supposed to have been fired from a large caliber smokeless gun.

Not to be confused with Frank Chávez, whose murder was reported earlier, José Francisco Chaves is the aristocrat whom we encountered as a political leader in the 1860's. He was born in 1833 and was one of a number of native aristocrats of that period who were sent across the Mississippi to be educated on the East Coast. According to the tradition in the Chaves family, on arrival in New York, José Francisco was tutored by a Delafield. In the Civil War he was commissioned as major and promoted to lieutenant colonel. He played a distinguished part in the early campaigns against the Navajos and later was a power and something of an autocrat in the state. His murder is commonly believed to have been arranged by political rivals. A $2,500 reward was offered for detection of the killer, but he was never found.

JANUARY 3, 1905:   COURT HOUSE ON WHEELS. Torrance County Ushered into Existence on a Santa Fe Railway Car. Officials Sworn in. Resolutions of Thanks to General Francis J. Torrance and Delegate-Elect W. H. Andrews.

Many striking and singular events are recorded in the history of the development of the west, but yesterday was probably the first time in its annals that a county was ushered into official existence and organized on a railway passenger coach. Such was the beginning of the County of Torrance, the twenty-fifth of the counties of New Mexico. The Thirty-fifth Legislative Assembly had decreed that the county seat of the new county should be Progreso. At that time Progreso consisted of the home ranch, now historic, of the late Colonel J. Franco Chaves. The ranch building is not even pretentious, merely a small frame house. It is over a mile to the next place. Soon thereafter, the Santa Fe Central Railway built a frame station over half a mile from the ranch and called it Progreso but soon abandoned it for there was no business to be gotten or to be created at Progreso. The county seat is marked on some maps but even there not accurately, and a few days ago the post office department asked: "Where is Progreso, the county seat of Torrance County?" But nevertheless, it is imperative that the board of county commissioners meet there and that the county officials transact their business there until the Thirty-sixth Legislative Assembly establishes the county seat elsewhere.

Senator W. H. Andrews, president of the Santa Fe Central Railway and Delegate-elect to Congress, resourceful and helpful, offered the new county a court house on wheels and promised to take it to the county seat at his expense whenever needed. It is true, it is only a passenger coach attached to a special train but it served its purpose well yesterday and the new county, although officially born on the morning of January 1, was brought into actual existence yesterday under auspicious circumstances and with due ceremony.

OCTOBER 11, 1905: WORSE THAN AN ARMY OF LOCUSTS.

New Mexico is deriving no benefit from the invading army of professional gamblers who have been driven out of Wyoming, Colorado, Texas and Arizona and now find that this Territory is about the only haven where they can ply their trade unmolested by paying only a small license fee. Even the slot machines ruled out of business in neighboring commonwealths are being shipped to this Territory to pick up every stray nickle or quarter. Of course, this invasion is not exactly to the liking of those members of the green cloth fraternity who have been established in business in New Mexico for years. Their only protection against the new comers is the exaction of high local license fees. Town and city authorities should not hesitate to impose heavy license fees upon slot machine operators as well as upon every other gambling device. In the meanwhile, the sentiment against gambling is growing in the Territory.

JUNE 15, 1906: NOW FOR STATEHOOD!

The hopes, the work, the prayers of fifty long years on behalf of statehood of the people of New Mexico, have been answered favorably at last by a Republican Congress and a Republican President. The courtesy has been extended to the people of New Mexico and Arizona to decide for themselves whether they will accept statehood now that it has been offered to them. To refuse the gift, the greatest that can be bestowed upon any people, would be nothing short of folly. The NEW MEXICAN which has taken the patriotic stand for single statehood for New Mexico under its present name until the last ditch, is now ready to lend its voice and its influence for the acceptance of joint statehood by New Mexico and Arizona under the conditions of the Hamilton bill just passed. This bill, with its generous provisions, grants New Mexico and Arizona all that they have ever asked in connection with statehood, and even more. On the other hand, it asks New Mexico to give up its cherished name and to amalgamate with a neighboring Territory. It is a big sacrifice to surrender a name that has been hallowed by deeds of valor and thrilling events of almost four centuries, but New Mexico is willing to pay the price in order to become an active and an essential part of the greatest and most glorious nation on the face of the earth, and to have its citizens enjoy all the political rights and privileges bought so dearly by tremendous sacrifices in blood and treasure. Arizona is not asked to pay as heavy a price for the boon as is New Mexico, for Arizona's euphonious name is to be bestowed upon the new state and Arizonians, though greatly in the minority numerically, are admitted into the partnership upon the same terms as New Mexico, and will receive an equal share of the same blessings. The gift of $5,000,000 in cash and $30,000,000 in lands to the public schools of the proposed state, is in itself, a princely donation that it would be stupid to decline except for the weightiest of reasons. Such reasons no longer exist and the NEW MEXICAN feels certain, that after a vigorous campaign, such as will be made during the next few months, the statehood proposition will carry in both territories, in New Mexico by an overwhelming majority and in Arizona by a vote that will be a revelation in view of the commonly accepted opinion that the Arizonians are unalterably opposed to union with New Mexico. All that it will take, is a united pull, a long pull and a strong pull of all the friends of statehood, and on the seventh of November the tidings will be shouted from Phoenix to Clayton, from Carlsbad to Yuma: "Hail to the newest of the states, the great State of Arizona!"

Arizona voted overwhelmingly against the proposal of joint statehood, which killed it.

JULY 18, 1906: WOMAN SOLDIER DYING HERE. Was Spy and Nurse in Southern Army. Mrs. Dietz' Strange Life of Thrilling Events—Captured by Union Troops. Knew Jesse James.

Mrs. A. W. Dietz, formerly Miss Georgia T. Read, a cousin of Attorney Benjamin M. Read, and at one time a wealthy southern girl, later a spy in the Confederate Army, under Generals Lee, Price and Boone, is dying of paralysis in a little adobe house in the rear of the home of David Gonzales, 302 Palace Avenue.

Miss Georgia T. Read (Mrs. Dietz), was born in Indiana, just across the river from Louisville, Kentucky. Her mother died when she was only six years old. With her father she moved to New Orleans where he established a large wholesale drug business. Her father became wealthy and the young girl was a member of the best social circle of Crescent City. When General Butler, with his northern troops, occupied New Orleans, the drug store owned by her father was confiscated and all of his property destroyed. The girl, thus suddenly made poor, taught in private families for a living. Her brother and father entered the southern army, the latter as a chaplain and hospital attendant.

The girl, then just entering womanhood, promptly enlisted as a nurse in a hospital corps, it is believed, with the troops of General Lee, in the Army of Virginia. She was present at the battle of Gettysburg and other historic fights between the north and south. The work of a nurse was too confining for the brave southern girl, and she became a spy for the southern generals. Disguised as a soldier with her hair cropped close to her head, or dressed as the widow of a fictitious soldier, with her face veiled in crepe, she many times, entered the Union lines and secured information of the greatest value to the South. She served at various times with the troops of General Boone and General Price. It was while with the latter general on a raid through Kansas and Missouri that she was betrayed by a relative in Westport Landing, now Kansas City, Missouri, and was captured by the Union troops. She was sent to St. Louis with other prisoners and placed under guard there until the close of the war.

While in Missouri, she met and became well acquainted with Colonel Mosby, the great guerrilla leader, and Jesse James and the Younger boys, outlaws.

Upon the conclusion of civil strife, she again became a teacher at Fredericktown, Missouri. Upon her refusal to take the oath of allegiance to the United States, she was ordered to leave the state and went to Illinois where she continued teaching. In 1866 she met and married A. W. Dietz, a wealthy miller, who owned large flouring mills near Lincoln, Nebraska. Fire destroyed the mills.

SEPTEMBER 18, 1906: THE AUTOMOBILE WOULD NOT RUN. Secretary Raynolds and Commissioner Seligman Have a Tough Time en Route to Albuquerque.

At 7 o'clock this morning the long distance telephone rang in the editorial office of the NEW MEXICAN. "Albuquerque wants on," said the female voice. At the telephone was County Commissioner Arthur Seligman, who gave information that Territorial Secretary Raynolds and he had arrived in the Duke City late last night. They had a real nice time on their automobile trip from Santa Fe via Kennedy, Golden and San Pedro to Albuquerque, that is in some respects. In others it was not as nice as it might have been. In place of making the journey in six or eight hours as they thought, it took them two days and one night. The automobile insisted on breaking down and needing repairs; at times they became confused as to roads and directions and yesterday spent five hours in the beautiful scenery of the Ortiz Mountains trying to find a road that would lead them from the Golden mining camp into the fertile Rio Grande Valley. The more they repaired the automobile, the more it insisted on breaking down, but as all good things must come to an end, they finally reached their destination somewhat tired, rather dusty, travel stained, dirty, thirsty and hungry. All's well that ends well and they expect to return this evening via the Santa Fe Railway and will reach town between 11 and 12 o'clock tonight, if there are no other accidents. Hale and hearty, yet they are somewhat browned up, but none the worse for their experience. The NEW MEXICAN violates no confidence in saying that it will be some time before they will again travel via automobile to Albuquerque via Kennedy, San Pedro and the Ortiz Mountains, a distance of 72 miles. The automobile will likely be left in the Duke City to be disposed of if a purchaser can be found.

MAY 28, 1907: HUGE SNAKE THAT FEASTS ON BABIES. Preposterous Story about Pueblo Indians Which Finds Believers among Credulous Easterners.

Sensational eastern papers tell a story that Catholic priests have complained to U. S. Attorney W. H. H. Llewellyn that certain Pueblo Indians of New Mexico pursue an ancient practice of feeding new born babies to serpents and that Major Llewellyn not having jurisdiction has referred the matter to U. S. Indian Attorney A. J. Abbott or Acting Governor J. W. Raynolds so as to have the Territorial authorities act and bring indictments. Numerous ridiculous tales have been told about the Pueblo Indians by romancing newspaper correspondents and magazine writers but this is the worst that has been perpetrated upon them.

Judge Abbott declares the Pueblo snake story to be an ancient absurdity repeated twenty years ago by Mrs. Wallace in her book on the Pueblo Indians and re-published again and again by the sensational seeking eastern press, the snake being located differently at Zia and at Acoma.

Several years ago the story was given such credence that Judge Abbott was asked to investigate the matter at Acoma and of course found it to be absolutely without foundation. Since then the snake story has been localized at Zia.

Clinton J. Crandall, superintendent of the northern Pueblos

and also of the United States Indian Industrial School in this city, says that the stories of human sacrifice to serpents among the Pueblo Indians crop up at frequent intervals and that generally tenderfeet are the victims of such stories, but not always, and the grand jury at Albuquerque several years ago investigated the story of a priest that the Pueblos at Zia sacrificed children to a huge serpent kept in the estufa. The grand jury found no evidence, of course, on which to base an indictment.

Samuel Eldodt, the merchant at Chamita, near San Juan, tells the story of a twelve-foot serpent which workmen killed in recent years while building a house for Mr. Eldodt, but whether it was a serpent that had escaped from an estufa or not, Mr. Eldodt was unable to determine. There is no doubt that a trace of a serpent worship is to be found to this day among the Pueblo Indians, but there is no evidence that any human beings were sacrificed to the serpents within the past century. Mr. Crandall has been in practically all of the estufas of the northern Pueblos and never found serpents in any of them.

Estufa, "stove," is the old Spanish name for what we now commonly call a kiva, the subterranean, or semi-subterranean, ceremonial chamber of the Pueblo Indians.

This absurd story of sacred snakes to which babies are sacrificed has surprising vitality. I heard it brought up, with great credence, in 1956 by a well-educated resident of New Mexico.

FEBRUARY 29, 1908: "PAT" GARRETT SHOT TO DEATH. Killing Takes Place near Las Cruces. Quarrel Led to Murder. Wayne Brazil, Young Ranchman, the Slayer—Latter Now in Jail.

Special to the NEW MEXICAN.

Las Cruces, N. M., Feb. 29—Patrick F. Garrett, a resident of New Mexico since the latter seventies, and who sprang into fame as the slayer of "Billy the Kid" a notorious southwestern outlaw and desperado, was shot and killed about noon today by Wayne Brazil, a son of the late Captain W. W. Brazil, of Lincoln county, while on the road to the Organ mining camp in a buggy with a companion by the name of Miller, at a point about five miles from here. Brazil is now in the jail at Las Cruces.

The trouble between Garrett and Brazil arose over a lease on Garrett's ranch which Brazil held. They had been quarreling along the road, Garrett being in his buggy and Brazil on horseback. Finally Brazil told Garrett that he wanted to talk to him privately. Garrett got out of the buggy and was shot twice, one shot taking effect in his head and the other entered his chest. He expired in a few minutes.

NOVEMBER 3, 1908: COWBOY ROPES MAN OFF MOVING TRAIN: FALL KILLS HIM.

Engle, N. M., Nov. 3.—Jesse Ake, a cowboy, said to have been considerably the worse for a load of whiskey is a fugitive in the mountains and officers are hunting him on a murder charge.

As a Santa Fe work train was passing between Lava and Crockett, loaded with laborers, Ake, it is said, rode up on his horse and roped Ramon Aragon, whom he dragged from the train.

Aragon was instantly killed in the fall, as the train was running at the time at the rate of twenty miles an hour.

Ake galloped off towards the Organ mountains and officers at Hillsboro, Las Cruces and elsewhere are now on his trail.

DECEMBER 9, 1908: PROHIBITION FOR NEW MEXICO.

The question of the prohibition of the sale of intoxicating liquors in the Sunshine Territory and future state is being strongly agitated all over New Mexico and the best and the most solid citizens favor absolute prohibition and a statute making the engaging in the liquor traffic a misdemeanor punishable by a fine and penitentiary imprisonment. There is no question among the sensible and patriotic citizens here that absolute prohibition would be the best for all concerned and forbidding the sale of any kind of liquor within the confines of New Mexico would greatly conduce to the benefit, welfare and comfort of the people, especially the common people, and in a few years would materially show for the better in the character, habits and well-being of the citizens of New Mexico. If prohibition cannot be obtained a local option law should be passed and no liquor of any kind should be allowed to be sold in communities that contain less than 1,000 people. The time has come in New Mexico when a firm stand on this question must be taken and the sooner this is done, certainly, the better for the coming state.

JANUARY 21, 1909: EDITORIAL ANNOUNCEMENT.

At a meeting of the directors of the New Mexican Printing Company held yesterday afternoon, it was announced with regret, that owing to illness, Colonel Max Frost, for so many years president of the company and editor of its publications, desired to retire from these positions and sought to sever his connections with the enterprise. Mr. Paul A. F. Walter was elected president of the company and editor of its publications, and Mr. John K. Stauffer, was re-elected secretary and treasurer with the duties of business manager.

APRIL 10, 1909: A MAGNIFICENT IDEA.

The Museum to be established in the Old Palace in this city will not be a local nor an insignificant affair. That much is plainly apparent from the plans outlined before the meeting of the Archaeological Society last evening. Already arrangements have been inaugurated which will result not only in the exchange of specimens with all the important museums of the world, but for the direct gift of duplicate, but nevertheless priceless exhibits, from the National Museum at Washington. These exhibits will be mounted, arranged and displayed by master hands, men who have made museum work their life study. The Old Palace will be fitted up and decorated so as to attract attention the world over. Not with iconoclastic hand but reverently and always with a view of illustrating the period in which it was built and the period of civilization the particular room shall illustrate. Painters of renown and decorators of international repute will place upon the walls scenes from the cliff dwellings or place upon the tables plaster models of the ruins, which the objects exhibited will illustrate further, thus bringing to the eye and mind vividly the particular period and the particular locality so that it may be compared with the civilization of another period or of another place. The great educational value of such exhibits can hardly be gauged by dollars and cents. The museum will offer a priceless educational facility to local schools and colleges and will attract visitors the world over. As one of the speakers remarked last evening: Santa Fe will certainly do as well as a certain place in Europe at which 6,000 Americans registered in the first three months of the year. It is wonderful this vista of usefulness and of greatness, that is unfolding itself for the museum, and as the idea progresses it brings forth new suggestions and plans which prove verily that New Mexico had never before done so great a thing for itself, as when it invited the School of American Archaeology to locate at Santa Fe and founded a museum in connection therewith.

MAY 31, 1909: THE LOCAL OPTION BATTLE.

A sidelight upon the local option battle at Santa Fe comes from the outside. Says the Roswell Register-Tribune:

"That local option fight over at Santa Fe is assuming national proportions. The begining of the scrap was when the Women's Christian Temperance Union secured the passage of an ordinance by the Santa Fe city council, giving the saloons a time limit of December 31 to get out of business. The booze men contended that the people did not want the drink dispensaries closed, and sought to have the ordinance repealed. The city council then called an election to let the people vote on the matter. The saloon men, backed up by the Albuquerque 'Personal Liberty League' sought aid of Attorney General Clancy and Governor Curry by the injunction route, their contention then being that the council had no rights to use city funds for defraying the expenses of the election. The W.C.T.U. saw their bluff and also raised the bet by promptly putting up the funds to pay for the election, showing at the same time that the city had no funds, and that it was an act of charity to both the liquor interests and the city to thus provide the sinews of war. It is reported on good authority that the Governor informed the 'Personal' etc., people that under the circumstances, he would not only not interfere with the election called, but would vote for the closing of the dampness joints. He promised, however, to not use his influence either way in the matter. If the drys win, it will set a rather hard precedent for the whiskey men to overcome, for the drys having paid for the election, the wets will have to come along with a similar price before a reconsideration can be ordered. The New Mexican, The W.C.T.U., R. L. Baca, speaker of the 37th Assembly, Manuel R. Otero, receiver of the Santa Fe land office, Hon. Ben Read and many prominent citizens of the capital city are lined up on the side of temperance, and it looks so serious for the wets that they are seeking international intervention."

On June 7, Santa Fe voted wet. It was not, and is not now, a community that desires prohibition. One of the difficulties of editing a newspaper in Santa Fe (and of going into politics there) is that leading Anglo-Americans are inclined to converse almost entirely with others of their kind, along with a few Spanish-Americans who have been denatured and cut off from their people. This results in grave misapprehensions concerning the opinions and desires of the mass of the people.

JUNE 7, 1909:   [*Advertisement.*] FORD MODEL T CARS.

If you are interested in a 5 passenger touring car or a 3 passenger Roadster, do not buy a car until you have inspected our 1909 Models. The wonderful performances of this car over New Mexican roads should remove all doubt as to which car you should buy. Santa Fe to Las Vegas 4 hours, 40 minutes, carrying three passengers and 200 pounds luggage.

Los Cerrillos and return over mountain roads 52 miles on high gear, 2 hours and 3 minutes.

Climbing Fort Marcy and Tesuque Hill on high gear.

> Earl Mays,
> Ford Agency
> 102 E. Palace
> Santa Fe

JULY 27, 1909:   THE INDIAN DANCE.

On August 4, that is next week, one of the finest Pueblo dances to be witnessed, will take place at Santo Domingo, about forty miles south of Santa Fe. It is a gorgeous spectacle that is worth coming many miles to see and should be witnessed this year by all those who can possibly make the trip, for the Pueblo dance is distinctly a pageant of the past. Even now, at most of the pueblos, crudities are creeping into the ceremony and it is losing its original religious significance. It is, of course, proper that this is so, and still it is to be regretted, despite the iconoclasts who would root up the custom entirely and that without any further loss of time. Be that as it may, the Santo Domingo Corn Dance is one of the unique annual attractions of this part of New Mexico and a sight well worth while a long journey.

This and the following story make a fine pair. The editors could not quite be happy in praise of an Indian cultural manifestation but could go all out for the alienation of Indian land. The Santo Domingo Corn Dance remains to this day a demonstration of an absolutely sincere, devout Indian ceremonial and an artistic event of international fame.

AUGUST 12, 1909:   EDITORIAL.

It is good news which comes from the Navajo reservation in a roundabout way from Washington, that the Navajos are prosperous, that their flocks are on the increase and that they are taking greater interest in farming. The government has done much for the Navajos and the Pueblos, but the greatest thing it could do for them is to throw open their reservations to settlement and thus have the Red Man enter into active industrial competition with his neighbors. Possessed of valuable land holdings and of flocks and herds, the Indian would not be at a disadvantage and at the same time would benefit by the development which would come to his surroundings, if the land holdings he does not use were placed in the market. In land holdings, as well as in water rights, the maxim should be that lands not put to beneficial use should be thrown upon the market for acquisition by those who will use them. It is a doctrine adopted in Europe of late years, where the unearned increment in the value of lands, is taxed so heavily that land owners will put their lands to beneficial use or alienate them. In the United States too, reservations, such as those in the far Northwest, have been put into the possession of homeseekers without detriment to the Indians and to the manifest advantage of the country.

DECEMBER 31, 1909:   EDITORIAL ANNOUNCEMENT.

The New Mexican announces editorial changes that will go into effect in the New Year. Mr. Raymond Haacke, the past year, in charge of the city editor's desk of the New Mexican, will be advanced to assistant manager in the business office, succeeding Mr. William D. Hayes, who will return to the forest service to take charge of the new planting station on Pike's Peak, one of the most important projects undertaken by the service in the state of Colorado and for which he is splendidly equipped by training and experience. Both Mr. Haacke and Mr. Hayes have rendered the New Mexican Printing Company valuable service the past year and deserve the well wishes of the friends and patrons of the firm. Mr. Bryan Boru Dunne, who was in charge of the splendid New Year's edition of the New Mexican and through it has become acquainted with the business community, will take the city editor's desk. Mr. Dunne is practically an old timer in New Mexico and Santa Fe, although still a young man, and merely returns to the land of his father, after valuable training received on the Baltimore Sun and other eastern papers and considerable newspaper experience in western centers. He is a forceful writer and expects to contribute whatever is in his power to the upbuilding of Santa Fe and its best interests. Like in the past, the New Mexican aims to give first, the news; then to comment upon it fairly, incidentally seeking to advance the cause of Greater and More Beautiful Santa Fe. It will not intentionally falsify or distort the news to serve its own or any one else's interests and stands always ready to correct any error into which it may have fallen.

FEBRUARY 25, 1910: PRICE OF WOOD TO ADVANCE.

With the advance of the price of table board now comes the advance in another kind of board—fire-board, or the sticks that are brought to the city on the backs of the patient burros, ever ready to stop at your door at the sound of their master's sneeze.

But no more will the burros kneel down in homage to the fire-god for 35 cents. He is on a strike. He must get for his master 40 cents per load.

This was made officially known today by Supervisor Stewart of the forestry office. Mr. Stewart hasn't got it "in" for the people of Santa Fe who burn wood in their stoves and have no steam or water heat to take the chill off their rooms in any other way. He has simply acted on behalf of the government and has had to inform the woodmen that they will surely have to "spare that tree" or battery of trees in the Pecos forest unless they offer consideration to the tune of 25 cents a cord for the wood they hew.

That is the way it has come about. And the woodmen in reply say they will have to raise the price of wood for food is very high and both they and the patient sneeze-obeying burro must still eat.

JUNE 20, 1910: SANTA FE IS WILD WITH JOY.

All New Mexico today rejoices over the signing of the statehood bill by President Taft.

In fact the joy making has not been of today only but has been really "triduum" in variety, for it began in Santa Fe Saturday afternoon when the New Mexican announced the news flashed from Washington that the House had concurred in the Senate bill. This city witnessed a demonstration of the people's joy Saturday night when a mass meeting was held in the plaza and presided over by Acting Governor Nathan Jaffa, who introduced many well known speakers. Every orator was greeted with shouts from the large crowd which assembled and cheered itself hoarse over the victory for which New Mexico has been fighting for three score years.

Santa Fe

The exponents of art, science, literature, law, medicine, politics and culture in its true sense, formed an interesting gathering at the famous Old Palace when the formal opening of the Museum of Archaeology, rich in art and historic treasures, took place on Saturday evening.

The affair, which took the nature of a reception, brilliant from every viewpoint, held in the presence of so many distinguished people from all over the world was eloquent testimony of the appreciation of the work of the School of American Archaeology and of the Archaeological Society of New Mexico of the work of the Ladies' Museum Committee and of the Woman's Board of Trade all harmoniously building up interest in that antiquity which makes Santa Fe unique.

The affair described was the beginning of the development of the nexus of state museums, which by 1955 included the Historical Museum and Library and Ethnological Museum in the restored Palace of the Governors, the State Art Museum next door, and, on the Old Pecos Road, the Laboratory of Anthropology (primarily a research institution) and International Folk Art Museum. The work of the museums is affiliated with the School of American Research and the state Historical Society. Adjacent to the Folk Art Museum is the privately maintained Museum of Navajo Ceremonial Art. Out of this complex of institutions and the now defunct Indian Arts Fund developed an important and fruitful alliance and interchange between art and anthropology.

OCTOBER 3, 1910:

CONSTITUTION MAKERS OF NEW MEXICO ASSEMBLE
AT THE CAPITOL.

Hall of Representatives Scene of Historic Gathering—
Charles A. Spiess Named for President; George W. Armijo
for Chief Clerk; H. N. Whiting for Sergeant at Arms;
Cesario Pedregon for Interpreter and Rev. Julius Hartman
for Chaplain.

NOVEMBER 21, 1910: THE CONSTITUTION.

The constitution formulated by the convention which closes today contains 20,000 words, 130 sections grouped into twenty-two articles. Probably no other commonwealth ever was confronted by the peculiar difficulties that faced the constitutional convention when it convened. Unique and paramount, despite repeated denial, was the race and language question. The 135,000 people in New Mexico who are of Spanish-American descent justly demanded protection of their equality before the law, retention of their ancient rights and privileges. Suspicious on account of the clause of the Federal Enabling Act which demands that all the state officers and legislators must speak English, they insisted upon guarantees that were difficult to formulate without giving them a wider intent in other directions than that proposed. This task was made no easier by the fact that one-half of the Republican majority were of Spanish-American descent, while the Democratic minority had but one delegate of that race. The convention also bore in mind the advice of President Taft to formulate a safe and sane constitution, a constitution unlike that of Oklahoma, as well as the many restrictions and conditions imposed by the enabling act. It too had to take into consideration the insistent demand for progressive features, a demand out of which the Democratic minority, naturally, made the most political capital. The convention was compelled to listen to the plea of vested interests and capital, that New Mexico needs railroads, capital for development and that nothing should be done to hamper future development. The various debts of the counties which the new state is to assume, the regulation of the land donations of 13,000,000 acres, the regulation of the liquor traffic, and kindred questions had to be dealt with. As a result, a constitution following the older models was adopted, with these salient and new features: An elective corporation commission having no judicial powers but nevertheless the right to regulate rates for transportation and transmission companies, to grant charters and to supervise corporations. An automatic arrangement immediately takes the decisions of the commission up to the state supreme court which must pass upon them judicially without delay. The initiative was rejected but a referendum clause was included which enables 25 percent of the voters, upon petition, to suspend a law within ninety days of a legislative session, and ten percent of the voters, upon petition to submit a law passed by the last legislature, to a popular vote at the next election while the constitution is made easily amendable, only a majority vote of the legislature being required to submit an amendment to the people. Prohibition and local option were excluded but the way was left open to the next legislature to deal with these questions. The constitution raises a boundary dispute with Texas and Colorado; it provides for an elective judiciary from top to bottom and for elective state officers. It limits the tax rate to twelve mills the first two years and ten mills after that; it grants to women the right to vote at school elections and makes them eligible to be school directors and school superintendents of counties and it also abolishes the fee system at present the rule. It includes a stringent anti-pass clause. It prohibits separate schools for Anglo Saxons and Spanish-Americans and provides for the payment by the state of the railroad bond indebtedness of a million dollars through the sale of a million acres of land granted by Congress. No distinction is to be made in the franchise, in jury duty, in holding office other than that of state and legislature on account of inability to speak English. Outside of these clauses, the constitution resembles very much that of the United States and of the older states, being much briefer than those of Oregon or Oklahoma. In short, the convention believes that it has formulated a fundamental law that will be ratified by the people and approved by Congress and President.

The New Mexican's *account fails to bring out some of the most interesting features of the new constitution. Although a simple vote of the legislature may submit a constitutional amendment to the people, the majority of counties, and majorities within counties, required before amendments to many sections can be adopted make alteration of the constitution in those respects so difficult as to be virtually impossible.*

A very large number of executive offices are elective, with the result that the governor has virtually no choice of who should be on his cabinet. This weakens the governor's office and makes it possible for his opponents, securely entrenched, to be his principal quasi subordinates. Thus, in the 1950's, during six years we have had a Republican governor with an entirely Democratic administration "under" him. "Under" has to be put in quotation marks.

There is neither language nor literacy requirement for voting, and voters may request a helper to enter the booth with them and show them how to mark their ballots. This has been a fruitful source of corruption. What has gone on since 1948, with some 10,000 illiterate, non-English-speaking Navajos of voting age in the northwestern corner of the state, when truckloads of them were hauled in to rural polls, is grotesque. The purpose of this provision, of course, was to prevent any device for preventing Spanish-Americans from voting, and at the time the constitution was written, it was probably necessary.

Alas for high hopes, the constitution as drawn up at this convention was found unacceptable in certain matters and was sent back to the Territory for revision, thus prolonging New Mexico's very long wait yet another year.

MARCH 31, 1911: KIDNAPING AT LAS VEGAS. Waldo, Three Year Old Boy of A. T. Rogers, Jr., Ransomed for $12,000.

"The three-year-old grandson of Judge H. L. Waldo was kidnapped at Las Vegas and ransomed for $12,000." Such were the sensational tidings that reached Santa Fe this morning.

The story reads like an episode out of a dime novel. Night before last, two masked strangers entered the house of Attorney A. T. Rogers, Jr. at Las Vegas, the son-in-law of Judge H. L. Waldo. Mr. Rogers was away at Raton attending the session of the district court. The intruders invaded the room of a brother, William Rogers, and compelled him to give up a revolver. They then forced their way into the apartment of Mrs. Rogers and demanded Waldo, her son. Mrs. Rogers was helpless. She pleaded and implored. She offered all her jewels, all her money, all her property, but one of the villains replied:

"To hell with your jewels, I want the kid!"

Despairing Mrs. Rogers begged for permission to clothe the child warmly and comfortably. This was granted, while the robbers coolly waited. The mother hugged and kissed her darling in frantic farewell until the criminal tore the boy out of her arms, mounted a horse and was off in the dark, leaving a letter of instructions, in which a demand was made for $12,000 in cash. Who can describe the agony of that mother? Her despair? Mr. Rogers was reached as soon as possible and he came home yesterday morning on the flyer. No time was lost in securing the money and setting in motion every agency possible to recover the child. The letter of instructions had directed:

"If you are ready to deliver the money, set a red light in a certain window at 10 o'clock in the evening." It then directed that the money should be taken to a certain spot in a road, 11 miles from Las Vegas that same night. These instructions were followed. Mr. Rogers in his automobile made the trip to the lonely spot and there met his man. He delivered the money but the child was not there. "The child is in Kearny's Gap," he was informed. Two horses were standing in the road and two men galloped away. Will Rogers speeded to Kearny's Gap. There the child was found in the road. It was wrapped in a blanket.

"Is that you, Uncle Will?" the youngster chirped. "I am awful hungry. I had nothing to eat all day." What a family reunion there was last night when the boy was returned to his mother's arms.

APRIL 12, 1911: WIGGINS AND ROGERS CONFESS.
Kidnapers Caught.

Will Rogers and Joseph Wiggins, arrested last night at Las Vegas, have confessed to the kidnaping of 3-year-old [sic] Waldo Rogers, son of A. T. Rogers and grandson of Judge H. L. Waldo.

The ransom of $12,000 was recovered intact in the chimney at the home of the parents who are prostrated with grief.

Wiggins was the first to confess. He had been sentenced to the penitentiary from Socorro for life for murder. He was pardoned out in 1909 by Governor Curry.

When the confession was shown to Will Rogers, the latter too, confessed. He is a brother of Attorney A. T. Rogers, father of the boy, and he was in the home of his brother during the kidnaping, while the latter was in court at Raton. He was arraigned this forenoon.

There will be no compromise in the case and the two men will be prosecuted to the full extent of the law.

Governor Mills, who returned this noon from Las Vegas brought with him copies of the confession of both men.

AUGUST 19, 1911: SANTA FEANS WILD WITH JOY.

Five minutes after the United States Senate passed the Flood Statehood resolution with the Arizona recall of judges eliminated, called the compromise measure, the Santa Fe New Mexican had a bulletin out announcing the news yesterday afternoon. The bulletin was posted at 4:19 p.m. and within five minutes the New Mexican's whistle spread the good news.

President Taft formally proclaimed New Mexico the forty-seventh state of the Union on January 6, 1912. The state's first governor, William C. McDonald, was inaugurated on January 15.

The new state legislature promptly met and proceeded to put on a fine demonstration of New Mexico politics at its fruitiest, as the following stories show.

MARCH 19, 1912: FOUR LEGISLATORS ACCUSED OF SOLICITING AND TAKING BRIBE.

With four members of the House in jail charged with accepting decoy bribes, with the Republicans unwilling to have the caucus decide the U. S. Senatorships, with the Spanish-Americans abandoning their attempts to center on a Spanish-American for one of the Senatorships and with several of the Democrats declaring they would get into the game, the Senatorial situation this forenoon was turbulent even beyond former anticipations.

MARCH 27, 1912: FALL AND CATRON ELECTED SENATORS AFTER
MILLS AND ANDREWS WITHDRAW.

Amidst scenes of indescribable enthusiasm, Albert [B.] Fall
and Thomas B. Catron were elected to the U. S. Senate today.
The fate of the latter hung in the balance when the roll had been
called—he lacked four votes of election but before the result
was announced, enough legislators rose to change their votes to
Catron, to put him safely across the wire. It was the Spanish
Americans on the Republican side who changed their mind at
the critical moment. The vote as finally announced, thirty-five
being needed for election, was as follows:

Republicans—A. B. Fall, 39; T. B. Catron, 38; L. Bradford
Prince, 3; O. A. Larrazolo, 2; Eugenio Romero, 1; William J.
Mills, 1; Jose D. Sena, 1.

Democrats—Felix Martinez, 25; A. A. Jones, 23.

Progressive Republicans—Herbert J. Hagerman, 3; W. H.
Gillenwater, 2.

For an hour before the ballot, the Hall of Representatives was
a seething mass that was milling to and fro, apparently purpose-
less, as viewed from the outside, but with grim determination and
with a well laid plan in view as those on the inside saw it. Up
to the last moment, National Committeeman Solomon Luna
pleaded with Speaker Baca to cast his vote for Thomas B. Catron,
but fruitlessly, up to the last moment Felix Martinez exhorted
the Spanish Americans not to vote for Catron and Fall; up to the
last moment, Thomas B. Catron and his son, Rep. Charles C.
Catron, sought to persuade the four votes lacking to fall into line;
and others, Republicans, Progressives, Democrats, Spanish Americans, were frantically making a last appeal.

Up to the last moment, the four legislators accused of bribery,
had determined to demand permission to vote, which would have
no doubt caused the U. S. Senate to take a hand later in the
Senatorship, for as Senator Root declared in the Lorimer case,
one tainted vote was sufficient to invalidate the election no matter how great the majority.

CHAPTER 4

PENS, PALETTES, AND POLITICOS

JULY 1, 1912:

Controlling interest in the New Mexican Printing Company was today acquired by Bronson M. Cutting. Details as to the future editorial policy of the publications of the company will be announced after the annual stockholders' meeting on Monday, July 8.

THIS simple announcement furnishes the perfect starting point for the next chapter in the New Mexican's, in Santa Fe's, and in New Mexico's history. Bronson M. Cutting, whom this notice first presents to us, requires somewhat more comment than can be extracted from the files of his own newspaper.

In 1912 and, for that matter, in the 1930's and later, New Mexico was still a frontier state. It was an ancient unit and it was rawly new. Its people had, and have, a roughness and virility about them, as well as a definite grace; in the first quarter of this century many an argument was settled in the broad light of day by bullet or knife.

To this state came Bronson Cutting for his health. He belonged to an old New York family of English and Dutch descent —of the same group as, for instance, the Roosevelts. He was educated at Groton School and Harvard. He had undergone a light case of what was then called infantile paralysis, which did not

207

cripple him but caused him to hold himself somewhat stiffly and awkwardly. He was a big man, who spoke with a very slight lisp. He was cultivated and something of an intellectual. On superficial acquaintance, he gave an impression of rather chilly correctness, curiously blended at moments with suggestions of the Mauve Decade.

With his intimates, he was a gay companion. He was ruthlessly competent in politics and intensely ambitious. His political career, as I look back on it, seems a blend throughout of genuine liberalism and unswerving personal ambition. Both were served by his considerable personal wealth. In national politics he won the respect and affection of the great progressives of the period, such as Borah and La Follette. In state politics his alleged liberalism had about it a certain smell of grabbing popular issues that the routine politicos of the state were too conservative, too committed, or too slow moving to take hold of. His enemies accuse him of having done more than any other one man in his time to fan the "race issue" in his courtship of the Spanish-Americans.

He was not responsible for the new cultural growth in Santa Fe that began with the establishment of the first museum, mentioned above, nor had he any real connection with the development of the art colony. But he and the newspaper which he controlled were naturally sympathetic with both, and it was fortunate that his rise to power coincided with Santa Fe's great period of artistic and intellectual development.

This man dominated, first, the Republican party in New Mexico, then both the Republican and Democratic parties. He towered over the state—a kind of man one would have thought licked before he started in such a community. The conservative and the correct hated him; many of the plain Spanish-Americans gave him something close to adoration. When he died, the New Mexican ran his will in full. It included nearly a full column of 6 point listing bequests of odd sums, almost all under $1,000 and many under $300, mostly to Spanish-Americans. These bequests covered the loans for which he held notes, and which were one of his means of insuring political support.

When he was senator, I had the interesting experience of work-

ing with him on some Indian legislation. His office in Washington was unlike any other senator's office I have ever seen. It was staffed entirely by men—most of them Harvard men and all, I believe, college graduates. They were agreeable, easygoing, and seemed hardly serious. In fact they were as smart a collection of henchmen as anyone could ask for.

In New Mexico he surrounded himself with a group of rubber men; they existed only because he inflated them. Under his orders, they seemed to be politicians; when he was gone, they ceased to exist.

JULY 4, 1912:   PLAZA FIESTA WILL BE GREAT.

The plans for the DeVargas pageant and Plaza Fiesta tomorrow are all complete. Every indication points to both events being a success that it will be difficult to duplicate or to excel in years to come. The program in detail for the pageant was published in Tuesday evening's New Mexican and will be adhered to in every respect.

The Plaza Fiesta will open prosaically with the rummage sale and will wind up poetically in the evening in the brilliantly illumined Plaza. In fact, all afternoon there will be throngs in the Plaza who will patronize the attractive booths that will face the Palace of the Governors on the north and will extend around to the east and the west.

There will be plenty to eat and to drink. Refreshments will be served and that at modest figures, on the east side of the Plaza. At the northeast corner will be the unique Mexican booth and on the NW corner the Indian booth. Between them will be the candy booth where homemade candy will find ready buyers, and the cigar booth that will prove attractive to the men. Nearby will be the flower booth at which fragrant nosegays and boutonniers will be on sale and the wearing of which will be the badge of honor and local patriotism for the day. The west side of the Plaza is reserved for amusements and fun. The band will be stationed part of the day near the Lamy fountain. In the pagoda will be the lunch counter at which sandwiches, wieners, doughnuts, delicious coffee, etc., will be served to all comers.

There is a common belief that the Santa Fe Fiesta has been celebrated annually, without a break, since it was instituted by De Vargas when he reconquered New Mexico in 1683. As a matter of fact, although there may have been some special annual mass in addition to the yearly procession of "La Conquistadora," the figure of the Virgin brought to Santa Fe by De Vargas, which is not part of the Fiesta, the popular celebration lapsed entirely for a long period of time, if indeed, it ever was of much importance. By 1912 a fiesta was being brought to life, largely as a matter of Anglo-American enterprise, although it was Spanish-American participation in it that gave it its quality and reality. By the 1920's this celebration had become known to the Spanish-speaking people as "las fiestas," in the plural. It was attached to the Labor Day weekend and extended over two and a half—now three and a half—days.

JULY 8, 1912:

[*Masthead:*]

SANTA FE NEW MEXICAN

Bronson Cutting	President
J. Wight Giddings	Editor
William F. Brogan	Associate Editor
Charles M. Stauffer	General Manager

AUGUST 30, 1912: SOLOMON LUNA IS FOUND DEAD IN DIPPING VAT.

Magdalena—Solomon Luna, the most prominent Spanish American citizen in New Mexico, Republican national committeeman, millionaire banker and for years a prominent leader in business affairs and in all public matters in New Mexico was found dead about seven o'clock this morning in a sheep dipping vat at one of his sheep camps, twenty miles from this town, according to a report brought in today by Elmer Fullerton, a cattleman, who lives in that vicinity.

Apparently Mr. Luna had gone to the vat early this morning to wash his hands or to get a drink of water. No one saw him fall into the vat so it is believed he leaned over the vat to wash his hands at a faucet and either suffered a stroke of apoplexy, heart failure or fainted, falling into the vat which was filled with three and a half fcct of sheep dip composed of lime, tobacco and water.

FEBRUARY 8, 1913:   IN PRISON ONLY AFTER MANY YEARS.

For a murder committed in 1890, one Octaviano Telles today began serving a three year term at the state prison and the history of his case and how he escaped punishment although sentenced in 1909, would read like fiction anywhere other than in New Mexico.

That the man reached prison at all, was only due to the perseverance of Governor W. C. McDonald, who said today that methods whereby this man remained at liberty, must stop in New Mexico if it were in the power of his office to stop them.

According to the investigation set under way months ago by the governor's office, there was a murder committed in 1890 in Valencia county. Telles, who was under suspicion, escaped and remained away for fifteen years. He then returned, was tried and in 1909 he was sentenced to three years in the state prison in this city. But Telles never reached prison.

A commitment was issued for him and the sheriff started for Santa Fe . At Albuquerque, a prominent politician met the sheriff and took the commitment from him on the pretense that he was himself going to Santa Fe to get a parole for Telles. The politician came to Santa Fe but if he got a parole, there is no record of it in the office of the governor nor at the state prison. The result was that Telles went back to Valencia county and lived there happily, until the case was called to the attention of Governor McDonald. The governor instituted a thorough investigation with the result that Telles arrived at the state prison today and is now starting out on his belated three year term.

A convenient form of patronage in the second decade of this century, in New Mexico, was the appointment of followers as coal oil inspectors. In the beginning of 1913, as Cutting's political power began to be felt, an attempt was made in the state legislature to strike at him through a special investigation of the activ-

ities as coal oil inspector of his city editor, Bryan Boru Dunne. Dunne had already established himself as a Santa Fe character, which he has continued to be for more than forty years, in addition to being an excellent newspaperman. The attempt to embarrass Cutting, the New Mexican, or Dunne failed, but the investigation led to what must have been an unusual hearing, briefly described below.

FEBRUARY 28, 1913:

That the testimony given by Brian B. Dunne, city editor of the New Mexican, before the oil investigation committee at the state capital was more interesting, more dramatic, more amusing than anything Ida M. Tarbell has written about "Standard Oil," was the declaration of members of the committee and of many of the listeners who filled the committee room where the committee met yesterday morning.

For one solid hour Mr. Dunne talked—and at times so rapidly that the stenographers were taxed to keep up with him. During that hour his narrative was uninterrupted except by violent bursts of laughter from politicians who held their sides or rolled over in their seats. As the witness drew picture after picture of the transactions he had had with certain well known "New Mexico statesmen". . . .

At the conclusion of his testimony, Mr. Dunne was surrounded by members of the committee who shook him warmly by the hand as did also visitors and his council, Judge L. C. Collins.

MARCH 11, 1913: ANTI-GAMBLING BILL IS MISSING FROM DESK OF HOUSE CHIEF CLERK.

Speaker Baca this morning named Rep. Nichols, Tully and Hilton as a special house committee to investigate the disappearance of the anti-gambling bill, the loss of a weights and measure bill at the last session and the disappearance of an emergency clause from the bill to abolish the coal oil inspector's office. This committee will proceed at once with the investigation.

Has someone "swiped" the anti-gambling bill?

The next item, if compared with those that closed the 1880 and introduced the 1890 periods, shows that an important change in point of view was occurring among the promoters of Santa Fe. This passage marks the beginning of the conscious intent to be old-style, and unlike other American cities, that has been the dominant theme in what the Chamber of Commerce calls "the City Different" (and many others, "the City Difficult") ever since.

JULY 18, 1913:   THE REAL OBJECT.

In the plans for the future building in this city, known as the "New–Old Santa Fe" movement, the ideas of the founders seemed at first to have been misunderstood, and a little friction was in a fair way to result.

It was never the intention of the city planning board or those interested in the endeavor to have Santa Fe retain those features which are natural to it, to dictate as to the materials used in residence or public building construction, or to interfere in any manner with mechanics or building contractors. There was no thought of abolishing brick cottages, or residences of any character, or commercial houses or public buildings. The only desire was to retain, as far as possible, the old Spanish style of architecture, including the stucco finish, which is a part of the ancient mode that has come down for centuries.

Happily this little misunderstanding has been adjusted and the real intent of the movers of the enterprise been clearly established. It was but a legitimate part of the publicity program. It was not to curtail building in Santa Fe, but to increase it. It was with the hope of making this old city distinctive in its character to such an extent that not only would tourists be attracted here, but permanent residents as well.

A modern style would not have a tendency to do this. Our very identity would be lost.

Would the historic relics in the Old Palace be as much admired if placed in a modern building? Would San Miguel church interest anyone especially had it been rebuilt on modern lines? Would guests from abroad going along our streets, stop and look at our homes in the old style architecture where the officers once lived, and admire them, were it not that they are built on the ancient plans? Would the Elks building attract the attention it does were it modern in form?

SEPTEMBER 17, 1913: SANTA FE IS DECLARED "THE OLDEST CITY" IN THE UNITED STATES.Chamber of Commerce Vote to Have That Legend Printed on the 68,000 Envelopes to Be Used by the Merchants and Others Who Strive to Swell the Tourist Crop.

Santa Fe was declared the "oldest city in the United States of America" (Baedeker's Guide Book, please copy) at an enthusiastic meeting held by members of the chamber of commerce last night in the Palace of the Governors which has come down the centuries to back the claim.

For some time the question of the "oldest" city has been of interest to Santa Feans when they discussed their city with tourists; but in the past few days the antiquity of Santa Fe has been of unusual interest because of the 68,000 envelopes which were to bear the slogan "Santa Fe, the Oldest City in the United States."

Some one who had heard of St. Augustine's claim to the "oldest city" suggested that the slogan be changed to "second oldest city"—but the merchants who ordered the envelopes said "Nay, nay." After all, what is the use of taking second place and telling the world about it?

So the matter was aired at the meeting last night. Colonel Ralph E. Twitchell, historian and lawyer, and former Governor L. Bradford Prince, president of the New Mexico Historical Society, rallied to the support of the "oldest city" boosters, and declared:

"There is no documentary proof there is any city in the United States that is OLDER than Santa Fe."

Sylvanus Griswold Morley, the Harvard scientist and authority on Central American history, took a different view and declared that in his opinion Santa Fe lacks evidence that it is the oldest European city in the United States.

MARCH 2, 1914:

[*Masthead:*]
THE NEW MEXICAN PRINTING CO.,
Publishers.

Bronson M. Cutting	President
Charles M. Stauffer	General Manager
E. Dana Johnson	Editor

E. Dana Johnson is still warmly remembered in Santa Fe as an able editor and delightful person. Under him, the paper acquired a liveliness it had not had since the days of Manderfield and Tucker.

MARCH 2, 1914:   BURY IT.

The New Mexican does not wish to be unpleasantly or unduly critical, but there is a dead rooster at the corner of Palace and Lincoln Avenues which has lain there unburied for three consecutive days.

There is no doubt about that rooster's death. No physician's certificate is required, as the passerby may testify. He has passed away. Now, while one rooster occupies comparatively little space, and while a casual visitor to the city might not notice him, the principle of the thing is wrong. One tourist might see that rooster and fail to see the Old Palace; and his report on Santa Fe would feature the fact that it had no facilities for interring or removing defunct roosters.

Let no visitor to the Oldest-Newest city in the United States see unburied roosters on our street corners. It is the little things that go to make the big impressions. Every rooster removed and buried makes Santa Fe one rooster the cleaner, one rooster the brighter and more attractive.

Let us let no dead rooster escape—or any other debris, animal, vegetable or mineral, on the streets of this beautiful capital city of New Mexico.

On April 31, 1914, a man held in the city jail for the murder of his wife was taken from the jail by masked men, who murdered him in revenge. This event led the New Mexican *to make a list of the killings that had occurred in the district in which the man and wife had lived. The people involved have many decent, law-abiding relatives now living, to whom it would be extremely painful to have the old report reprinted; therefore only a summary is given here, for the purpose of showing the element of violence that has always been, and still is, a characteristic of Santa Fe. These killings run back to fifteen years before the two mentioned above and took place within a small neighborhood.*

Two men were stoned to death. Two others, besides the man who was taken out of jail, killed their wives. One man shot a companion when both were drunk. The total of known murders for the fifteen years is seven, in addition to a suspected, but unproven, case of infanticide.

MAY 1, 1914:   THE SUFFRAGE MEETING.

The New Mexico Woman's Suffrage league is to hold a mass meeting tomorrow evening in the Old Palace, at which the campaign for ballots for women in nation and state will be officially launched in New Mexico.

That the New Mexico women are going at the matter sensibly and wisely is indicated by the statement made by an official of the organization that the suffragists in New Mexico are in no sense of the word "suffragettes." The women of the state who want the ballot intend to convince the electorate logically and earnestly of the justice of their cause, without any fireworks, without any spectacular demonstrations or anything of the kind; and there is no better way to go about it. That they have unanswerable arguments makes it the more unnecessary to employ any pyrotechnics in placing their case before the voters. That the women of New Mexico are as well able as those of any state in the union to use the ballot rightly and intelligently has already been amply demonstrated in school elections in the state; and that the organized women of the state are becoming a powerful influence no one will deny in view of the progress made in the woman's club movement throughout New Mexico in the past few years.

This meeting tomorrow night is one that should be attended by every man or woman interested in matters of government and in progress, whether or not you are a believer in woman's suffrage. At least, if you are a fair minded person it is well worth while to go and hear the woman's side of the case.

JANUARY 19, 1915: THE THEATERS.

The managers of the two Santa Fe theaters are to be congratulated on the remarkable enterprise they have shown in the effort to bring to the people of this city the very best possible attractions. Likewise the amusement seeking public is to be felicitated on the opportunity given here to see such good performances and top-notch movies. The advertising campaigns being carried on in the NEW MEXICAN are a sufficient testimonial to the up-to-dateness and enterprise of both these play houses. It is hard to exaggerate the importance to a city of this size of the progress which has been made in the motion picture world. To be able to see Tom Terriss and Ethel Barrymore and such dramatic stars, to become familiar with the greatest plays and players thus intimately for popular prices and to have this never-failing source of amusement and mental stimulus in Santa Fe is a real blessing and one that the generous patronage given the theaters demonstrates is appreciated. Not only so, but considering the fact that Santa Fe is off the main line in the far SW, the class of plays brought to the local opera house is most excellent. Certainly the local impresarios are deserving of all the patronage the theaters get and we would be hard put to it for amusement in Santa Fe were the playhouses to be eliminated from the scheme of things.

FEBRUARY 1, 1915: ELFEGO BACA HELD CHARGED WITH MURDER IN PASS CITY.

Elfego Baca, former district attorney in Socorro county, deputy sheriff in that county, lawyer, candidate for Congress and who some years ago sought the nomination for district judge at Albuquerque, is in jail in El Paso charged with the murder of Dr.

Celestino Otero, formerly of Albuquerque. It is believed the shooting was a case of self defense. It is also believed that it was the outcome of the determination of the Villa faction to "get" Baca for his friendship with General Jose Inez Salazar, an enemy of Villa who recently escaped from the Bernalillo county jail while awaiting trial in the U. S. court on the charge of perjury. Baca has been attorney for Salazar and closely associated with him. Both men spent considerable time in this city some months ago, Salazar as defendant on a charge in the U. S. court of neutrality violation in shipping arms and ammunition across the border, and Baca as his attorney.

As has already been noted, the frontier lingered until recently in New Mexico and is perhaps not entirely gone even now. However, in 1958, the point had been reached at which Walt Disney Productions had come to Santa Fe to make a picture about Elfego Baca. That gentleman, a highly controversial character, was a genuine New Mexican frontier product. We get news of him, in the item above and those that follow a little later, only in the sunset of his career. As deputy sheriff and district attorney in Socorro county, he reversed the usual formula and was the heroic "Mexican" lawman who stood up against the lawless, treacherous Texans at the constant risk of his life. In one famous fight, single-handedly he stood off a band of armed Texans variously estimated at from twelve to eighteen.

FEBRUARY 11, 1915:   THE ONLY THING.

The only thing that prevents the New Mexican from saying more about the unspeakable, inexcusable, appalling condition of the streets of this city is the fear that it MIGHT HURT THE TOWN.

We should hate to say anything which might induce the Visiting Legislator, who daily wades painfully through the bottomless mud and filth, to believe that our streets were not in faultless and immaculate condition. We would not for the world lead the Solon who slips on the ice and pushes his countenance into the slop to

218

believe that Santa Fe has not an efficient and watchful city government. That would be Playing Politics.

APRIL 12, 1915:   SIX INDICTED FOR AIDING IN ESCAPE OF SALAZAR.

The story of the conspiracy in connection with the escape of General Jose Inez Salazar, Mexican revolutionary from the Bernalillo county jail at Albuquerque, last November and which was outlined by the New Mexican more than a week ago, "broke" late Saturday evening when six indictments were returned by the Federal grand jury here. The men indicted for alleged connection with the Salazar conspiracy are:

District Attorney Manuel U. Vigil, Albuquerque

State Game Warden Trinidad C. de Baca of Santa Fe

Elfego Baca, of Albuquerque; counsel for Salazar

Monico Aranda of Albuquerque

Carlos Armijo, of Albuquerque; deputy sheriff and jailer at the time Salazar escaped.

Porfirio, alias Perfilio Savedra, of Albuquerque.

The six men were indicted on two counts, both alleging conspiracy against the United States in the rescue and release of a prisoner from the custody of the U S marshall.

Armijo, the former deputy sheriff, is definitely charged with opening the cell in the Albuquerque jail and allowing Salazar to be taken out.

State Game Warden Trinidad C. de Baca and Monico Aranda, together with Celestino Otero, the Spaniard killed by Elfego Baca in El Paso, are charged with having taken Salazar out of jail, thereafter removing him to a "place of concealment."

The charge against Elfego Baca and District Attorney Manuel U. Vigil is simply conspiracy.

Among American Indians having a pattern of secrecy concerning their religious beliefs and practices, little sophistication, and a sense of humor (which few tribes lack), the inquiring ethnographer runs a constant risk of being taken for a dreadful ride. This happened to Matilda Coxe Stevenson, an ethnologist of consider-

able standing, when she came among the Tewas, and led to the
editorial below. If I remember correctly what I was told by Tewas
some thirty years ago, the humorist who made a gull of Mrs.
Stevenson was considered to have gone too far, since the tale
received wide publicity that the Indians considered harmful, and
was disciplined.

APRIL 30, 1915: THAT PUEBLO STORY.

The New Mexican would like to see the bureau of Indian affairs take the trouble to carefully investigate the annually recurring story that the New Mexican Pueblo Indians maintain the practice of human sacrifice to appease their gods. If the periodical tale is true the government ought to be able to find it out and put a stop to the practice by whatsoever means are necessary; if it is not true the story ought to be "scotched" for good and all as it gives New Mexico a vast amount of unfavorable advertising year after year. Every so often some correspondent, when news is dull, digs up the lurid legend of the sacred serpent, anywhere from ten to forty feet in length which wriggles in its noisome lair until the picturesque red man with mysterious incantations offers up the squalling papoose and the shrieking squaw to placate the voracious reptile.

The New Mexican has considerable respect for the work done by Mrs. Matilda Coxe-Stevenson [*sic*] as an ethnologist. Like the rest of us, it is possible that she may be mistaken. Her report, however, which has been widely published in eastern newspapers, and which repeats circumstantially the story of human sacrifice, is ample justification for an official investigation which will definitely and finally clear up the matter.

DECEMBER 20, 1915: NOT GUILTY, IS VERDICT IN CASE OF MEN
CHARGED WITH CONSPIRACY. CLEAN BILL GIVEN ELFEGO, ET AL. BY
SPANISH-SPEAKING JURY.

The jury, composed entirely of Spanish-Americans, in the alleged conspiracy case at 6:10 Saturday night acquitted Elfego Baca, Trinidad C. de Baca, Manuel U. Vigil and Carlos Armijo of complicity in the successful plot to liberate General Salazar from jail in Albuquerque on November 20, 1914.

Who did liberate Salazar: who were the masked men who, Jailer Carlos Armijo alleges, overpowered him and tied him to a post, who concealed the general and who engineered his flight to Mexico thus remain deep dark and unsolved mysteries and so far as known are likely to remain so and take their places with the most baffling enigmas of history.

DECEMBER 4, 1915: SOUL OF SOUTHWEST LAID BARE IN 35 BEAUTI-
FUL PAINTINGS BY WALTER UFER HUNG YESTERDAY IN GOVERNORS'
PALACE.

"The Soul of the Southwest," is what one finds in the 35 paintings hung yesterday in the reception room of the Palace of the Governors by Walter Ufer, the Chicago artist. The pictures will remain up only until Monday noon and the Santa Fean or the sojourner in Santa Fe who does not seize the opportunity of seeing and studying them, misses a treat.

Mr. Ufer paints the Indian as he finds him in his native habitat. He does not pose him; there is nothing artificial about his noble Red Man. That is why he reveals glimpses of San Juan one had never suspected, picturesqueness and beauty that we, too, will see next time we go there, after having viewed Mr. Ufer's pictures.

Mr. Ufer is distinctly modern in his technique. His skies, the daintiness of his fields of flowers and textures, are achieved with careful hatch and stipple. The aim for decoration and design is so skillfully disguised as not to obtrude itself but his pictures are perfectly balanced in their masses.

JANUARY 15, 1916: CASSIDY EXHIBIT OF PAINTINGS AT OLD PALACE
ARTISTIC EVENT OF THE WEEK.

As a portrait painter, Gerald Cassidy, whose exhibit opened at the Palace of the Governors this week is rapidly acquiring fame. He catches with rare cunning the spiritual light that reveals the soul. It is a wizardry of drawing, color and the indefinable something that men call genius whether it is manifested in poetry or in music or in painting. And Cassidy is among that few in whose pictures even the layman recognizes the touch of genius.

The art colony at Taos can be traced back to 1898, when Bert Phillips and Ernest L. Blumenschein, en route from Denver to Mexico City, stopped there. The story that their decision to stay at Taos was caused by the collapse of a wagon wheel at a particularly beautiful spot may be apocryphal; it is too good and too reasonable to reject.

Santa Fe got going much later. Its beginning as a center of the arts is in the last two items above. Ufer was a Taos artist. Cassidy was one of the first to settle in Santa Fe, where he became a major figure. His widow, Ina Sizer Cassidy, is a writer and local historian and has been a most effective leader in bringing about the preservation of Santa Fe's antiquities and its native style.

JANUARY 17, 1916: A TIMELY ACTION.

The resolutions passed by a number of Spanish speaking New Mexicans in this city the last of the week, re-iterating fealty and loyalty to the United States government were timely and admirable. The wisdom of taking every opportunity to call the country's attention to the fact that New Mexicans are citizens of the United States is apparent to almost any one who has been bored while in the east by the continual necessity of explaining, to supposedly intelligent persons, that Villa is not encamped in Santa Fe canyon, and no massacres by Zapata bandits ever occur in Albuquerque.

These resolutions, we believe, express the real feeling of the mass of the Spanish speaking citizens of New Mexico; citizens who love New Mexico and take the deepest interest in all that concerns her and whose patriotism, as pointed out, has been immortally demonstrated on the battlefield. As a matter of fact, but for language, Old Mexico is as foreign a country to most of New Mexico's citizens as to those of Arkansas or Wisconsin.

MARCH 10, 1916: ENOUGH.

The armed invasion of the United States and the state of New Mexico by a thousand bandits under Francisco Villa; the murder of nearly a score of Americans and the burning of American property constitute the final and incontrovertible evidence that Carranza, whose government has been recognized by the U S, is unable to restore or maintain order in Mexico or to prevent revolutionaries in that country from endangering the peace and safety of the people of the U S.

The order for U S troops to enter Mexico was absolutely inevitable.

It was not conceivable that any self-respecting president or secretary of state who claimed a spark of manhood or of Americanism would wait for further demonstration of this inability on Carranza's part.

This is the last straw. The American people have watched the killing of their countrymen by scores in Mexico with patience and forbearance for years; when New Mexico and American soil must contribute burnt offerings to Watchful Waiting the limit has been reached.

At this writing United States troops are in Mexico in pursuit of the murderers. The U S government should re-inforce these pursuers with every soldier it owns and send them clear to Yucatan if that is needed to catch and punish Villa and his band of criminals.

This newspaper believes we have had enough of mere "punishment" after the fact, what we want is punishment that will mean prevention. Nothing short of the death of Villa and every one of his followers involved in the raid will be adequate measures in this case. They should be shot down with no more consideration that that given a Gila monster or a rattlesnake. Villa has roamed unhindered across Mexico in the fact of opera bouffe opposition by Carranza troops; the Mexicans fear him like a devil and his removal from the scene is the only method of eliminating the most formidable menace to the peace of Mexico and the safety of Americans both north and south of the line.

APRIL 1, 1916:   WORK OF WILLIAM PENHALLOW HENDERSON RANKS
VERY HIGH IN BEST AMERICAN ART.

The arrival here of Mr. and Mrs. William Penhallow Henderson, of Chicago and formerly of Boston, has been hailed with
delight by local artists and art lovers. Mr. Henderson's work has
been highly praised by some of the great newspapers of this country, from coast to coast. The following critical study from the pen
of a Chicago writer in the "Evening Post" may prove of local
interest:

William Penhallow Henderson, painter in oils and etcher,
opened to view an exhibition of original pastels in the galleries
of Albert Roullier in the Fine Arts building this afternoon. There
are twenty-five lyrics in color of famous gardens in estates along
the north shore, Lake Forest, Lake Bluff and Lake Geneva in
Wisconsin, and nearly two score sketches of cities, portraits, fan-
tasies and figures. The viewer is tempted and dares to write that
the association with the gardens of growing flowers has stimulated
an efflorescence in Mr. Henderson's productions.

*Mrs. Henderson was the poet, Alice Corbin, one of the founders
of* Poetry *and a figure of international stature. She was responsible
for the coming to Santa Fe of such poets as Carl Sandburg, John
Gould Fletcher, and Witter Bynner and, obviously, played an
important part in the development here of a center of writers as
well as of painters.*

*William Penhallow Henderson was an artist of considerable
versatility. He became a builder and architect, as well as a cabinet
maker. The very distinctive Museum of Navajo Ceremonial Art
in Santa Fe is the best evidence of his architectural originality.*

*The Hendersons were the first to settle on what had originally
been called Corral Road, but had become Telephone Road because the telephone line into town followed it. The Hendersons
had no intention of living in a place like Santa Fe on a street with
such a name, so they renamed it Camino del Monte Sol, a street
that has since become fairly famous for the artists living along it.*

They set about a vigorous exploration of the Spanish and Indian

region of northern New Mexico and Arizona, later in company
with their daughter Alice, and few members of the art colony
knew the country better, from the Hopi villages in Arizona to
the mountain Spanish settlements behind the Sangre de Cristo
Mountains.

JUNE 30, 1916: FOUR VILLISTAS ARE HANGED AT DEMING THIS
MORNING.

Four Villistas who took part in the Columbus raid were executed by hanging in the county jail here today. The men were put
to death in pairs. Euisiero Renteria and Taurino Garcia were
placed on the scaffold first. They were not pronounced dead until
after twenty minutes had passed. Jose Nangel and Juan Costilla
were next. Their necks were broken and death was almost instantaneous. This completes the disposition of the cases of the
Columbus raiders. Jose Rodriguez recently was granted a stay of
execution and is serving a life sentence.

Two other Villistas had been hanged on June 9. The charge
against them all was of murdering certain citizens of Columbus.

JULY 31, 1916: REVIVAL OF DE VARGAS PAGEANT TO BE AGITATED
BY COMMERCE CHAMBER.

That Santa Fe is going to be placed most decidedly on the map
before another year passes seems assured by a recent movement
for which the Chamber of Commerce stands sponsor. This movement which has been the subject of a number of conferences between the chamber officials and some of the local business men,
has for its object the revival on a stupendous scale of the De
Vargas Pageant, which was last staged in Santa Fe in 1912. A
great deal of interest in this proposed revival has been shown by
local people lately, all of whom seem to think that it is about
time local activities should be directed toward the permanent
establishment on a large scale of some distinctive annual celebra-

tion or fete that will be a typical Santa Fe affair and bring crowds from "all over."

The "immemorial" Santa Fe Fiesta is still in process of being brought to life, for entirely laudable commercial reasons.

AUGUST 26, 1916:   SANTA FE ARTISTS EXHIBIT PAINTINGS PORTRAY-
ING VARIED ASPECTS OF NEW MEXICAN LANDSCAPE AND SANTA FE
TYPES.

Among the artists showing pictures at the Old Palace are several old residents of Santa Fe who need no introduction. These are Carlos Vierra, Kenneth Chapman, Gerald Cassidy, Sheldon Parsons and Sara Tudor Parsons. The best introduction to the other artists is a visit to their several canvases in the exhibition. The pictures shown present a wide variety of subject matter and method, and as the artists have drawn their inspiration from the familiar landscape and characteristic types of this neighborhood, the pictures have a local, as well as an artistic interest for the people of Santa Fe.

Also showing in this exhibition was Robert Henri, who had become a member of the colony.

Cutting and his newspaper were beginning to make themselves felt in New Mexico. They were upsetting to politicians reared in firm doctrines of total party regularity. Cutting was influential enough to have been appointed a colonel on the Governor's staff, which explains the military title given him below. He set up a convention of "Progressives and Independents," which, on September 1, 1916, endorsed the entire state Democratic ticket, while leaving itself uncommitted concerning the national slates.

At the same time, the paper set about walloping local Republicans, and it hurt. Frank A. Hubbell, Republican candidate for senator, filed a $50,000 libel suit against the New Mexican. This was followed by the action reported below, also involving $50,000, the account of which gives a sample of the paper's style in full combat. It sounds like old times.

226

OCTOBER 11, 1916: EX-PENITENTIARY WARDEN AND CZAR OF SO-
CORRO FAILS IN ATTEMPT TO PUT PRESIDENT OF NEW MEXICAN IN
JAIL.

H. O. Bursum, removed by Governor Hagerman as warden of
the state penitentiary because of the disgraceful mess uncovered
in that institution; H. O. Bursum, who paid $88.26 of his per-
sonal taxes of $5,000 in ten years; H. O. Bursum, connected with
beneficent Republican legislation of the Hawkins bill stripe for
many years; H. O. Bursum of wild animal bounty fame, whose
store got $10,000 of $27,000 spent on the Mogollon road; H. O.
Bursum, kingpin of as sweet a smelling political organization as
ever disseminated its fragrance in the west, is still at work trying
to gag the press and put the lid on his own highly perfumed record
in the desperate attempt to squeeze himself and his bunch into
power in this state. Mr. Bursum is working this time through one
of his tools named Henry Dreyfus, his city marshal in the town of
Socorro, where they bulldoze bill posters and crippled movie proprietors and threaten their livelihood if they dare to exhibit Democratic bills or slides. This city marshal is the gentleman whom
Mr. Bursum ran for sheriff in 1911 and who was repudiated by the
dear voters. Mr. Bursum, through Mr. Henry Dreyfus and through
Honorable Judge Amos Green, a Bursum justice of the peace,
through an illegal warrant, today sought to seize and capture the
person of Col. Bronson M. Cutting, president of the New Mexican Printing Company, and hale him in chains, manacles, fetters,
and disgrace, to Mr. Bursum's Socorro county jail. The chains,
however, failed to clank.

Sheriff Emil James, of Socorro county, arrived today at noon
and served a warrant on Col. Cutting, sworn out by Honorable
Judge Amos Bursum Green, on complaint of one Henry Bursum
Dreyfus, charging Col. Cutting, who returned yesterday from El
Paso, with wickedly libeling Dreyfus by reason of a statement
printed in this paper Saturday to the effect that "a Bursum henchman named Dreyfus in the days of Governor Hagerman, tore
down the American flag in Socorro and stamped on it," and otherwise desecrated it. It will be remembered that the infamous inci-

dent of flag desecration in Socorro was one of the things used with telling effect by Governor Hagerman and newspapers in the campaign which defeated Bursum in 1911. Mr. Bursum, through Henry Dreyfus, who thus claims that he is the "Bursum henchman named Dreyfus" mentioned, also brings a civil suit for libel damages in the modest sum of $50,000, papers in this case being served today on President Cutting and Secretary Dorman, of the New Mexican Printing Company.

JANUARY 19, 1917: STAFF OF THIS NEWSPAPER CRIMINALS, IS CHARGE. New Mexican Thoroughly Indicted by Grand Jury of Socorro on Libel Charges.

The Santa Fe New Mexican herewith formally announces the following indictments, returned by the Grand Jury of the County of Socorro, State of New Mexico, against persons connected with this newspaper, the charge being criminal libel:

BRONSON M. CUTTING, President New Mexican Printing Co. Four True Bills.

EX-GOVERNOR M. A. OTERO, Treasurer New Mexican Printing Co., whose speech-making campaign was largely responsible for the defeat of H. O. Bursum, Republican candidate for governor. Two True Bills.

RALPH M. HENDERSON, Business Manager, Two True Bills.

E. DANA JOHNSON, Managing Editor, Two True Bills.

AUSTIN C. BRADY, Member Reportorial Staff. Two True Bills.

So far as the New Mexican is advised, none of the bookkeepers, department foremen, printers, linotype operators, newsboys or the office "devil" has been indicted up to the time of going to press.

It is presumed, although the New Mexican has not been advised of the specific charges, that these indictments are an aftermath of the late campaign of this paper against H. O. Bursum, of Socorro, defeated Republican candidate for governor.

Further comment upon the indictments at this time would be improper and highly unnecessary.

SEPTEMBER 11, 1917:   NEW MEXICAN EDITOR GETS 30 DAYS IN JAIL.

E. Dana Johnson, editor of the Santa Fe New Mexican, was sentenced to thirty days in the "common jail" of the county of Valencia yesterday afternoon at Los Lunas by the Honorable Merritt C. Mechem, judge of the Seventh judicial district, on the charge of contempt of court. After stating he did not believe the case appealable, Judge Mechem stated he would allow an appeal to the supreme court and fixed the supersedeas bond at $500.

SEPTEMBER 12, 1917:   THE CONTEMPT CASE.

As the public was advised through the news columns of the New Mexican yesterday, the editor of this paper has been convicted of criminal contempt and sentenced to jail by Honorable Merritt C. Mechem, judge of the seventh judicial district sitting in Valencia county because of the publications made in this paper on March 30 last at the time when it was discovered that Merritt C. Mechem had filed an affidavit with the state board of bar examiners in support of the exoneration of M. C. Spicer, one of the attorneys for Henry Dreyfus in the libel suit brought by Dreyfus against the New Mexican Printing Company and others, which affidavit cast doubt upon the credibility of the affidavits filed in the same proceeding by Bronson M. Cutting, Mrs. Justine B. Ward, his sister, Miguel A. Otero, Jr., Chaves Armijo and Francis C. Wilson, in which they charge Spicer with wig-wagging signals to Dreyfus while he was under cross-examination with the intent to indicate to Dreyfus what answers he should make to the questions being propounded to him.

The contempt-of-court charge, based upon a news story highly unpalatable to Judge Mechem, was soon cleared away. The libel case dragged on until finally dismissed by the state supreme court on October 23, 1919.

Mechem and Bursum are respected dynastic names in New Mexico Republican politics. Cutting and his paper were no respecters of persons.

SEPTEMBER 14, 1917:   SECRET BALLOT BOOTH TO BE USED FIRST
TIME IN NOVEMBER.

Booths for secret balloting will be used in New Mexico for the
first time at the election on the "dry" and other proposed constitutional amendments on November 6. General provisions for
secret balloting are contained in the Australian ballot law passed
at the regular session of the last legislature, and Chapter 17 of the
laws of that session makes special provision for booths and a
secret ballot at the November election. It is provided that the
booths must be supplied by the county commissioners of each
county, and that in each precinct there shall be one for every 100
votes cast at the last election.

NOVEMBER 7, 1917:   THE "DRY" VICTORY.

New Mexico yesterday entered the "dry" column by an overwhelming vote.

It was a landslide for prohibition. Even the most optimistic
champions of the amendment had not anticipated it.

It marked the greatest stride that the state has so far made. The
economic value of the victory, particularly at this time, is great,
but far greater is its value in public decency, in better citizenship,
in better homes, in happier and more contented and more prosperous people.

New Mexico voters struck a great blow for New Mexico yesterday.

The New Mexican *had been ardently dry for some years and
was to continue so for some little time to come. Cutting maintained perhaps the finest wine cellar in the Southwest.*

*As readers will have gathered, the Palace of the Governors,
having passed from federal into state ownership, had been turned
into a museum. Under the energetic leadership of Dr. Edgar L.
Hewett, whom we find promoting many things, it became also
the headquarters of his School of American Research. With stead-*

*ily increasing activity in historical studies and collections, archae-
ology, ethnology, and a growing art colony, the Palace was soon
overcrowded.*

A second museum, now usually called the Art Museum, and
containing the St. Francis Auditorium, was built across Lincoln
Avenue from the Palace, relieving the strain. The person who
made himself conspicuous in connection with this achievement,
at the opening functions as reported below, was Hewett. Actually,
Robert Henri and George Bellows provided a good deal of the
spark, and Frank Springer, lawyer and paleontologist of Cimarrón,
New Mexico, was the principal contributor to the cost. His part
is suggested in one of the New Mexican's headlines but explained
nowhere in the text, notably not in Hewett's address. His own
speech was extremely modest.

The State Art Museum is unique in many respects. Built under
the influence of Carlos Vierra, it is an architectural curiosity.
Made of cement, hollow tile, and plaster, it attempts unsuccessfully to imitate true adobe. As Hewett indicates in his speech, the
workmen "freed themselves from plumb-line and square," in
short, were under orders to lay up the courses out of true, so as to
give the effect of adobe after it has settled. The exterior details of
the Museum are copied from a number of mission churches, portions of Indian pueblos, and other sources. The total effect is
stagey and not particularly interesting; nonetheless, this building
was beneficially important in leading to the development of the
modern Santa Fe style.

With the exception of the period of occasional juried or invi-
tational exhibits, the Museum's walls are available to anyone who
applies for space. It is merely a matter of waiting one's turn. The
resultant shows are sometimes startling, sometimes laughable,
sometimes fine; proposals to modify this "open door" policy have
always met with extremely vigorous and successful opposition.

New Mexico now had in its capital city an anthropological, historical, and art museum and an auditorium, all under one board
of trustees, with a complicated extra factor in the independent
School of American Research, the director of which is head of the
museums. Since then, two more institutions have been acquired

by the Museum of New Mexico—the Laboratory of Anthropology
and the International Folk Art Museum. The resultant complex
is unusual and culturally important.

NOVEMBER 26, 1917: [*Banner headline.*] NEW MUSEUM BUILD-
ING FORMALLY DEDICATED; EDUCATORS GETTING BUSY. GOVERNOR
LINDSEY IN FITTING PHRASE FORMALLY ACCEPTS MUSEUM FOR
STATE. HIGH SPHERE OF INSTITUTION EMPHASIZED BY EXECUTIVE;
DR. KELSEY PAYS TRIBUTE TO MEN WHO HAVE MADE GREAT ACHIEVE-
MENT POSSIBLE.

"Mine eyes have seen the coming of the Glory of the Lord,"
the audience that filled the St. Francis auditorium Saturday night
sang under the leadership of Mrs. R. M. Henderson and a trained
orchestra and choir. "The Battle Hymn of the Republic" has not
meant so much to the nation for 50 years and more, as it does now
and the great crowd realized it as it joined in the Hallelujah
chorus of the grand old hymn. It was a fitting opening for the new
museum building to the public, and the thousand and more people who had gathered for the occasion felt it.

Dr. Edgar L. Hewett presided during the exercises, which were
simple, but nevertheless most impressive. His introductory address appears in another column. . . .

SANG "THE MARSELLAISE."

Mrs. Maude McFie Lansing, daughter of Judge John R. McFie,
was accorded the honor of singing the first solo in the new auditorium. She chose "The Marsellaise," that patriotic hymn of the
French, the accepted battle hymn of democracy the world over.
Mrs. Bloom [*sic*] sang it in French and with a spirit which emphasized its fire. Her sister, Mrs. Lackey, accompanied her.

MEMORIAL TO THE FRANCISCANS.

The closing address was by Secretary of State Antonio Lucero.
It was a scholarly paper that he read on the early history of New
Mexico, emphasizing especially the part that the Franciscans took
in bringing civilization to the Southwest, beginning as early
as 1539, and ending in glorious martyrdom during the Pueblo

Revolution of 1680. It was a deserved tribute to the order, to the memory of whose martyrs the new building is an imperishable monument.

OPENING OF ART EXHIBIT.

From the auditorium, the throngs poured into the art galleries and lingered to admire the art exhibit, the significance of which Dr. Hewett had pointed out. The Woman's Museum board, assisted by the artists and their families, received. It was a much appreciated opportunity that the visitors, especially the educators, whose names stand at or near the head of American art and whose pictures made the exhibit the greatest of Southwestern art that has ever been attempted anywhere [*sic*]. Artists like O. E. Benninghaus [*sic*, for Berninghouse], came direct from St. Louis to attend this opening of the exhibit, and among them Mrs. Robert Henri, Mr. and Mrs. Julius Rolshoven, Mr. and Mrs. W. P. Henderson, Mr. and Mrs. H. Paul Burlin, Arthur F. Musgrave, Sheldon Parsons, Miss Sara Parsons, Mr. and Mrs. Carlos Vierra, Ralph Myers, Mr. and Mrs. K. M. Chapman and others almost as well known, and whose paintings are among the finest on exhibit.

NOVEMBER 26, 1917: [*Banner headline and subhead on page one, Section Two.*]

NEW MUSEUM THE NOBLEST, SIMPLEST AND MOST IMPRESSIVE TYPE OF CHRISTIAN ARCHITECTURE ORIGINATING ON THIS CONTINENT.

———

SPLENDID MONUMENT TO THE PIONEER SOLDIERS OF THE CROSS IN NEW MEXICO TO BECOME HOME OF SCIENCE, ART AND EDUCATION, HON. FRANK SPRINGER, WHOSE GENEROSITY AND EFFORTS MADE THE BUILDING POSSIBLE, POINTS OUT IN DEDICATION ADDRESS LAST NIGHT; DESPITE THE WORLD CONFLICT, FLAGS OF SCIENCE AND ART MUST BE KEPT FLYING, HE DECLARES, AS A SACRED DUTY TO FUTURE GENERATIONS.

(Address of Hon. Frank Springer at the Dedication of the New Museum Sunday [*sic*] Night, November 25.)

Santa Fe

NOVEMBER 26, 1917:
(Address of Dr. Edgar L. Hewett at
Opening of New Museum, Satur-
day Night, November 24.)

It is my privilege to announce the opening of a new institution
—the New Mexico Art Museum. For many months the eyes of
our people have turned daily toward this place. They watched the
old military headquarters disappear, the new walls rise, the great
timbers swing into place. Out of unrelated elements, clay, lime,
wood and iron, this edifice emerged which certainly has some
characteristics of a great work of art. There has been an organiz-
ing and relating of crude material into a structure which we expect
to stand for ages, a monument to a noble past, an inspiration to
future builders of a great state.

One thing we especially like about this building—so many have
had a helpful part in it. People ask, "Whose conception is this?"
"Who did this remarkable work?" Time was when it existed
only in the minds of two or three people, but it quickly became a
matter of organization and cooperation of many minds and hands.
All honor to those who endowed it with funds; to legislators and
regents and building committees who put the resources of the
state back of it; to architects, superintendent of construction and
artists, but equal honor to the workmen whose hands produced
the results you see here. To do this, they had to give up traditions
of their craft, to free themselves from plumb-line and square and
level, and work with the boldness of master-builders. And how
well they did it! They became more than artisans; there are the
strokes of their axes, gouges, trowels, brushes. I leave it to you to
say if the work is not a master work. On the role of honor let
us inscribe the names of the carpenters, bricklayers, plasterers
and painters.

234

Then too, the spirit of the contributors who gave the School of American Research the initial sum with which to put up this structure, is built into it. In their donation, they say: "This fund is contributed by a small group of men and women residents, of or interested in the state, who desire in this manner to attest their loyalty to New Mexico, their solicitude for its progress and their appreciation of the benefits which its opportunities have afforded them." If patriotism does not mean gratitude for the opportunities afforded by one's country, it is an empty word.

How fortunate, too, for us that a great institution, the Archaeological Institute of America, gave its sanction to this enterprise. Without it, there would have been nothing of this that we celebrate to night.

NOVEMBER 26, 1917:   A MAGNIFICENT MONUMENT.

Entirely without exaggeration it may be stated that there is nowhere else in the United States the equal of the new New Mexico state museum. It has been a marvelous revelation to Santa Fe people no less than to Santa Fe guests. With its beautiful gems of art, its priceless treasures of science and history, its unique architecture, its perfection and artistry of detail, its interior and exterior, it is an institution without a parallel in the country and a prize whose value the city and state are just beginning to realize. The dedication exercises have been most impressive and appropriate and fully in harmony with the spirit of the entire enterprise. That the art gallery ranks with the Carnegie gallery in Pittsburg, the Chicago Art institute, the Corcoran Art gallery in Washington and others, no one who has had an opportunity for comparison will deny. But after all, the New Mexico museum is so entirely different, so completely in a class by itself, and is in itself such an artistic achievement that no comparison is really possible.

NOVEMBER 26, 1917:   [*Box.*] SCIENCE CONGRESS. College and High School Section. New Mexico Association for Science— School American Research.

In St. Francis Auditorium at 9:45 a. m., Tuesday and Wednesday Forenoons. Tomorrow's Program.

235

"Spanish Colonization and the Founding of Ciudades and Villas In the Time of Don Juan de Oñate"—Ralph E. Twitchell, Esq.

"Opportunities of the New Museum"—Dr. Clark Wissler of the American Museum of Natural History, New York City.

"A Navajo Medicine Pouch"—By Dr. Edgar L. Hewett.

"The Symbolic Man of the Osage Tribe"—By Francis La Flesche (of the Omahas), Bureau of American Ethnology, Washington, D. C.

Either Tuesday or Wednesday forenoon, the Ildefonso Indians will give the Eagle dance on the rostrum of the auditorium, Mrs. Natalie Curtis Burlin explaining it and also presenting a number of Indian songs.

The program announced in the last item shows that the opening of the doubled museum was an affair of some scientific quality. Ralph Emerson Twitchell is still rated as New Mexico's principal historian. Clark Wissler was then the leading authority on the general anthropology of the North American Indians, and the first proponent of the theory of culture areas. Francis La Flesche was the first American Indian to become a fully trained, professional anthropologist. He was killed not long after this celebration, in the course of field work in the Philippines.

APRIL 11, 1918: GERMAN TAKEN OUT OF SCHOOLS.

The German language has been taken out of the public schools of New Mexico and no longer will be even an elective study.

This action was decided upon by the state board of education before it adjourned late yesterday afternoon, and takes effect September 1. The state board has supervision of the courses of study in the public schools, grammar and high, and when it no longer prescribes German as a course of study it virtually removes it from consideration by the pupils.

From about 1916 on, the New Mexican *showed, in addition to its good-natured enlightenment in respect to such matters as the*

*Santa Fe architectural style and the developing art colony and its
unrestrained and apparently deeply relished political battling, a
sad tendency to succumb to extremes of the popular hysterias of
the time. It appears at first in regard to the situation in Mexico and
the Mexican "threats" to the United States, and in regard to
"Huns" at home and in Europe. An example of the latter follows.
More will be said about the paper's (or its editors') frame of mind
later, at the beginning of 1920.*

APRIL 18, 1918:   FEW WHOLESOME EXAMPLES.

To be quite brutally frank, what America most needs at home
right now is a considerable number of Hun tombstones.

We are daily interning Huns for offenses which if attempted by
Americans in Germany would result in the instant summons of a
firing squad. They blow up our factories and burn our wheat and
we award them a vacation with plenty of appetizing food and all
the delicacies of the season. In the past few weeks scared citizens
have brought into the New Mexican office and into the offices of
the food administration samples of flour thought to contain powdered glass, which happily turned out to be particles of sand or
mica or celluloid or other foreign substances such as inevitably
work their way into flour. Compelling victims to eat powdered
glass is one of the most fiendish tortures ever devised in the Orient.
That Americans should even be subjected to the fear of such
torture in their own country is a rather serious reflection upon
our national virility. The German is essentially a coward. It should
be quite easy for the government to so put the fear of God into
the hearts of all Germans in this country that one would not dare
even to contemplate in secrecy attempting to poison food or drink,
to use the torch or dynamite. And it would protect loyal men of
German extraction from hysterical mob violence.

APRIL 27, 1918:   VIERRA ENCOURAGES SANTA FE STYLE.

The Santa Fe style of architecture—the kind that is so much
admired by the artists and people of artistic temperament who
come here, will get a big boost in a plan which is to be carried out

237

under the direction of Carlos Vierra, artist and well known resident of this city.

In order to see a group of Santa Fe style cottages built, with no discordant architectural note struck nearby, Mr. Vierra has purchased, through H. H. Dorman, real estate dealer, property along Buena Vista Loma, opposite the Wiley property, and he has decided to sell lots only to those builders who will erect cottages in this style. He has sold the first lot to Mr. Brief of the Toltec Oil Company. This lot is 75 by 230 and on it Mr. Brief will erect a Santa Fe style cottage. Other lots probably will be sold in the near future as there are many persons desiring comfortable cottages which they can own and thus keep permanently.

The "Santa Fe style" is any one of several variants upon that same shapeless adobe construction that, in 1890, was destined to be replaced as rapidly as possible. Vierra's influence in getting it generally accepted was most important. His concept of it was rather eclectic, combining features to be found in the old church architecture, others in multistory Pueblo Indian construction, and others in more Spanish-derived, residential architecture, all in one building. The best example of his influence is the State Art Museum on Palace Avenue.

NOVEMBER 11, 1918:   ALL SANTA FE TURNS OUT WHEN WHISTLES ANNOUNCE END OF THE WORLD WAR AND JOIN IN FETE.

Santa Feans were whistled out of bed at 6 o'clock this morning to celebrate the end of the world war.

By 6:30 o'clock scores were parading in the streets and by 7 there were hundreds carrying flags, cheering and shouting in a frenzy of delight.

It was the news of the signing of the armistice which brought the belief that at last the sacrifice of human lives, the destruction of property and the starvation of nations, had come to an end.

The news of the signing of the armistice was sent from the Santa Fe New Mexican to the Water and Light company and to the City Hall, and at 6:00 a.m. two whistles announced the glad tidings. At first people who had forgotten the announcement that these whistles would tell the hour of cessation of hostilities thought there was a fire. But as the shrill whistles kept tooting, and as church bells began to ring, it was realized that at last the news of Germany's collapse had arrived.

There were wild scenes all forenoon around the plaza.

Every motor car in town was in motion, and every one of them decorated with bunting, and the occupants carrying flags—flags of the U S, of Italy, of France, of other allies. A few of the motors were draped in flags, and a particularly large and beautiful flag of Italy was seen, to recall the great work of General Diaz and his soldiers in pushing back the Austrians and breaking the last prop of the hated Huns.

Kids on bicycles sped by, carrying a small flag in one hand and endeavoring to steer their speedy machines with the other hand. These wobbling cycles added to the merriment and occasionally to the alarm.

One of the prettiest sights was a little cart drawn by a Shetland pony. The cart was draped with bunting and contained no fewer than six children, waving flags and shouting themselves hoarse.

DECEMBER 11, 1918: THE PATH ON THE RAINBOW.

Much needed and much wanted has been an anthology of songs and chants from the Indians of North America and here it is even more beautiful than any one had dreamed possible. It is a joy to behold the book with its cover of black upon which is printed a totem pole embellished with Indian symbols in gold, but it is even a greater joy to examine and drink in the contents. The compilation is by George W. Cronin and the introduction by Mary Austin, at present writing in Santa Fe. The names of the contributors are familiar in Santa Fe. Some of them like Mrs. Alice Corbin Henderson and Natalie Curtis Burlin live here; others like Mrs. Matilda Coxe Stevenson and John Peabody Harrington have worked here; still others like J. Walter Fewkes and Washington Matthews have visited here; while the rest are nearly all personally known to the workers in archaeology and anthropology of the Museum. Mary Austin too, contributes a sheaf of songs, which possess that mark of distinction which make her a fine interpreter of the Indian spirit and so great a writer.

Mary Austin could be said to have been for years the leader of the prose writers of Santa Fe, as Alice Corbin was of the poets; as we shall see later, she was also a leader of the artists as a whole. Natalie Curtis (Burlin) later published The Indians' Book, *an anthology of importance. Mrs. Stevenson we have already met, in connection with serpents and human sacrifice. Harrington and Fewkes were anthropologists of the highest standing, and Matthews was the army doctor whose publications on Navajo myths, religious poetry, and ceremonials remain ethnological and literary classics. The publication of* The Path on the Rainbow *marks, I believe, the beginning of the union between art and anthropology that has been so fruitful in Santa Fe.*

DECEMBER 13, 1918: THAT AERIAL MAIL SERVICE.

Santa Feans who credulously for four days turned their faces toward the heavens every time it was reported that the airplanes were coming did so because, in 99 per cent of the cases, they wanted to see one fly. Although there had been some unobtrusive reference to the mission of the aviators, scant attention was paid to it. Those who knew in an indefinite way that it had something to do with a more or less chimerical aerial mail service, did not gather than Santa Fe was especially interested or important in that connection.

Lieutenant Hancock, who is in command, however, states that there was a fixed purpose on the part of the government to scout out a route for mail service of which Santa Fe has all along been regarded as the inevitable western terminus. That puts a different face on the matter.

JANUARY 7, 1919: BATTLESHIP NEW MEXICO SPEEDY MONSTER SAYS THE NEW YORK SUN.

Through the courtesy of Mrs. Ina Sizer Cassidy, long a resident of Santa Fe, but now living in Harrington Park, N. J. we are enabled to republish the following story on the battleship New Mexico:

"Probably the great new dreadnought New Mexico, now lying in the Hudson off Grant's Tomb, is the most interesting vessel of all the great fleet from the point of view of naval men.

"For the New Mexico represents something entirely new in propulsion and on the success of this experiment may rest the revolutionizing of engine building for all future warships. The New Mexico, flagship of Vice Admiral Albert W. Grant, is the first big ship in the navy to be electrically driven. The quadruple screw turbines, electrically driven, which propel the great 32,000 ton war machine, were given their first speed tests. When the engineers "opened up" the 28,000 h.p. engines the big ship easily went over her required speed.

"Several times the speed went up to nearly 23 knots. This was done with the four shafts running at 175 revolutions a minute. The engineer officers figure that only 3/4s of the big ship's power had been developed on the Rockland trials."

JANUARY 25, 1919: MRS. AUSTIN FINDS US AMAZING; SPIRIT OF MODERNITY SURPRISES COMMUNITY THEATER MEMBERS, DESIRING MORE DIGNIFIED PUBLICITY, ARE TOLD THERE'S NO SUCH THING AS A DIGNIFIED INFANT.

Some members of the Community Theater, deeply interested in its success, were disturbed at the cheerful, not to say facetious manner in which the staff has set about the initial program. They hunted up the dramatic editor in her den in one of the chancel rooms of the St. Francis Auditorium to ask what she thought about it.

"Don't you think it ought to be more dignified?" they anxiously inquired. Mrs. Austin laughed.

"Who ever heard of a dignified infant?" she said. "The Community Theater is only about six weeks old, you know. As a matter of fact, nothing could be more promising than the gaiety with which it sets out. One of the dangers of all young things is taking themselves too seriously. I am delighted to see this youngster to whom I seem to be elected godmother, kick up its heels."

"You Santa Feans are a most amazing people," Mrs. Austin said, after a moment's silence. "Here where I least expected it, where all the traditions are against it, I find the utmost modernity of spirit. Outside New York, I doubt if there is a community in the United States which could have gone at this business of the theater in a manner so identical with all that the phrase, modern art movement, implies. In all my twenty-three years' of experience I have seen nothing resembling it, except the beginning of the Washington Square Players at New York."

MARCH 4, 1919: NEW MEXICO ART FEATURED IN SCRIBNER'S MAGAZINE.

"Rear Platform Impressions of the Southwest," by Lawrence Perry, the leading article in the March Scribner's Magazine, is illustrated by ten reproductions of paintings by members of the Taos Society of Artists. The paintings reproduced are:

"Twilight, Taos Pueblo," by E. Irving Couse, awarded a silver medal at the San Francisco Exposition.

"The Goat Herder," by Robert Henri, the model being a Santa Fe boy.

"Deer Track" and "War Cloud," by Julius Rolshoven.

"A Mood of the Mountains," by O. E. Berninghaus.

"The Start for the Hills," by Ernest L. Blumenschein.

"View from the Studio of the Copper Bell," by J. H. Sharp.

"In the Land of Mañana," by Walter Ufer.

"Looking Backward," by Bert G. Phillips.

MARCH 22, 1919: BAUMANN HANGS NEXT EXHIBIT.

Tuesday a new exhibit by Gustave Baumann will be hung in the Tewa gallery. It will include the first production of color prints from his press in his studio on Canon road and will deal with New Mexico subjects, including the Rito de los Frijoles and Taos. It is quite an item for Santa Fe to be the center where these beautiful wood block prints in color are produced by an artist in such high standing. The Rito de los Frijoles pictures especially are impressive and brilliant and include a free reproduction of the fresco of "The Deer Hunt" discovered in one of the caves by the Springer expedition.

MAY 2, 1919:   ALL BRANCHES OF LEARNING IN STATE MUST BE
TAUGHT IN ENGLISH, STATE BOARD POINTS OUT.

Reports have reached the capital that in some parts of New Mexico, there were public schools where all the courses were taught in some other language than English. But such schools have no reason to exist in the opinion of the state board of education, which passed a drastic resolution dealing with the matter at its meeting held here recently. The text of the resolution was given out for publication:

"The law of our State is mandatory, in its provisions to the effect that all branches of learning taught in our schools be so taught in the English language, and in this regard it properly interprets the spirit and purpose of our institutions. This does not exclude the teaching of foreign languages, which indeed is quite commendable, but it certainly is opposed to the establishment and maintenance of primary schools where all branches of study are taught in a foreign language, and where the language of our country, which is the English language, is only incidentally taught."

MAY 30, 1919:
VILLA THREATENS REPRISALS ON UNITED STATES
BANDIT CHIEFTAIN TO KILL GRINGOS IF SOLDIERS PASS.

———

Will Not Be Responsible, Says Pancho, for Lives and Property of Americans in Chihuahua if Carranza Is Given Permit to Transfer Troops from Sonora to Juarez Across U S Soil; Murderer of Columbus Naively Declares that He Will Be Unable to Control His Men.

———

Defies Government Which Sent Two Million Soldiers to Fight in France; Charges Mr. Wilson with Bad Faith.

JUNE 4, 1919: A REAL MENACE.

It is hard for the ordinary citizen to take much stock in the theory that organized anarchy exists in the United States in sufficient measure to demand a nation wide government campaign of extermination. It is time however for the American people to realize that the forces of destruction are sufficiently strong and well organized to merit serious, organized, systematic and stern attention from the nation.

Quickly following the carrying out of a plan aimed at the assassination of prominent men by bombs sent through the mails, comes a series of explosions of infernal machines also intended for leading representatives of law and order and government. That none of the intended victims was slain is not because the plot was not well laid. The thing to think about is that it is possible for such conspiracies to reach their culmination and for one such demonstration to follow immediately on the heels of another.

What we need is a few hangings, very public hangings. . . .

At midnight, June 30–July 1, the wartime prohibition law went into effect, to be succeeded on January 1 by the Volstead Act, based upon the Eighteenth Amendment to the Constitution. The New Mexican was enthusiastically dry.

JULY 9, 1919: CONGRATULATIONS.

Las Vegas is again entitled to congratulations on the success of her annual cowboys' reunion. Despite wretched roads and a superfluity of precipitation, Las Vegas got by this year in good shape, with a large attendance and a splendid program of western sports.

Since the old days of the territorial fair at Albuquerque, which used to bring the most famous ropers and riders from all over the west, the responsibility of keeping alive frontier sports and exhibitions in New Mexico has fallen upon the shoulders of Las Vegas and she has made good. The prizes and glory available to the festive cowpunch at "li'l ol' Vegas" furnish an effective incentive to the boys of the tall grass to do their best and to perpetuate the things which we hate to see pass with the coming of more fences and Fords. Las Vegas is helping keep alive the traditions and atmosphere of the good old western days and those responsible for the success of the reunions are entitled to considerable credit. . . .

Long life to the cowboys' reunion. Meanwhile Albuquerque has her state fair and it is up to Santa Fe to put her own unique celebration, the Santa Fe Fiesta, on a par with these other annual events.

In connection with the reference to Santa Fe's Fiesta just above, we may as well note here that in 1919 it was in full process of being firmly re-established—or simply established. The affair, however, had little relation to a Latin-American fiesta, being run by a group of historically minded Anglo-Americans, and the carefully staged pageants and performances being walled in, accessible only to those who could afford to pay the admission.

JULY 30, 1919:   BEAUTIFUL MODERN HOMES BEING BUILT IN SANTA FE; VIERRA DWELLING FINE SAMPLE OF PICTURESQUE STYLE.

Despite the high cost of building material, plumbing and fixtures, of furniture and carpets, of almost everything that goes into, onto or under a house, there is a building boom in Santa Fe. The after-war prices have not been sufficient to stop it; there is the feeling that while building is expensive it will be years before the prices tumble.

The southern part of the city is the scene of this building activity. Don Gaspar and Santa Fe avenues and College street are showing several new houses.

One of the largest and in many ways most artistic houses is that which Carlos Vierra, the artist, is building south of Don Gaspar avenue, with a superb view of the Sandia mountains. In fact, all of the surrounding mountains can be seen from the Vierra house. . . . It is two stories high, in the Santa Fe style of which Mr. Vierra is an apostle, and is of adobe with various layers of brick. It promises to be "the last word" on original Santa Fe style houses. . . .

This is to be one of the most attractive and, perhaps expensive of the many fine houses. It may cost $8,000 to $10,000.

AUGUST 4, 1919:   SPEAKING OF ART.

One of the good brothers[1] has put up a sign in front of San Miguel church that he who runs may read. In fact, he who shoots by in an auto at 60 miles per may read. The sign is clearly legible from the top of the Jemez mountains.

We admire his enterprise. The Oldest Church has long needed some designating mark. The sign, however—and under the circumstances we hate to say it—is a deplorable disfigurement to one of the sights of America. It ruins the picturesque old corner and fits into the scheme of things artistic in beautiful and artistic Santa Fe about like a jazz band in the Choir Invisible.

Brother, we implore you take it down and put up one that fits the subject and doesn't deface one of America's greatest treasures. We ask Colonel Twitchell, the Art Colony and the Ancient and Honorable Society of Santa Fe Style Boosters to intercede and have this sign changed. The city or the Chamber of Commerce should reimburse the well-intentioned brother for the expense of the change, if necessary. . . .

While on the subject—

Let's have no Billboard Nuisance in the city of St. Francis, St. Michael, De Vargas, Onate, Kit Carson and General Kearny. The tourist en route to the City of the Holy Faith, filled with anticipations of the glamor of romance and the glory of tradition, picturing the ancient crosses of the Franciscans and the monuments of the mail clad conquistadores, approaches the city and his eye is greeted by a succession of lurid hoardings, blocking the vista of the mountains and mesas, advertising HOODLUM TIRES, CHOKEM'S GASOLINE EMPORIUM, SAM SWIGGIN'S SWELL SWEATERS, and so forth and so on ad nauseam. If the traveler must know where the garages and the stores are, the drug palaces and the booteries, let's put up a presentable directory of commercial establishments at the gateway to the city which doesn't shriek its desecration of the landscape to High Heaven and do away with the eyesores which make the Santa Fe Trail in the environs of Santa Fe look like the railroad entrance to Junktown, O., or the goat district of Millville, N. J. . . .

[1] San Miguel Church is under the care of the order of Christian Brothers.

DECEMBER 3, 1919:

FALL DEMANDS U. S. BREAK RELATIONS WITH CARRANZA.
New Mexico Senator Charges Mexican Embassy and Consulates
in New York and San Francisco Have Been Peddling Bolshevik
Propaganda and Resolution Asks President to Sever Relations.

DECEMBER 14, 1919: NEW MEXICO CAPITAL TO HAVE ONE OF FIN-
EST HOTELS IN WEST. SANTA FE'S LOYAL CITIZENS RAISE THE $200,000
PROMPTLY.

"Gentlemen, the child is born!"

In these picturesque words Levi A. Hughes, president of the
First National Bank of Santa Fe, Saturday night at the Business
Men's Association dinner at the Woman's Board of Trade Library, announced the completion of the subscription to $200,000
worth of bonds to finance the building in Santa Fe of one of the
most modern and beautiful hotels in the Southwest.

The achievement is one never before equaled in New Mexico.
In two weeks' time a community of not over 8000 souls all told
raised nearly a quarter of a million dollars to boost the Old
Home Town.

They had able assistance from outsiders; but they went after
this assistance and got it. The result is the biggest thing Santa Fe
or any other town its size has ever done and assures the steady
growth and prosperity of the city.

*This was the inception of La Fonda, still the best hotel in Santa
Fe. The enterprise in time proved too much for local management and financing and was taken over by the Fred Harvey system.*

DECEMBER 27, 1919: SANTO DOMINGO PUEBLO INDIANS DISARM
POLICE. Bloody Battle Narrowly Averted When 17 Mounted
Policemen, Seeking Hides of Alleged Rustled Cattle, Surrender
to 200 Infuriated Braves Disturbed at Fiesta; Officers Allowed to
Depart with Weapons; Indian Service Officials Deny Right of
State Authorities to Invade Reservation.

A pitched battle between 200 Santo Domingo braves and a

mounted police posse of seventeen men that probably would have resulted in the massacre of the small posse was narrowly averted at the pueblo in western Sandoval county on Christmas day.

The first word of the clash reached here today when Mounted Policeman Alfred Montoya, of Peña Blanca, leader of the posse; R. H. Hanna, of Albuquerque, attorney for the Pueblo Indians; and Leo Crane, of Albuquerque, superintendent of the Pueblo agency, came here for a conference with Attorney General O. O. Askren.

SHOT BY MONTOYA PRECIPITATES ATTACK.

The posse had gone to the pueblo for the purpose of making a search for hides. It was said that four head of cattle had been butchered not far from the village the day before Christmas and it was suspected that Indians had done the slaughtering. The Santo Domingos were holding a fiesta when the possemen arrived and surrounded the pueblo in a thin line. There were only 17 of the police.

The Indians continued their dancing, ignoring the fact that they had been surrounded, until one of their number, according to possemen, attempted to break through the line, carrying a bundle of hides under his arm. The possemen had been instructed to prevent any one escaping with hides and one of them fired a shot. Montoya said he fired in the air. The Indian dropped the hides. They were old. The shot precipitated trouble for the posse.

The braves stopped in the middle of their dancing, as if the shot was a signal, rushed into their houses, got their weapons and charged the circling line. The Indians came at the possemen waving long rifles, hatchets, knives and even bows and arrows. The situation was critical and only the coolness shown by Montoya, the posse leader, and the control held by the Indian governor over his braves prevented bloodshed and probably the annihilation of the outnumbered posse.

The possemen retreated, according to the Indians, and concentrated on a hill a short distance from the pueblo. The braves then surrounded them and called upon them to give up their rifles and

248

revolvers. Resistance was useless. It could not have gained anything but the massacre of the posse and they complied with the Indians' demand. No shots were fired and no one was wounded, but a hasty act on either side probably would have started a battle to the death.

After the posse had been disarmed the Indians were willing to make peace by negotiation. They offered to deliver the seized arms to Montoya if he would take his posse away and not molest them. Their terms were accepted. The Indians returned the guns and the posse went away.

The discovery of the entrails of four slaughtered head of cattle near the pueblo the day before led to the encounter. Montoya suspected the Indians were responsible. He suspected they had killed the cattle for their fiesta and he got a search warrant from the nearest justice of the peace. He then went to the pueblo, armed with the search warrant, but he was refused admittance so he went away and returned the next day at the head of the posse.

Judge R. H. Hanna, attorney for the Pueblos, questioned the legality of Montoya's warrant. He had not seen it but the mounted policeman informed him that it was a blanket warrant giving him authority to search any house in the village and it was for that reason that Hanna doubted its propriety.

Montoya didn't give up his attempts to find fresh hides in the pueblo. He went back Friday, but found Mr. Crane, the pueblo superintendent there. The head men of the village had sent for him. Mr. Crane met the mounted policeman outside the village and after a conference it was decided to lay the case before Attorney General Askren, asking him to give an opinion as to the state officials' rights to invade the pueblo.

Indian service officials were said to be opposed to any clash with the state's officers and to desire merely to insure their charges of protection in their legal rights. The right of state's officers to make arrests on Indian reservations is doubted by them. They believe that Deputy United States marshals should be called upon for that and that is one of the points that Attorney General Askren is expected to cover in his opinion.

The Santo Domingo Indians were entirely within their rights in repelling this invasion of county officials, who, unless deputized as federal police and equipped with federal warrants, were simply armed trespassers upon what lawyers call "Indian country," in this case the Santo Domingo Grant. The Indians, fortunately, showed great restraint and the posse great discretion; had shooting started and anyone been hit, the consequences would have been serious.

With certain exceptions since the passage of Public Law 280 in 1953, "Indian country," that is, land within the exterior boundaries of an Indian reservation or grant, or land allotted in trust to an Indian by the United States, is exempt from state and local jurisdiction so far as the Indians on it are concerned. Law enforcement is divided between the tribe for most matters and the federal courts and police agencies for certain major offenses.

This is a portion of the home rule which tribes retain as a fragment of their lost sovereignty. The Indians regard it as a vitally important protection against the prejudice and mistreatment they commonly encounter in dealings with local police and local courts. Tribal-federal jurisdiction is constantly under attack by local forces; less so in New Mexico, perhaps, than in most Western states. The entry of a Sandoval County posse into Santo Domingo is an unusually flagrant instance of such attacks. The firmness and control shown by the Indians was and still is characteristic of this particular tribe.

DECEMBER 28, 1919:   OVERALLS OR BLANKETS.

George Vaux, Jr., of the U S Board of Indian Commissioners, believes the artist colony at Taos has a deleterious and undesirable effect upon the Pueblo Indian in that it encourages him to retain his immemorial manner of dress and spoils him by offering him easy money to pose for paintings when he might be better employed at the handles of a plow, tickling the fertile earth on his reservation in order that it may produce corn, wheat, chili, pumpkins, cantaloupes, enchiladas and other forms of fruit. We rather gather that Mr. Vaux simply has no flair for the arts at all so far as the Indian is concerned; and that the painters are merely clogging the wheels of progress by making the Indian lazy and shiftless.

It is a little difficult to see why the Pueblo Indian may not till his fields to a reasonable extent and employ his leisure hours in posing for the insistent artist. The two vocations seem quite compatible, if properly adjusted. Certainly any Indian, no matter how industrious agriculturally, has plenty of leisure time. Approaching the matter from another angle, if the Pueblo at Taos can make more money posing for the ubiquitous painter, is he not making commercial progress—developing into a more successful business man—becoming more prosperous, even if he hires some one to plant the unpicturesque potatoes? . . .

Why any human being brought up differently should be made to wear American pants is a mystery. How considerations of morality or enlightenment or the uplift in general are subserved by empanting the American Indian is beyond us. Let the Pueblo wear his white drawers and his moccasins and his blanket until the last dance is danced and the last governor is gathered to his fathers. He is picturesque, even beautiful, in his native and historic garb; why make him commonplace and ordinary and submerge his individuality in pants? We have many lofty things in our civilization; but the pant is not one of them.

Earlier, I mentioned a certain hysteria that developed in the paper, beginning in 1916. By 1920 the New Mexican *seemed almost schizophrenic. The liberal, humorous, mature point of view typified by the editorial just above on "empanting the Indians" consorted ill with phobias concerning the "Huns," the "Reds," the Mexicans, and the difficulty of getting servants to work for a dollar a day. The general political and social outlook of the paper at this time casts a curious light on its owner's later liberalism.*

Many of these phobias and hysterias were current throughout the country. "Reds"—the term embracing everything from Anarchists to moderate Socialists, and making no distinction whatsoever between them—were believed by many to be about to overthrow the government. The excitement, and the lawless actions of officials against the "Reds," quite eclipse what we ex-

perienced during the heyday of McCarthyism, although it was over much sooner.

It was at this time, too, that one heard in all parts of the country indignant talk about how working men were buying silk shirts and automobiles, and many were horrified at labor's demands for an eight-hour day.

A good many people, mostly in Texas and the Southwest, wanted us to invade Mexico. Senator Albert B. Fall of New Mexico installed himself at El Paso, where he opened a farce of hearings into Mexican offenses against Americans. Mexican officials, naturally, refused his summonses to come and testify, and his hearings provided a sounding board for the wildest allegations of interventionists, quite secure against refutation. This testimony provided excellent material for headlines, which the New Mexican gladly gave him.

We were also going through a phase in which all military personnel who had not served overseas were damned as slackers, and the issuance of decorations to any of them aroused strong protests. To this, too, the New Mexican lent itself.

It was a curious, brief period. Prohibition had just gone into effect; the first bootlegging and first arrests were occurring. The women's suffrage amendment was in the course of adoption. We were having a depression. It was a campaign year, with a dying man in the White House. "Flaming Youth," F. Scott Fitzgerald, and the "Lost Generation" were bursting upon their astonished elders; in 1920, in Providence, Rhode Island, I believe, debutantes first started checking their corsets before the start of a dance.

One who reads several months' issues of the 1920 paper at a sitting is left with an unpleasant impression, for all the urbanity and agreeableness of most of the local news. The paper was ugly. Its front page was a hodgepodge of headlines in several different styles, over too many articles, long and short. Halftone cuts were poor; in fact, the actual printing and inking was usually poor. There was nothing left of the handsome appearance of the 1849 publication, or of the days of Manderfield and Tucker.

For some months in 1919 and 1920, the paper ran a Sunday

rotogravure section, devoted largely to booster picture-surveys, one by one, of the towns of New Mexico. Most of these towns were small, fairly new, none too prosperous, dusty, and sun scorched. Their frame houses, brick blocks, and turn-of-the-century public buildings look drab indeed to a mid-century viewer. In January, and continuing until the section was abandoned in the middle of the year, it was alleviated by half a page of photographs of works of local artists, beginning with a number of portraits by Randall Davey in the January 18 number.

Elaborate patent medicine advertisements, especially for a thing called Tanlac, were run in exactly the form of news stories, sometimes occupying well over a column. A very small "adv." might be run at the end but was often omitted.

A symptom of a quite different nature was the appearance of a regular weekly summary of developments in the oil business within the state.

To give an idea of the phobic-reactionary side of the paper and have done with it, we run here a selection of headlines and editorials before returning to more local materials in chronological order. The first group relates to Victor Berger, Socialist, pacifist, and alleged pro-German. He was elected to Congress from Wisconsin, but the House of Representatives refused to seat him. In a second election, to fill the vacancy thus created, he ran again and again was elected.

JANUARY 8, 1920: ENCOURAGING.

Victor Berger was driven out of Jersey City when he attempted to hold forth on his disloyal doctrines there.

Five socialist members of the New York assembly by an almost unanimous vote were refused seats pending an investigation of their disability. The socialists, when they showed a disposition to make a noise, were escorted out courteously by the sergeant-at-arms.

That is the way to handle them.

Santa Fe

JANUARY 11, 1920:

BERGER

TILL HELL

FREEZES.

———

DISLOYAL WISCONSIN YET

FLAUNTS TREASON

BEFORE NATION.

———

BOUND TO HAVE

FRIEND OF HUN.

JANUARY 12, 1920:

[*Extract from an editorial on Berger's re-election:*] That Wisconsin is reeking with treason has become a fact known to every part of the nation.

JANUARY 6, 1920:   MASS SHOOTING.

On their own showing, the Lenine-Trotzky soviets, not content with making Russia run red with blood, aspire to extend their benevolent system to the entire world, which is to be made an "international soviet republic." Their program contemplates the spread of civil war to all corners of the globe; and "mass shooting" is urged as one of the favorite and most efficient means of propagating the Bolshevist gospel.

In short, so far as we can make out, the idea of the Bolshevist is to turn the world into a shambles and keep up the "mass shooting" until all the population of the world is exterminated save the mass shooters who can do the greatest execution. It is a bloody, violent, murderous cult which has declared war on the civilized world; and the challenge should be accepted promptly, especially in the United States. The present movement to ship all the mass shooters back to Russia, to mass shoot and get mass shot there, is an excellent one; but it might be improved upon by the passage of a law providing for the mass shooting of all mass murderers

254

here at home. These "Reds" are guilty of assault with intent to kill the government of the United States; by the profession of the leaders of their own cult they are all potential murderers; they are rattlesnakes coiled under the shelter of the American flag waiting only the opportunity to strike; and when caught they should have but the barest protection by the laws and the government to whose destruction they are committed.

JANUARY 2, 1920:

200 RADICALS IN
JAIL IN CHICAGO;
CLEAN-UP OF REDS
IS MADE THOROUGH.

———

SPECIAL GRAND JURY TO
INVESTIGATE ENTIRE
"RED" SITUATION.

JANUARY 3, 1920:   [*Banner headline.*]

ARMY OF 6000 "REDS" ROUNDED UP IN NATION-WIDE RAID
UNCLE SAM HITS
U. S. BOLSHEVIKI
A KNOCKOUT BLOW.
GIANT DRAGNET PULLED IN ALL OVER COUNTRY AT NINE
O'CLOCK LAST NIGHT FILLED WITH SCUM AND RIFF-
RAFF OF EUROPE CHARGED WITH PLOTTING TO OVER-
THROW AMERICA'S GOVERNMENT BY FORCE AND
VIOLENCE; ANOTHER SOVIET ARK TO BE CRAMMED
TO GUNWALES WITH "UNDESIRABLES" WHO WILL
FOLLOW GOLDMAN AND BERKMAN TO RED RUSSIA.

In late 1919 the United States put 249 "undesirable aliens" on a military transport and shipped them to Helsinki in Finland, whence they were taken under guard by Finnish and American troops to the Russian border. The last stage of this pilgrimage drew the following headlines:

255

Santa Fe

JANUARY 18, 1920:

REDS ON
TRAIN TO
RUSSIA.

———

ANARCHISTS ON WAY TO
FRONTIER AT LAST;
WELL GUARDED.

———

UNWASHED KEPT
BETWEEN DECKS.

FEBRUARY 6, 1920:

BIG ARMY
OF RED
DEVILS.

———

HALF MILLION ORGANIZED
IN NEW YORK ALONE
FOR VIOLENCE.

———

VIEWS DIFFER
ON NEEDED LAW.

*The following headlines relating to affairs in Mexico were
hardly less startling.*

JANUARY 7, 1920:

AMERICANS
BEING SHOT
DAILY IN
MEXICO.

———

U. S. CITIZEN SLAIN BY
CARRANZA SOLDIER
AT TUXPAM.

256

NOTE DEPARTMENT
IS BEING KEPT BUSY.

———

USUAL FORM OBSERVED
IN CASE OF DEATH OF
RONEY, BOWLES.

The text of this story claims that a total of twenty Americans were killed in the Tampico area between April 17, 1917, and the date the story was filed.

FEBRUARY 3, 1920:

BRUTAL MURDER OF
AMERICANS DESCRIBED
TO FALL COMMITTEE;
PROPERTY DESTROYED.

———

ONE GRINGO SHOT IN THE
PRESENCE OF DAUGHTERS,
VEATERS SAYS.

———

HELP MEXICANS,
SAYS MARK SMITH
VILLA JUSTICE PREFERABLE
TO THAT OF CARRANZA
ENGINEER'S VIEW.

JANUARY 22, 1920:   [*Banner headline.*]
PRESIDENT CARRANZA BACK OF PLAN TO SEIZE NEW MEXICO.
MEXICO EXECUTIVE
IN PLOT TO INVADE
SIX STATES OF U. S.

———

TREACHEROUS VENUSTIANO, IN POWER BY VIRTUE OF
AMERICAN RECOGNITION, SHOWED GRATITUDE BY
AIDING PLAN OF SAN DIEGO AND SAN YGNACIO RAID

IN WHICH AMERICAN SOLDIERS WERE SLAIN; DELIB-
ERATE ARMED ATTACK ON BENEFACTORS EXPOSED IN
EVIDENCE BEFORE FALL COMMITTEE.

COOPERATED WITH ZIMMERMAN[2] AND
HUNS TO STAB THE UNITED STATES
IN BACK, DECLARES VALLS OF TEXAS.

JANUARY 23, 1920:

EARS OF
GRINGOS
CUT OFF.

EXAMPLE OF FRIENDSHIP OF
CARRANZA TOWARD THE
UNITED STATES.

RAIDS DIRECTED
BY PRESIDENT.

HUNS IMMUNE WHEN
AMERICANS ARE SHOT
BY FEDERALS.

*Mexico in the period between the fall of Diaz and the acces-
sion to the presidency of Obregón was a rough place. Even after
the administrations of Obregón and Calles, it was not entirely
calm. During the years of World War I, bloody war flamed all
over the Republic, and American bystanders, their country not
being much loved in Mexico, often got hurt. There is no need to
whitewash the Mexicans, but we should recognize also that not
all the Americans were innocent bystanders—far from it. In any
case, Fall's committee daily slaughtered, and the* New Mexican
*daily mourned, a number of Americans somewhat in excess of
the total that had visited Mexico during the period under investigation.*

2 German ambassador to Mexico.

258

The paper's last major phobia, in which also it went along with a considerable segment of national opinion, was in regard to servants. A news story and an editorial suffice to cover the subject.

JANUARY 4, 1920:   SEVEN-DOLLAR HIRED GIRL TO RETURN.

Chicago, Jan. 3.—The day of the $7 a week servant girl who would cook, sweep, mind the baby, wash dishes, run the laundry and do odd jobs of calcimining in her spare time, is coming again, according to Miss Elizabeth Moynihan, of the travellers' aid society.

Every boat from Europe is bringing hundreds of Scandinavian, Irish and English and Italian girls eager to do housework, Miss Moynihan says. The travellers' aid society is assisting scores en route from New York.

"I expect that in three or four months," one employment agent said, "we will have almost the old conditions back—girls willing to work for $7 or $8 a week, instead of 'highty tighty' dusters willing to aid in housework for $15 a week."

Admittedly, this was a wire story from Chicago, not a local expression. It was run on the front page, however, and should be read in the light of the next item, an editorial.

JANUARY 18, 1920:   NOWADAYS.

Sophie Hodowsky, a waitress, was fined $2 by a New York magistrate after pleading guilty to violating traffic rules with her $4,500 automobile. She got a salary of $12 a week, she said, and averaged $80 a week in tips, making a remuneration of nearly $5,000 a year.

And then some people say there isn't any servant problem.

Who would teach the young idea earnestly how to shoot, trudging to and fro on foot to the house of learning, or who would be a college professor with a flivver, or who, forsooth, would seek to be a respectable worker with the high forehead when one can be a low brow and shoot biscuits for $5,000 a year, or a janitor with gold hardware in his private flat, or a profligate bricklayer with a sea-going yacht, or a laundry-wagon driver with a Long Island estate and three butlers in the front hall? And where shall the modest $2,500 a year clerk and his wife appear, hiring a $5,000 a year domestic, and whose social aspirations culminate in the ambition to have the iceman condescend to speak to them as he passes by?

Lord, send those Scandinavian girls we heard about—send fourteen million of them, ready to work for sax dollar a mont, and bust the servant girl market wide open.

If the country goes on like this there will be a violent eruption and somebody will get hurt.

FEBRUARY 18, 1920:   THE HEALTH LEVY.

Sixty people all sick with the flu in Rociada, a San Miguel county hamlet, and dying off without doctors or nurses.

One little incident which would seem to make it unnecessary for advocates of public health to work very hard to get the special health levy through at the extra session. With an efficient health organization in every county, made possible by money to pay for it, such things couldn't happen.

With a state health department to supervise, we've only made a start. It has to have somebody to supervise and do the work.

MARCH 28, 1920:   30 INDIAN DRAWINGS ARE ON DISPLAY; NEW ART INDIGENOUS TO THE SOIL; APPRECIATED BY THE KEENEST CRITICS.

Thirty Indian drawings by various Indian artists hang in the Museum in the Indian alcove. Our citizens in Santa Fe may not realize it, but they have here in the southwest, in these Indian paintings, an art indigenous to the soil. A true art. As fine an art in many ways and as sincere as the primitive art of the early European civilization. It would be a pity to educate the Indian (civilize they call it) to the detriment of his truer self. How few of our painters can express as sincerely and with as close a technique the things of every day life as have these Indians with their dances and occupations. They paint their ceremonies with the deep feeling that is a part of their religion, and which it is. It is a reverence that lasts through every day of the week.

The development of Indian painting, which now, in the 1950's, has spread to Indians all over the United States, began with an attempt by Kenneth M. Chapman and other anthropologists to salvage some record of the San Ildefonso Pueblo ceremonial before the entire tribe died out, as it then seemed likely to do (since 1930, its population has slowly increased and its ceremonials are still going strong). The figures, done in crayon or water color by a few young Indians, were so handsome that they immediately caught the attention of the artists. Encouraged by both artists and scientists, the painters went on to start an entirely new movement, the first formal recognition of which is noted above.

APRIL 8, 1920: SEWER DIGGERS DISCOVER PREHISTORIC REFUSE HEAP; PROOF INDIAN PUEBLO PRECEDED ANCIENT SANTA FE.

That the areas close to the public plaza in Santa Fe were the site of an ancient Indian pueblo has been established beyond any doubt. While digging the trench for the new sanitary sewer on Johnson street, two blocks from the New Museum building, the workmen at a depth of approximately four feet encountered a pueblo refuse heap extending for a distance of more than 300 feet, its western end being about 150 feet from the Denver and Rio Grande railway tracks at the foot of Johnson street, and the eastern end being opposite the property of William E. Griffin.

APRIL 22, 1920: CREEDS OF HATE.

We are not in the habit of printing or commenting on anonymous letters; but the one from "A Switchman's Wife," printed in another column, seems to merit being an exception to the rule, as the sincerity of the writer is evident. The switchman's wife, who is trying to stretch a dollar into two or three dollars, is going through the same struggle as every one else; but the rest of us do not have the opportunity nor power to go on strike, to stop the operation of trains, to make thousands of other poor people go hungry and cold, to take a union club and crack our fellow citizens over the head with it to enforce our demands and give force to our complaints; and in so doing again add to the increasing cost of their living.

In a part of the letter, which is not printed, as it does not seem germane to the subject, churches are attacked for the diversity of their alleged narrow beliefs and their "creeds of hate." A "creed of hate" is what our correspondent is preaching vehemently in her letter. She classes men engaged in a certain form of labor—always the men in the unionized trades, as "laboring men"—all others are malefactors engaged in crushing the "laboring man." As a matter of fact this town, for instance, is full of laboring men, most of whom have no connection with unions. They are working on the streets, on their farms, in their shops, in stores and offices and counting rooms and as a rule they do not make wages comparable to those paid to railroad men. When the cost of living rises they have to pay it; they have no means of making their neighbors pay it for them.

This is the creed of hate which has been demonstrated almost every week since the war ended—"we'll get an increase or starve the country. While we're getting it we'll paralyze business and production and industry so that every one else, in addition to helping pay our increase, will have to pay more for his bread and potatoes." They even threatened to lose the war for America when the crisis was greatest—and the threat worked.

This is no time to talk of the downtrodden "laboring man," especially the railroad man. He has used his club regularly since the war and has almost invariably got what he asked. What happened to the rest of us was none of his concern.

MAY 4, 1920:   NEW MEXICO VERSE.

"Poetry" for May is particularly rich in contribution by members of the New Mexico literary crowd. The leading place is given to Marsden Hartley's "Sunlight Persuasions." He opens with "The Festival of the Corn," which some readers may call "grotesque," but which those who have felt the indescribable swing of the chorus and the fervor of the dance at Santo Domingo on August 4, will acclaim a wonderfully realistic and impressionistic word picture. The very rhythm, accentuated by the marvelously skilful choice of words—each crisp phrase bringing up a picture, a phase, of the kaleidoscopic scene of the great Indian summer ceremony—make the poem a powerfully dramatic piece of work. It sets the stage with a few terse descriptive sentences:

> The black horse and the ochre horse
> Were prancing on the front wall
> Of the little mission,
>> The dark red boy sat upon the roof,
> Waiting for the first gunshot
>> To strike the hammer on the bell.

MAY 15, 1920: GOAT HERDER IN CHAVES MOUNTAINS HAS NEW DISEASE.

The Malta fever has appeared in New Mexico—officially. The state health department has suspected for some time that there were isolated cases in the state, but until today it has never received an official report of a case.

The first victim reported to the department is a goat herder in the mountains of Chaves County.

The disease is carried by goats, according to Dr. George S. Luckett, chief of the division of preventable diseases, and naturally goat herders are the usual victims. The disease is said to be common on the Mediterranean coasts, particularly on the African coast, but comparatively rare in New Mexico.

The fever is sometimes fatal, but the percentage of mortality is not high. An effective curative serum has been found, but it is doubtful if there is any in the state. If there is, none of the health department officials know of it.

MAY 17, 1920: LAND DISPUTES ON INDIAN RESERVATIONS IN STATE
HEARD BY SUBCOMMITTEE OF HOUSE AT TESUQUE; 2,000 CASES FORM
A PROBLEM FOR INDIAN BUREAU. Five Pueblos Represented at Conference Yesterday; Solons Say Carter Bill Makes Little Difference in Indian Status; Gets Vote If He Wants It.

Non-Indian possession of the Indian reservation lands, transferred by Pueblos who the government holds have no individual title and can not legally transfer the lands, has given rise to a serious situation which engaged much of the time of the house sub-committee on Indian affairs on its visit to Santa Fe and environs yesterday.

The committee spent the morning at Tesuque Pueblo interviewing Indians from that Pueblo, San Ildefonso, Taos, Santa Clara and San Juan and also the non-Indians interested in the controversy. The problem is not easy of solution. It is said there are some 2,000 disputes, in some cases non-Indians having had peaceable possession for as long as 200 years.

It is said this alienation of lands by [*sic*] the Indians has been in progress for the past ten years. An instance is that of the Bond & Nohl Company of Espanola, an Espanola delegation having appeared before the committee. Bond and Nohl acquired land in 1880 from a native, to whom or whose predecessors in ownership the Indians had transferred it. Possession has never been disputed and the title to the land was supposed to be indisputable. Now, wherever non-Indians have secured a footing, their tenure is being questioned. A. B. Renehan acted as legal representative to the Espanola defendants, largely Spanish Americans. Suit was recently instituted to quiet title to these lands.

The story above introduces a controversy of which we shall hear more, and out of which in the end came unexpected results. The Pueblo tribes held the greater portion of their lands, including all the land surrounding their actual pueblos or villages, by grant from the King of Spain. Under the Treaty of Guadalupe-Hidalgo with Mexico, the United States was pledged to respect and protect these grants.

In many cases, as time passed and the Pueblo population, now an expanding one, decreased, many tribes found that they had more land than they needed. Relations with their Spanish-American neighbors and fellow Catholics were friendly on the whole. In some cases they simply made no objection when an acquaintance moved onto an unused part of their land; in other cases they sold it, unaware that they had no right to do so. There were also instances in which powerful individuals, Spanish or Anglo-American, moved in and made themselves so tough that the Indians could not drive them out. All of these occurrences involved failures in duty on the part of the United States, the Indians' trustee.

With the land go the rights to the water for irrigation. That is, if a certain amount of water is usually delivered to a certain field, whoever owns that field has the right to that water. As the Pueblos lost land, they lost water with it. The combination was serious and by 1920 was working severe hardships on a number of tribes.

OCTOBER 7, 1920: [*Seven-column banner headline.*] SANTA FE DEMANDS ACTION OF THE MAYOR AND THE CITY COUNCIL ON TYPHOID.

Eight new cases of typhoid fever were reported in the southeast section of Santa Fe in the past 24 hours. Two deaths have occurred. Physicians say unless remedial measures are taken the disease will show a recurring outburst every two weeks. In the face of a deadly epidemic the Santa Fe city government has sat idle for weeks; it has failed, neglected and refused to take any preventive measures whatsoever. It shows apparent utter indifference to a grave public crisis.

The time has arrived for the people of Santa Fe to let the mayor and council know that they have got to move. The New Mexican, speaking the public sentiment of the community demands that Mayor T. Z. Winter get a quorum of the council together NOW and take action to stay the spread of this disease. Never mind the politics. This is a question of public safety and human lives.

If it costs somebody votes to protect the poor people of this city, the votes will have to go. The community doesn't want any more pitiful excuses. It wants ACTION—and it wants it NOW.

DECEMBER 28, 1920: TWO VIEW-POINTS.

There appear to be two viewpoints regarding the Villistas pardoned by Governor Larrazolo. One is that they are murdering bandits and should be hanged or imprisoned for life because they took part in the Columbus raid, whether or not they committed murder during that raid; that the ordinary processes of justice do not apply and that in their case even the supreme court of the state need not observe that impartial attitude which is supposed to characterize such a tribunal in ordinary matters. We cite the court's action in passing upon a question of law in their case, in going outside the record to denounce Villa as a "notorious bandit" and the Villistas as "Bandits." The difference is easily seen when one tries to imagine, for instance, the action of the court in the case, let us say, of John Jones, who alleges he was arrested in an illegal manner. If it should rule that Jones was not properly served and add that he was a well-known wife-beater the bar would experience mild surprise, of course.

The governor shows symptoms, in his statement published today, of surprise of this kind. He likewise proceeds with voluminous detail to prove what everyone knows, that Pancho Villa was head of an organized revolutionary army under a provisional government and thus as much an "organized military force" as ever devastated hapless Mexico. Personally we regard Villa as a "notorious bandit."

JANUARY 15, 1921: NOW GO AHEAD.

The Deming "Graphic" is somewhat persistently and excitedly seeking to misrepresent the attitude of this paper in the matter of the sixteen Villistas pardoned by Governor Larrazolo and to reflect upon the New Mexican's Americanism in this connection. Incidentally the Deming paper makes it clear that it advocates a fair and impartial hanging of the Mexicans without any unnecessary delay, and points with pride to Deming's charitable action in not lynching them.

We are not particularly interested in the Graphic's attempted preachments on patriotism but to keep the record clear on this matter, we reiterate emphatically that it was improper and undesirable to saddle the board and keep of these ignorant human animals, "tools of a murderous 'master mind'," at a rate of $6,000 a year upon the taxpayers of New Mexico for the rest of their natural lives while the archcriminal is subsidized, lionized as a hero and permitted to exist in immunity and luxury; that their deportation to Mexico would have been far more desirable; that their cases should have been handled summarily by the federal administration whose incompetence made the raid possible; that the expense of their trials should never have been laid upon this state; and that their execution will in no wise expiate the crime of Columbus. While their extermination may be just as desirable, it will no more satisfy the claims of justice than killing a rattlesnake which has bitten you and ignoring the person who dropped it down your neck.

So the Graphic may go ahead and insist on the hanging. But let it devote its attention to the hanging and not to seeking to pose as a monitor on Americanism.

MAY 20, 1921: CONGRATULATIONS.

The Business Men's Association of Santa Fe raised promptly among the business men of Santa Fe the $1,200 needed to secure the new municipal tourist camping ground.

The association and the contributors are to be congratulated on another demonstration of the new Santa Fe pep. Time was when financing a project of this kind would have been a long and wearisome task. The new Santa Fe does these things with snap and whiz.

There was vast encouragement yesterday afternoon in the spectacle of a dozen busy business men of Santa Fe, taking an hour or two off from their private affairs to go down and inspect the new camp ground and holding a snappy session of this live organization in the middle of an alfalfa field. That's the new Santa Fe spirit, the old Santa Fe spirit renewed and revived, and it's bound to get the answer.

The new camp ground is a prize which any city in the southwest would pay liberally for. It is a beautiful natural park, half in alfalfa, lined with magnificent old cottonwoods, a mountain stream dashing its full length, traversed the same distance on the other side by the main street of the city, five minutes from the heart of Santa Fe, level, supplied with a ditch which makes any part of it irrigable, with beautiful vistas of mountain and river and city; an absolutely ideal site, where a thousand automobiles may be parked with comfort. It will combine the advantages of a city park with an outdoor caravansery for tourists, and its purchase will expedite the completion of the river boulevard and park system. Not only so, but it will stimulate development of the Agua Fria section as a residence district. The high ground along the river on the south side in a few years' time must logically develop into a beautiful home section. The old adobes one by one will come down and modern dwellings will take their places.

AUGUST 16, 1921:   A WARNING.

The recent raid on bootleggers in this city by federal prohibition officers merely touched the surface. Four small fry were rounded up. It is estimated that there are a dozen or more moonshine stills in operation in the immediate vicinity of Santa Fe. Everyone knows that more rot-gut whiskey is being sold and drunk in Santa Fe than before the days of the Volstead act.

We imagine the attitude of mind of the local authorities is to "Let George Do It." George being Uncle Sam. Yet no one doubts that the sheriff's office and the police of the city could easily furnish the federal officers sufficient evidence to put a crimp in the whole bootleg industry here if they so desired.

There was a revolution in Santa Fe some years ago. Hundreds of citizens who were in the habit of drinking whiskey joined in a determined campaign to drive out the dives that were poisoning and killing young men and old, and stop the sale of all liquor. If the present situation continues public sentiment is going to wake up again and something will have to move. If the local authorities consider that they have an alibi because federal authorities are entrusted with the job they may eventually find it cuts no ice with the community.

At least two persons in Santa Fe are commonly reputed to be the leaders of the bootleg industry. Nearly any well informed citizen knows their names. The local authorities undoubtedly know their names. It strains our credulity to believe that evidence could not be secured against them were any sincere effort made to do so. The thing is notorious. The apparent immunity of these and others from arrest is the subject of daily humorous comment on the streets. The humor will inevitably disappear when the ravages of bootleg booze pass a certain stage in Santa Fe.

We respectfully submit these suggestions to the mayor, the city attorney, the chief of police and the sheriff of Santa Fe county for their earnest consideration. The City Different is gaining unenviable fame as a bootleg center. The people will stand it only up to a certain point.

OCTOBER 29, 1921: BEGINNING OF GREATER ART COLONY ON CAMINO MONTE SOL. Interesting Group of Studio Homes on Picturesque Thoroughfare; Young Painters Flocking to Spot to Build Dwellings.

By Ina Sizer Cassidy.

If to have an art colony it is necessary for the artists to live in a certain community, then Santa Fe, which has thought it had one before, is truly now to have one, which may be the beginning of a great colony. Who can tell?

Out along the Camino del Monte Sol, the real name of the road familiarly called "telephone" road, there is rapidly growing an interesting group of studio homes. Of course, William Penhallow Henderson first started it, after the Great Artist had first laid out the landscape with its far reaching view of snow clad mountains, and volcano scarred plain, sweeping over it all a refreshing breeze of pure air.

269

Then came Frank G. Applegate, of ceramic fame, who came to Santa Fe for a week and became so enamored that he decided to make his home here. So he bought a strip of land and commenced his house. In this he is to place some of the tiles which have made him famous, and here he will build a kiln and show what can be done with Santa Fe mud. Truly Santa Fe is to be congratulated upon the acquisition of Mr. Applegate. Then as though a fairy had waved her wand, other artists came to this spot and commenced studio homes, until now the Camino has somewhat the appearance of an enormous anthill in summer time. Will Shuster, whose interesting canvases, "Nativity" and the "Rainmaker" were recently sold to a New York collector, is one of the builders. J. G. Bakos of Buffalo, another young enthusiast, from Buffalo, whose paintings are familiar to museum visitors, is busy modeling a home of adobe, and El Paso has lost her talented young painter, Fremont Ellis to the charms of the City Different, and he is building a home along Camino also. Willard Nash, the idealist from Detroit, who has an alcove of attractive canvases in the museum this week, will also build in the same locality. So by mid winter, travelers to Sunmount will see all sorts of artistic life along the way. This little group of homes means much to the art future of Santa Fe.

The story above makes the first mention of four of the five young painters who called themselves Los Cinco Pintores—*Shuster, Bakos, Ellis, Nash, and Walter Mruk, not named here.*

JANUARY 21, 1922:   VOLUNTEER FIRE DEPARTMENT IS RECOGNIZED BY THE CITY.

By the terms of a new fire ordinance passed last night by the city council, the volunteer fire department of Santa Fe, headed by Chief Ashley Pond, is officially recognized "as a functioning part of the civic body of the City of Santa Fe."

The department is now fully organized, in two companies of ten each, with Ashley Pond as chief, W. H. Roberts assistant, Carl Bishop fire marshal, and E. L. Thomas, inspector of equipment. Mr. Higley is assistant fire marshal.

FEBRUARY 14, 1922:   THE HOTEL FINANCE.

Close to $170,000 has been subscribed and paid in by residents and friends of Santa Fe—almost entirely by local people— to pay for the beautiful new La Fonda hotel, now approximately completed, one of the handsomest hotels in America, and which is destined to be a tremendous factor in the future growth of Santa Fe.

Total subscriptions were some $200,000. It is declared that by the time the last effort has been made the record will be a ninety per cent collection of pledges. But even at eighty per cent the record is a magnificent showing of loyalty by the people of this city, of demonstrated confidence in the future of Santa Fe. We challenge any other community of this size to do better.

In case the impression has gone forth by reason of the receivership proceedings, that Santa Fe has "fallen down" on her hotel enterprise, Santa Feans should keep in mind the facts and publish abroad the remarkable community feat which has actually been accomplished.

The statement published in today's paper is a workmanlike product, showing clearly where the money went, and being largely a summarizing of statements which have been published from time to time in the New Mexican about the progress of the work.

The reason for the criticism voiced by certain stockholders is not clearly apparent, nor is there evident anything about the whole procedure which prevents the owners from doing exactly what they like with the property.

The New Mexican tomorrow will publish the entire list of subscribers to "La Fonda" and the amounts which they have subscribed and paid. The list of fully paid up subscribers is a splendid proof of the public spirit and the loyalty of Santa Fe citizenship. It is a list to which Santa Fe can ever after point with greatest pride. In publishing the lists of those who have partially paid and those who have paid nothing the New Mexican will of course make no invidious comparisons nor attempt to say whether any of these subscribers have fallen short of the effort made by the paid-in-full men.

Meanwhile we make a final urgent appeal to those who have not "Come through" to Do It Today. At least make a supreme effort and pay up every dollar you can raise so that the number of suits brought shall be as small as possible. The hotel is virtually completed. We want to come clean on the whole proposition without another day's needless delay; get "La Fonda" in commission and begin to reap the reward of our enterprise and our financial effort. For everyone knows that the results, when a beautiful and commodious modern tourist hotel is started here, will be immediate and substantial. The results in fact have come already and other hotels are getting the benefit of the business which came expecting to stop at the new caravansary. They will continue to get additional business because of the new hotel even after it is filled up. And bear in mind that you are "letting George do it" if you permit your neighbor to pay up in full when you have failed to do your own best.

MAY 3, 1922:   PAINTERS OF WEST TO OPEN BIG EXHIBIT HERE THURSDAY.

The first Annual Exhibition of Paintings by western artists has arrived at the Museum and will be opened to the public Thursday evening, May 4th, at 8 p. m.

This notable exhibition, which will completely fill the Museum galleries, consists of the work of 78 artists, each being represented by one picture. It is sent out on a circuit of the larger western cities by the Western Association of Museum Directors, of which the Museum of New Mexico is a member.

The exhibition will remain for a month and will afford the people of Santa Fe and New Mexico their first opportunity to compare the work of the ten local artists, represented in the collection, with that being produced in the other art centers of the west.

. . . Landscapes and portraits predominate in the exhibit, although such fine Indian subjects as "Irrigating His Corn," by J. H. Sharp, and "Her Oven," by E. S. Weinberg are admirable. One of the most interesting character studies is "Senor Martinez," by Will Shuster. Alice Klauber, Carl Oscar Berg, Joseph [*sic, for Jozef*] Bakos, O. E. Berninghaus, Blanche Grant, William P. Henderson, Sheldon Parsons, William [*sic, for Willard*] Nash, John Sloan, Theodore Van Soelen, Allen True, and others well known in Santa Fe, are among the contributors. The exhibit opens Thursday evening, May 4, with a reception by the Woman's Museum Board.

SEPTEMBER 6, 1922: A MARVELOUS PEOPLE.

Talk of decadence of Indian arts and crafts has rather disappeared since the opening of the First Annual Southwest Indian Fair in connection with the Santa Fe Fiesta this year. The fair, according to Turin B. Boone of the Indian office, is the most remarkable, complete, varied and beautiful collection of the product of the Indian's skill ever assembled in this country. When it is considered that this wonderful showing is possible at the first attempt, with only limited time for preparation, and with all the difficulties of preliminary organization, the possibilities of this great enterprise are apparently unbounded.

That the Indians of the southwest are a most marvelous people is impressed on the visitor at the Indian fair as never before. Their art is unique, absolutely distinctive; there is nothing like it in the world; it is a genius for decoration unequaled by any nation of people, inherent and inherited, cropping out, as shown in the exhibits, in the drawing of little Indian children seven and eight years old. This art is one of the world's greatest treasures; it is a priceless possession of America and America is to be congratulated that its value has received final recognition and that every effort will be made by the government and other agencies to foster and preserve and develop it.

We call these people "untutored", and yet, to watch a dark-skinned desert dweller spill varicolored sands between his fingers into a magic pattern on the ground glowing with color and beauty; to see rich designs springing from under the flying fingers of a Navajo woman seated impassive before her loom; to see the cunning of the silversmith; enigmatic pictures evolving in beads and straw, sheer beauty flowing from the finger tips of this strange race of men and women, to study their symbolism and listen to their age-old traditions, is to be lost in wonder. Their mystery baffles us, the profundity of their simplicity fascinates us. It would be civilization's misfortune if they and their works should be lost to us. Santa Fe and the Indian office have commenced a tremendous service to the world. We repeat, its possibilities are unlimited, and it is with satisfaction that we observe this great movement is starting along right lines, eliminating carefully all that which is not truly Indian and fostering and encouraging that which is the real thing.

SEPTEMBER 20, 1922: THE INDIAN BILL.

The New Mexican publishes in full in today's paper the Bursum bill, passed in the senate, and now reported held up in the house, designed to settle the long standing controversy between Pueblo Indians and non-Indians regarding title to lands adjoining the Indian villages.

We publish this so that every person interested in securing justice in this controversy, and the general public, may have a full opportunity to read the bill. It should be read carefully and analytically. This bill is of tremendous, far-reaching importance. On the law to be finally enacted depends very largely the future of the Pueblo Indians, the ethnological treasure of the continent, a priceless asset to the southwest, a race which, balancing precariously between growth and decline, will vanish like a wraith and become merely memory and legend in America unless given every possible chance to remain.

Not since the days of Custer has it been necessary to "protect" non-Indians in this country against the Indian. The steady pressure of encroachment has borne them backward and further backward everywhere. The Indian is the most historic of all under dogs. The plain intent of such sweeping legislation as this before us must be positively to protect the Pueblo Indians in the possession of every foot of land which is justly theirs. If deprived of a tithe of an acre unjustly half a century ago the Indian should have his land restored to him. Enough has been said about "relief" for the non-Indian settler on Indian land. It is time to keep an eye on the other side of the equation.

Wading through the maze of legal phraseology in this bill, we do not gather that it is giving the Pueblo Indian any the best of it. There is much that sounds like the same old squeeze. Just at this time, with a great movement under way to re-energize the creative arts of the Pueblos and make Santa Fe the focus and beneficiary of the movement, Santa Fe is particularly vitally interested in any legislation which so deeply affects the fate of these people. They cannot develop their ancient arts and crafts for the delight and education of the world unless they can continue their communal existence under favoring conditions. They must have enough to eat. They must have the compact lands to which they are justly entitled and which are vital to their life, and they must not be deprived of all irrigation water necessary to farm their lands.

SEPTEMBER 25, 1922: EFFECT OF INDIAN BILL WOULD BE TO CRIPPLE, DESTROY SOME OF PUEBLOS, SAYS.

"The effect of the Indian bill would be to cripple some of the Indian pueblo communities and at an early date to destroy others."

This is the opinion of John Collier, research and publicity agent for the Indian welfare department of the National Federation of Women's Clubs, now in Taos, who was here recently and has been making a thorough investigation of the provisions and effects of the measure drawn by C. C. Catron, R. E. Twitchell, A. B. Renehan and others, introduced by Senator Bursum and passed in the senate, but which was held up in the house.

As stated in this paper Saturday, large numbers of people here have taken up the protest against passage of the bill in its present form and the bill was analyzed and its defects pointed out by Attorney W. J. Barker at a meeting of objectors held at the McComb residence, Sunday afternoon.

The threat of action in the federal courts on behalf of the

Pueblo Indians, to recover the lands within their grants then being occupied by non-Indians and the irrigation water that went with the land, alarmed influential people. The Indians had no vote in New Mexico. The adverse occupants were voters. The Republican party was then in power in the state, and many of these occupants were devotedly Republican Spanish-Americans—some of them local political leaders of importance.

To forestall the possible effects of such action, Senator Holm O. Bursum, who had been appointed by Governor Merritt C. Mechem, introduced the "Bursum Bill." In effect, this bill would have confirmed the title to land and water of almost everyone who had settled upon Pueblo Indian land. Albert B. Fall of New Mexico was secretary of the interior; the office of commissioner of Indian affairs was purely political. Without opposition, this bill slipped smoothly through the Senate before it was noticed.

A reaction occurred that astonished the politicians, as the "yearners"—the artists, anthropologists, and their friends—took up the cudgels. These people, whose respect for Indians and Indian rights ranged from the purely scientific to the extremely sentimental, had long been regarded with amusement and derision; they came to be looked upon with anger and fear.

Under the leadership of John Collier, who first appears in the story just above, public opinion was mobilized all over the United States. He also mobilized the Indians. From time to time, officers of the nineteen pueblos had met, usually at the call of the Indian agencies. Now they began meeting at their own call—or Collier's. They met at Santo Domingo, both because that place was fairly central and because its people were less inhibited than most about throwing out unwanted visitors. The Indian Service made attempts to prevent these meetings, or to capture them, but was unsuccessful. Out of them, in time, came the All-Pueblo Council, an officially recognized, continuing body.

Collier took a group of leading Indians on a tour of the East and to Washington. He demonstrated for the first time that when the Indians themselves unite and find means to catch the attention of the American people, they can do much to protect themselves.

Even before they had finished with the local issue, the "yearn-ers" were beginning to think in broader terms. John Collier him-self brought to the Indians' cause an unusual dedication and a new high level of thinking, along with unusual talents for making, and keeping, both friends and enemies. The story of the develop-ment of an alert, informed, democratic public interest in the American Indians in general is marred by an early history of bitter, often ridiculous, feuds. Out of the interest first generated among the "yearners" of the Santa Fe–Taos region came, eventually, the appointment of Harold L. Ickes as secretary of the interior and of Collier himself as commissioner of Indian affairs, leading to pro-found changes in all matters affecting our Indians.

From the original interest of the General Federation of Wom-en's Clubs, which can be attributed to the presence in Taos and Santa Fe of a few influential Federation members and the found-ing of the New Mexico Association on Indian Affairs in Santa Fe, came the establishment of a number of pro-Indian organizations. In the course of time the strongest of these united to form the Association on American Indian Affairs, a truly national organiza-tion which continues to wield an important influence for the benefit of the Indians.

NOVEMBER 6, 1922:   INDIAN BILL WILL DESTROY PUEBLO LIFE, SAY INDIANS IN MEMORIAL TO COUNTRY.

United in action for the first time since they arose and drove out the Spaniards in 1680, nearly one hundred delegates, travelling afoot and on horseback, and including eight governors, represent-ing the eight thousand Pueblo Indians in nineteen pueblos in New Mexico, assembled at the pueblo of Santo Domingo on Sunday, adopted a memorial to the American people "for fair play and justice and the preservation of our pueblo life."

The appeal is the result of the passage by the U. S. Senate of the bill known as the Bursum Indian bill, which purports to effect a final settlement of the century-old controversy between the pueb-los and their non-Indian neighbors over the land and water of the Indians. Alleging that they have not been consulted, that official explanations have been refused, that the bill will destroy them as a people, that it will make them dependents of the government, that it will force them to go into courts to settle tribal matters they have always adjusted among themselves, and that the government to which they look for protection in their rights has deserted them, they say in conclusion, "The bill will destroy our common life, and rob us of everything we hold dear; our lands, our customs and our traditions. Are the American people willing to see this happen?"

DECEMBER 12, 1922:   FROM HEADQUARTERS.

Proponents of the now celebrated Bursum Indian Bill—those few who have ventured to defend the bill publicly—have rather caustically charged or implied that "propagandists" have been responsible for the allegation that the Pueblo Indians have been made the gradual victims of squatters through the negligence, or indifference, of the government agencies whose business it is to look after them.

However, we now have the statement, explicit and unequivocal, direct from headquarters—in the report for 1922 of the United States Board of Indian Commissioners to the Secretary of the Interior. This board, which is charged with the work of investigating conditions among the Indians, includes members who have served on it from ten to forty years. It is the last word in official data upon the Indians. Regarding the Pueblos north of Santa Fe it says:

"The Indian pueblos north of Santa Fe, N. M., viz., Taos, Picuris, San Juan, Santa Clara, Nambe, San Ildefonso, and Tesuque, were visited by Commissioner Scott in October, 1921, and the people generally were found to be well housed, law abiding, and industrious, but very poor.

"These Indians claim ownership of their lands from original occupation, by Spanish grants guaranteed them by the United States, in the treaty of Guadalupe Hidalgo with New Mexico, in which the United States affirmed their ownership. The government has never really protected them in their rights for it has by inaction allowed Mexican squatters to occupy large areas of their grants by encroaching continually thereon until the Indians have but one or two acres of cultivated land left, per capita, an insufficient amount for maintenance. Because of this non-interference from the government, the squatters claim rights, and although many of these Mexican claims are considered preposterous, the claimants have been permitted to remain unmolested and to encroach more and more from year to year. The Indian, helpless to protect himself in a lawful way, looks to the department to protect him, as its duty requires. This land question is at the bottom of most of the continual clashes and squabbles over trespass. There are many cases pending in the courts against the squatters. This whole question can be settled by promptly pressing the suits to trial and judgment.

"In every conference which the Indians held with Commissioner Scott they expressed dissatisfaction with the appointment of the tribal attorney whose duty it is to look after their land interests and to attend to the adverse condition surrounding their land grants. They insisted they ought to be consulted in the selection of their legal adviser so they could be certain he would be a man who would be free from all influences which might be antagonistic to their interests.

"The Pueblos complained that in all the years of government supervision they have never been consulted in the matter of the appointment of the tribal attorney. Commissioner Scott is of the opinion that this common dissatisfaction of all Pueblos in the northern jurisdiction has created a condition which should be inquired into by the department. If the Indians are right in their contention prompt remedial action should be taken."

DECEMBER 13, 1922:   INDISCRETION.

The folly of equivocal defense of the Bursum Indian Bill, by Mr. Bursum, Indian Commissioner Burke and others is hard to understand in view of the action already taken by the United States Senate on the ground that the bill was misrepresented to it, and that it does in itself settle titles to contested lands by legislation. Even if the public couldn't read the English language, it would be inclined to take the word of the United States Senate against that of Mr. Bursum and Mr. Burke. Their wisest policy would be the golden one of silence.

MARCH 1, 1923: BURIES BURSUM BILL, ABUSES SLAYERS. Snyder House Committee O. Ks. Substitute, Takes Hide off Those Who Got It. PROPAGANDISTS LIARS; BUREAU GIVEN HALO. Lenroot Measure Passes the Senate, Likely to Get Over in House Today.

Washington, D. C., March 1.—The Lenroot substitute for the Bursum and Jones-Leatherwood Pueblo Indian land bills passed the senate and is expected to pass the house today.

The house Indian affairs committee, Homer P. Snyder, chairman, yesterday put the Bursum and Snyder bills into the waste-basket and recommended passage of the substitute accompanying the report with a violent attack on the individuals and agencies who supported it or a similar measure and who brought about the discarding by the committee of the Bursum and Snyder bills.

ALL ATTACKS MALICIOUS AND FALSE, SAYS COMMITTEE.

The report of the Snyder committee besides the vitriolic attack on the Bursum bill opponents sets up an elaborate defense of the conduct of the Indian bureau and the government treatment of the Pueblos.

The report believes the Lenroot substitute "is a fair solution of the many complicated problems involved and under it the rights of the Indians are fully protected, as well as the equitable right of the Indian claimants."

After praising the substitute which omits practically all the features of the objectionable Bursum bill fought by the national federation of women's clubs [*sic*], Catholic agencies, scientific societies, archaeologists, Indian defense organizations, eminent writers, artists, and the press of the country including practically all the leading metropolitan dailies, the house committee report proceeds to lambaste most unmercifully and bitterly the people who made the substitute possible. Among the targets for attack are Mrs. Atwood, chairman of the Indian welfare department of the national federation of women's clubs, which took a leading part in the fight; John Collier, research agent for the federation; Father Fridolin Shuster, Franciscan missionary; Judson King, of the Popular Government League and Francis C. Wilson attorney for the federation [*sic (punctuation)*].

In the early 1920's, the Indians needed friends. In addition to Fall as secretary of the interior, under him as commissioner of Indian affairs was Charles H. Burke, a small politician with an abysmal outlook. The Bursum Bill was only one example of legislation to plunder Indians that was approved by an acquiescent Bureau of Indian Affairs and Department of the Interior.

At the same time, the Bureau renewed with extra vigor its long-standing war against Indian religious practices, as evidenced by the following story. Burke's letter to the Indians was most fortunately timed. It further aroused public opinion in favor of the Indians and was a factor in leading the Indians' friends to look to the whole Indian field, not merely the Southwest. The Bureau of Indian Affairs was routed in this sector after a brief but stimulating battle.

MARCH 7, 1923: BURKE WOULD STOP DANCES BY THE PUEBLO INDIANS.

Indian Commissioner Burke has issued a fiat to the Pueblo Indians which if obeyed would mean practically the wiping out of the ceremonial dances of this people. The communication received by the Indians follows:

"TO ALL INDIANS:

"Not long ago I held a meeting of Superintendents, Missionaries and Indians, at which the feeling of those present was strong against Indian dances, as they are usually given, and against so much time as is often spent by the Indians in a display of their old customs at public gatherings held by the whites. From the views of this meeting and from other information I feel that something must be done to stop the neglect of stock, crops, gardens, and home interests caused by these dances or by celebrations, pow-wows, and gatherings of any kind that take the time of the Indians for many days.

"Now, what I want you to think about very seriously is that you must first of all try to make your own living, which you cannot do unless you work faithfully and take care of what comes from your labor, and go to dances or other meetings only when your home work will not suffer by it. I do not want to deprive you of decent amusements or occasional feast days, but you should not do evil or foolish things or take so much time for these occasions. No good comes from your 'giveaway' custom at dances and it should be stopped. It is not right to torture your bodies or to handle poisonous snakes in your ceremonies. All such extreme things are wrong and should be put aside and forgotten. You do yourselves and your families great injustice when at dances you give away money or other property, perhaps clothing, a cow, a horse or a team and wagon, and then after an absence of several days go home to find everything going to waste and yourselves with less to work with than you had before.

"I could issue an order against these useless and harmful performances, but I would much rather have you give them up of your own free will and, therefore, I ask you now in this letter to do so. I urge you to come to an understanding and an agreement with your Superintendent to hold no gatherings in the months when the seedtime, cultivation and the harvest need your attention, and at other times to meet for only a short period and to have no drugs, intoxicants, or gambling, and no dancing that the Superintendent does not approve.

"If at the end of one year the reports which I receive show that you are doing as requested, I shall be very glad for I will know that you are making progress in other and more important ways, but if the reports show that you reject this plea, then some other course will have to be taken.

"With best wishes for your happiness and success, I am,

"Sincerely yours,
"Charles H. Burke,
"Commissioner.

"February 24, 1923."

*As noted from time to time in the course of these comments,
New Mexico politics were—sometimes still are—on the gaudy
side. The conviction and sentencing of the editor of the* New
Mexico State Tribune *is so juicy an example of a political judge
in action that a notice of it must be included. The story covering
the Governor's reversal of the court wraps it up neatly.*

*In fairness I should add that, although still popularly elected,
state judges in New Mexico today are far less political and hold
themselves to a commendable standard of ethics.*

JULY 16, 1923:   [*Banner headline.*] MAGEE GIVEN FULL PARDON.
TRIAL CONSPIRACY AND PERSECUTION, DECLARED BY GOVERNOR
HINKLE. CARL C. MAGEE, ALBUQUERQUE, EDITOR OF THE NEW MEX-
ICO STATE TRIBUNE, WHO RECENTLY WAS SENTENCED BY JUDGE
LEAHY OF THE DISTRICT COURT IN SAN MIGUEL COUNTY, TO THE
STATE PENITENTIARY FOR A YEAR TO A YEAR AND A HALF FOLLOW-
ING HIS CONVICTION ON THE CHARGE OF CRIMINALLY LIBELLING
CHIEF JUSTICE FRANK W. PARKER OF THE SUPREME COURT, AND 360
DAYS IN THE COUNTY JAIL OF SAN MIGUEL COUNTY AFTER BEING
FOUND IN CONTEMPT OF COURT WAS PARDONED BY GOVERNOR
HINKLE ON BOTH SENTENCES TODAY.

. . . In the pardon on the penitentiary sentence, the governor
gave as his reasons that the indictment on which Magee was tried
was obtained without the knowledge or consent of the party "supposed to be libelled;"

That the trial was held in a district where neither Magee nor
Parker lived;

That the bringing of Magee to the bar seemed "to be a conspiracy, and more of a persecution than a prosecution."

In the second pardon, relieving Magee of the necessity of going
to the San Miguel county jail for nearly a year, Governor Hinkle
also remits fines and costs of $7 imposed upon Magee for the al-
leged contempt, on four citations, and also all fines imposed upon
his newspaper, The New Mexico State Tribune, for the same reason, totalling $4,050.

Santa Fe

Governor Hinkle, in the second pardon, says he is "of the opinion the contempt cases were also a persecution; that the sentences are harsh and beyond reason; that this whole procedure is a disgrace and blot upon New Mexico, and the good people thereof."

NOVEMBER 11, 1924:   AN ELECTION LAW.

The election just held in New Mexico demonstrates again and more forcibly than ever before the need for a sweeping reform in election laws in this state.

Present methods are archaic, clumsy, out of date, antiquated, inefficient and ought to be discarded without further delay.

They are an invitation to fraud, prolific of controversy, and in about forty-eight other ways are undesirable.

The place to begin is with registration. The registration methods used in Santa Fe this year were enough to cause any civilized community to blush. Citizens resident here for a decade couldn't find the registration books, didn't get registered and had to swear in their votes. In other states registration is surrounded with all the restrictions of judicial procedure; the place of registration is known, the voter has to register in person and he has to show that he is entitled to register. As an indication of the slipshod methods used, nobody is ever able to give even approximate figures on registration in New Mexico. The custom is to add ten percent to the vote shown at the last election. If the population has fallen off twenty percent, the estimate stands. It is all guess work.

At the polls in any modern commonwealth, voters are held in a straight and narrow line and if anyone outside of that line ventures within fifty feet of the polls he is promptly placed under arrest. No one is permitted to enter a booth and assist a voter in marking his ballot. The vote is secret from the time it is placed in the voter's hand to the time he places it himself in the ballot box. In this state there is every opportunity for half a dozen persons to inspect the ballot. The voter goes into an open booth in plain sight of anybody and everybody, surrounded with a litter of used, halfused or discarded ballots, anybody who can put it over marks his ballot for him.

Days and days are spent in counting ballots which in the east are enumerated by the time the polls close. Ballot boxes in remote precincts are surrounded by a fog of mystery; nobody knows what they are doing, rumors persist that they have been tampered with and generally it would be hard to prove that they have not. A week after other states have forgotten the election, the New Mexico returns are being slowly and laboriously brought in.

Nobody has any faith in the integrity of the voting methods obtaining in the aforementioned remote precincts. All we know is that in years past gross frauds have been perpetrated and there is no particular valid assurance that the practice has died out.

Perhaps it is a cruel slander to charge even the possibility of tampering with the ballots in this state. The fact remains that we must get rid of a system which always gives rise to this suspicion and uncertainty. We must have a secret ballot in New Mexico, an efficient method of gathering election returns promptly, a system sufficiently well safeguarded to eliminate doubt. Right now the whole country is wondering what in blazes is the matter with the returns in New Mexico. The metropolitan dailies wiring impatiently for final returns, can't understand how we do it.

This is not a partisan editorial. We are commenting on a condition that is known to everybody and which has exasperated the public this year more than ever before. It will be to the advantage of all parties and all voters to get behind a concerted movement to reform the New Mexico election laws.

The New Mexico seal and coat of arms consists of the American eagle sheltering the Mexican eagle, complete with cactus and serpent, under its wing. It is elaborate, not easy to read, and makes an unsatisfactory flag. Suggestions were invited for a simpler state flag and symbol, leading to the eventual adoption of the Zia Indian sun symbol in red on a yellow ground—the old Spanish colors. This device was first proposed by Dr. Harry P. Mera of the Laboratory of Anthropology. Its actual adoption by the legislature was not without some debate.

MARCH 5, 1925: ZIA SUN FLAG HOUSE CHOICE; ALBUQUERQUEANS
PUT UP FIGHT.

That the flag selected in the Daughters of the American Revolution contest is the choice of the House for state flag was shown
late yesterday after a lengthy discussion in the committee of the
whole. By a vote of 28 to 8, the committee decided to make a
favorable recommendation to the house, despite efforts of the
Bernalillo county delegation, which favors a design submitted by
the Business and Professional Women's club of Albuquerque, to
block a vote.

The flag picked by the house is the Zia Sun symbol in dark red
on a Spanish yellow field.

The galleries were crowded with a number of Albuquerque
women present and Mrs. A. T. Hannett, the governor's wife, and
Mrs. Estella Westfall, her mother, sat at the speaker's desk with
Rep. Daniel Boone of Curry county who presided as chairman of
the committee and ruled in a way that would have given a pointer
or two to "Uncle Joe" Cannon when he was going at his best. Only
members, however, were permitted to take part in the discussion.

MARCH 5, 1926: LA FONDA.

"Fred Harvey is to get La Fonda June first."

This announcement has an effect on the Santa Fe public similar
to that of the forthcoming work on a new city reservoir.

It is one of the most gratifying that has ever been published in
this newspaper. It means the realization of a 20-year ambition. It
means not only the long wished for Harvey House in Santa Fe,
but we are quite confident it means also the jewel of the entire
collection of railroad hotels in the Southwest. The present building is quite unique; it lends itself, in the expected remodeling
process, to the task of completing a hotel here which shall be
indeed monumental among Harvey hostelries.

Harvey hotel service, Harvey hotel food, Harvey hotel standards
—these are fixed and unchangeable and their fame is as wide as
travel itself. In setting the Santa Fe Harvey Hotel, La Fonda, will
be the superior of them all; the very location is the most historical

along the Santa Fe Trail in that it is the End of the Santa Fe Trail. As the headquarters point for the most notable departure in modern railroad tourist traffic, the Indian Detour, this hotel will have an added distinction, one will advertise the other, and both will work for the greater fame of the Oldest City.

Here as elsewhere, the building of every new hotel means more business for every other hotel, present or future. The citizens of Santa Fe who have worked together so loyally to bring about this consummation will reap the benefits of their foresight for years to come.

The coming of the Harvey hotel system into this capital is one of the milestones along the route of Santa Fe's progress. It is cordially welcomed. Santa Fe has made good her promise to co-operate with the interests represented by the Indian Detour project. She will continue to co-operate in the future. It is a matter of mutual benefit all the way through.

Above I have mentioned the combination of Santa Fe people who led the opposition to the Bursum Bill. Practicing artists and writers, sympathetic anthropologists, and amateurs of the arts and of the special qualities of Santa Fe and New Mexico—these last in many cases quite wealthy—all could be classed together as the Santa Fe art colony. It was not in such a group to be unanimous. It was made up of strong individuals, who split off from the main body and reunited with it as agreements or disagreements might indicate. In the main, the larger group followed the lead of the artists. Its influence was perceptible shortly after 1910; between the mid-1920's and early 1930's, for a little less than a decade, it was the most influential single group in the city.

One of the first demonstrations of its power in local affairs was in regard to "the Texas ladies' Chautauqua" in 1926, which furnished a beautiful example of a first-class tempest in a teapot.

Apparently at least partly due to the initiative of the Santa Fe Chamber of Commerce, supported by Dr. Edgar L. Hewett, director of the Museum of New Mexico and of the School of American Research, a project was developed with the Southwestern Federation of Women's Clubs, including Kansas, Louisiana, Mis-

souri, Arkansas, Colorado, Arizona, Texas, Oklahoma, New Mex-
ico, and Mississippi, to establish a "culture colony" of women at
Santa Fe. The colony incorporated as the Cultural Centre of the
Southwest. The Santa Fe Railway supported the scheme, a dele-
gation reached Santa Fe on April 15, and on April 23 the City
Council voted to offer the colony land near Sunmount, at the
southeastern edge of town, at a nominal consideration. From the
New Mexican's accounts, it would appear that the proposed col-
ony would be made up largely of Texans.

The first serious opposition to the project developed on April
23.

APRIL 24, 1926:   OPPOSITION TO CLUB CULTURAL COLONY HOLDS
MEETING AND PETITIONS THE CITY COUNCIL. Move to Get Land
Back of Sunmount Results in Mass Meeting at Which Speakers
Say Project Is Not Desirable; Old Santa Fe Association Formed.

The move to secure land as a site for the proposed cultural colony or Chautauqua in the cove in the foothills just east of Sunmount Sanitarium resulted in a mass meeting at Sunmount last
night which petitioned the city council for a special meeting at
which objections and protests against the establishing of the colony here could be heard. At the meeting, attended by between
60 and 75 persons, tentative organization was also effected of the
Old Santa Fe association.

TO PRESERVE THE BEST OF OLD SANTA FE.

The brief statement of purposes to which the organizers attached their signatures, in order to get the tentative organization
going, was as follows:

"We, the undersigned, do hereby organize ourselves into a permanent body to be known as the Old Santa Fe Association, for
the purpose of working for the preservation of Old Santa Fe, and
of guiding new growth and development and advancement in
material welfare, in such a way as to sacrifice as little as possible of
the unique charm and distinction of this city, born of age, tradition and environment, and which are Santa Fe's most priceless
assets." . . .

ALWAYS DISASTROUS DECLARES MRS. AUSTIN.

... Mrs. Mary Austin, the novelist, ... reviewed what she said had been her personal experience with cultural colonies at Monterey, Calif., Carmel-By-The-Sea, and in New Jersey. In each case she said the project was impermanent, resulted in construction of flimsy buildings because they were only used a few months in the year, brought little money to the community and created an atmosphere which in Monterey resulted in the disappearance of all the old processions, religious observances, and customs which made Monterey 25 years ago very similar to Old Santa Fe. ...

... She alleged from her experience in buying and selling property in Monterey and Carmel that such a colony raises property values for the first two years to a certain extent, after which they deflate. ...

"The Chautauqua type of colony never has helped any city at which it has been located," she said. "I do not mean to say that Chautauquas do not do fine work; my mother helped establish one, and it was of great service to many people of the kind who seek culture en masse, rather than through individual initiative."

A number of others made remarks to the effect that the colony would be unattractive, of no advantage to the town, and that it was time to take action against it.

On April 26 the Chamber of Commerce came back with a mass meeting which developed into a free-for-all. Accounts of the proceedings occupied considerable space in the New Mexican *for April 27 and 28. C. E. Doll, president of the Chamber, seems to have been taken quite aback by the intensity of the opposition. The editor of the* New Mexican *(Dana Johnson) resigned as a director of the Chamber "after C. E. Doll's outburst" (April 28). The April 27 story quotes Mr. Doll in part as saying, "For God's sake, give us credit for being able-bodied men; we're not children. ... You have no right to repudiate the good work of the Chamber. ... These people have money. You don't dare stop people from coming in and investing their money. I know I mean business; you stand behind your Chamber of Commerce. We want to give them a site of 15 acres on the ridge north of the city."*

On the same day, the City Council refused to reconsider its action. Letters to the editor were pouring in. The paper, which up to this point had been shilly-shallying, now took a definite stand.

APRIL 28, 1926: THE SITUATION.

The proposal to bring a "cultural colony" here has split Santa Fe wide open.

The unity of spirit on which this city has prided itself has been blown up in a few days' time.

If the proposition goes forward, this breach must inevitably widen. No one can predict the result. There is only one conceivable thing to do, and that is to drop it like a hot potato.

What is proposed is an institution. Every man and woman in this town has a right to favor or oppose it. The past few days have demonstrated perfectly that the opposition failed to crystallize earlier because no one knew what it was to be. It is idle to say that it has had publicity; the meeting Monday night showed a dozen different convictions as to its character. People also have a right not to be bound to any hospitality which others have offered in their behalf. This can be put on the basis of neither hospitality nor personality.

No one can forbid any individual or group to come here and buy land if he or she can secure it. The City of Santa Fe CAN through its government and Chamber of Commerce, refuse to commit its people to a project when a large element is against it, and when it is a demonstrated cause of disastrous and deplorable dissension.

The New Mexican, like hundreds of individuals wavered in its judgment of this enterprise because of the conflict in the claims of what it really was. Our final conclusion is of little importance compared to the actual existing situation in this town.

The city council and the Chamber of Commerce have no recourse but to inform the projectors that the people are so seriously divided on the matter that they cannot assume authority to offer inducements from the city of Santa Fe.

Slurs on those citizens, tax payers, property owners, home

builders, investors of over a million dollars who are against the proposition, are futile.

The situation is that neither the council nor the Chamber of Commerce can assume such authority, in the light of what has happened. The New Mexican is ready to meet any abuse which this editorial may provoke. We are stating a truth that every person in Santa Fe knows and we would not support any enterprise on earth which came here under such conditions. We are willing to accept our share of the unpleasantness, believing firmly and honestly that our position is the only one that could be rightfully taken under the circumstances.

The city council should rescind the action it took last night.

APRIL 29, 1926:   ASSETS.

The present controversy in Santa Fe has revealed what is to this paper the surprising fact that a considerable number of merchants have not the slightest objection to Santa Fe's being exactly like Bucyrus, O., or Wigginsville, Ind., so long as they get More Business.

This seems astonishing.

It is a fact which must be faced. It is tremendously important that these business men be enlightened.

We are speaking for an institution which distributes $50,000 annually in Santa Fe; . . . which has been a heavy contributor to the Chamber of Commerce . . . ; which has given it and the School of American Research acres of publicity. . . .

Santa Fe, we will say, is in competition with other towns for business. . . .

The merchant with the goods his competitor lacks advertises them. So with a city. . . . Santa Fe has special assets which all our business competitors lack. These are:

Antiquity;
Old landmarks;
A stirring history;
A foreign flavor;
A Spanish atmosphere;

Pueblo Indians;

A unique type of architecture;

Traditional and picturesque customs;

A group of creative people, artists, writers, sculptors, musicians, architects;

Individuality, unconventionality and picturesqueness in dress;

A remarkable array of native talent;

A center of scientific and historical research;

A cosmopolitan population;

A democratic social atmosphere founded on individuality and not money.

The factors, or any one of them, have brought Santa Fe its present growth. . . .

This is the kind of growth and the kind of business that is making Santa Fe substantial and prosperous, without impairing the assets. . . .

It brings not only More Business, but far more important, Better Business. This is the thing which must be taught many business men here.

MAY 17, 1926:   UP TO THE CHAMBER.

It has now been fairly well demonstrated that half the population of Santa Fe, to put it conservatively, is opposed to the much discussed "Culture Colony." The two leading Spanish American civic and fraternal organizations, El Centro de Cultura and La Union Protectiva, have gone on record, the former with one dissenting vote and the latter with complete and enthusiastic unanimity, with their protest against the proposition. These organizations—the latter with its auxiliary has 400 members and the former 165—furnish conclusive proof of the attitude and sentiments of the Spanish speaking people.

As previously stated, the opposition includes also a score of members of the Chamber of Commerce, members and officers or ex-officers of the Kiwanis and Rotary clubs, Women's Board of Trade, Santa Fe Women's club, State Federation of Women's Clubs, leading educators, business and professional men, heavy property owners and taxpayers, heavy contributors to the Chamber of Commerce. These people do not claim to be the cream of Santa Fe. They do claim to be on a parity, in civic leadership and town building, with any of those trying to push this thing over in the face of a tremendous sentiment against it. They have not tried to run the town; they have merely insisted they have an equal share and voice in community invitations or settling community problems with the group who have attempted to ignore and override them. . . .

To continue the effort to bring these women here, thinking they have a community invitation, is false pretenses and grossly unfair to the women.

To continue the effort is calculated to jeopardize the success of the Fiesta and the other pressing business of this community. To maintain the present attitude is to invite a further and more determined fight by the opposition, to invite more additions to its ranks, to widen the breach in this town, and cause ultimate consequences which will be of the gravest detriment to Santa Fe's progress. To continue is to invite people to leave, who have come here and invested, made good citizens, and joined in building up Santa Fe.

This peculiar conflict led to the realization, on the part of the newspaper and many individuals, that the "amateurs" mentioned earlier, many of them rich, or at least well heeled, were important contributors to Santa Fe's economy who would be lost if the city lost the special character that had caused them to settle in it. Other news stories and editorials stated that there were people who projected building residences at a cost of $50,000 and considerably more, who were suspending their plans until they saw what was the final decision on the culture colony.

The uproar received national attention. The unusual point of view of the opposition tickled the fancies of many. The New Mexican *quoted editorials and articles not only from leftish publications such as the* New Republic *and* Nation *but from as solid a pillar of respectability as the* New York Herald-Tribune. *Letters from notable personages who had visited Santa Fe kept coming in. There seems to have been no final decision, properly speaking; the project simply died away in the face of the hostility it was arousing. By the time Sinclair Lewis expressed his opinion, the battle was pretty well over.*

JUNE 5, 1926: CULTURAL COLONY WOULD MAKE CITY "FLIMSY FAIR GROUND." Sinclair Lewis, Author of Best Sellers, Joins Array against Project.

That it would be nothing but a "ghastly misfortune" to permit the establishment of the proposed Cultural Colony here is the opinion of Sinclair Lewis, author of best-sellers, including Main Street, Babbitt and Arrowsmith, for which he recently turned down the $1,000 Pulitzer award.

Mr. Lewis expresses his views of the situation in a message addressed to the Old Santa Fe Association.

He says:

As one who has seen the unspoiled beauty of Santa Fe I believe that it would be nothing but a ghastly misfortune to hand the town over to the hordes of seekers for predigested culture—to change it from a dignified and distinguished city, admired by all the world, into a flimsy fair-ground. And as to financial gain, very little of that will go to the authentic citizens of the town; most of it will be expertly seized by the shrewd speculators who follow such carnival-like affairs.

> Yours sincerely,
> Sinclair Lewis

As we have already seen, the Santa Fe Fiesta was begun—or possibly revived, a question for historians—about 1912, let lapse, staged again in 1916, and continued, under the leadership of Dr. Edgar L. Hewett and his colleagues of the Chamber of Commerce, frankly as a device to promote Santa Fe's appeal as a tourist center. In the early 1920's, the principal part of Fiesta was a historical pageant, featuring, but not confined to, the re-enactment of De Vargas' reconquest of the city in 1692. The front of the Palace of the Governors, which had become the historical and anthropological museum, and adjacent parts of the plaza were cut off by a palisade. Stands were erected inside, and the pageant was run off for those who could pay the price of admission. The aver-age Spanish-American could afford no such thing, so that the descendants of the conquistadores *were left to peek through the cracks in hope of a glimpse of the portrayal of their ancestors. (See Shuster's reminiscences under March 12, 1950.)*

Once again the art colony rebelled and in 1926, on short notice, organized and put on an open celebration for all comers, follow-ing the "closed" fiesta, which they called El Pasatiempo. *The Hysterical Pageant mentioned in the accounts below was con-ceived, obviously, as a parody of the Historical ditto but grew far beyond that. The burning of Zozobra, nowadays not twenty, but forty, feet high, has become an event famous enough to claim international reputation. This was Shuster's concept, but Shuster says that Baumann gets credit, which he has not received, for mak-ing the first head.*

The first Pasatiempo *ended closed functions for the few, then and there. The remarkable project was executed by the Old Santa Fe Association, which had been formed only a few months earlier, in the course of the fight against the Ladies' Culture Colony. The initiation of a real Latin fiesta, then, must be credited to Anglo-Americans. The Spanish-Americans, however, joined in with verve, and it was their wholehearted participation that gave the thing its character. Now Santa Fe has tripled in size, its Spanish-speaking population seems to be less spontaneous and more self-conscious, and in its Anglo population the art colony is hopelessly outnumbered by people who habitually wear business suits. Cos-tuming has all but died out, no one dances in the streets, and the celebration consists more of watching spectacles, less of being part of spectacles. Still, it remains truly a fiesta and strongly Latin.*

The New Mexican *ran lists of contributors too long to include in this book, as also would be a full list of those who were active in putting on the* Pasatiempo. *The artists were all in it, of course, and old-timers would insist on special mention of John Sloan and his wife Dolly, an unstoppable little package of dynamite. The leading merchants of the town responded warmly to the call for money and prizes. Among other supporters, we find the all-important amateurs, led by the Misses Martha and Amelia Elizabeth White, and from the political side, Bronson Cutting.*

In the stories that follow, there is mention of a new personage, Martin Gardesky, as a major figure in El Pasatiempo. *Gardesky had come to Santa Fe in 1924, and with his friend, assistant, and successor, Morris Yashvin, ran the Capital Pharmacy on the plaza. He spoke Spanish, knew Mexico, and had a deep feeling for and relish of the special character of Santa Fe. He also had a wonderful sense of fun. It came naturally to him to be one of the cornerstones of Fiesta, and he fitted easily into the activities of the art colony.*

Yashvin told me a story that illuminates both men's characters. One day there came into the store a tall, blond salesman, whom Gardesky spotted immediately for a Jew pretending to be a Gentile. Gardesky put Yashvin onto his idea with a word and a look. Suddenly, to his distress, the salesman found that these two men spoke and understood nothing but Yiddish. He had business to do, and in the end he broke down and made his sale in that language. They were equally capable, if it suited the occasion, of being able to understand nothing but Spanish.

FRIDAY, SEPTEMBER 3, 1926: PASATIEMPO NOW HERE.

El Pasatiempo is here. After the burning of Zozobra this evening at 8 P. M., the town will be dedicated to jolly fun. Any Santa Fean who is suspected of harboring dull care after that hour, or even of thinking a serious thought, will be liable to a fine, not to exceed five hundred dollars, same to be paid to the Pasatiempo committee.

If you can't wear a rose in your hair, and you haven't got a lace mantilla you can get out your white duck trousers and tie red cheese cloth around your middle. If Paddy's pig were here he'd be more Spanish than Irish tonight. Then of course there is considerable latitude. If you would rather be a Mayan noble see Doc Morley and learn how to turn egg beaters into earrings and pie tins into armor. If you want to be a bad man get the forty-four from under the mattress, find a neck cloth and a big hat and join the forces of Billy, the Kid.

Speaking of Billy the Kid, the public ought to know that nothing but a miracle will prevent the hanging of one of our most promising young citizens on La Fonda roof tomorrow night. It is hoped to avert all tragedies but it's hard to tell what will happen when leading citizens turn desperado, and genteel creatures like Margaret, Cissie and Jane become dance hall sirens.

A three ringed circus won't have anything on the plaza shows tomorrow night. Singing and dancing, plays and stunts, burlesques and drama and trovadores contests. There will be new groups and single stars. See your program and pick your places.

FRIDAY, SEPTEMBER 3, 1926: BONFIRE AND BAILE TONIGHT; COUNTY FAIR OPEN TODAY. Plaza Beautifully Decorated for Pasatiempo; Elaborate Spanish Program Saturday Night; Dancers Tonight Should Wear Old Native Costumes; Parade, Bull Fight, Saturday.

El Pasatiempo has started.

The Plaza is gorgeously decorated, the county fair is open this afternoon, Zozobra, El Rey de los Diablos, better known as Old Man Gloom, will be burned in effigy at the city hall grounds at 8:00 p. m. tonight and the big Spanish baile at the Armory will also be held at 9:00 o'clock tonight.

The county fair will be open at 8:30 Saturday.

Isidore Armijo will act as auctioneer at 9:30.

The Gallo Race will happen on Lincoln Ave., at 10:00 a. m.

The Burro Parade on the Plaza at 10:00 a. m.

The Burro Race at 11:00 a. m., on the Plaza.

The wood-loading contest at 11:30 a. m., Lincoln Ave.

The Band plays in the Plaza at 1:00 p. m.

The Hysterical Pageant leaves St. Michael's College grounds via Manhattan Ave., at 2:30 p. m., and comes down town, around the Plaza, down San Francisco to Galisteo, thence to Water to Don Gaspar to Alameda to College and back.

Bull Fight at College grounds at 4:00 p. m., in charge of Martin Gardesky.

Carnival on Plaza starts 7:30 p. m.; Spanish competitive entertainment stunts at 8:00 to 9:30 p. m.; Virginia Reel and street dancing follow.

SATURDAY, SEPTEMBER 4, 1926: [*Under two-column cut of "The Santa Fe Kid."*] PASATIEMPO BAILE CROWDS ARMORY, ZOZOBRA IS BURNED. With Marcy Street a Solid Mass of People for a Block Watching the Obsequies over Zozobra, the Monster Gloom Condemned to Be Burned at the Stake, and the Armory Packed to the Doors at the Gran Baile del Pasatiempo Last Night, the Opening Night of the Carnival Was All That Could Be Desired.

Following vespers at the Cathedral, a long procession headed by the Conquistadores' Band marched to the vacant space back of the city hall, where Zozobra, a hideous effigy 20 feet high, produced by the magic wand of Will Shuster, stood in ghastly silence illuminated by weird green fires. While the band played a funeral march, a group of Kiwanians in black robes and hoods stole around the figure, with four others seated before the green fires. When City Attorney Jack Kennedy on behalf of the absent mayor, solemnly uttered the death sentence of Zozobra, with Isidoro Armijo as interpreter, and fired several revolver shots at the monster, the green fires changed to red, the surrounding ring of bonfires was ignited, red fires blazed at the foot of the figure and shortly a match was applied to its base and leaped into a column of many-colored flames. As it burned the encircling fires blazed brighter, there was a staccato of exploding fireworks from the figure and round about, and throwing off their [*b*]lack robes the specters emerged in gala costume, joining an invading army of bright-hued harlequins with torches in a dance around the fires, as the band struck up "La Cucaracha." Following which the crowd marched back between bonfires lining the streets to the armory and the big baile was on. It brought out the biggest crowd of native merrymakers seen here for years.

OLD-TIME DANCES.

George Armijo, announcer, with a big megaphone called the dances and announced the individual events, and he and Mrs.

Adelina Otero Warren, the latter in a beautiful old-fashioned costume of Spanish colonial days, led off with a graceful polka. Spanish comedians kept the crowd in a roar of laughter while Adolfo Camillo's orchestra of accordeon [*sic*], drum, guitars and violin played old tunes for the old dances. After an hour the crowd around the edge of the hall pressed in so closely it was impossible to dance. Everybody, however, had a gorgeous good time and Dan Ortiz and Brison Yontz, in charge of the baile, received many encomiums. By courtesy of Paul Walter of the Museum staff the patio of the Old Palace was thrown open, and there and in the Plaza the Kiwanis Cantadoes [*sic*] with a group of Spanish trovadores and Misses Katherine Van Stone and Mary Von Nyvenheim singing and playing guitars, furnished a share of the musical entertainment.

The ballroom afforded a spectacle picturesque and animated, and the gente had the time of its life.

MORNING PROGRAM.

The Plaza with its brilliant decorations was a beautiful sight again this morning, El Dia de Los Burros, and although the man in charge of the burro events was unexpectedly absent, Ike Alarid, George Armijo, John Conway and others took charge, and the burro parade and races, while only a few burros appeared, furnished a lot of fun. The mounted mayordomo [*sic*] on prancing chargers with silver harness, and wearing gorgeous colored shirts, clanking spurs and big sombreros, together with Ashley Pond's mounted Pasatiempolice, added to the colorfulness of the scene.

COUNTY FAIR.

As in the case of the burro revue, the short time of preparation made it impossible to have many exhibits of fruit and vegetables, but those present were very fine, and County Agent Ramirez, in charge, believes the foundation has been laid for an exhibit next year which will be a whiz. Isidoro Armijo acted as auctioneer of some of the exhibits and the judges inspected them to decide upon the prize winners, which will be announced later.

A CHILDREN'S FETE.

The morning program around the Plaza developed into a children's fete, with hundreds of urchins and little girls, Spanish and Anglo, crowding around the burros and hooting and yelling frantically as the races were put on. The wood-loading contest in front of the Palace was the premier morning event, causing much excitement as the judges held their watches on the men expertly piling fuel on the wondering burro used as the vehicle of the prize-seekers.

The gallo race around the federal grounds was another exciting event. George Armijo kept up a running fire of wheezes as he announced the various events and their results which kept the crowd in a joyful humor.

AFTERNOON.

The afternoon program was the main works, with the grand Hysterical Pageant and bull fight as centers of interest. A full account of these epochal events will appear in Monday's paper.

CHILDREN'S SHOW.

The Children's Pet Stock show held yesterday in front of the Palace in charge of Miss Alison Sommerville, was a complete success, and one of the interesting events of the festival. All the kids got prizes and the full list of entries will be published later.

TUESDAY, SEPTEMBER 7, 1926: FEARFUL AND WONDERFUL SIGHTS APPEAR IN HYSTERICAL PAGEANT OF EL PASATIEMPO. Carnival Procession Generally Voted Most Astonishing to Date; Thousands Make Merry at Plaza Carnival Saturday.

That the Hysterical pageant of El Pasatiempo Saturday was the most hysterical in history was unanimously voted by the crowd who witnessed the big feature of the carnival. The bizarre, the comic, the grotesque, the beautiful, had full sway and there were more laughs to the lineal foot in the long and colorful procession than one could imagine possible. Following the parade, the scene at the College grounds was a striking one, the grandstand packed full of people, hundreds flocked on the field, a complete ring of automobiles all the way round in a gigantic circle, and the parade participants in a grand and gorgeous review in the arena between.

Considerable excitement was caused and Gus Baumann, maker of the bull nearly fainted when Matador George Armijo mounted on a big black mare started to drag the bull-carcass off the field and the mare commenced pitching and kicking the bull. The latter was seriously injured but can be repaired.

NIGHT CARNIVAL.

The Saturday night Plaza carnival presented a gay and animated scene, colored lights in the Plaza, illuminating the many-colored banners, Spanish dancing and singing by Jose D. Sena's and Miss Velasquez' pupils on raised platform and the bandstand, where Miss Angela Garcia sang dramatically La Paloma and Chaparrita and a number of other Spanish songs. The band played all afternoon and evening and never covered itself with greater glory. Hundreds joined in the street dancing.

Thomas Wood Stevens and troupe put on a spectacular melodrama on the roof of La Fonda, depicting hair-raising adventures in the career of Billy the Kid. . . .

Many declared the crowd in the Plaza largest ever assembled there. There was no disorder of any kind all through the Pasatiempo and so far as can be learned there was no drunkenness, and everybody was happy. Securing a list of all participants in the parade is a difficult job, as there were several hundred, but the New Mexican will attempt to give a complete resume of the hysteria tomorrow.

PRIZE WINNERS.

There was some delay today in securing a list of the prize winners and these also will be published tomorrow.

TUESDAY, SEPTEMBER 7, 1926: [*Editorial.*] EL PASATIEMPO.

El Pasatiempo de la Gente is generally agreed to have been the most brilliant and picturesque carnival Santa Fe has seen. Sponsored by the Old Santa Fe Association and its expenses chiefly underwritten by members of that organization, it was arranged as an opportunity for the Spanish speaking people of Santa Fe and the nearby plazas to hold their own fiesta. How eagerly they accepted the opportunity and with what enthusiasm they put it over is history. How the business men of Santa Fe appreciate it was [*sic*] shown by their generous response when it was announced that donations for prizes and expenses would be gratefully received. The Pasatiempo demonstrated again moreover that the stimulus of such an occasion gets results out of the unique cosmopolitan Anglo population of Santa Fe that can't be duplicated anywhere else in America. Globe-trotters said Saturday they had never seen anything to compare with El Pasatiempo at home or abroad, not excepting the New Orleans Mardi-gras, in beauty, fantasy, art, cleverness, in humor and delightful co-operation, in spontaneity and color and sheer picturesqueness.

It seems to us this impromptu carnival, done with only two weeks preparation, proved more strikingly than ever before the pricelessness of the treasure of Spanish culture here. The rare, quaint, old costumes of the grandmothers; the graceful old dances, the beautiful mantillas and shawls, the haunting old melodies, the happy children in their bright-hued finery, the white haired women in black shawls watching with shining eyes the merrymaking of the young people; candles burning on house-tops, gay banners in the sunshine, children shrieking at a burro race, heirloom silver bridles clanking on prancing steeds, grotesquerie and fun—the picture is one that lingers, and to draw and keep the community together, nothing else has such a magic influence as making merry together.

Santa Feans know and understand each other better as a result of El Pasatiempo. All Santa Fe is happier for the two weeks of work and the two days of play, and we have found out a whole lot about the values in other folks. We believe El Pasatiempo de la Gente was a complete expression of the genius of Santa Fe, and the exemplification of those things which make life so rich and well worth living here.

SEPTEMBER 15, 1926:   SANTA FE GOES OFF RAILROAD OCTOBER FIRST.

An epochal event will befall Santa Fe on October first.

The Ancient City will no longer be on the railroad.

This is in a manner of speaking, as freight will still travel in increasing quantities over the Lamy branch, and no tracks will be uprooted. But all passenger, mail and baggage service will be via Harveycars [*busses*] to Lamy.

OCTOBER 12, 1927: ARTISTS OBJECT, STATUE IS FORFEITED; MRS. AUSTIN, APPLEGATE PROTEST.

The Santa Fe Associated Press correspondent sends out the following tale of the statue that didn't stop in Santa Fe:

Its colony of artists protested in the name of art and Santa Fe lost a $10,000 statue which was to be presented to it as a gift.

The Daughters of the American Revolution are placing a number of statues called "Madonna of the Trail" to mark national old trails across the continent. The one proposed to be erected here was to mark the Santa Fe Trail, of which Santa Fe was the terminal.

Mrs. Mary Austin, writer, and Frank Applegate, artist, were among those who appeared before the D. A. R. committee here when Santa Fe presented its claims for the monument. Applegate said Santa Fe artists did not want it.

In a report made by J. D. De Huff, Chamber of Commerce secretary, who attended the meeting, he said in part:

"Mr. Applegate made a statement something to the effect that he had canvassed all the artists and writers in Santa Fe and that none of them wanted the monument here, that it was not artistic, and Santa Fe did not want something unloaded on it that it didn't want.

"Mrs. Austin made a few remarks, the tenor of which was that the so-called Pioneer Woman monument did not represent the real pioneers of this region at all, that the real pioneers were Spanish people and that they had not been consulted and were not represented at all.

"Mrs. Moss (member of the D. A. R. committee) was infuriated with the tenor of Mr. Applegate's remarks and asked him to leave the room or make an apology. He left the room.

"The actual members of the deciding committee then went into executive session and the vote was taken, resulting in a vote of five to two, in favor of Albuquerque."

OCTOBER 18, 1927: LET US FORGET IT.

A communication in today's paper from Mary Austin, the novelist, lends color to the well-known maxim that no two people can see a dog-fight and relate the same version of the facts. Not that we would by any manner of means compare the late session on the lamented D. A. R. statue to a dog fight, but that is the saying.

Mrs. Austin, than for whom we have greater regard for none, feels that instead of any discourtesy on her part or that of Frank Applegate at the conference on the statue, the discourtesy was on the part of the D. A. R. lady and the Chamber of Commerce, which she feels, also, is stupid and makes Santa Fe ridiculous. Mr. Applegate, also an esteemed citizen, has a communication which will be published tomorrow, and if we may be allowed to intervene with a few words, we hope the controversy will end with Frank's letter tomorrow, which is neither libelous nor inflammatory.

May we not first say that the gentlemen of the Chamber of Commerce are not, as alleged, stupid nor do they make Santa Fe ridiculous; as far as that is concerned many of us occasionally do that. Let us add our conviction that the Chamber of Commerce is a very intelligent and representative body of men with a secretary who is an excellent spokesman for our fair city.

This being said, let us further opine that here we have excellent citizens and citizenesses on both sides the fence, none of whom we regard as prevaricators, and all of whose motives and sincerity are above question.

Thus we conclude that there has been an honest misunderstanding; we all differ from one another in temperament and glory, and even the stars vary in magnitude. It is quite possible that the matter of a statue of the Pioneer Mama is much more serious to the artistic temperament than to the common or garden temperament of the casual habitant of the Land of Little Brain.[3]

[3] *The Land of Little Rain* is one of Mary Austin's best known works.

If the statue were erected as per schedule, the artists might perchance have even had a trifle of fun with it, unbeknownst to the D. A. R., though in any case we could never approve painting it up the way some local Old Master decorated Nate Salmon's well-known Assyrian lions. Nor is this discussion to be repeated to the Revolutionary Daughters—a splendid, fine patriotic organization, my dears, which as such could not possibly imagine it was discourteous in having these statues erected along the Trail. Here being another Point of View to be included in our perspective. There are all kinds of people in the world and twice that many varieties in Old Santa Fe.

We fear that just today, neither Mary nor Mac will accept the olive branch which the editor has the temerity to wave. If they enquire how the stones get in the olives, we can only respond, What is your idea in bringing that up? But eventually with a legal publication every Tuesday for a period of two months in advance and service on all parties concerned, we may form the habit of having the debate before the night of the dance and avoiding our public misunderstandings. We can't make sculptors out of Charley Proebstel and Dad Kaune, so it looks as if we would have to make a special drive to get more artists in the Chamber of Commerce.

When the smoke clears away, we are going to discuss seriously getting up to date with an advisory board of the best qualified people in the town to work with the city council on skyscrapers, trees, architecture, statuary offenses, and city beautification in general. This will be an unobtrusive way of having the artistic temperament seep through us lowbrows. Town growth is accelerating so fast it is going to get away from us if we don't get together, business man and painter, architect and grocer, and take it in hand with a vision of the Santa Fe that is going to be or not be 20 years hence.

DECEMBER 29, 1927:   CUTTING APPOINTED U. S. SENATOR.

Bronson Cutting of Santa Fe is the New United States senator from New Mexico to succeed the late Senator A. A. Jones.

Santa Fe

Governor R. C. Dillon signed the appointment and commission at 10 a.m. today in the executive office in the presence of a small group of people.

After making the appointment the governor issued the following statment:

"I appointed Col. Cutting to the United States senatorship because he had an overwhelming and statewide indorsement from citizens in every walk of life. In addition to this a great majority of the ex-service men backed him. Col. Cutting at no time made application for the place and the appointment was made on popular demand.

"I consider Col. Cutting admirably qualified for this distinguished post and am convinced that he will be able to give New Mexico high class and effective service in the national congress.

R. C. Dillon."

Old-timers who were politicos of importance in the 1920's have told me that Cutting was appointed to the Senate because it was expected that he would contribute generously to the Republican party and that the party's big wheels believed him a playboy whom it would be easy for experienced, hard-bitten politicians to manipulate.

Cutting's title of colonel came from one of those political, half-humorous appointments to a previous governor's staff. He had ingratiated himself with the American Legion, however, and had built up an important reputation as a great friend of the Spanish-American people. The politicos were soon to find that they had caught themselves a tartar.

AUGUST 9, 1928:   TURQUOISE TRAIL.

Alice Corbin's long anticipated "Turquoise Trail; An Anthology of New Mexico Poetry" (Houghton-Mifflin, $2.00) has appeared on the news stands—a treasure-trove housed in turquoise blue, all the beauty and lure of the land voiced by those fortunate ones who can express what the rest of us feel.

Alice Corbin has apparently overlooked none of them. Thirty-seven are represented in the book and every one who has come and fallen under the spell, or has felt it from afar, will find the volume beyond the price. The name is inspired by that Turquoise Trail over which the Spaniards—including Villagra, the Homer who made of New Mexico a poetical First Frontier, came from Mexico to New Mexico, and to the still-producing mines of the sky-blue gem at Santa Fe's door.

The author uses "New Mexico" in its full and wide regional personality significance of Spanish exploration days, the old province of Nuevo Mexico, that took in California, Arizona and Texas and fringes of northern states. "It is now," she says, "however, only in New Mexico and particularly in the region about Santa Fe, where time has so largely stood still, that this older meaning of the word persists; and it is only here indeed that one still finds the essence of the original province."

The first poets of New Mexico, she tells us, are the Indians; their poetic tradition reaches back into nebulous antiquity, but their orally transmitted poetry is a "vital, contemporary expression of the soul." On the common ground of poetry the living Indian poets and the Anglo-American poets of New Mexico now meet in friendly contact."

"Atmospherically New Mexico is still a remote outpost and survival of the transplanted Golden Age of Spain in the United States."

A third source is the cowboy lyrics. Summing up she says that "the subliminal influences of soil and atmosphere inevitably affect the expression of any poet or artist who consciously or unconsciously is submerged in a new environment, particularly when that environment is as strange as it is new, as liberating as it is primal."

The Turquoise Trail *still stands up as a fine collection of poetry and a most satisfactory poetic statement of New Mexico. It is interesting to note the names of famous contributors, most of whom came to Santa Fe because of Alice Corbin Henderson— Witter Bynner, John Gould Fletcher, John Galsworthy, Vachel Lindsay, Edgar Lee Masters, and Carl Sandburg, to mention only a few, the last three of whom had begun their careers under Mrs. Henderson's encouragement. D. H. Lawrence, also represented, was brought to New Mexico by Mable Dodge Luhan, as everyone knows. Mary Austin, characteristically, arrived entirely under her own steam, as did Willa Cather.*

DECEMBER 31, 1928: A SIGNIFICANT MOVEMENT.

The announcement of Mr. John D. Rockefeller's gift of a total of $270,000 to the Laboratory of Anthropology for Santa Fe is the most important that has been made for many years in New Mexico.

We are confident that his further conditional gifts will be made; that the "probationary period" of the great scientific enterprise will be much more than satisfactory, and that its growth in usefulness to society will go hand in hand with a growth in financial resources that will make it the outstanding institution of its kind in America.

Certainly no more desirable accession to Santa Fe could be conceived. Nothing could more firmly fix Santa Fe's fame as the seat of a culture, nor be more potent to help guide this capital's development along the proper lines, and bring the most desirable kind of people, interested in Santa Fe's one greatest resource.

One need hardly refer to the fact that our solid growth as a unique city has been due to the lure of the story of pre-historic, and historic man and his works in the American Southwest; to our museums and Indians, our archaeological treasures, our remains of ancient cities, the architecture and handicraft of red men and Spanish-colonials, the cliff homes that once teemed with a race now vanished.

The scientific world, as represented in great universities and museums, is now saying: Let Us Go to Santa Fe to Study Man; to the place where his most fascinating story is to be learned, where the ruins of his handiwork stand, where there is the most remarkable survival of the primitive; study him where he lived in antiquity, study him amid his own environment.

This to us is the significant meaning of this Laboratory enterprise, which holds promise of in reality reversing the present order, so that New Mexico and the Southwest will no longer be carried off to the scientific student and investigator, but he will come here to probe into their mysteries. The possibilities of such a movement are unbounded. Its benefits will accrue to every existing agency in the Southwest, notably our present museums and educational institutions, in particular the University of New Mexico and the State Museum, which so recently effected a co-operative arrangement with the same end in view—Southwestern scientific research and education in the Southwest, on the ground.

It is unnecessary to stress the importance of the action of America's greatest philanthropist in placing the stamp of his approval on this whole movement.

His estimate of its importance is worthy the serious thought of the people of New Mexico, in their support of their own agencies engaged in this kind of work.

Old bones, in sooth, are an asset, not merely playthings for highbrows or "nut professors." There is no limit to our resources of this kind, no limit, save that of our own vision, on their exploitation.

The initial impetus leading to the founding of the Laboratory of Anthropology came from the Indian Arts Fund, a local group in which artists and "yearners" were important. They had a concept of a dynamic institution with, among other things, a positive program in support of contemporary Indian arts.

The Laboratory was built and stands as the next important milestone after the Art Museum and the first portion of the new La Fonda in establishing the new-old Santa Fe style. The architect was John Gaw Meem, who became the outstanding exponent and elaborator of that style. Avoiding the hodgepodge effect of the two earlier buildings, he made sound use of the New Mexico variant of Spanish mission design, producing a structure that is handsome, traditional, yet free of the effect of false antiquity. He was particularly successful in developing the pattern of a number of simple planes, which is one of the most interesting elements of the old New Mexican architecture. Once again hollow tile was used, and once again, as in the case of the new museum, care was taken to achieve an effect of irregularity.

From the Laboratory came a number of excellent publications, but it turned away from the original inspiration in favor of a rather dry type of anthropological study with a highly local point of view. It seemed to suffer from the lack of a staff that had received broad formal training in the discipline, and at the same time it kept the "amateurish" Indian Arts Fund group at arm's length.

The Rockefeller contribution diminished yearly, in the anticipation that the Laboratory would find increasing support from other sources. This it failed to do, and after lingering on into the 1950's as an independent institution, it finally was absorbed into Santa Fe's remarkable system of state museums. Under state control, it continues as a sound, unexciting research institution.

In 1929 occurred the death, at Taos, of Arthur R. Manby, who may or may not have been murdered. The story that resulted is so bizarre as to merit the running at this point of a number of selections from the New Mexican *for that year and 1930, grouped together. These selections do not clearly bring out the fact that Manby was a British subject and that the renewed official interest in his death was stimulated by representations from Britain to our State Department.*

John Young-Hunter, whose house was robbed and burned, happened also to have been English. He continued as a member of the Taos art colony until his death some twenty-five years later. He was noted for his rather illustration-like, romantic paintings of Indians, many of which were reproduced and distributed by the Santa Fe Railway.

Manby's body was found on July 3. There was no paper on the Fourth, so that the first notice appeared on July 5, on page five.

JULY 5, 1929:   FIND MANBY DIED FROM NATURAL CAUSE. Head Pulled off Body by His Dog, Left in House Three Days without Food. CORONER'S INQUEST BLASTS MURDER THEORY.

Taos, N. M., July 5 (AP)—Excitement here over the finding

of the decapitated body of A. R. Manby of Taos ebbed today with the announcement of the verdict of the coroner's jury that Manby had died from natural causes, and that the body had been decapitated by his dog which was locked in a room with the body for three days without food.

With the arrival here today of J. B. Manby, a brother, of Malta, Colo., a nephew and brother-in-law, the case turned to probate court this afternoon where a hearing was conducted for the appointment of a temporary administrator to open Manby's private safe and look into his papers.

Manby, according to medical testimony at the inquest, was 70 years old and had been in ill health for some time. The room in which the decomposed body was found was heavily screened and the doors were hooked from the inside.

FAILED TO GET "BALM."

One claim against Manby's estate if any is disclosed is that of Miss Margaret Waddell, now living some place in California, who several years ago sued Manby for $25,000 breach of promise. The suit was tried in Santa Fe and she was awarded a judgment of $12,000 which she has never been able to collect. Only recently she brought a new action in federal court here in an attempt to collect the money.

Manby was an Englishman and Miss Waddell came to the United States from Scotland. During the breach of promise suit, the late A. B. Renehan of Santa Fe who represented her described her as a "Scotch lassie, strong of mind and body."

FLESH EATEN OFF.

Because the body was decapitated, the Taos police officials first believed that Manby had been slain. The medical testimony, however, was that the dog had torn the head from the body for food. All of the flesh had been eaten from the head. The decomposed state of the body prevented a thorough medical examination, but no instruments, vials or weapons were found which would lend credence to a suicide theory, and the fact that Manby had locked himself in his room disposed of the belief that he had been attacked by some other person.

WELL KNOWN HERE.

A. R. Manby—such was his name and not "J. R. Mamby," as published in morning newspapers—was well known in Santa Fe. He had lived for decades as a rancher in Taos, and for years he kept a rather elaborate establishment with several servants, it is said, and entertained many friends not only with his hospitality but with his anecdotes of the "old days" when they visited Taos. He was a neighbor of another great story teller, Dr. T. P. Martin, of Taos. . . .

HAD SERVANTS.

Friends in Santa Fe expressed surprise that Manby could have died alone. He usually had several servants in his household, one an old Indian who worked in his garden, they said. Sometimes, however, they said, he liked to do his own cooking and he may have decided to lead a solitary life for a while.

Mr. Manby had a big house of 15 or 16 rooms. It stands opposite the residence of Bert Phillips, the artist.

Mr. Manby had a dog, a pet, which he kept for years. It is not known, however, whether this is the animal that, according to the verdict of the coroner's jury, attacked his dead master.

Mr. Manby, an Englishman, was an admirer of horses and usually had several about his place.

OF PROMINENT FAMILY.

Coming to this country from Lestershire, Eng., more than 30 years ago, he apparently was of good family. He brought with him some fine tapestries, mahogany furniture and old paintings. He was considered a fair critic of objects of art.

He owned hot springs near Taos and one of his chief ambitions is said to have been to develop them. Victor Morowitz [*Morawetz*], former chairman of the board of directors of the A. T. & S. F., used to go there to take the bath.

A BULL MOOSER.

Mr. Manby at one time took an active part in New Mexico politics, being identified with the Bull Moose movement in 1912.

He is said to have been married twice.

JULY 27, 1929: [*Editorial.*] WHAT IS GOING TO COME OUT OF
THE MANBY MYSTERY?

From all the reports coming out of Taos, and from sketchy exhibits which the New Mexican has seen in connection with the
alleged death of the possibly late A. R. Manby of that place, the
New Mexican is convinced that here is a real mystery, worthy of
the talents of a Sherlock Holmes or a Lecoq, or the pen of Edgar
Allen Poe or E. Phillips Oppenheim.

Apparently there is already a full set of circumstances, replete
with weird and astounding detail, to support almost any theory
one wishes to adopt—murder, suicide, substitution and disappearance, hallucination or esoteric machinations, anything you
like. One cannot help believing that something has been going on
in Taos which when revealed will amaze the world. The mere
surface facts—if any two people can agree even on them—are
incredible. What is known of the life of Manby intrigues the
imagination enormously.

A resident of Taos in a letter to the New Mexican today
demands a real investigation, beginning with exhuming of the
remains and a searching examination and analysis in order to
prove or disprove that this decapitated corpse is that of Manby.
Certainly this at least should be done. As a matter of fact, the
best detective ability available in America would not be wasted
on ferreting out the truth of this baffling mystery, in solving this
dark riddle. Too many things remain inexplicable.

New Mexico is not unused to such mysteries. The Armour case,
which grew, because of the tenacity of a New Mexican reporter,
from a casual news item into one of the most celebrated murder
cases in criminal history, embellished with every imaginable sensational incident and development, is only one of many. Truth is
so much stranger than fiction that the most lurid fiction magazines reject it because their readers won't believe it.

We may be wrong, but we predict in this instance a similar
series of astounding developments.

As the matter now stands, the Taos writer is apparently correct
in saying that everybody is on the quivive with curiosity and specu-

lation except the authorities who should be leaving no stone un-
turned to get at the bottom of this strange case. If possible the
governor might do a public service by turning his official attention
to the matter in whatever way is proper.

FEBRUARY 14, 1930:   NEED OF AN AUTOPSY.

It has been customary in the United States for the coroner to
hold an autopsy or post-mortem wherever there is a suspicion of
mystery concerning a death. It is the custom in many cities and
towns to have the coroner at least view the body of any person
who dies suddenly in the streets.

Manby's death was reported July 3 of last year and there appears to have been ample time in which to make a post-mortem
and naturally the public would like to hear the report in view of
the conflicting rumors concerning the disappearance of the eccentric old Englishman.

WHAT WILL AUTOPSY SHOW?

There are reports that the ferocious police dog severed Manby's
head from his body after Manby had died a natural death at the
age of 80 [*sic*]; that Manby was murdered and his head cut off
with a sharp instrument; and, finally, that Manby is still alive, and
that the body left in the Manby house was not his but a substitute,
with suggestions that it was a body that had been buried and
disinterred. It is easily understood therefore, why people interested in the Manby mystery might like to read the results of
the post-mortem.

There is a rumor that the post-mortem will show that Manby's
head was cut off with some sharp instrument. Such a find would
naturally strengthen the theory that Manby was murdered in his
own home despite the fact that he was old enough and perhaps
sick enough to meet a quiet death at any time.

MARCH 11, 1930:   NOT TOO LATE.

A midwestern newspaper with half a million circulation has
published all the details of the Manby murder mystery, not leaving out of the picture any of the results of the investigation by

Detective Martin, and laying bare a situation which as presented by the Star constitutes a terrific arraignment of justice, law and order in New Mexico.

The NEW MEXICAN with other newspapers has been charged with "trying the Manby case in the newspapers." The NEW MEXICAN, it may be stated here, has been in possession of every line of information printed in the Star story and has withheld the bulk of it from publication in the vain hope that something definite would be done by the constituted authorities, with the evidence or alleged evidence at its disposal many months ago.

It is not entirely too late for New Mexico to make a demonstration of some kind, just because the British government has had to appeal to the federal authorities to get action.

We suggest a preliminary move today. That is to place in the state penitentiary at once for safe-keeping two persons arrested in Taos on the charge of robbery and receiving stolen goods. One of these persons was found in possession of many articles known to have belonged to the late A. R. Manby. A $500 bond in a $10,000 robbery case is hardly adequate.

The limit has been reached if no state action is taken now in view of the Kansas City Star publication, the intervention of the federal government and the arrests made in Taos.

The failure of justice to move so far has done incalculable damage to the reputation of New Mexico in the United States and abroad.

MARCH 12, 1930:   OPEN COURT BATTLE FOR ESTATE OF MANBY. TERECITA IN COURT.

Terecita Ferguson, about 40, a blackhaired, blackeyed little woman with a wary expression, sat at the table with Crist and Pacheco. She wore a black felt hat with a black figure on it, a black plush coat, serge dress, and tan oxfords. She was Arthur Manby's "Princess Terecita" and after his death was elected president of the Colonial Bond and Security company. At present she is under arrest charged with willful possession of property stolen from the Taos home of Mr. and Mrs. John Younghunter [*sic*] of New York.

Likewise in the courtroom was Mrs. Felix Archuleta, a very pleasant rather large woman and well dressed, who operates a restaurant in Taos. She is one of the stockholders of the Colonial Bond and Security company. Outside the rail was John Strongberg, of Taos, an angular western type of fellow with thin face and blonde hair. Also present was Private Detective H. C. Martin of Santa Fe who conducted the initial investigations for Taos county and the state of New Mexico in the Manby decapitation case.

MARCH 17, 1930: MANBY PROBERS BARE HUGE BUNCO SCHEME. VICTIMS TELL OF TERRORIST METHODS USED.

Taos, N. M., March 17 (AP)—Handwriting comparisons were being made today in an attempt to definitely establish that the mysterious "United States Secret Civil Service Society," was a glorified bunco game manipulated by using fictitious persons as officers.

These fictitious characters are "Severino Gutierrez," or "S. G." leader of the S. C. S. to whom the late A. R. Manby and his "Princess Terecita" Ferguson addressed a huge volume of letters, and "Craig Kenneth" who was represented to be one of the organization's great detectives.

CHEETHAM GETS FACTS.

This latest information in the Arthur Manby decapitation case was dug out by Capt. Herbert Cheetham, former secret service operative, who said he has received proof from members of the society that one certain family was buncoed out of $14,000 over a period of three years.

The spell of fear which has closed the lips of certain persons in Taos, Captain Cheetham said, has been broken and the local leaders of this purported society have been revealed as the late A. R. Manby, the Ferguson woman now at liberty under $1,800 bond in connection with the Younghunter [*sic*] and Archuleta robberies; her common-law husband, Carmen Duran, in jail on similar charges in default of $5,100 bond, and George Ferguson, in jail on those charges and also held for highway robbery.

FICTITIOUS PERSONS.

The fictitious Gutierrez was represented to be the head of the "Self-supporting branch" of the society which comprised Wyoming, Colorado, New Mexico and Arizona. No one has ever seen either the alleged Severino Gutierrez or Detective Craig Kenneth, members of the society have told Captain Cheetham.

"We believe beyond doubt," Cheetham said, "that the handwriting of Severino Gutierrez, Craig Kenneth, and one of the members of the Manby-Ferguson circle are the same." There are two other sources of investigation in the case whose findings are the same as those of Cheetham.

"Certain members of the society," Cheetham's informant said, "were called on constantly to pay assessments represented to be the traveling expenses of Severino Gutierrez and the society's detectives, and also to advance loans to designated members of the Taos branch. The organization was represented to be a branch of the United States secret service and the invitation to join appealed to patriotism with the additional promise of untold millions of dollars to be paid by the United States government.

"Meetings were held in the home of Terecita Ferguson," Cheetham was told by this person who attended many of them. "The Taos members sat in one room and it was represented that Gutierrez and other high officers, whose physical appearance was kept secret, were in an adjoining room. Business matters were then placed before the Taos group after which Terecita would go into the adjoining room to talk with the high officers. The Taos members could hear Terecita talking about the business transacted but no one was every heard to answer her. After a few minutes Terecita would return and report on what the high officers desired the 'local members' to do."

JUNE 19, 1930: REQUIESCAT IN PACE.

Two leading and honored citizens of Taos, the Hon. Terecita Ferguson and the Hon. Carmel Duran, are reported peacefully and industriously at work plastering up the residence of the late Arthur Rochfort Manby at Taos.

It will shortly be a year since the deceased was butchered.

We merely mention the present activities of these eminent citizens as analagous or symbolic of the work of Father Time in plastering over the memory of this grisly and unpunished murder. His trowel eventually ought to cover up a lot of evidence. Naturally, perhaps, the authorities regard the healing, oblivion-bringing activities of Fr. T. as something inevitable. Nature taking her gradual and biological course, against which any puny activities of man would be unavailing and futile.

The NEW MEXICAN for some time has been mentioning the affair monthly. For the comfort of the apprehensive we can only say that hereafter we shall probably mention it annually.

Further references will be in the nature of historical allusion, just as one mentions Jefferson Day and Old Home Week. Nor need we conceal the fact from anxious anonymous ears and eyes that we haven't the slightest idea that anything will ever be done to bring the murderers to justice.

JULY 26, 1930: "PRINCESS TERECITA" IS FOUND GUILTY. . . .

Raton, N. M., July 26 (AP)—"Princess Terecita" Ferguson of Taos, N. M. and Manby case note, and her common-law-husband, Carmen Duran, have both been found guilty in connection with the robbery of the studio home of Mr. and Mrs. John Young-Hunter, prominent artists of New York, who spend part of their time at Taos.

Miss Ferguson was found guilty of possessing stolen property late last night 30 minutes after the jury received the case. Duran was convicted of the robbery two days ago. George Ferguson, who also participated in the robbery and burning of the home, turned state's evidence against his aunt and Duran.

The loot from the Young-Hunter home was traced last March to the Ferguson home by Captain Herbert Cheetham, private citizen, where he found the stolen property hidden in the house and buried in boxes and trunks in the orchard, chicken yard and under the back porch. The loot contained nearly 200 articles valued at $10,000.

Duran will now be tried on a charge of arson for setting the Young-Hunter home afire.

The arson charge against Duran was shortly dropped. Nothing more was ever done about Manby's death nor about the Secret Civil Service Society.

OCTOBER 28, 1929: JUSTICE AND MERCY.

The claims of justice have been satisfied in the case of Albert B. Fall.

Never in history has there been a more dramatic, impressive, painful or pathetic spectacle than the conviction of this man, who in his rise and fall achieved more national prominence than any other citizen of New Mexico.

Fall, as thousands of editors and reports have said in the past week, is a crushed, disgraced, broken, enfeebled man, where once he was a commanding, truculent figure. He has been branded by a jury of his peers as receiver of a bribe as a member of the cabinet of the President of the United States; and by the supreme court of the United States, which we are wont to regard as the most august tribunal in the world, as a "faithless, public servant." An appeal is at best a forlorn hope, holding out the prospect of many more months of suspense and mental anguish, a prolonged further ordeal for the defendant, his family and friends. Even a reversal on technical points could not affect the writing of the Moving Finger that the secretary of the interior received $100,000 from a man who stood to benefit by the action of such official and who in truth did become the beneficiary of such an action. This fact in itself is permanent, inescapable and unexplainable.

But fine or imprisonment would add nothing to expiation, already made, material penalty nothing to the spiritual and mental punishment Fall has received and which has been shared to the dregs by his devoted family. The quality of mercy is not strained, and the government of the United States needs no pound of flesh.

Justice can ill afford to become vengeful. A prison sentence for this defendant would be brutal.

Hysterical denunciation of the court and jury by the defense may be regarded tolerantly, in view of the circumstances. As to the court's instructions, the record as published shows that counsel on both sides agreed to the instructions, 13 of them drawn up by the defense and 15 by the prosecution. As to the verdict, the jurors fought it out for hours among themselves before an unanimous vote was polled. In a country where the legal system gives the defendant always the best of it, this was beyond dispute a fair trial, and the jurors, whose sympathy for Fall is shown in their unanimous recommendation of mercy, are entitled to praise for doing their duty despite that sympathy.

It seems to us that A. B. Fall has squared his account. On his shoulders fell a heavier load of official punishment than on those of any other member of the ill-fated Harding political group, and in a sense he is the scapegoat. He has paid his shot, and he and his family should have the boon of privacy and peace. We are sure the people of New Mexico will treat him with friendliness and respect, and let the dead past lie buried. We leave it to those who are pure and unspotted of conscience and conduct to cast the first stone.

Fall was sent to prison and served his time—New Mexico's first cabinet officer and the first such officer to wind up in the federal pen.

The following excerpts are of interest chiefly for the profound change they illustrate in the attitude, not only of the New Mexican, *but of the nation generally, toward Mexico and her presidents. Ortiz y Rubio's visit across the border was also an important first.*

On January 8 a news story appeared at the bottom of page one concerning the Governor's train ride with the Mexican President-elect and the presentation to the latter at the Belen stop of a scroll containing greetings from the Mexican colony of Albuquerque and a "floral offering" to his wife by a committee of New Mexico women. This must have been written before the events but was presented as a report.

JANUARY 9, 1930: SENIOR RUBIO AND PARTY MEET ACCLAIM IN CROSS-STATE TRIP; BOND OF FRIENDSHIP SEALED. Reception Extends throughout Journey; Culminates with Crowd of 2,000 People in Belen; Governor Introduces Famous Visitor to Waiting Throngs; Mexicans Deeply Touched at Sight of Rio Grande; Exchange Gifts with Governor; Ask Endless Questions about Spanish Colonies; Deeply Interested.

(By Dana Johnson.)

Pascual Ortiz y Rubio, a dignified, attractive, polished gentleman apparently in the early sixties, and one who on February fifth next will become the president of the Republic of Mexico, made a fast friend of New Mexico with a smile yesterday. He was the first Mexican executive to make a formal good-will tour of New Mexico.

On the other hand, the distinguished visitor, who assumes an office next month which he terms, with a shake of the head, "muy dificil," spent in New Mexico yesterday one of the happiest days of his American journey. And this has been a journey marked by a continued series of ovations and the highest honors the United States can tender such a visitor.

The president was aided in no small degree in the splendid impression he made by the graces of his charming black-eyed wife . . . ; by the irresistible smiles of his beautiful children . . . ; and his nephew . . . , a slender youth. . . .

FUN AT VAUGHN.

. . . There the visitors amused themselves walking up and down the platform with the governor [*Dillon of New Mexico*] and engaging in a vigorous snow-ball fight which caused much excitement. . . .

SCROLL FROM THE COLONY.

Manuel Garcia . . . presented to Sr. Rubio a scroll bearing greetings from the Mexican colony in Albuquerque, with a basket of flowers for the presidente's [*sic*] "esposa". . . .

LADY CORONEL UNUSUAL.

. . . The feminine contingent was much intrigued to meet and talk in Spanish with a "mujer coronel"—such is unknown in Mexico as yet—Mrs. Otero-Warren, wearing her insignia of rank. . . .

The president and party were much pleased to be able to converse in Spanish with Governor Dillon, and gazed with great interest upon the village of Encino, scene of the halcyon days of the state executive, who told them about his experience with "borregos" and pointed out his store. The visitors were likewise interested to find many Spaniards and Basques in the groups which greeted the train in the Encino country. . . .

JANUARY 13, 1930:   TWO SANTA FEANS ARE ON THE "NATION'S" HONOR ROLL FOR YEAR 1929.

"The Nation," famous high-brow magazine, pays little old Santa Fe a signal honor, placing the names of two of its residents on its "honor roll" for 1929.

The Santa Feans thus honored are:

Evelyn Scott for her book "The Wave", described as a great novel about the Civil war.

U. S. Senator Bronson Cutting, for his public service in battling against the present system of letting government clerks tell Americans what they may read.

Senator Cutting led the fight against an extreme provision for the censorship of imported books, included in the pending tariff bill by Senator Reed Smoot of Utah. This battle did much to make Cutting's national reputation and to establish him in the group of progressive Republican senators.

JANUARY 24, 1930:   LABORATORY OF ANTHROPOLOGY FIGHTS EROSION, POT-HUNTERS.

Clearing house for all institutions studying the records of man in this country, the Laboratory of Anthropology at Santa Fe is starting immediately in an energetic fight against the depredations of progress and nature, to map and save as far as possible the hundreds of surviving Indian habitations of antiquity, says a bulletin issued by the laboratory, as follows:

Gifts of $155,000 to hasten research in the vanishing traces of American Indian life, now a race against time, are announced by the Trustees of the new Laboratory of Anthropology at Santa Fe.

FEBRUARY 4, 1930:   LAUGHING HORSE FEELING ITS OATS; WILL HA-HA BOOK CENSORSHIP IDEA.

"The Laughing Horse", much talked of but slightly dilatory Journal of the southwest, will publish a special issue on the subject of censorship before the end of February, it was announced today, much to everybody's surprise. There has not been an issue of the Horse since last fall at Fiesta time, but since the publication of this magazine has become annual, instead of quarterly, as announced, literary circles are aghast at this premature effort, especially in view of the fact that a spring issue is also forecasted [*sic*].

The question is: Can local talent stand the strain? With so many members of the literary colony lecturing in the east or wintering in Mexico and California, where is the material coming from? But the question will probably be answered soon.

The censorship issue, according to the editor, is being rushed for immediate publication because of the timely element involved —the censorship clause in the tariff bill being a vital controversy in the United States senate which will probably come up for a deciding vote within the next few weeks. This issue of the Horse is of course a New Mexico gesture in support of Senator Cutting who has been responsible for the revival of the question in congress and who is making such a laudable fight for a sensible revision of the present law.

A few of the contributors who have already been announced include many local people: Margaret Larkin, Cyril Kay-Scott, Mabel Dodge Luhan, Witter Bynner, Mary Austin, Harry Mera, Andrew Dasburg, Harry Behn, and Ward Lockwood of Taos; and other famous names on the list include Will Irwin, Alfred A. Knopf, New York publisher, Henry Goddard Leach, editor of the Forum, Arthur Davison Ficke, and many others.

Santa Fe

Willard, better known as "Spud," Johnson is a poet now estab-
lished in Taos. His early reputation was won by his book, Hori-
zontal Yellow. *His erratic* Laughing Horse *was to be found, to my*
personal knowledge, on art colony tables as far away as New Or-
leans. He now gets it out weekly as a supplement to El Crepusculo,
the Taos newspaper. The special issue described above drew con-
siderable attention.

APRIL 1, 1930: BE FRANK.

"Is your complexion natural, or acquired?"

"Are you true to your husband? (or wife?)"

"When did you quit having birthdays?"

"Do you buy of chain stores, or home-owned?"

"Do you use your husband's safety razor without asking permission?"

Answer all questions politely and frankly when the census man
comes around. He is starting out today, if he can get time off from
the election. Do not regard it as superfluous or silly when the
enumerator inquires whether or not your grandmother knew how
to skate.

Question number seven is "what is your sex?" Reply to this
honestly, please, and do not attempt to deceive the government.

As to your relationship to your family, if you are not related to
it, say so. You might as well be candid about these matters.

JULY 30, 1930: NON-INDIAN COMPENSATION MAY BE PUT UP TO
CONGRESS; PUEBLO BOARD TO END WORK.

The Pueblo lands board, created by an act of Congress in 1924
to clear up a 300-year-old controversy over title to Pueblo Indian
land, will conclude its labors within the next two or three months.

Its record will be unique in that it will go into history as a government commission that finished its job in the allotted or expected time—and one of the few that has actually completed the
work assigned it.

Its most important final act will be to recommend to the Secre-

324

tary of the Interior, who will pass it on to Congress, a plan for reimbursing the non-Indian claimants, in the majority of cases Spanish-speaking settlers, who have lost title to land held in good faith. The lands board act provides for this tentatively but an act of Congress will be required. This means possibly as much as $100,000 will be distributed among non-Indians in the Pueblo county of New Mexico.

The Pueblo lands board has finished up its regular reports, after an immense amount of detailed labor, on all but Pojoaque and Pecos pueblos, neither of which now has remaining inhabitants. These reports will be filed shortly. . . .

Entrusted by Congress with the work of clarifying the title controversy, dating back to the times of the Spanish conquerors, the board tackled a herculean job. It entailed minute surveys, involving tracts of land of all sizes, shapes and degrees of obscurity of ownership, endless complicated maps, plats and descriptions, laborious field work, voluminous evidence, lengthy hearings, and accumulation of a huge mass of data. Abstracting was a monumental undertaking; some deeds go back to 1540. The work has covered the land tangles about the pueblos of Laguna, Isleta, Santo Domingo, Sandia, Zia, Santa Ana, Jemez, Cochiti, San Ildefonso, Santa Clara, Tesuque, San Juan, Taos, Picuris, Nambe, Pojoaque, Acoma, San Felipe and Pecos.

AUGUST 7, 1930: OVER 200 HEAR SOUTHWEST POETS AT M'COMB HACIENDA; INDIAN WELFARE BENEFIT.

Thirteen failed to prove a hoodoo at the McComb residence on the Alameda yesterday afternoon when that many southwestern poets read selections from their repertoires for the interest and pleasure of a crowd of over 200 people, which filled the large living room and overflowed into the Green Garden and the stone-flagged placita, as well as into other rooms. No more delightful nor fully Santa Fe-flavored affair has occurred in town for a long time.

The "Poets' Round-up" was for the benefit of the New Mexico Association on Indian Affairs, a dollar admission was charged at the corral gate and exactly $212 in receipts was reported by Mrs.

Francis Proctor, treasurer. The event was entirely western in atmosphere. Miss McKittrick, chairman of the association in range togs had charge of the door to the "chute" and announced the various outlaws as they were successively admitted into the arena, at the west end of the living room. Her introductions, in cowboy lingo, were most clever and witty. The performers wore sombreros, chaps, spurs, boots, brilliant blouses, overalls, neckerchiefs or Indian trappings. Some were "bawn and bred on this here range," some were "bad actors," others were wandering riders from afar. Their joint product constituted an impressive and most enjoyable anthology of southwestern verse, some of it by writers of national fame.

Spud Johnson, supposed to break the hoodoo, regrettably failed to make conections with the party. The others and their offerings were:

Ina Sizer Cassidy—The Red Man's Altar, The Warrior's Invocation, The Valley of Nar-Su-Sa.

Earl Scott—The Haunted Rider, Chiquita, Boys, She's West.

Peggy Pond Church—Admonition (her famous Santa Fe poem), Old House, Tourist, Burros, At the Cloud's Edge, If I Had a Young Son.

Mary Austin—Western Magic, Black Beetle, Dead Water, Santa Doucelina (from The Children Sing in the Far West).

Witter Bynner—Rain at Cochiti.

Langdon Mitchell—I am the Monk Voltramos (from the German), Farewell to the Court (from the French), Deor's Lament (from the Saxon).

Leonora Curtin, II—Mesa Verde, Eloquence of Wind, Kiva, Navajo.

E. Dana Johnson—Hiawatha, With Apologies.

Alice Corbin—Three Men Entered the Desert Alone, Juan Quintana, Cundiyo, Essential Wish.

Gladys Campbell—Not With Our Hearts, Remembered Landing, Prairie River, Without Gift. (As she was a visitor, one may discriminate and say her poems were among the most pleasing heard at the roundup.)

Maurice Lesemann—Sheepherders.

Evelyn Scott—The Owl.

Margaret Larkin—She sang, with guitar accompaniment, two thrilling plaintive old songs of the range, My Love Is a Rider and the Chisholm Trail.

Refreshments were served the throng in the dining room, Mrs. McComb being assisted chiefly by Misses Isabel and Mary Eckles.

Over 100 cars were parked on the grounds during the party, in charge of an efficient corps of attendants. The poets had a private corral from which they were released into and out of the chutes. It rained during the round-up but failed to dampen the enthusiasm.

Margaret Larkin was of valuable assistance as press agent for the affair.

AUGUST 27, 1930:   RENAISSANCE OF THE SPANISH COLONIAL ARTS AND CRAFTS REMARKABLE; SHOP PILED HIGH.

Surprise is the general reaction to the display of Spanish hand work in the Sena plaza. Since the first of May, when the shop of the Spanish Arts opened, new workers have been bringing in their hand-made articles, until now the shop is brimming with blankets, carvings, embroideries, furniture and many other things.

Even Santa Feans are amazed at the variety and originality of individual wood carvers, like Celso Gallegos of Agua Fria, and Jose Dolores Lopez of Cordova. The work of these two men is as distinct as the work of two men could be, but in one thing they are alike: an amazing fertility that derives more from a spirit of play than from any utilitarian motive. The shop in the Sena plaza contains a great many carvings of the saints, for Mr. Gallegos is the last of the santo-makers. Just yesterday some visitors from Texas carried away a dusty San Ysidro with his plow and two noble oxen. Almost every day, beautiful carved birds or amusing little pigs, made by Jose Dolores Lopez or his daughters, are purchased as souvenirs of this country.

Just now the shop is piled high with blankets, rag rugs of many kinds, pillows of patchwork and pique: these things have been brought in for sale during the Fiesta and in the hope of winning some of the annual prizes that are offered for the best hand work done by Spanish people in different fields. There is one blanket of pure angora wool, entirely handspun and dyed with vegetable dye. This blanket sold the very day it was brought in but is being held until after the award of prizes by Mary Austin on Monday. There are three carved pieces from Cordova, one that is almost like a religious symbol, with delicately patterned beauty, and two others that represent bands of animal musicians—conceptions of amazing humor.

For several years the Spanish Colonial Arts society has been offering these Fiesta prizes and selling the hand work that was brought in. So great was the response shown on the part of both workers and buyers, that the plan of a year-round shop, for the display of native things, exclusively, was formed. This shop is to be a center for the distribution of Spanish articles, for which there is a growing demand, not only in Santa Fe, but wherever fine hand-made articles are appreciated. Carved doors are being shipped this fall to Pennsylvania and to California. So the work of the local craftsmen spreads.

During the 1930's there was a noteworthy revival of Spanish-American, or "native," crafts in New Mexico. The revival was facilitated by the depression, for the same reason that hard times caused a revival of small-scale gold mining—when the need is great enough, people will put in long hours of work for a small return. The activity of the Spanish Colonial Arts Society, which provided guidance, encouragement, and a market, was also an essential factor. The driving individual behind that, in turn, was the same Leonora Curtin mentioned just above, in connection with the Poets' Roundup.

The business eventually got somewhat too big for Miss Curtin, and, through no fault of hers, it was overexpanded and then fell off. For reasons that are not clear, native craftwork died away rapidly in the last years of the decade. In the 1950's there is little left worth mentioning—a couple of gifted wood carvers, a very few tin workers, and one or two old men who still know how to work in iron. The spinning and dyeing are dead; of the weaving remains only the work at Chimayo, which seldom has any aesthetic appeal.

There is one factor that bears upon this change and also upon the changing character of the Santa Fe Fiesta. The culture of the Spanish-Americans was a quasi-medieval folk culture with a good deal of peasant subsistence economy, preserved by extreme isolation. The isolation, linguistic and geographic, has ended; a cash and wage economy is taking over; ancient graces and ancient sufferings are disappearing; and the people themselves are changing. The woman whose husband has bound himself in peonage to a television set bought on installments will not put flowers behind her ears, drape herself in her grandmother's silk shawl, and dance in the street during Fiesta. She knows better. Nor does she find it a creative pleasure to wash, card, and dye fine wool and spin it into a soft, strong yarn. If the return for all that trouble works out at about ten cents an hour, she will have none of it. The same thing is happening to her Navajo and Apache sisters; it is an inescapable part of what we cherish under the name of Progress.

FEBRUARY 13, 1931:   FRANK APPLEGATE.

A lover and preserver of beauty is lost to Santa Fe in the death of Frank Applegate. His contribution to the sum total of those things which make living in Santa Fe a privilege and a pleasure was tremendous. The renaissance of beautiful native Spanish and Indian arts; the architectural movement which has made Santa Fe a city unique in the world; the literature of the southwest, the "little theater" movement, painting,—all these owe Applegate a heavy debt. He was in the widest and best sense an artist. His fight for landscape beauty was determined and persistent; he was a consistent enemy of the ugly and the sordid, and his sturdy and kindly personality was a tower of strength to every one interested in these causes.

The sum total of his aid and encouragement to struggling artists and writers and the needy ambitious in many lines will probably never be known. It is most lamentable that he did not live to finish the work he loved, in its innumerable ramifications, when he was just getting into his stride.

Applegate's capable, busy and tireless hands used pen and brush, trowel and chisel with equal facility. He molded adobe and clay, wood and metal, the thoughts of those around him, public sentiment, into forms of grace and beauty. He was in the highest sense a builder, and a strong and helpful friend.

His end could have been no more fitting than to pass away peacefully in an easy chair before his fireplace content with another artistic endeavor faithfully executed to give pleasure to others.

The Republican and Democratic parties in New Mexico were, and still are, pretty good examples of what Franklin D. Roosevelt meant by "Tweedledum and Tweedledee." In 1930 both were conservative. If, under the influence of the New Deal, the Democratic party acquired a certain liberalism, that has in good measure been cured by the continued immigration into New Mexico of hereditary conservative Democrats from the regions immediately east of the state.

The powers in the Republican party found themselves stuck with a senator who had become a firm member of that progressive Republican group, led by such figures as Borah, Norris, and La Follette, which was doing much more than the official Democratic opposition in the Senate to make the unfortunate President Hoover's life a misery. The state leaders did not like him as senator; they did not like his power in the state. Senator Cutting, for his part, found it necessary to do some tricky footwork to keep that power.

He formed what was, from time to time, according to his convenience, a Progressive wing of the Republican party, or a Progressive party. Through the Progressive machinery he made a deal with the state Democrats which put their candidate, Arthur Seligman, in the governor's chair. In 1932 he found it politic to support the Democrats all along the line, which, among other things, resulted in the defeat of the incumbent Republican congressman, Albert Sims, by Dennis Chavez. The other senator, Samuel Brat-

ton, was a Democrat. *We then had the engaging spectacle of a Democratic governor, senator, and congressman, all under the leadership of the one major Republican office holder.*

If the old guard was angry in 1931, by 1933 it was in a frenzy. Conservatives of both parties united then to overthrow Cutting's amazing empire, leading to the developments recorded in due course below.

FEBRUARY 14, 1931:   OLD GUARD ATTACKS CUTTING AND SELIGMAN. CLAIM STATE VOTE BOUGHT IN ELECTION.

By Harry E. Shuart.

In its second orgy of "personal privilege" speeches of the week, the state senate yesterday turned its back once more on the state's business that is before it for consideration and devoted its time to an old guard Republican attack on the administration and on United States Senator Bronson Cutting.

The undercurrent of petty political bickering that has been existent since the legislative session opened was brought to the surface in a session that was marked by bitter attacks made by Senators Thomas Hughes, A. M. Edwards and Z. B. Moon, the latter two charging, in substance, that Senator Cutting had aligned himself with Gov. Arthur Seligman and "bought the 1930 election in New Mexico."

Perhaps no more maudlin collection of implied indecencies has ever been forced upon the ears of the senate and its galleries than that uttered by Senator Moon in his attempt to justify his desertion of his party and align himself with the old guard opposition to the administration and its policies.

Of such a nature were his utterances that publication of them would be an insult to clean-minded citizens of New Mexico.

The rites of the religious organization of Spanish-Americans commonly known as Penitentes *are dramatic and strange, their music unusual, and, until very recently, their self-inflicted penances gruesome to outsiders. The sum total was the kind of thing that thrill seekers consider spectacular. There grew up among cer-*

*tain Anglo-Americans a sport known as "Penitente hunting" or
"Penitente chasing," which led to a great deal of hard feeling before it was suppressed, in part by the court action described below,
in part by vigorous and direct actions of the Penitentes themselves.*

APRIL 4, 1931:   PROTECTING PENITENTES.

It is reliably reported that several carloads of callow youths
parked their autos close up against a morada or Penitente chapel
at the settlement of Hernandez the other night, commenced making merry and that when a group of natives appeared and asked
them what they were doing, one bright boy drew a revolver and
discharged the same in the general direction of the residents.
"Penitente chasers" are forming the habit of making a Roman
holiday out of the Easter week observances of this religious sect
and it is growing worse year by year.

The action of the district court here in warning that a law will
be invoked which protects religious rites from disturbance, is commendable in the interest of peace and order, because the molestation of or interference with these people by jeering or merely
curious sight-seers is bound to lead to serious trouble, if not tragedy. Without entering into the question of approval or disap-
proval of this kind of penance, it is recalled that several years ago,
when the brothers permitted a hundred Santa Feans to crowd into
their Abiquiu chapel for the "tinieblas" or extinguishing of the
lights, they most courteously made the sole stipulation that the
visitors be quiet and respectful. Since that time there has been an
increasing tendency on the part of sightseers to try to make a
circus out of the performance. There is only one moral and that
is that the large number of millionaires in this country almost all
got that way by attending to their own business.

When uninvited thrill-hunters invade somebody else's community, in the face of the natural resentment of the residents, to
entertain themselves with someone else's business, they are looking for trouble; and as we interpret the action of Judge Otero, he
is seeking to prevent it. Which is certainly in the best interests of
all concerned.

JULY 23, 1931:   VILLAGE GOSSIP.

Wanted—Information leading to disclosure of the identity of the unprincipled person who sent Santa Fe's leading novelist a cake of Fairy soap on Wednesday.

On November 15, 1931, a man with a long prison record raped and murdered a girl, injured her mother, and shortly thereafter— early on the morning of November 16—beat the night attendant at a garage into insensibility. He was arrested that day, and he confessed to assaulting the attendant. The berserk former convict happened to be a Negro. The event led to the publication of an editorial that, in a newspaper that was the personal organ of an outstanding progressive, is astonishing.

NOVEMBER 16, 1931:   A LESSON.

Santa Fe for the first time has gone through the indescribably sickening shock of having the Negro Crime committed at her own doors, under circumstances which almost numb the average person with horror.

We believe the first time will be the last.

Two things are involved—barring in future of negroes from this town, save for its old timers, a thing possible here because Santa Fe is yet a small town; and immediate deporting of discharged convicts to their homes or at least out of Santa Fe.

Some months ago the NEW MEXICAN warned that this community which has inherited no black and white problem, should not allow itself by negligence and indifference, to acquire one.

The city, chamber of commerce, police and sheriff's office must establish a perpetual community rule that negroes are not desired here. Visitors from Texas or elsewhere should be told that we do not care to have them bring negro chauffeurs or other servants here and that if they insist upon it, their room is better than their company.

The practice of bringing in such servants has been largely responsible for a recent substantial increase in the number of col-

333

ored people. There is ample unemployment among our own people to absorb any such demand.

Santa Fe has had always a few respected and often much beloved colored citizens. But for 300 years we have escaped this particular social problem.

No further warning will be needed as to the necessity of stamping it out in infancy, than the inconceivably frightful thing of last night, which has seared the soul of the community like a branding iron.

The thing to do is to keep them out. It can be done, peaceably, officially, in an orderly manner, and especially with wide publicity. They do not belong here, they bring a racial conflict even more intense than elsewhere, we do not need them economically.

This editorial was vigorously challenged in letters that would be expected from members of a community such as Santa Fe had become, and the editor ended by wriggling away from the position he had taken.

APRIL 8, 1930: SOLOMON SPIEGELBERG WAS FIRST JEW IN NEW MEXICO; HE ARRIVED IN YEAR 1846.

Solomon Spiegelberg, arriving in 1846, was the first Jew to come to New Mexico, according to Bernard Postal, writing in "The Day", New York Jewish newspaper. How the early Jewish peddlers and small business men invaded the wild southwest of the middle of the past century is told in interesting fashion by this writer, and sheds further light on the real hardy pioneering spirit of these merchants who helped bring civilization to the wilderness.

Their monuments are found all along the trail, not only in thriving towns which they helped to found, but in names which have stuck through the century—as for instance the ancient village of Ehrenberg on the Colorado river and Seligman in the more northern desert. . . .

HERE SINCE 1846.

New Mexico, the most Spanish of the 48 states, has had Jews

The Sena Plaza, on Palace Avenue in Santa Fe, built as a private home about 1840, is an excellent example of Territorial architecture. Today, the old building houses shops and offices.

Photograph by D. Orton Smith; Courtesy the Historical Society of New Mexico

The Carlos Vierra house. Vierra was a prime mover in the return to building in the Santa Fe style, and his house was the first modern residence in that style.

Will Shuster, one of the foremost members of the now famous art colony. He was the inventor of Zozobra and still makes him for the Fiesta.

Zozobra, or Old Man Gloom, at the moment just before the dancer facing him, Jacques Cartier, touches him off, thus starting the Santa Fe Fiesta.

A religious procession which is part of the Santa Fe Fiesta, held each year over Labor Day week end, heads toward St. Francis Cathedral.

Courtesy the New Mexico State Tourist Bureau

The queen who presides over the Fiesta must be of Spanish descent. Here, the queen and her court take part in the Sunday morning procession.

Courtesy the New Mexico State Tourist Bureau

Parades and pageants are among the features of the Fiesta, which is in celebration of the reconquest of New Mexico by Don Diego de Vargas in 1693. This is one of the floats of the *Hysterical* Parade.

During Fiesta, the Indians bring in their arts and crafts to display under the *portal* of the old Palace of the Governors. This open-air mart is frequented by many hundreds of people each day. Here, an Indian woman offers pots of intricate design and workmanship for sale to interested visitors.

within its borders since 1846, two years before it became American. Solomon Spiegelberg, who arrived in America in 1842 at the age of 16, was the first Jew in New Mexico. Heeding the call of the west, he journeyed to Leavenworth and from there joined a wagon train bound for Mexico. On this trip he enlisted with the command of Colonel Doniphan going to Chihuahua. So popular did he become with the officers that on their return they appointed him sutler at Santa Fe where he soon established a general store. In the 1850's he brought out his five brothers.

The young men who clerked in the Spiegelberg store became the nucleus of the present New Mexican Jewish community. Among them were Simon, Bernard and Adolph Seligman and Jacob Nussbaum, who later became postmaster of Santa Fe. In the 1850's the success of the Spiegelbergs attracted other ambitious Jews, and Nathan Jaffa, Louis Zeckendorf, Nathan Eldot and the Bibo brothers came into the territory. Solomon Bibo, the son of a Westphalian rabbi, married the daughter of an Indian chief of Pueblo [sic] and in later years when he became governor did much to improve the conditions of the Indians.

Another Jewish pioneer in New Mexico was Sam Dittenhoefer, who because of his familiarity with the Indian language was nicknamed Navajo Sam by the "Redskins" with whom he was very friendly. Jewesses, too, were among the pioneers. Mrs. Betty Spiegelberg, wife of Levi Spiegelberg, came to Santa Fe in 1860 after braving the privations of a trip by ox team for two long months across the Rockies and the prairies. The wife of Solomon Spiegelberg and Mrs. Fannie Zeckendorf made the same trip.

NATHAN JAFFA.

The record of the New Mexican Jewish pioneers would not be complete without mention of Nathan Jaffa, an enterprising proponent of irrigation and later secretary of the territory, Ernest Meyer and Charles Roseman, members of the territorial legislature, Henry Jaffa, the first mayor of Albuquerque, Philip Prager one of the contractors during the construction of the Santa Fe railroad, Charles Ilfeld, Herman Wertheim, Jacob Wertheim and Sidney Prager.

The classic description of the pioneer Jew and the part he played in opening, and civilizing, the West is in Edna Ferber's Cimarron. Most Americans, including the Jews themselves, seem quite unaware of the part that race played in the history of our frontier.

FEBRUARY 8, 1932: PROGRESSIVES WIN DAY IN G.O.P. MEET. CONVENTION TO BE HELD IN SANTA FE. OLD GUARDERS GO DOWN FIGHTING MOVE TO HAVE CONFAB WHEN SENATOR IS HERE. LOSE ON APPORTIONMENT. DILLON VOTE IN 1928 BASIS OF DELEGATIONS; ABOUT 880 ELIGIBLE FOR MEET.

By Arthur N. Morgan.

Progressives had their way at the meeting of the Republican state central committee in the Elks' club room Saturday afternoon on the apportionment question and March 26 was fixed as the date for the "delegate" convention, in accordance with the wishes of Sen. Bronson Cutting, as they were conveyed to the "junta" by State Chairman Carl P. Dunifon.

The old guard didn't surrender but died—and on a battleground of their own picking at that. The personnel of this central committee was named by the state convention of 1930 which was the O. G.'s own; inasmuch as they are out of step with popular sentiment in New Mexico today, a sizeable part of the members might be classified as lame ducks.

MARCH 28, 1932: OLD GUARD HOPELESSLY DEFEATED. STATE SENDS UNINSTRUCTED DELEGATION TO CONVENTION. HOOVER GIVEN 'FAINT PRAISE' IN RESOLUTIONS; SENATOR BRONSON CUTTING AND MRS. MARGARET MEDLER NAMED TO NATIONAL COMMITTEE; ELECTION IS BY ACCLAMATION; SENATOR SAYS WILL RESIGN POSITION IF MEETING DISAPPROVES STAND; ONLY CLASH ON REPORT OF CREDENTIALS COMMITTEE.

By Arthur Morgan.

United States Senator Bronson Cutting was chosen as national committeeman, Mrs. Margaret Medler of Albuquerque as committee woman and nine instructed delegates to the Chicago national convention were elected at the Republican state convention, an enthusiastic gathering, which finally got down to business after 10 o'clock Saturday night and wound up some time after 1 a. m. Sunday at Seth hall.

One of the most significant things about this convention was Cutting's speech after he was elected national committeeman. It was an elegant bit of straddling, in which he said no good of either Hoover or the national Republican party and made a good many digs at the Democrats. At the end he said, according to his newspaper, that "if the convention felt it had misplaced confidence in him, after hearing his platform, he hoped somebody in the hall would arise and move to reconsider his election."

His Progressives dominated the meeting, and the response to this challenge was a warm demonstration of support. Thus he stood formally at the head of his party in the state, in a position to support or bolt the national party as he might see fit, and this with the support of that portion of the state party that controlled the convention—in appearance, of the whole party.

After this meeting began the rallying together of conservatives from both parties, at this time in a somewhat tentative manner. The new alignment was strong enough to carry the Santa Fe city elections that spring, electing David Chavez, brother of Dennis Chavez.

APRIL 6, 1932:   OH, VERY WELL.

Our side got licked.

The Republican old guard in Santa Fe—which for years denounced the insurgents bitterly as "double crossers" when they joined forces with the Democrats—finally took a leaf out of the progressive book, foreswore sacred party allegiance, joined up with the enemy and took the progressives to a most workmanlike, complete and efficient cleaning.

The old timers made the best possible use of their expert, well oiled and traditionally effective capacity for organization.

337

They took all possible advantage of over-confidence, inadequate organization and strategic blunders on the part of the opposition.

The winning combination this time was unique, unprecedented and in spots both amusing and bewildering to the innocent by-stander accustomed to partisan classification in this town.

We acknowledge the beating handsomely, pay our tribute to the snappy come-back of the old guard and are sure we voice the general admission when we say they are entitled to anything they want at the hands of the Democratic administration which they put in office.

JUNE 16, 1932: DOING THE SPLIT.

The G.O.P. elephant at Chicago did a straddle which makes the Colossus of Rhodes look like a paralytic.

The agitated pachyderm now has two feet planted in wet states, where party spellbinders may sound the slogan of "resubmission" and state's rights.

Supporting a precarious equilibrium, the two other elephantine feet are stretched across a sea of bootleg booze to the arid bank where campaigners may shout "No repeal" and "down with the liquor traffic."

Meanwhile the party platform plank promises strict enforcement of the prohibition laws and disapproves its own action by declaring prohibition is a matter of individual opinion and should not properly be put in a platform as it distracts attention from pressing national problems.

The Republican platform makers have made a notable contribution to the gayety of nations.

JULY 2, 1932: ROOSEVELT.

The name is one to conjure with, and while there is little resemblance in the two personalities, the presidential nominee of the Democratic party will find that name working for him effectively.

Franklin Roosevelt is a big man, a clean man, an able man.

He might perhaps be placed in the category of "safe" men.

His integrity and character are unchallenged.

Whether he has the capacity for leadership, the aggressiveness, the backbone, the initiative, the hard fiber, the driving force to pull America out of the slough, is the question.

Governor Roosevelt will have to answer that question to the voters as convincingly as he can between now and November.

SEPTEMBER 23, 1932: CUTTING DEFIES OLD GUARD ROLLER. SCOURGES CHICANERY. SENATOR AT 12-COUNTY CONFAB ASSAILS RULE BY RUMP CONVENTIONISTS AND FRAUD. PEOPLE THWARTED. URGES FOLLOWERS TO VOTE SOME OTHER TICKET IF BOSSES CARRY OUT HIGH HANDED SCHEME.

By Brian Boru Dunne.

Albuquerque, Sept. 23—War was declared this morning in the Republican party before the big convention opened for its job of naming a ticket reported to be a job of putting over ex-Governor Dick Dillon with such old guard leaders as Holm O. Bursum and other veterans driving the steam roller.

United States Senator Bronson Cutting, who is also Republican national committeeman shortly after 9 o'clock went before hundreds of Republicans, representing at least 12 counties, gathered in the court house building, as hundreds of other Republicans waited at the armory for the convention to open.

He declared he would not stand for fraud and political chicanery. Cutting said that by the action of the central committee, seating delegates from rump conventions, the wishes of the people, the qualified voters, had been thwarted and he was not going to stand for it. He said he believed the way is open to vote for any ticket put in the field after such action, but he did not urge voting for the Democratic ticket.

Cutting made it clear he is ready to step out as national committeeman, as was hinted in the Albuquerque Journal article this morning.

Santa Fe

The Republican state convention at Albuquerque came to an exciting if premature close last night when Senator Bronson Cutting tendered his resignation as national committeeman and the regular Santa Fe and Rio Arriba county delegations, augmented by the Miera faction from Socorro, said "good-bye" to the assembly.

After this the nomination of former Governor R. C. Dillon was a mere matter of routine. It was made by acclamation and the convention recessed until today.

The walk-out was the result of the convention's action in sustaining the credentials committee, 682½ to 368½, in the Rio Arriba, Santa Fe and Socorro county contests.

"Act calmly," advised Judge Luis E. Armijo, advising the convention not to accept the resignation. "We need all the Republicans in New Mexico to win."

Armijo's motion not to accept was ruled to be lost by Chairman Dan Kelley on an aye-and-nay vote. Nobody made a motion to accept it.

The "old guard"—perhaps they could as well be called the "regular Republicans"—had recaptured the formal machinery of the party. With a strong personal machine, and an understanding with the Democrats, Cutting was far from defeated. At the time it looked to many as if he had never been stronger.

He proceeded to campaign openly and vigorously for Roosevelt. In November the state went overwhelmingly Democratic, with Congressman Dennis Chavez leading the ticket, even running slightly ahead of Roosevelt. Chavez was, and is, a competent machine builder on his own account. His victory, following upon his brother's election as mayor of Santa Fe by a conservative coalition, gave him a new independence. Nonetheless, Cutting's contribution to the New Mexico landslide was impressive.

340

NOVEMBER 30, 1932: CUTTING TO TALK WITH ROOSEVELT. SENA-
TOR INVITED TO CONFER WITH PRESIDENT-ELECT AT WARM SPRINGS,
GA. RUMOR OF CABINET PLACE. INDICATION ALL REPUBLICAN-INDE-
PENDENTS MAY BE ASKED FOR OPINIONS.

Senator Bronson Cutting, before leaving here last night for
Washington, announced that he had accepted an invitation from
President-elect Franklin D. Roosevelt to stop off at Warm
Springs, Ga., and confer with him.

Rumors have been rife recently that the senator would be offered a place in the cabinet of the new president, but Senator
Cutting refused to comment on the rumors, or to say anything
about his visit to Warm Springs except that he has accepted
the invitation.

DECEMBER 3, 1932: TO DUST RETURNEST.

A negro attendant of a Santa Fe garage yesterday found by
accident the unconscious form of an unknown man lying bleeding and blackened in dirt and darkness, in a grimy coal-basement,
hurt unto death. It was found he wore clerical garb. His identity
was unknown until a summoned priest discovered it. No one
seemed to remember having noticed an unobtrusive little man,
with twinkling eyes behind his glasses, walking busily into the
place preoccupied about some information concerning the leaving time of a bus.

Probably no part of his life so became the Archbishop of Santa
Fe as his manner of leaving it.

Modest and inconspicuous, he was on foot and alone going
about his Father's business, and bemused with the welfare of his
people, he stumbled, rapt, into eternity.

A prelate of the Church, head of one of its largest subdivisions,
this Franciscan remained a humble exemplar of the faith of the
founder of his order. Through his life he labored selflessly in the
Dust. His passing was in no stately taper-lit chamber; he lost his
conscious hold on life in a dingy cellar and the final spark left
him as he lay on a hospital cot.

The grandeur of his humility looms only after his death. Kind-

ly, humorous, democratic, at times crisp, practical, endowed with
rare common-sense, his spirituality was cloaked with a matter-of-
fact demeanor.

FEBRUARY 18, 1933: SEN. CUTTING REFUSES JOB. NEW MEXICAN
PREFERS TO CONTINUE IN SENATE; REJECTS CABINET PLACE.

Washington, Feb. 18 (AP)—Senator Bronson Cutting, (R.,
N. M.) was understood among his friends on capitol hill today
to have declined the portfolio of secretary of the interior in the
Roosevelt administration.

Returning to his senatorial duties today after a train-conference
with the president-elect yesterday, he himself refused to comment on the rumors linking his name with the cabinet.

His friends feel that he prefers that any statement on the subject should come from the president-elect.

*The last item has more significance than appears on the face of
it. Both Cutting and Hiram Johnson of California, another Progressive senator, were interested in the Department of the Interior
and in Indian affairs; the latter were probably more important to
the New Mexican than to the Californian. In connection with
Pueblo land legislation and various other matters, Cutting had
been in contact with John Collier, then executive secretary of the
Indian Defense Association, and through him seems to have had
some dealings with the former Bull Mooser, Harold L. Ickes, who
was president of the Association's Chicago branch.*

*At the time, the persistent rumor was that Ickes was under con-
sideration for commissioner of Indian affairs, and he may have
first been suggested for that post. At any rate, starting from the
protests of the Indians themselves in 1922 against the Bursum Bill
and the row kicked up by the art colonies of Santa Fe and Taos,
circuitously, through Cutting's unusual political maneuvers, the
sequence of events led to the appointment of about the most colorful secretary of the interior this country has known.*

*This in turn led to Collier's appointment as commissioner of
Indian affairs, and the Ickes-Collier combination resulted in*

changes in the condition of our Indians that cannot be treated here.

Relations between Spanish- and Anglo-Americans in New Mexico are commonly referred to as "the race question," although, regardless of some actual racial differences, the only significant differences are cultural. The subject is extremely delicate, feelings are easily inflamed, and the Spanish-Americans, not without reason, are touchy. In 1933, working through Dr. George I. Sanchez of the University of New Mexico, the leading living student of the Spanish- and Mexican-Americans, the Rockefeller Foundation started an inquiry into racial attitudes in the state. An important part of the inquiry was the circulation to the public schools of questionnaires. Violent protests resulted—so violent that the Governor intervened.

MAY 5, 1933: THE VARSITY INQUIRY.

Any reasonable person should be convinced from the evidence before the committee investigating the University race attitude quiz, that it was not prompted by race prejudice; that it was not intended as race prejudice propaganda, but the reverse; and that the motive behind it was to combat race prejudice.

Those in charge of the enterprise, conducted it appears, in the approved scientific method used all over the country in such surveys overlooked the following facts:

That the average person, here, Spanish speaking or otherwise is not familiar with "scales" or scientific sociological technique and would naturally assume that derogatory statements to be checked off in a printed form were the opinions of somebody.

That some of the words used were traditional terms of opprobrium used against Spanish speaking people, rightly regarded here as insulting epithets, and that their appearance in print for any purpose is certain to be offensive and inflammatory.

That the native people are naturally sensitive in such matters, and their sensitiveness was known to have been made more acute by recent occurrences brought to the attention of the legislature;

343

That, rightly or wrongly, the recent fraternity discussion convinced many natives that they were being discriminated against at the university and made the victims of prejudice there; and thus anything emanating from the university touching upon racial differences would probably be dynamite.

This seems to us a fair statement both of the apparently innocent motives and the serious lack of discretion which marked the unfortunate handling of this survey.

We still hold the opinion that the way to bring further solidarity of the two language elements of our people is not to hunt out prejudice, put it under a microscope and let everybody take a look at it, but to do and encourage the doing of the things which bring us together and wipe out prejudice, making us mutually forget it. This psychology may not meet latest theories in high research quarters, but it is the only kind that works in New Mexico.

Kindness, consideration, courtesy, mutual respect, acquaintance, co-operation are more effective than analyzing each other's peculiarities. A survey no matter how scientific could discover no other practical means.

The valuable university, even if it has meant the best in the world, has created a prejudice against it in the minds of the Spanish speaking half of our population. Removal of this prejudice is now more important than an abstract study of race attitudes elsewhere.

The regents, president and faculty should make it their first business to restore the confidence of Spanish speaking taxpayers in a state institution which must serve all the people; and which, we repeat, has a special opportunity and obligation of service to the natives, for generations deprived of equal educational opportunity through the negligence of federal and territorial governments.

The reader will recall how ardently in favor of prohibition the New Mexican *was in the years leading up to adoption of the Eighteenth Amendment. But local sentiment had changed greatly, and the paper had changed with it, becoming frankly wet when its owner came out for Roosevelt, who campaigned on a*

344

platform with a forthright repeal plank. The story that follows contrasts sharply with those of the second decade of the century.

SEPTEMBER 20, 1933: NEW MEXICO VOTE GIVES WETS 31 STATES. SANTA FE GOES 15 TO ONE FOR PROHIBITION REPEAL. VOTE IN COUNTY IS WET AS THAT IN CITY; CURRY AND ROOSEVELT COUNTIES ONLY TWO IN STATE TO GO DRY; WET MAJORITY THREATENS TO PASS THREE TO ONE ESTIMATE; ALL PROPOSALS ON BALLOTS PASS EXCEPT INCREASING NUMBER OF JUDGES; LOCAL OPTION WINS BIG VOTE.

If Santa Fe voters were not the most dripping wet in the state at the repeal election yesterday they were certainly among those deserving consideration.

The vote in the city was 2,768 wet against 201 dry, or about 15 to one wet. The vote on local option and state repeal showed a discrepancy of about 100 votes. There were about that number of citizens who wanted to see the state dry amendment repealed and the city permitted to sell liquor who did not vote on national repeal.

The poll in Santa Fe county was just about on a par with that in the city. With 15 of the 24 precincts in the county reported the wet vote was carrying at about 14 to one.

All the proposals before the voters of the city carried by large majorities except the one to increase the number of judicial districts in the state to 12. This was overwhelmingly defeated.

SEPTEMBER 25, 1933: GOVERNOR SELIGMAN DIES. DOCTOR SAYS CHIEF EXECUTIVE HAD SUDDEN ATTACK OF ANGINA PECTORIS. WAS IN ALBUQUERQUE FOR MEETING OF BANKERS ASSOCIATION WHEN DEATH ARRIVED; STRICKEN IMMEDIATELY AFTER ADDRESSING SESSION AT FRANCISCAN HOTEL; APPEARED IN GOOD HEALTH.

Albuquerque, N. M., Sept. 25 (AP)—Gov. Arthur Seligman of New Mexico died suddenly in a hotel here this morning of what physicians described as an attack of angina pectoris.

The governor had come here from Santa Fe to attend a meeting of the New Mexico State Bankers association of which he was a member.

I well remember the stunning effect of the news reported above. It meant the collapse of Cutting's empire. All around Santa Fe that day, one encountered groups of politicos conferring —some in deep gloom, some in triumph. Arthur Seligman the human being, a good man, sensitive to beauty, and a connoisseur of Indian crafts, seemed quite forgotten. He was succeeded by A. W. Hockenhull, the lieutenant governor, an upright, non-political figure who, having no desire to be re-elected, could not be reached. At about the same time, Senator Bratton was made a federal judge, and Hockenhull appointed in his stead Carl W. Hatch, best known for authorship of the Hatch Act restricting political activities of federal employees. Thus the whole line-up changed.

FEBRUARY 13, 1934:   JOBLESS MEETING HERE BREAKS UP IN ROW OVER SINGING INTERNATIONAL.

An attempt to sing the Soviet "International" hymn of revolution while the American flag was hanging in Gonzales hall last night led to the breaking up of an alleged meeting of unemployed in a near riot. A move to turn it into a Communist meeting was blocked.

The paean of class hate was finally merely read after Capt. Seymour I. Hess, lately of the U. S. army, objected six times to the proposed song unless the U. S. flag were hauled down, holding that no revolutionary ditty should be on the program of a meeting held under the protection of the stars and stripes. He was supported by groups of workers, including a delegation of Portales farmers who left the hall in disgust. They said they wanted relief for the needy but wanted it under the U. S. flag.

The meeting struck its first snag when Capt. Hess stopped talk of a "fight" and "revolution" by wanting to know how this subject came up in a meeting ostensibly called to discuss unemployment insurance.

The meeting had been advertised as an attempt to organize the jobless of New Mexico and their sympathizers, to secure state operated unemployment insurance.

346

Up to the end of the session nothing had been said about insurance.

When the meeting resumed today the American flag was still in place.

From early spring until after Election Day in 1934, the newspapers of New Mexico gave much space to the complex local political fight. Cutting was up for re-election. The reports in his own paper were partisan, verbose, and none too reliable; the editorials, read many years later, are often dull. The best procedure is to summarize the story, with pertinent quotations.

Cutting's Progressives were strong—strong enough to reject an invitation from the regular Republican organization to be absorbed as a minority. Instead, they proposed that they be allowed to remake the party. This, on May 16, the New Mexican presented as being much more than part of a local struggle for power; it claimed that it was "an issue which is national, not merely local; the situation, elements, the lineup are the same here as everywhere.

"The question is far bigger than compromising 'factions' or a division of spoils; one that involves not mere temporary advantage but the whole future of the Republican party."

This solicitude for the party's future faded away when it looked as if Cutting might receive the President's endorsement, as had Johnson of California, and with that could have made another combination with the Democrats. On July 2 the paper was suggesting that Senator Hatch be shelved, for a Democratic-Progressive ticket with Cutting and Chavez as the two senatorial candidates.

Relations between Roosevelt and Cutting had soured, apparently because of a clash of personalities. Gradually it became clear that the Senator could expect no endorsement and that a fusion with the Democrats could not be arranged. On July 25, Governor Hockenhull issued a special statement to the effect that any debt his party had owed the Progressives had been paid.

Cutting was tough. He now set out, quite simply, to capture the Republican party, and, furthermore, he succeeded.

Santa Fe

SEPTEMBER 26, 1934: *[Seven-column banner line.]* BRONSON CUTTING HEADS REPUBLICAN TICKET.

Forced to continue into the small hours of this morning by contests for every place on the lower part of the state ticket, except those of state treasurer and corporation commissioner, the Republican state convention wound up shortly after 2 a. m. today at Seth Hall.

Despite the long, gruelling hours, the convention had practically a full attendance at the finish, holding all but a few of the tired delegates in their seats to the last minute, and despite the struggles to make the ticket, the close was harmonious.

The last roll call showed 824 still on the job although the Colfax county delegation was absent, caucussing, it was said, over the county's selections for the state central committee.

*The Progressives' triumph meant that most of the Republican stalwarts went over to the Democrats, to do state-wide, if they could, what they had once managed to do in the Santa Fe city election noted above. The Democrats, then, had behind them all the drive of the New Deal, as well as the help of a considerable faction of Republicans. Once again the state went heavily Democratic, and in a sour editorial entitled "*OH VERY WELL*," the New Mexican conceded this victory on November 7. It did not mention the senatorial candidates, who were Hatch and Chavez, so even then it may have been cherishing a hope that Cutting, at least, would win through. On November 9 it appeared that, indeed, he had—a tremendous feat, even discounting the* New Mexican's *stuff about a "moral majority."*

NOVEMBER 9, 1934: UNBEATABLE.

On the face of present returns, if last minute ballots do not overturn his majority and if the election is not stolen, U. S. Senator Cutting has beaten the most formidable collection of adversaries ever deployed against a candidate in New Mexico, by a moral majority of over 41,000 votes.

348

For in starting the count you begin with the Dennis Chavez' 1932 majority of 41,000 which Cutting wiped out.

The senator emerged from a national ocean of Democratic victory running 10,000 to 20,000 ahead of his state ticket and carrying two-thirds of the counties of his state.

In doing so Senator Cutting beat the following:

He beat a national Democratic tidal wave that exceeded the 1932 deluge and drowned old guard Republicans in nearly every state.

He beat the vast power of the presidential office.

He beat the heavy squeeze of the Tammany-Farley national Democratic steam roller.

He beat the pipeline of money from Washington.

He beat the dug-in state Democratic machine, commanding an army of job-scared state employes, a regiment of state cars, armed with half a million debenture money;

He beat the hunger-club that coerced ten thousand destitute relief rollers and unemployed.

NOVEMBER 21, 1934: CUTTING IS ELECTED BY 1291 VOTES.

Final official election returns by The AP election bureau show Senator Bronson Cutting, Republican, elected by 1,291 votes over Cong. Dennis Chavez, his Democratic opponent.

The last official count was available today from Rio Arriba county, where the absentee vote had not been available before. The new totals, official from the entire state, gave Cutting 76,245 and Chavez 74,954.

Not unnaturally, in view of the closeness of the election, Chavez contested it. The Secretary of State at the time was Marguerite P. Baca, a Democrat, widow of former Lieutenant Governor José A. Baca. Mrs. Baca was subjected to extraordinary pressure to find that the Democratic contestant had won, but she certified Cutting on December 31. Chavez then took his fight to the Senate, but before the question could be decided there, it was settled in a most unexpected manner.

Santa Fe

[*Banner line.*] CUTTING KILLED.

Washington (AP)—THE OFFICE OF SENATOR CUTTING OF NEW MEXICO REPORTED TODAY AN UNDERTAKER AT MACON, MISSOURI, HAD REPORTED CUTTING WAS KILLED IN AN AIRPLANE CRASH NEAR THERE THIS MORNING.

EDGAR F. PURYEAR, SECRETARY TO THE SENATOR, TALKED WITH THE UNDERTAKING ESTABLISHMENT BY LONG DISTANCE TELEPHONE. THE UNDERTAKER REPORTED, HE SAID, THAT THE SENATOR HAD BEEN IDENTIFIED BY A CARD WITH HIS NAME ON IT AND A PICTURE OF HIS MOTHER IN HIS BILLFOLD.

PURYEAR DEFERRED NOTIFYING SENATOR CUTTING'S MOTHER, WHO IS IN WASHINGTON, UNTIL MORE DEFINITE NEWS WAS RECEIVED.

SENATOR LaFOLLETTE OF WISCONSIN WITH WHOM CUTTING HAD ENGAGED IN MANY A SENATE BATTLE FOR LIBERAL LEGISLATION, WAS STANDING BESIDE THE SECRETARY'S DESK AS HE TALKED WITH MACON. HE WAS DEEPLY GRIEVED AT THE NEWS.

MAY 6, 1935: EDITORIAL.

Twenty years personal contact with and deep affection for a considerate employer and loyal never-failing personal friend and an unspeakable sense of personal loss make impossible here any measured editorial tribute to the character and accomplishments of Bronson Cutting. Our only suggested index to his character is the perennial devotion of everyone closely associated with him, which probably had its root more than anything else in the fact that he was instinctively, automatically and intrinsically a gentleman.

Meanwhile it is our job to "get out the paper." If it has any deficiencies today, we are sure they will be overlooked.

350

Dennis Chavez was appointed senator in Cutting's place, and that was that. Since then he has run for re-election a number of times and won, usually decisively.

Cutting had a friend and protégé, Jesus Baca, whom he seemed to look upon as his political heir, the man who would carry on his policies and, above all, become the champion of the Spanish-Americans. To him he made by far his largest bequest; his house and land in Santa Fe, the sum of $150,000, and the New Mexican. *Within two years Baca had sold the paper to a Kansas chain headed by O. S. Stauffer.*

JUNE 29, 1937:   IN NEW HANDS.

Retiring after twenty-five busy and enjoyable years, the editor of the New Mexican takes sincere pleasure in introducing his successor and friend Mr. Rolla Clymer, who has come to Santa Fe from Eldorado, Kas., to take over the job of managing and editing the Santa Fe New Mexican.

Mr. Clymer, who is co-owner of the property, takes active charge tomorrow.

He has had a long and thorough training in the newspaper business. At the age of eighteen he went to work for William Allen White on the Emporia Gazette. This is a coveted start in the profession and in Kansas is regarded as a prime qualification for success. He was in Mr. White's employ for seven years.

The new editor once told me, apropos of a big fight going on over the current handling of the Navajos, that it was the policy of Stauffer's chain "not to get into controversies." In his notes, Morgan remarks, "Editorials became fatuously point-with-pride-ish. They never viewed with alarm, except on some distant, non-controversial scandal, and then only in the mildest terms."

The policy of the paper was Republican if it was anything. It lost all character, and its make-up, which had become lively and attractive in the last ten years, became ugly.

Santa Fe

DECEMBER 10, 1937:

FORMER EDITOR OF NEW MEXICAN DIES.
E. DANA JOHNSON IS HEART ATTACK VICTIM IN
CALIFORNIA TODAY.
HAD GONE TO WEST COAST TO RECUPERATE FROM LONG ILLNESS;
WIFE AT BEDSIDE WHEN END COMES; FUNERAL TO BE HELD HERE;
BODY TO BE BROUGHT TO SANTA FE IMMEDIATELY; WAS POWER IN
POLITICAL AFFAIRS OF NEW MEXICO; CLOSE CONFIDANT OF
SENATOR CUTTING.

CHAPTER 5

PROSPERITY AND ATOMS

JUNE 1, 1940: RAND FIRM PUBLISHES PAPERS.

The Santa Fe New Mexican today began publication under the presidency of Frank C. Rand, Jr., who early this week announced the purchase of the New Mexico Publishing Co. stock.

At the same time, The Capital Examiner, published by the New Mexico Publishing Co., and edited by Alex Barnes, made the first appearance on the streets. The paper is served by the United Press. Barnes, formerly city editor of the Santa Fe New Mexican, is a Santa Fe resident of 20 years.

Will Harrison, formerly editor of the recently suspended New Mexico Sentinel and an Associated Press employe became editor of the 91-year-old New Mexican.

FRANK C. RAND, JR., a young man, was a strong, conservative Republican. The New Mexican *had been supporting Willkie for president, in its tepid manner. As soon as Rand acquired it, it became violently anti-Roosevelt. It compared the Roosevelt administration with that which led to Hitler's dictatorship.*

Under the previous ownership, the editing of the paper had a quality of remoteness from Santa Fe, as though the paper were published in Kansas and shipped in from there. Will Harrison, Rand's editor, was well soaked in the Santa Fe tradition. Under him, for all its political conservatism, the New Mexican *once more*

353

*became lively, its make-up improved, and it recaptured the feel
of the city.*

*Between 1920 and 1950 a number of attempts were made to
establish rival newspapers in Santa Fe. But the city, which in
1950 fell just short of 30,000 population, could not support two
papers; one had to fold. Quite contrary to its practice in the nineteenth century, the* New Mexican *ignored its rivals. None of them
lasted long. From June 16 until the end of 1940 the Sunday paper
was issued as a joint effort of the* New Mexican *and the* Capital
Examiner, *mentioned above. By the end of the year the older
paper had absorbed the* Examiner *entirely.*

The editorial that follows gives an idea of the New Mexican's
*sociopolitical outlook in this period. Governor John E. Miles,
named therein, was an old-line Democrat but no New Dealer.
Madrid was a company town, notorious for the extreme poverty
of its miners and the wretched conditions under which they lived.*

MAY 25, 1941:   [*Front-page editorial.*] PATTERN FOR ROOSEVELT.

Following a riot at the Madrid Mines two weeks ago, in which
about 55 strikers and 150 workers participated, the New Mexico
State Police refused to allow picketing. Governor Miles, in commenting on a letter of protest against this action, which he received from Mr. Frank Hefferly, district president of the United
Mine Workers of America, made one of the strongest public
statements of his career. Governor Miles said:

"I don't want to interfere with any of labor's rights, but I am
going to see, if it is possible, that men who want to work have the
opportunity to do so. And if we don't have enough police to see
to this, I will call in more.

"I want labor, as well as capital, to enjoy whatever rights they
have; but I feel at the present time, in view of turbulent world
conditions, with a lot of our boys making sacrifices, leaving their
jobs for the army at $21 a month—I feel, that other people can
make a little sacrifice along with them."

This statement is probably the most American statement, made
by a public official, we have been privileged to read for some time.

If there is any one thing which might be called an individual's fundamental right in our democracy, it is certainly the right of any individual to work as he chooses without interference by force or name-calling from any person or group of persons. The statement of Governor Miles might well be taken by our president as a sound model for solving the national labor mess which he and Madam Perkins have created by their sugary labor policies. President Roosevelt and his New Dealers have pampered and wooed organized labor for the purpose of political exploitation. In the past the administration's "bigwigs" have encouraged and protected strikes and strikers, even though such protection and encouragement resulted in the destruction of property and loss of life. The outcome of such protection has been, that even those willing to work begin to fear for the safety of their homes and families.

AUGUST 19, 1941:

200TH PACKS

UP TO LEAVE

BLISS SEPT. 1.

Destination Unan-
nounced, but Reported
To Be Alaskan Post.

AUGUST 23, 1941: NEW MEXICO'S OWN.

New Mexico's own—the 200th. coast artillery anti-aircraft—has set sail for parts unannounced and with it goes the love and admiration of every citizen of the state.

The 200th., formerly the 111th cavalry, is considered one of the finest regiments in the newly formed army of the nation. It left Fort Bliss where it has been stationed for many months, for an unannounced destination, but whatever or wherever that destination is the men were happy in the thought that they will be of value to the defense of their nation.

New Mexico is proud of its regiment and rests secure in the knowledge that wherever it lands it will soon have the situation well in hand.

SEPTEMBER 3, 1941:   STATE'S OWN FACES WEST.

FT. BLISS, Texas. Sept. 3. (AP)—The 200th coast artillery of the New Mexico national guard, faced westward today towards a distant and secret destination.

For years a cavalry regiment, the 200th has been in active training as an anti-aircraft unit only since last January.

Officers did not conceal their pride in the fact that the 200th was chosen for a potentially dangerous assignment over other anti-aircraft regiments with longer records of service and training.

Col. Charles G. Sage, commander, is a New Mexico publisher who has never lost his World war interest in soldiering.

He served nine months in France during the World war and has been a national guardsman virtually ever since the armistice.

When the regiment changed from cavalry to anti-aircraft less than two years ago Colonel Sage readily adapted himself, as did other officers of the regiment.

During the last two years, while on active duty, Colonel Sage has scarcely seen his newspapers in Deming, Lordsburg and Silver City. Since Uncle Sam will not let women folks go where the 200th is going, Mrs. Sage will remain in New Mexico to supervise the three newspapers.

The 200th, its two sections united in San Francisco, is understood to be sailing this month. The regiment's strength is about 1875.

The 200th's destination was the Philippines. As was finally told much later (see November 11, 1945), it played a gallant part in the defense of Bataan, and its members then underwent the horrors of Japanese prison camps.

SEPTEMBER 2, 1941:   WRECKING CREW ON CHILI LINE.

Antonito, Colo., Sept. 2 (AP)—Crews were to start ripping out the rails of the chili line today, leaving Santa Fe, N. M., the only state capital in the nation without passenger train service.

The last train over the Denver and Rio Grande narrow gauge

line puffed into Antonito from Santa Fe last night—a mixed train of three freight cars, combination mail and baggage car, two passenger coaches and two private cars.

Contending there wasn't enough business to justify its continued operation, the company has abandoned the line—a step continuously opposed by residents of the upper Rio Grande valley whose chili peppers and onions the line carried.

Filled with sentimentally attached passengers and trainmen, the train stopped yesterday at Espanola and other points to pick up agents' equipment. It was 18 minutes late on its 125-mile run.

What the AP man called "private cars" were parlor cars, equipped with comfortable wicker armchairs, which were not fastened to the floor, and beautifully polished, nickel-plated, asbestos lamps overhead.

The timing of the destruction of the Chili Line Branch was superb. The rails were pulled up just in time to be sold to Japan— or so everyone around Santa Fe understood. Once the thing was done, gasoline rationing came in after Pearl Harbor, which would have boosted the Branch's business considerably. Furthermore, the line passed just at the foot of the climb up to a boys' school called Los Alamos in the Jemez Mountains. Had the rails remained, at least the portion between that point and Santa Fe would have been, and would still be, very busy hauling goods for the atomic city that was founded there in 1943.

Everyone missed the line. The whistle of the northbound train as it came around the cliffs near Otowi was the signal for San Ildefonso and Santa Clara Indians and the Spanish-Americans near by to leave their fields and go to lunch. As one Indian told me, once the train stopped running, they would either have to buy watches or go back to the ways of their ancestors and plant sticks in the ground to tell them when it was noon. I am only one of many whose pack outfit, horses and mules, spooked and scattered into the hills at the sound of that same whistle. In a very real sense it was part of the valley, part of the local community all the way north from Santa Fe.

The first trip from Santa Fe to Española is described earlier,

357

under January 10, 1887. The line had lasted not quite forty-four years.

SEPTEMBER 24, 1941: MRS. BALLARD, HEAD OF 'I AM' CULT, SON HERE.

Screened from publicity, cloaked in silence, shrouded in mystery, was the brief visit "like that of a royal guest" of one of the most talked of women in the world today—Mrs. Edna Ballard of Los Angeles.

The internationally known leader of the religious or philosophical cult called "I AM," accompanied by her son, Donald, rested at a local hotel on a motor tour of the Southwest. Friends of Mrs. Ballard said the famed religious leader, head of the organization of a million members called "I Am," was passing through Santa Fe and New Mexico on "a vacation" and there was no statement to give out. A quiet vegetarian dinner party, a visit to Indian pueblos, art museums, were hinted—but the air of mystery was maintained.

The "I Am" cult mentioned above claims as its authority a new revelation by Saint Germaine, which complements and to some extent supersedes the Christian revelation. After her husband's death, Mrs. Ballard became the sole leader of it. This item about her visit to Santa Fe is of interest because the city—and the newspaper—were to see a good deal more of her and her followers, then concentrated mostly in California.

DECEMBER 7, 1941: MISUNDERSTANDING?

That Japan is hesitant to start war against the ABCD powers is patent on the face of last reports. We notice that Japan has indicated through official sources a desire to prolong peace negotiations with the United States and suggests that the "utterably impossible" position taken by Washington was due to a "big misunderstanding."

There is every reason to believe Japanese officials are correct in their statement, but they failed to add that the "big misunderstanding" was not on the part of the United States but on that of Japan who misunderstood America's willingness to back up what it believed right and decent. Nippon has drifted so far from the straight and narrow that it fails to realize that honest, fair and decent people still exist in this war-torn world.

DECEMBER 8, 1941: THE MANAGEMENT SAYS THANK YOU!

Loyalty, efficiency, and initiative are things you cannot buy and the staff of the Santa Fe New Mexican showed plenty of all three of these things yesterday afternoon. When the news of Japan's dastardly attack on the Philippines broke, the president, the general-manager, and the editor were out in the country trying to bring home some ducks and could only be reached by a special messenger. Pending an O.K. of their work by telephone, the staff went right ahead with the preparation of the momentous news for the Sunday extra. It is difficult to fully express the deep gratitude of the management for the great job which yesterday was enacted by the Staff of The New Mexican and by the close friends of the paper. To the staff and to our friends, thank you.

Outbreak of war, and false alarms about Japanese planes over the West Coast or Japanese submarines just off it, brought a movement of "refugees" from California to the Santa Fe region. Most of these were wealthy people, but the "I Am" organization also selected the city for an inland center, bringing to it an influx of believers, for the most part elderly people of modest means.

FEBRUARY 3, 1942: HUNDREDS OF I AM ON WAY.

The movement of I Am members from the west coast to Santa Fe continued today and members predicted it would not stop until there are "hundreds of us together."

Real estate agencies continued to receive inquiries for houses from the new residents and it was learned that members of the activity had unsuccessfully negotiated for leases on the Santa Fe Inn and Bishop's Lodge.

359

*During the war years the paper was shorthanded both in the
shop and in the editorial room. War news dominated the space.
One of the readers for this collection, himself a newspaper man,
comments on this period that the paper had "three stock editorials: anti-Roosevelt, anti-Labor and anti-Roosevelt-anti-labor
(a combination). Only the wording or the 'angle' of these were
changed from day to day."*

AUGUST 7, 1944: TERRITORIAL GOVERNOR OTERO DIES AT 84.
AUTHOR OF VIVID HISTORIES.

Miguel A. Otero, for nine years the territorial governor of New
Mexico, died in his sleep early today at his home at 354 East
Palace. He was 83 years old and though bedridden for three years
was as mentally alert as in the days when he fought the territorial
bad men into submission to law and order.

Governor Otero died peacefully. His son Maj. M. A. Otero, Jr.,
inquired about his father shortly before 7 a. m., and was told that
he was sleeping quietly. A half-hour later he was dead. . . .

Governor Otero served as New Mexico's chief executive longer
than any man in modern history. He was appointed governor by
President McKinley in 1897 and was reappointed by President
Roosevelt, retiring in 1906.

From 1943 on, the staff of the New Mexican *was involved in a
major suppression of news. Near the beginning of that year, A. J.
Connell, the headmaster of a ranch boarding school for boys at
Los Alamos, informed the paper that a deal was pending for sale
of the site to the government for military purposes. When the
deal was made, fairly high army officers came to the* New Mexican
*office with Connell and said that nothing about the sale was to
be printed.*

*Morgan comments on the matter of secrecy: "Just about every-
body on the* New Mexican *knew what was going on at Los Alamos,
especially after an Army private gave it out in a barroom that a
cyclotron had been moved up to the Hill. This naturally was not*

mentioned. Nor were other and similar leaks. The paper even had to give the location of auto accidents on the Los Alamos road as 'somewhere north of Santa Fe.'"

On July 16, 1945, there was a two-inch story on page six, headed "MAGAZINE LETS GO AT ALAMOGORDO." *That was the treatment of the experimental shot at Trinity. It must have been a considerable strain on newspaper men who had an excellent idea of what had happened.*

AUGUST 6, 1945: [*Banner headlines.*] LOS ALAMOS SECRET DISCLOSED BY TRUMAN. ATOMIC BOMBS DROP ON JAPAN. [*Two-column headline.*] DEADLIEST WEAPONS IN WORLD'S HISTORY MADE IN SANTA FE VICINITY.

Santa Fe learned officially today of a city of 6,000 in its own front yard.

The reverberating announcement of the Los Alamos bomb, with 2,000 times the power of the great Grand-Slammers dropped on Germany, also lifted the secret of the community on the Pajarito Plateau, whose presence Santa Fe has ignored, except in whispers, for more than two years.

Decision to locate the Atomic Bomb Project Laboratory on a mesa an hour's drive from Santa Fe, meant that it was necessary for the Army Engineers to construct an entirely new town to house the workers and their families. Primary reason for selection of the isolated site was security.

RANCH SCHOOL SITE.

When the Army took over the property early in 1943 there were a few buildings which had been occupied by the Los Alamos Ranch School. New buildings began going up at once. Today there are 37 in the main technical area and about 200 others on the property used for the project itself. Three hundred buildings containing 620 family units, also were constructed, as well as military barracks, hospital buildings and structures for administrative offices.

AUGUST 6, 1945: [*Five-column headline.*] NOW THEY CAN BE
TOLD ALOUD, THOSE STOORIES[1] OF 'THE HILL.'

By William McNulty.

The secret of Los Alamos is out and The New Mexican staff
and other newspapermen through New Mexico can heave a sigh—
sigh nothing; it's more of a groan—of relief.

President Truman's revelation today that it was an atomic
bomb THEY were working on on The Hill ended what was probably the strictest censorship ever imposed upon the press of this
state. There was practically no limit to the lengths that the guards
went to and the situation at times became fantastically involved
including the famed "Battle of the MPs".

Notwithstanding the censorship, the news of Los Alamos had
scarcely raced about the Plaza this morning when the membership of the "I-Knew-It-All-Along" club began growing by leaps
and bounds. As a matter of record, the most recent rumor, No.
6,892—straight from the horses' mouth last week—was that Alamos was working lickety-split, night and day, in the production of
windshield wipers for submarines.

The taboo on the mention of Los Alamos was final, complete
and until today, irrevocable and not susceptible to any exceptions whatsoever.

A whole social world existed in nowhere in which people were
married and babies were born nowhere. People died in a vacuum,
autos and trucks crashed in a vacuum and the MPs baseball team
materialized out of a vacuum, trained in a vacuum and after their
games at Fort Marcy Park, returned to the vacuum. Even the
graduates of Los Alamos Ranch School, the institution which
preceded Uncle Sam's Atomic Bomb Project Laboratory, ceased
to be graduates of Los Alamos; they bounded direct from Public
School No. 7 clear into the classrooms of Harvard and Yale.

And on days when the Alamos experimenters threw their
atomic bombs about a little too vigorously and the windows of

[1] The spelling "stoories" is probably intentional, fitting, as it does, McNulty's
fondness for introducing a touch of brogue.

362

Santa Fe rattled ominously, this paper's phones would ring but the whole staff could just "no speak English".

The chain of secrecy about the project was maintained from the big cities in the East where workers were recruited clear through to the delivery of these same workers on The Hill. The Alamos Bus stop was at Sena Plaza and people, laden with luggage and youngsters clinging to their arms, frequently barged into offices of that Plaza and inquired, "Where do we go to work?" One of the earliest bits of Alamos lore was that of the dude Wac who had never been farther west than Albany, N. Y.; she chose the moment when The Hill bus was turning the highest point on the Jemez mountains to peek out—and fainted dead away.

Under these conditions of secrecy rumors multiplied like maggots in one of Mel Hagman's garbage cans. Gas warfare, rockets, jet propulsion, death rays and—atomic bombs—were among the guesses most frequently voiced. During the last Presidential campaign, Alamos—no foolin'—was sometimes a Republican internment camp.

In the early days of the project, even the "outside employees" who knew no more of what was going on than the Japs in the foxholes of Guadalcanal, were sworn never to reveal what they didn't know anyway, for the rest of their lifetime. Our own B. B. Dunne got tangled in the wringer for so much as mentioning that "there were a lot of scientists in town".

Then there was the time when the New York Daily [*News*] was whipping up a Sunday feature on Nobel prizewinners in the U. S. It queried The New Mexican for a brief summary of what Prof X was doing now. The staff recognized the Alamos postoffice box number—that famous postal box where babies were born and to which whole crateloads of furniture were assigned—but it was decided to give the professor a whirl anyway on the old "You can't shoot me for trying" principle. A letter went out to Professor X in which an interview was asked.

The next morning at 8:09—their watches must have been slow, —two guards jumped the cityroom. After a heap of protestations and avowals of innocence, it was agreed that the following telegram could be sent the News:

"Your man working for Mr. Whiskers on extremely hush-hush project. No soap."

The telegram was delivered in New York by a Western Union boy flanked by a covey of guards. These men then began spilling all over the News cityroom like oranges out of a busted crate.

How, they wanted to know, did the News staff explain such Dick Tracy huggermugger stuff?

The News' difficulty was that the girl who had sent the telegram had gone on vacation and couldn't be reached. The News explained it after two clouded weeks in which, by report, you couldn't toss a cigaret in a wastepaper basket without setting fire to a guard.

The tantalizing little that Santa Feans knew about The Hill, only heightened their interest. There were the lights to be seen from miles away; there were the days when fires raged and smoke billowed in the mountains and always the mysterious explosions— (Lady Holmes moved to Tesuque and had moments when she thought she was back in bomb-shattered London).

The payoff, however, came in the "Battle of the MPs". More than a year ago a boxing card was arranged in which the Santa Fe High athletes took on the Alamos MPs. The sluggers from The Hill must have been missing out on their vitamins or the Demons were packing an atomic punch because the MPs were knocked cold, two or three of them in one round and one punch practically.

Unfortunately for Mel Rhine and his Santa Fe MPs—as distinct from the Alamos MPs—soldiers read the sports pages and the next Saturday night, there was an epidemic of free-swinging in the bars and restaurants.

Frantically Rhine demanded that The New Mexican print an explanation that the one-round pushovers were decidedly NOT his MPs but he ran smack into the Alamos secrecy ban.

For hours Rhine sweated over a document which, by the time it complied with censorship requirements, rambled for no less than 700 words or so—and meant exactly nothing to anybody. It was a masterpiece of obfuscation. Of course, the boys were still swinging at the so-called "one-round MPs" for weeks before they discovered their mistake.

The return alive of about half of the members of the 200th Coast Artillery, many of them still feeble and ill, touched off a special welcoming celebration. The army's Bruns General Hospital had been established in the city, and that was the natural point to which to ship the men as they came out of the Japanese prison camps in the Philippines and gained strength enough to go anywhere. The fiesta staged for them was under Will Shuster as general chairman. Captain A. B. Martinez of the state police, later Santa Fe's chief of police, was in charge of the parade.

The New Mexican *came out with a special "Bataan Edition," in such a state of enthusiasm that the edition had no masthead, no date appeared on it anywhere, and there were no page numbers. It is clear, however, that it came out on Sunday, November 11, 1945. People still faintly remembered that November 11 had formerly been known as Armistice Day. The celebration took place on Monday, November 12.*

[November 11, 1945:] BATAAN EDITION. [*Banner headline.*] WHEN IT LOOKED AS IF THE WAR WERE NEW MEXICO VS. JAPAN. 200TH 1ST AND LAST TO FIGHT; IN FRONT LINE WHEN BATAAN FOLDED.

NEW YORK, Dec. 8 (UP)—The NBC Manila Correspondent reported today that the Japanese planes which attacked Clark Field this morning were driven off but that 300 casualties were reported at the big U. S. army base. Some 25 American planes were reported destroyed by the Japanese attack.

By Art Morgan.

The New Mexican splashed the entire foregoing dispatch across the top of the front page in 30-point Italic type, above the banner line for the day. It was full of unwritten portent for Santa Fe readers.

The War Department had banned any mention of the location of U. S. troops. However, the families of 80 Santa Fe men and boys knew they were stationed at Clark Field, north of Manila. They were in Battery C, Santa Fe's own battery, 200th Coast Artillery (Antiaircraft).

The 200th had embarked late in August or early in September at San Francisco for the Philippines. A New Mexican National Guard regiment, the 200th had been called into federal service early in 1941, trained in the interim at Fort Bliss, Tex.

UNDER FIRE.

Unofficially two reasons have been widely quoted among the folks at home in explanation of the Army's choice of the 200th for Luzon. One is that many of the gunners spoke Spanish fluently, would be able to get along well with the Filipinos. The other was their gunnery record for accuracy. Later reports lent color to the latter version. The 200th had had but little time to fraternize with the Filipinos before the war was upon them.

The Dec. 8, 1941, bombing of Clark Field was the "baptism of fire" for New Mexico's now most famous regiment. From that day until April 9, 1942, when the Japanese finally overran the lower tip of Bataan Peninsula, most of the 200th were in the thick of the fighting. One battery escaped to Corregidor, the rock fortress in Manila Bay, and fought on until May 6 when Lt. Gen. Jonathan Wainwright capitulated, ending American resistance on Luzon except guerilla warfare.

Guam and Wake fell; Hong Kong and Singapore, fabulous British stronghold, fell. The Japanese gained footholds on New Guinea and in the Solomons, threatening the U. S. lifeline to Australia, which was to be Gen. Douglas MacArthur's springboard for his return to the Philippines. Still Bataan held out. In those dark days it looked almost as if it were a war of New Mexico against Japan. The 200th was almost exclusively New Mexican. There were many lads also from this state in the 515th Coast Artillery (AA), a scattered few in other outfits on the peninsula.

The 515th was split off the 200th in Luzon and the two regiments made up the Provisional Philippine Coast Artillery Brigade (AA). Col. C. G. Sage, Deming newspaper editor, commander of the 200th when it reached the islands, was placed in command of the brigade. Col. Harry Peck of Albuquerque took over command of the 515th and Col. Memory Cain, also of Deming, succeeded Sage in command of the 200th.

REPORTS ALARM.

The 300 casualties reported in the Clark Field attack carried an ominous ring for the home folks. So did later reports of heavy losses on Bataan. The folks did not know at the time that it was the 19th Heavy Bombardment Group, formerly stationed at Kirtland Field, Albuquerque, that had taken the heavy punishment at the base.

It was many months afterward, when stereotyped postal cards began to trickle back to the States from prison camps, that the soldiers' families began to realize that most of them had survived Bataan and "The Rock". Colonel Sage, who arrived recently at Bruns General Hospital, estimated the 200th fatalities did not exceed 20 up to the time of the infamous "March of Death".

But the 200th did not get off lightly. More than three years in enemy prison camps, with their starvation diet and barbarism, took a severe toll. The sinking of enemy prison ships by U. S. forces, as the Japanese hurried their prisoners northward before the reinvading American armies, took an even heavier toll of life.

IRONY OF FATE.

It was an ironic fate for the men who went down with these ships. They had lived through the hardships of prison life to witness the promised return of MacArthur, but to die before their liberation, by drowning or shot by Japanese as they struggled in the water.

The 200th was 1,400 strong when it went to the islands, including men received from the draft at Fort Bliss to bring the regiment up to full strength. Carl Whittaker, liaison officer of the New Mexico Veterans War Information Bureau at Albuquerque, said on Oct. 22, this year, that 577 of the 1,400 were dead, including 488 New Mexicans 422 were still listed in his files as prisoners, including 263 New Mexicans; 48 as missing, including 27 New Mexicans, and 821 as returned to the States, including 638 New Mexicans.

Explaining the large numbers still recorded as prisoners, Whittaker explained that his information was about a month behind that given next of kin by the War Department. . . .

After it was all over, a citation of the 200th and 515th announced by the War Department in the name of President Franklin D. Roosevelt, gave the 200th credit for covering the retirement to Bataan, "contributing in a large measure to the successful execution of the difficult maneuver that made possible the prolonged defense of Bataan."

[November 11, 1945:] BATAAN EDITION. HALF OF SANTA FE'S BATTERY LISTED AS LOST.

Battery C. 200th Coast Artillery (AA)—Santa Fe's three-inch ackack battery—lost approximately half of its original strength in the war against Japan, Carl F. Whittaker, . . . has disclosed.

Of the 149 enlisted men of this battery who went to the Philippines in the fall of 1941, 58 are listed as dead on the WVIB's records. Fourteen others are still recorded as prisoners, three as still missing in action.

The 149 included men added to the battery by the draft after the regiment went to Fort Bliss, Tex., early in January, 1941, for training having been called into federal service.

69 LIBERATED.

Of the 149, 69 have been liberated from Japanese prison camps after more than 3½ years of starvation and brutality. Seven were released before the war, being in the over-age group.

The 69 liberated, however, do not include all Santa Feans at Bataan and Corregidor, who have come home. There were other boys from the Capital City in these battles who belonged to other outfits; Whittaker's figures apply only to the one battery.

Of the officers who went to Bliss with the battery only one has returned—Maj. Gerald B. Greeman, then a lieutenant, who is now at Bruns General Hospital here. Capt. James Sadler, who commanded the battery at that time as first lieutenant, is dead. So is Capt. A. B. Melendez, previous battery commander, who had been transferred to regimental headquarters. These bring the battery's known dead to 60.

NOVEMBER 13, 1945:   SANTA FE PAYS RECORD TRIBUTE TO BATAAN MEN.

The 200th Coast Artillery (AA) found out how the hometown felt about it yesterday when thousands of Santa Feans marched in cheering tribute past the Plaza reviewing stand packed with survivors of Bataan.

Young and old, many defying a nipping wind to wear Fiesta costumes, joined in the procession which oldtimers declared the most impressive patriotic ceremony in memory. One or two of the Fiesta parades in the early 20's may have topped yesterday's in elaborateness and length but it was conceded that the 1945 program will go down as the city's most spontaneous Armistice Day demonstration.

PARADE STANDS OUT.

The parade was the stand-out feature of a Welcome-Home celebration which included religious services of prayer for the dead and thanksgiving for the nation, presentation of souvenir ring certificates to liberated Bataan survivors of Santa Fe County, a football game in which Santa Fe High toppled Las Vegas High 13 to 6 at Magers Field and a cocktail party and supper dance at the Elks Club.

The turnout by the veterans, many from out of town, was as much a matter of mutual jubilation as the unprecedented turnout of Santa Feans for the parade. Three trucks, 90 feet long, furnished a reviewing stand that was jampacked with returnees who, hailed by each contingent as it marched past, ribbed and greeted friends in the line of march.

APRIL 29, 1946:   26 MAKE HIKE TO CHIMAYO. 500 JOURNEY TO SANTUARIO FOR MASS.

More than 500, probably the largest congregation ever to attend services in El Santuario, Chimayo's famed chapel, were present at 10 a. m. High Mass yesterday which culminated the weekend pilgrimage of veterans to that tiny community.

Twenty-three veterans—all but two members of New Mexico's 200th coast artillery (AA) which was captured on Bataan—made the 26-mile march, the last 11 miles of which was over open, mountainous terrain. Besides, three women, two of them wives of participating veterans, and Fuzzy, a little, shaggy, white-and-yellow-haired terrier, owned by S/Sgt. Gavino Rivera, 326 Staab street, completed the hike.

At yesterday's service, the pewless, earthen-floored shrine was packed by families of the veterans with an honored place given to those who had lost sons and brothers on Bataan and in Japanese camps. The crowd overflowed until the 50-foot patio in front of the church was more than half-filled. The narrow streets and yards of the rolling hillside confronting the church were filled with other groups and autos parked every which way. At times during the hour-and-a-half service rain sprinkled on the crowd.

The Mass was sung by the Rev. Salvador Gene, pastor of Santa Cruz church, who has jurisdiction over the chapel. The choir of St. Anne's church, Santa Fe, under the direction of Nat Chavez, sang. According to old custom, the women stood on one side of the church and the men on the other; the altar was decorated with blue and gold streamers and rosettes. Santo Nino and other prized wooden statues were in holiday array.

The crowd was so large in the tiny edifice that it was difficult to kneel; there was a single, backless bench but one old woman had brought two kitchen chairs.

After the service with its sermon in Spanish had been completed, those in the patio surged into the chapel and the little side shrine was crowded with a patient stream of supplicants who gathered handfuls of the soil from the dry well which supposedly has curative powers.

Autos had been piling into the hamlet since early morning and the crowd was enlarged by the arrival of approximately 70 in a large bus provided by Bruns General hospital. The bus was late in arriving at the meeting place, in front of the Old Governors palace. But the occupants were then given a fast, roller-coaster ride over the hills, the kids, most of them riding in an army vehicle for the first time, had a wonderful outing. For the return home a second bus was at hand and children, deserting their own family cars, filled this one, too.

The effect of the long hike on the pilgrims varied markedly. The three women, Mrs. Arthur B. Smith, Mrs. Eddie Tafoya and Miss Teresa Mahboub were limping but considering that they were entirely unused to that sort of thing, they appeared to have come through quite well. One or two of the men—the heftier ones—were utterly fatigued; the faces of others bore haggard lines yesterday after a night's sleep. And others went to a village dance Saturday night. . . .

The usual route to Chimayo is 31 miles but the pilgrims, taking a cut-off near Cuyamungue, theoretically shortened the distance by five; the gain was questionable since they were committed to dusty wagon roads winding up and down hills and around mesas.

The patron of the miraculous shrine, Santuario, or "Sanctuary," is known as Santo Niño, the Holy Child. Actually it is, or was originally, the Black Christ of Esquipulas, in Guatemala. The cult of the Black Christ, with its special feature of a deposit of clay which the devout scrape up and take away much as one might take holy water, was brought to Chimayo in the late eighteenth century, when a group of Mexican weavers were colonized there.

The Santuario was built by private individuals, who maintained it for more than a hundred years. In the early twentieth century it was neglected and falling into serious disrepair. A group of artists and their friends, led by Mary Austin and Alice Corbin, bought it and presented it to the Roman Catholic church, which has since maintained it.

DECEMBER 10, 1946: HEALTH DEPARTMENT FACTS BELIE TIME'S ASSERTIONS.

State health department records expose as replete in factual errors an article in Time's Dec. 9 issue which pictures Santa Fe county as Death valley for infants, only a little better for new mothers. The article tells of the Medical Mission sisters' work at their maternity institute, 417 E. Palace avenue. It says they came here "one bleak November day in 1943 . . . because of a grim fact." The reason for their coming, Time adds, was that "Santa Fe county had the highest infant mortality rate (111 per 1,000) and the second highest maternal death rate (over 50 per 10,000) in the U. S."

The official records of the health department show Time's figures to be grossly inaccurate. The infant mortality rate in Santa Fe county was 82.7 per 1,000 livebirths. There were at least 13 other counties in New Mexico with a higher rate, San Juan topping the list with 171.

In other states many individual counties had higher rates than Santa Fe county. Dr. Marion Hotopp, head of the maternal and child welfare division of the state health department, is the authority for this statement. She referred particularly to some of the border counties of Texas, others in the Deep South.

At least eight states had a higher maternal death rate than New Mexico, official statistics show. For New Mexico counties the rate ran up to 13.11 per 1,000 live births. In this county it was 5.48. Dr. Hotopp said, in the light of these facts, she was quite certain this county's rate was not the nation's second highest.

Nearly one hundred years after their first mention in the New Mexican, and eighty years after that paper had described their misery in the exile at Bosque Redondo, the Navajos were in the news again. For generations the majority of Navajos had resisted having their children educated, nor, regardless of the provisions of the Treaty of 1868, had the government ever seriously tried to get all children of school age into school. As a matter of fact, nobody had the faintest idea how many Navajos there were until the issuance of ration books in World War II forced recognition of the startling fact that they numbered at least 60,000. The 1958 estimate is about 80,000, and the rate of increase is in the neighborhood of one thousand a year.

An exploding population on a large, but largely desert, tract of land combined with mass illiteracy and ignorance even of the

*English language to create a desperate situation that had been
disguised, first by WPA, CCC, and other depression measures for
making work and wages, then by the income from military service
(a family receiving $70 a month from an enlisted son was well off)
and war work.*

*The editor of this collection, as it happens, was invited to Win-
dow Rock by the then superintendent, James Stewart, who rubbed
his nose in the economic facts, so that it fell to him to break the
Navajo story, which soon became of national interest.*

*After several years of agitation, Congress enacted the Navajo-
Hopi Rehabilitation Bill (the Hopis did not want to be rehabili-
tated, but since they live directly in the middle of the Navajo
country, they had to be included). This, a sharp increase in tribal
(not individual) income from oil and uranium, and a crash program of developing school facilities by every possible means carried out by Commissioner of Indian Affairs Glenn L. Emmons in
the Eisenhower administration have done much to alleviate the
condition of the tribe.*

SEPTEMBER 27, 1947: LA FARGE DECLARES NAVAJOS EXIST ON
LESS THAN GERMANS. Author Urges U S Program for Industry.

Navajos are subsisting on 1,200 calories a day, 300 less than the
amount allotted to individuals in Germany, Oliver La Farge,
author, told an open meeting of the N. M. Association on Indian
Affairs last night in the Hall of Ethnology.

La Farge, discussing newest phases of the Navajo problem,
cited the need for educational and medical facilities and declared
that the intention of the Department of the Interior to develop
a long-range program of industrialization offers at least "a hope
and a possibility."

Without such development, the reservation can provide for
about 25,000 leaving the remaining 35,000 in need, the speaker
said. As an example of the possibilities, he said the tribal sawmill
this year for the first time in a number of years, is turning a profit
but at most only 200 are employed.

Mrs. C. H. Dietrich, association president, also stressed the need for a specific program to present before the next Congress. She suggested that the government might encourage investment of private capital under arrangements similar to those with Latin-American countries by which a specified amount of Navajo labor would be employed.

JANUARY 15, 1948: NEW MEXICAN HITS 9,000, RECORD PRESS RUN PEAK.

Nine thousand copies of this issue of The Santa Fe New Mexican—an all-time record—were run off the presses today.

The New Mexican's circulation steadily has advanced since the late war years. The figure today is almost exactly twice the average daily press run for July 1943, and represents an increase of 3,100 over the total for January 1946.

In 1926 the mayor of Santa Fe, Ed Safford, appointed a city planning commission. Despite lack of interest, entire lack of authority, and other discouragements, the commission kept plugging away, until in 1948 its labors bore important fruit. Meantime, in 1947 the state legislature had passed an act authorizing the establishment of such commissions with real authority. During the ensuing ten years, despite political opposition, the planning commission developed itself into an influential and effective body.

APRIL 15, 1948: COUNCIL OK'S CITY ZONING ORDINANCE. REVISIONS ARE MADE TO MEET OBJECTIONS RAISED BY RESIDENTS.

. . . The long debated, and amended, ordinance was passed last night. John Gaw Meem, who appeared with Daniel T. Kelly for the city planning commission, has suggested that such action would be a fitting farewell from the outgoing city administration [*under Mayor Manuel Lujan*]. It had sired the idea. . . .

The ordinance had been revised to meet, as far as possible, written objections made by citizens at public hearings last fall, Meem said. . . .

As chairman of the planning commission, Meem also sub-

374

mitted a completed copy of the city plan, two years' work, prepared by Harland Bartholomew & Associates in cooperation with the commission. . . .

Thanks was given by the commission to Bartholomew, the city, school board, Chamber of Commerce, state and Old Santa Fe association, all of whom had contributed to the work. The council gave the commission a vote of thanks. . . .

Meem pointed out that under the enabling act of the 1947 legislature it will be necessary to name a new planning commission. The present one was created before the enactment. . . .

Almost as soon as Indian veterans began returning, they agitated for the right to vote, denied them in New Mexico by an attorney general's interpretation of the phrase in the state constitution, "Indians not taxed," a "term of art" appearing in the Fourteenth Amendment to the U. S. Constitution and having a special, tricky meaning. Suits in the state courts, sponsored by the American Civil Liberties Union, were frankly and unconscionably delayed. Finally the late Felix S. Cohen, the greatest authority this country has ever had on law affecting Indians, entered a suit in federal court in the name of a former marine, with the result described below.

Arizona had already conceded the vote to Indians, on the basis of a decision of its state supreme court. This, I believe, left Idaho and Rhode Island as the only states that denied the vote, and both soon remedied the inequity—in Rhode Island it was purely a matter of sentiment and of clearing that state's record.

AUGUST 3, 1948:   [*Six-column banner.*] INDIANS AWARDED VOTE RIGHTS; STATE BAN SAID DISCRIMINATORY.

Pueblo- and reservation-dwelling Indians have the right to vote in New Mexico, a three-judge U. S. district court held today. The court voided a provision of the state's constitution disfranchising "Indians not taxed." This ban, the court found, contravenes the 14th and 15th amendments to the U. S. constitution, being discriminatory on account of race.

U. S. Circuit Judge O. L. Phillips [*of Colorado*] announced the decision. Sitting with him were U. S. District Judge Bower Broaddus and Royce H. Savage, both of Oklahoma.

However, many New Mexico Indians may not be able to vote this fall, although the court has held they are entitled to. In fact, none may get to vote then.

The court enjoined County Clerk Eloy Garley, Valencia county, from refusing to register Miguel H. Trujillo. The injunction is effective only in Valencia county; Garley was the only county clerk "before the court." Other county clerks may accept or refuse to accept the court's ruling, until the U. S. supreme court passes on it.

Secondly, state's attorneys may get a stay, pending an appeal to the U S Supreme Court. They indicated in court this morning that they would appeal. That alone would not act as a stay.

The state did not appeal the decision, nor did any county clerks ignore it.

When the New Mexico state constitution was being drafted, the state still contained a fair number of illiterate Spanish-Americans and yet a larger number who spoke no English, all of whom were accustomed to exercising their rights as citizens as had their ancestors since Spanish times. The constitution, therefore, permits no requirement of literacy or ability to speak English as a qualification for voting.

The court's decision meant that in northeastern New Mexico somewhere in the neighborhood of 10,000 Navajos, most of whom could not read or write or speak any tongue but their own, could vote. Further, there is the curious fact that the overwhelming majority of Indian traders dealing with the Navajos are confirmed Republicans. With a few outstanding exceptions, Navajo Indian traders have, and deserve, the friendship and trust of their customers.

New Mexico law allows a voter to take an adviser with him into the voting booth to help him mark his ballot. The Democrats saw all too clearly what would happen: truckloads of Navajos being delivered from the various trading posts and advised by

Navajo-speaking Republicans as they marked the straight ticket headed, in 1948, by Bidugai Atsisi, "Little Mustache." This provision particularly affected the Democratic District Attorney for the counties with a large Navajo population, leading him to some extraordinary actions. The two key reports of his endeavors are run here together, out of chronological order.

SEPTEMBER 10, 1948: GUTIERREZ OVERRULES U. S. COURT.

Marcelino Gutierrez, district attorney and a candidate for re-election, has instructed county clerks of his district to deny some 10,000 residents and citizens of the district the right to vote.

In an opinion released yesterday he held that the recent ruling by a three-judge federal court which declared invalid a New Mexico ban against Indian voting, applied to only some Indians. Not included among the voters, according to the district attorney, are the thousands of New Mexico Navajos, practically all of whom live in the district attorney's district. They are excluded, he explains, because they live on a reservation.

The federal court made no such distinction in its ruling. It declared invalid a provision in the New Mexico constitution which denied voting privileges to "Indians not taxed." U. S. District Attorney Everett Grantham, an active participant in the case, said the court action, in his opinion, extended the voting franchise to all Indian residents.

OCTOBER 29, 1948: DOUBLE LINES OUT—KEGEL; INDIAN RESENTS GUTIERREZ.

Double lines of voters at the polls are out, Assistant Attorney General Walter R. Kegel ruled today.

He was replying to an inquiry from District Attorney Marcelino Gutierrez, Gutierrez wanted to know if Indians who need assistance could not be culled out from "intelligent voters" to save time.

Kegel found in a seven-page opinion all election officials "must process each elector separately."

In reply to other queries by Gutierrez, Kegel said:

(1) Sheriff's deputies may be posted at the polls on an Indian

reservation, but they lack "criminal jurisdiction over incidents where Indians are involved, either as law violator or victim."

(2) Navajo interpreters may be used.

Kegel added it was the duty of election officers and peace officers "to keep the entrance to polling places unobstructed and to arrest any person obstructing the same." He added: "If the obstructing person were an Indian, serious doubts would arise as to the jurisdiction of any state or county officer to arrest such person, in view of the limited jurisdiction of the state upon the reservation."

Joe H. Herrera, a Cochiti Indian, today protested he was "capable of casting as intelligent a vote as the district attorney." He resented D. A. Marcelino Gutierrez's inquiry of the attorney general if two lines couldn't be formed at the polls—one for Indians needing assistance and the other for "intelligent voters."

The Republicans seized upon Gutierrez's endeavors with whoops of joy. Their net result was that he was soundly defeated in an election in which most Democrats won.

Meantime, the residents of Los Alamos were also having difficulties. It was the general opinion at the time that the politicians of both parties were terrified at the thought of the injection into their established situation of the votes of several thousand notoriously well-educated, intelligent, and independent people.

SEPTEMBER 21, 1948: [*Seven-column banner line.*] COURT VOIDS ALAMOS PRIMARY VOTE. DECISION INDICATES JUDGE ARLEDGE WINS DUKE COURT POSITION.

New Mexico's supreme court today disqualified all votes cast at Los Alamos in the recent primary election. But it held some residents of the AEC installation are legal voters. The disqualification came on the court's ruling that all polling place for the election were on lands acquired by condemnation. Such lands, it held, are not a part of the state for voting purposes.

The high court held:

1. Residence on lands at Los Alamos acquired by condemna-

tion will not meet constitutional requirements of "residence" for voting purposes.

2. That exclusive jurisdiction has not been ceded to the United States on lands acquired from public domain and that residents on such lands are entitled to vote.

3. But that since all polling places in the primary election were located on lands acquired by condemnation, all votes are invalid.

The decision apparently gives to District Judge R. F. Deacon Arledge of Albuquerque the Democratic nomination for district judge, second division, Second judicial district. If the Los Alamos votes had been held valid, his opponent D. A. Macpherson probably would have won.

SEPTEMBER 24, 1948: CAPITOL CHAFF. CANDIDATE SURVIVES BY HALF A MATTRESS.

By Will Harrison.

Betty McClendon, Los Alamos candidate for the legislature, has survived the supreme court's checkerboard ruling that some people up there are residents of New Mexico and some are not. She made it by half a mattress.

The court held that residents of lands at Los Alamos which were acquired by condemnation are not residents of New Mexico —those on other lands are. Candidate Betty, it develops, lives in a house at 3948 Trinity drive that is split in two by one of the dividing lines. Half of her house is citizenship territory, half alien. The line, as far as she and her scientist husband can determine, sweeps through the family's front bedroom which is occupied by Mrs. McClendon's parents, whacks on through the wall and across the room where the candidate sleeps.

"But the bed is on the citizenship side, at least my part of it," she said. "And besides, when I registered I was living on citizenship land in another house with no line through it."

She telephoned District Attorney M. Ralph Brown at Albuquerque and was told that she was still a valid candidate. "But he advised me," she said, "To sleep way over against the wall."

379

Santa Fe

Before the next general election the right of Alamites to vote had been conceded, and the Los Alamos area had been made into a separate county, thus getting all that brain power off the backs of the local politicos in Santa Fe and Sandoval Counties, within which the settlement had lain.

CHAPTER 6

JUST THE OTHER DAY

DECEMBER 1, 1948: ROBERT MCKINNEY TAKES OPTION TO BUY
NEW MEXICAN'S STOCK.

Frank C. Rand, Jr., president of the New Mexico Publishing
Co., which publishes the Santa Fe New Mexican, announced
today that Robert McKinney, Tucumcari rancher, has been
granted an option to purchase the stock of the corporation. Mc-
Kinney said he plans to exercise the option Jan. 15 for himself
and associates.

George Reynolds, formerly of Alexandria, Va., a representative
of the prospective publisher, will serve as acting general manager
during the option period.

UNDER McKinney and Reynolds, then under McKinney alone,
the New Mexican became Democratic, with a strong dash of independence. Until January 19, 1952, Harrison continued as editor.
As under Dana Johnson, the staff of the paper included many who
had long been steeped in the Santa Fe tradition and more who
were naturally sympathetic to it. A special effort was made to
stress Santa Fe's quality as an artistic and literary center, leading
in time to the setting up of a special Sunday page on artistic doings, under a special editor.

Will Shuster and the editor of this collection were taken on as
columnists, and for a time from the end of 1949 until late in 1951

381

members of the staff contributed what became known as "poor man's editorials"—short pieces of observation on the local scene, essays, reminiscences, and sketches. They were contributed simply for the fun of it, which in itself is a document on newspaper life in Santa Fe at the time. The literary level achieved was not high but better than one might have feared. Santa Fe has the characteristic of attracting and holding people of sensitivity who could do better financially elsewhere; this characteristic was reflected in the New Mexican *of the period.*

A conscious purpose of this final section is to reprint evidence that Santa Fe, with a population of 30,000, still retains a good bit of the special "oomph," the oddity, and the liveliness it had when all its people numbered 5,000 and that at the beginning of the second half of the twentieth century its newspaper, now thoroughly professional, bristling with wire services and other modern improvements, still relates to its community as intimately and informally as it did in the days of Manderfield and Tucker.

Some people are naturally Santa Feans; they become part of the city's character almost as soon as they arrive. Others, even some born here, simply cannot belong. There were numerous examples of the first group on the New Mexican's *staff in 1950. An outstanding case was William McNulty and his artist wife, Agnes Tait, who came here in 1941. McNulty was born in Lawrence, Massachusetts, and was a graduate of the* Providence Journal, *among other papers. It was he who named the "poor man's editorials," and his were the best. His treatment of the atomic secret appeared in the last section; if there is a good deal of him in the present one it is because, in the little more than a decade before his untimely death, he was an authentic part of what makes this curious city what it is, and his being on the paper gives us a rare X ray of a member of the club.*

JANUARY 22, 1950: A DOLLAR FOR JULIA.

By William McNulty.

Bear with me on this one as it is rather involved.

Before Christmas, The New Mexican printed letters from Children to Santa Claus and naturally I was given the job of being Santa Claus editor. (I say "naturally" because that's the kind of assignment I get around this place.)

Among the communications received was one from an anonymous Julia who felt that she and her sister had not been given a fair shake as regards the distribution of gum, the chubby old lad seeming to favor those younger than 8. In short, she told Santa to "blow back to the North Pole."

The story seemed to have appeal for people fed up with certain aspects of the holiday doings. The wire services picked up the yarn and it apparently made the national networks.

A contributor sent in two cartons of gum to Julia in recognition of her blunt, if somewhat undiplomatic stand. Thus, in claiming the gift, she was identified as the daughter of Mr. and Mrs. Tomas Gomez, 508 Doroteo Street.

In spite of what you might think, Julia is no brash youngster; instead it was hard work getting two words out of her.

So far so good, but a reader or a listener in California was so moved by Julia's intrepidity, that he sent her a dollar, presumably to buy more gum.

Here's where the problem arises. The dollar, new and crisp, lies in the top drawer of my desk; notice of the man's offering has been printed in the Mister Citizen column but Julia hasn't shown up yet.

Every time we open the drawer to get a paper clip or consult the weather data or hunt for a pencil stub, our eye falls on the dollar.

There are times, it is our shame to admit, when our luncheon money gets perilously low; it may be down to as little as 45 or 50 cents and always there is this dollar confronting us which, if put together with 45 or 50 cents would furnish a rum and water and the 85-cent special at La Cantina.

There it is Julia; so far we have refrained from embezzling your dollar by an unprecedented show of character. For three reasons:

1) Never let it be said that a McNulty embezzled only a single dollar; if I must face a term in the clink, let it be for some such sum as $125 or $150.

(One of our in-laws made Leavenworth. It was true he was only an in-law, one of the men whom the womenfolk, as the tolerant saying has it, bring into the family, but still, Leavenworth is no truant school.)

2) Never let it be said that a McNulty embezzled from an eight-year-old child.

3) Never let it be said that a McNulty embezzled from Julia Gomez, a person whose fortitude is so eminently admirable.

Still and all, while our principles are so firm, please, Julia, please come and get your dollar.

Relations between the ancient capital of New Mexico and the shiny new atomic city on "the hill" have mostly been good, but exceptions must occur. In 1950 the AEC authorities started selling off old temporary wooden buildings that had been erected in the days of the Manhattan Project. Because some of these buildings were in very poor condition, and because they were fire hazards, the Santa Fe city council forbade their use inside the city limits. This action, and an editorial about it, drew fire.

MARCH 16, 1950: A NEIGHBOR FROM LOS ALAMOS STATES HIS VIEWS ABOUT SANTA FE.

Editor, The New Mexican:

This is a letter of thanks and appreciation for proving one of my theories about the way the people of Santa Fe feel about Los Alamos and its residents. Your editorial about the "old type" buildings (March 9) being moved down the hill into your "beautiful and unprotected countryside" told the whole story very effectively.

For one thing no one is trying to deceive the poor and desperate people who need these "death traps." Cheating and deceiving are the tools used by Santa Fe businessmen and New Mexico politicians. Compared to some of the slovenly adobe pigsty's [sic] that are called home in Santa Fe, these buildings could be a gift from heaven with a little remodeling. Why should you gripe about a few of our poorer buildings when you have a city full of degenerate, disease infested shacks and mud hovels?

The "butter rich" city is shucking off some of its buildings for several reasons, but you might take a hint and start a clean out campaign of your own. Espccially after some of the filth and star-vation cases reported there recently. I personally don't see how these buildings could make Santa Fe any worse than it is now. The only way to clean up your filthy city different, would be to burn the whole city to the ground and start all over again. Even then there wouldn't be much improvement.

One other point I would like to bring out. I don't know where you get the idea that the residents of Los Alamos are rich, unless you have been around when some of the Santa Fe businessmen raised their prices when they heard that a Los Alamosan was com-ing in the door. We make a decent living wage here, but not high enough to cope with the ideas of some Santa Feans. I am happy about one thing though, and that is the gripes we are going to hear from these same businessmen when the University employees start working Saturdays. Imagine Santa Fe without the Saturday shoppers from Los Alamos. I can hear them crying already.

Victor F. Allen,

1075 Iris St., Apt. 15,

Los Alamos, N. M.

The New Mexican has a large number of communications re-garding the condemned buildings from Los Alamos—some like them, some don't. They will be published when space permits. Victor F. Allen's communication is put ahead. It might pop a blood vessel lying in a basket.—Ed.

MARCH 19, 1950: OUR LITERARY EDITOR DISCUSSES LETTERS-TO-EDITOR 'LITERATURE.' OFTEN NEWSPAPER CRITICS COMMIT VERBAL HARI-KARI.

By Oliver La Farge.

"Would that mine enemy would write a book"—or anyway a letter to the editor. The chances are ten to one that he will deliver himself into your hands, this writer not excepted.

Thursday's New Mexican provides an example of verbal hari-kari too beautiful to pass up. In search of clean fun, let us now consider the featured letter to the editor from a Hill resident who did not like the paper's front-page editorial about dumping those condemned houses on the county. It's a lulu.

Rhetorically, the letter starts well: "This is a letter of thanks and appreciation for proving one of my theories about the way the people of Santa Fe feel about Los Alamos and its residents." Good, sound sarcasm. If the writer had kept to this vein he might have given us real, creative invective.

How many of us read what we read? That sentence also inserts an absolutely false premise, upon which the rest of the letter is constructed. The editorial had nothing to do with "Los Alamos and its residents." It was aimed entirely at the atomic energy commission, whose rules enforce the sale of tumble-down firetraps. Thus, to the thoughtful reader, the letter disqualifies itself in the first sentence.

In the second paragraph one can watch a familiar process: an angry writer losing his temper in the enthusiasm of creation. We reach: "Compared to some of the slovenly adobe pigsty's (sic) which are called home in Santa Fe . . ." And a little farther on: ". . . a city full of degenerate, disease-ridden shacks and mud hovels."

The boy is in full swing now, and pretty good. He has begged the New Mexican's main question: the fire hazard of these buildings. He has also ignored the point, carefully made, that none of these buildings will be set up within Santa Fe. He is giving himself away pretty fast. The phrase "mud hovels" is a case in semantics; "adobe house" has no connotation, good or bad, but "mud" and "hovel" arouse emotions, they are technically known as "signal words."

As to the real point: I doubt if even our impassioned correspondent would argue that mud walls, 18 or more inches thick, able with fair maintenance to last for centuries, are as inflammable as the tar-paper and slat walls of condemned temporary buildings.

Following now a completely non-existent argument, in the next paragraph he writes: "The only way to clean up your filthy city different would be to burn the whole city to the ground . . ." In open debate, with fire hazard a principal question, no smart man would say that; it would lay him too wide open. Even in this letter, the self-betrayal is surprising. Alas, this is no longer the art of invective, but the indulgence of diatribe.

To a writer, the important thing is that by now our correspondent has defeated himself. The City Difficult has bad slums, true, but they were not under discussion. The city was not under discussion. Through sheer lack of control he has disqualified himself before most readers, regardless of their opinion of Santa Fe. It's a pity; this letter might have been good.

To my delight, he does not stop there. He writes of being on hand when Santa Fe merchants "raised their prices when they heard that a Los Alamosan was coming in the door." "Los Alamosan," incidentally, is quite a mouthful.

I see a fascinating picture. Taking a few from one block:— Messrs. Yashvin, Spitz, Moore, Kaune, and Zook, and the staffs of Woolworth's and Penney's, hurriedly altering price tags as the Alamite approaches. The Santa Feans, country shoppers, and tourists present look on smiling. They are in on the game; they will get a cut.

Did our correspondent ever wonder how we spot an Alamite on sight? I'll tell him. We, too, have a Geiger counter; but it is different. It was made in the dark of the moon following the winter solstice, in the Horned Husband Kiva at Awatovi. Set up in the Plaza, it can spot an Alamite before he rounds the federal building, by his high blood pressure and his disgust at our good village. Unfortunately, 98.833 repeating per cent of Hill people are agreeable, we like them, for all their justified gripes they seem to like us, and they come to town feeling pleasant. These the counter misses. Unless they will agree to wearing a scarlet A on their chests, we shall continue to miss a lot of chances to gouge them.

It is interesting and sad to realize that this letter has nothing whatever to do with the editorial it allegedly answers. The writer, his mind locked by pre-established angers, saw the words, but he never read them. Alas, all too much "debate" in this world goes on at this level. The Russians do it at Lake Success. Here, with the political or loony season coming up, even if we don't have the Hurley-burley of the last campaign, we are going to get a lot of it.

We need to hear and analyze what the other fellow says. We need even more to hear and analyze what we ourselves say, to learn whether we are thinking or are merely flapping our prejudices in the innocent air.

Early students of New Mexican Spanish found that it preserved in remarkable degree the speech of seventeenth and early eighteenth century Spain, "the Spanish of the Golden Age" of Cervantes and others. What is happening to it and to many other aspects of the old culture among the inhabitants of the ancient capital is epitomized in Calla Hay's article, "Ringeame."

The compound itself needs a bit of explanation. It is pronounced "reeng-eh-ah-may," with the stress on the last syllable. From the English verb "to ring" has been formed a pseudo-Spanish "ringear," the reflexive form of which as used by Mrs. Hay means "ring me."

MAY 28, 1950: RINGEAME.

By Calla Hay.

Russia may lay claim to the origin of the international language devised by its Dr. Zamenhof under the pseudonym of Dr. Esperanto. In Santa Fe, however, an entirely new language is growing up, nameless, and this might be a good time to nail it down before other claimants can put in a bid. What to call it, we do not know. "Amerspan" might do, or "Espanican", or almost any word which would signify a combination of Spanish and United States American. The suggestion of English and Spanish is necessary because this new speech is a combination of the two, with the worst from each frequently chosen.

Whether it should be taught in kindergarten is a moot question. Having learned it from the teen-ager set, we're not too sure whether the youngsters should be let in on it. They probably don't need to know that their older sister "tenia un date with that fello el Sabado;" nor that her best friend will query in awe and admiration: "Gee, kid, tuvieron good time?"

"Ringeame" will be the conclusion of this exchange, and it is this word that is the key to the way in which Amerspan is becoming widespread. We've been learning it via the telephone, not that we were ever great on listening to conversations that Marconi never dreamed of when he tinkered with an invention. Unfortunately, for the past five months we were stuck with a telephone line which was useless except as a lesson in the new language.

We never did find out whether our line was a two or four-party. If the latter, three-quarters of its subscribers were shut out by the one family which usurped all time on the line from the hour that the young people come home from school and/or work until they were bedded down or out on the town late at night. They visited over the wires by the hour, just as if their friends were in the same room rather than at the opposite end of a public utility. They laughed, they talked, they made love. They left the line open while they did errands. They returned, sometimes with the phonograph turned up loud in order that a new record could be heard across town. They sat in silence over and again, the long moments being filled only with the gentle rhythm of their gums pressing and repressing wads of gum. If, at such a moment, a fellow subscriber considered the silence a cue to click for an operator, their indignation knew no bounds. Gums would chomp chiquete like fury, over "There's someone on the line." But not yet would come the "Ringeame tomorrow—bueno goodbye" which concluded every call. No, the mere fact of someone else needing the line, put them on their metal. They got there first, didn't they? They weren't going to give up to any johnnie-come-lately.

In five months of paying for telephone service on a line that was impossible of use, one grows curious as to what these long conversations develop. Patching the bits together, we learned the new language somewhat as follows: "Halo honey, como estas: Fine an you? You know what, I have been so busy. Sabes que! Tonight voy al show con la sister de la Jennie. Oh you know what, la Jennie tiene un baby tan sweet. You know I don't like la sister de la

Jennie. Porque? O, she is muy traicionera. No, you don't know her, sabes que es tan nice."

Having disposed of Jennie and her sister, more important business arises.

"Let's go to the dance tomorrow en Pojoaque in my Foringo," the boy suggests. "Of course el starter y las brekas are not working very good, pero podemos tener un good time." Now this discussion is good for thirty minutes and before it is ended, "you know what? Tengo una leva, a new one, I am going to wear. Y tu?" She decides on what dress to wear, she wonders and asks, "Todavia me quieres?" And that proves to be good for an hour of love and jealousy.

"Oh you know que nomas tu dear; and you, do you still love me? Of course, tu solo tu. How can you say that when the other night andabas con el, with that pachuco? He is not a pachuco, he is my cozzen. How about you cuando estabas en el army? Tu le dijites al Jonnie que tenias dates with muchas gringas."

Forty minutes later, she is ready to admit of the pachuco, "Sabes porque lo quitie? Porque he only wanted to have dates alla en el Resvalon hall. Gee kid, hijole, they had so many fights there." Love's young dream is on the beam as she consents to being his little cucaracha at the Pojoaque dance. Reluctantly, they leave the line, but not without a few verbal passes at those who would take it from them, and final, "Ringeame."

For fellow sufferers in the City Different, for we found that ours was only one of many similar abused telephone lines, let us recommend this language study as an antidote for apoplexy when important calls demand making. For those who fail to find bilingual slanguage amusing, the only thing to do is to move into some other district where there will be a changed telephone service. We did. Now you can "ringea" us.

MARCH 12, 1950:

By Will Shuster.

In 1920 there were several small adobe houses opposite the museum where the Hudson Motor Co. is today. Each had two small rooms tandem-like, one in back of the other. They rented for $5 a month. I had one of these for a studio. It was close to the Art Museum and to the Plaza.

Mounted riders tied their horses to a post on the corner while they shopped or visited in town. Sheldon Parson's horse stood there frequently for long hours. The Hendersons, Whippy and Alice, with young Alice frequently rode to town together and would park their cayuses at that post. I dread to think of what would happen to any horse parked there now.

Old Abe Spiegelberg used to drop in regularly to keep an eye on the new painting and yarn about the old West. One afternoon I heard hoofbeats on the sidewalk. I was cleaning my palette and brushes at the end of the day. A voice shouted, "Is anyone in?" "Yes, come in." With that invitation a horse and rider complete with chaps rode right into the room through the open door, dismounted, extended his hand, saying, "I'm Mike Clancy, just dropped in to get acquainted, would you like a drink?" All in one breath. The horse stood there in the room and behaved himself while Mitch and I got acquainted. Life was just as informal as that.

That year, at Fiesta time, a high stockade was built of aspen poles extending from each end of the Governors' Palace across Palace Avenue and along the north side of the Plaza. It completely enclosed the street and the Plaza sidewalk. A long grandstand was erected on the Plaza side facing the Old Palace. Admission gates were placed at each end. It was gay and beautiful inside. The Fiesta was held within that compound.

Around the outside of the stockade, peering through the cracks between the aspen poles were the less fortunate children and gente of the town watching THEIR FIESTA. The gaiety was all inside. I made a satirical drawing of that subject.

I can recall the feeling of resentment that surged up in me over that Fiesta. It set off a chain reaction which has set me against that sort of thing and has made me stubbornly and consistently fight it. That is the reason that Zozobra has always been a free show. No paid admissions, no peeking through cracks, a free show for the whole town.

JULY 2, 1950:   NOW LOOK, MR. EDITOR!

By Art Morgan.

Being a newspaper reporter isn't just a job of meeting "so many interesting people." There are others.

A few years ago The New Mexican's news staff consisted of five men. Among them they could brag of only 3½ complete stomachs. Three had had the final degree of the great legion of ulcerites conferred upon them on the operating table.

They didn't get that way by meeting interesting people exclusively.

The newsmen back in Kansas may have trouble with their Smiths and Joneses, getting their initials right. They are having a summer of roses and wine, even if they don't realize it. Just wait until one of them gets a job in New Mexico and has to struggle with such names as Martinez, Gonzales and Chavez, which fill a large part of the city directory.

Back there seldom do the Joneses and Smiths have the same given names. Here it is different. The New Mexico equivalents of these surnames in many cases have the same given names. And if you bobble one sometimes you think the term "Christian name" is a misnomer.

Can you blame a typewriter-pounder rushing to make a deadline, for getting the deceased and the defendant mixed up? But, strange as it may seem, this often brings a protest—from the only party able to protest.

When the reporter gets the name correctly he can't get in a solid night's sleep. He knows what is going to happen the next morning. Sure enough, the phone rings as soon as he gets on the job.

"Your paper said that ———— ———— got sent to the penitentiary for 99 years," somebody says. "That's my name. I'm an honest man and I am on my job. My friends are asking me how I got out so soon. I want a correction."

One of the chief headaches is the people who want things they have written to appear in the paper word for word. If you save them from glaring grammatical blunders—that even a news writer couldn't fail to spot—do you get any thanks? You get "cussed out." Every word they write is, to them, a brain-child, even though Webster has another name for it.

Volunteer writers of eulogies are frequently fond of the phrase "sweet Christian character." If you leave it out you hear from them, and how. You can't be too harsh with them, however; they don't realize that the next time a well-known dipsomaniac passes on, his family will insist upon your doing as handsomely by him. If you demur, they point to the precedent: "You did it for so-and-so."

There also are gripes from people indignantly asserting they "didn't get nearly enough publicity" out of the demise of a distant relative.

Threats of libel suits are of almost daily occurrence. "If you print my marriage license, I'll sue you," says a sweet bride-to-be. Somebody ought to take her aside and inform her that courts have not so far held marriage to be a felony.

When you refuse a bit of free advertising, the usual retort is: "Don't you want the news?"

You're never fair to any political party unless you risk jail by libelling the opposing party.

Oh, well, it's all in the day's work.

For the new state capitol building, the architect commissioned a set of rectangular terra-cotta plaques, or spandrels, to be inset in the exterior walls. Six of these were designed by the sculptor, a number of casts being made of each. One, originally entitled "Earth," showed a nude female figure about as lacking in erotic quality as is possible. When the first of these was installed it drew fire from a shadow organization calling itself "The Ministerial Alliance," consisting, so far as I have been able to find out, either of the minister of the Berean Baptist Church alone, or of him and one other minister of another numerically minor denomination. In the first news story arising from this protest, McNulty, a creative reporter, named the figure "Miss Fertility," a name that stuck.

The row that followed was as lively as any in which the art colony was ever involved, but its outcome showed how greatly

Santa Fe had changed. In the end, the artists were routed by the Alliance, although the major Protestant churches firmly stayed out of the fight, and the Roman Catholic authorities issued a statement on permissible art that was tolerant, intelligent, and explicitly did not include objection to the panel. Mary Austin must have turned in her grave.

OCTOBER 3, 1950:   BEREAN BAPTISTS ASK REMOVAL OF NUDE ART ON CAPITOL WALLS.

By William McNulty.

Is "Miss Fertility" a symbol of uplifting art or is the brooding figure just a representation of a nude woman in a position too suggestive for display on a public building?

That's the question revolving around the oblong bas-relief panel fashioned by William Longley, young bearded Santa Fe artist and sculptor, for the exterior of the new capitol. The protest was made by a member of the Berean Baptist church.

As of presstime, Governor Mabry, while approving the fertility symbolism of the terra-cotta work, nevertheless ordered the removal of the sculpture after consulting with Willard Kruger of Willard Kruger & Associates, architectural firm who commissioned it. The governor's attitude was that he did not wish to stir any controversy.

However, Longley, who has just moved into a 'dobe home, which he himself built on Camino del Monte Sol, indicated that he may not let the matter rest. A member of Artists Equity, a New York organization corresponding to Actors Equity, in the protection of artists' rights, Longley said this noon, "I may yet get sore at this one."

OCTOBER 4, 1950:   CITY'S ARTISTS IN 'BATTLE OF NUDE' AS MABRY BALKS ON REMOVAL ORDER.

By William McNulty.

Gov. T. J. Mabry, after a conference with a group of artists this morning, decided to call a session tomorrow at 10 a.m. at which

394

the artists and the Rev. Robert J. Brown, Berean Baptist church, can thresh out a solution of the "Miss Fertility" plaque controversy which has attracted nation-wide attention. On the protest of one of his congregation of 80, the Reverend Brown yesterday prompted a move to have the panel, properly named "Earth," removed from the new capitol building.

OCTOBER 4, 1950: THAT BAD WOMAN.

Miss Fertility, or Mrs. it should probably be, was ordered banished from the wall of the new state office building yesterday because she didn't have any clothes on her plaster limbs and belly. A preacher complained that she was "suggestive" and down she comes rather than start a row.

We didn't think much of the relaxed matron either. It seems that after all these centuries sculptors would have thought up some symbol of fertility other than a buxom woman. Whether she's on the wall or not won't make much difference in Tom Mabry's new structure. It does make a difference, though, that all public statuary, murals and such must be tailored to fit within the pattern of the most extreme prudery, even in Santa Fe which likes to kid itself about being cultured and cosmopolitan.

In this art there are no thighs, no mammary glands, no navels. The human body is vulgar, sinful and suggestive unless disguised in shoulder pads and falsies.

The Fertility panel might be safely replaced by a bas relief pile of manure, a fertility symbol that wouldn't be suggestive of anything but fertility.

OCTOBER 5, 1950: FIERY ARTISTS SLAM MINISTERS' ATTITUDE.

By Art Morgan.

Whether "Miss Fertility," a terra cotta spandrel showing a nude woman, remains on the walls of the new state office building rests with W. C. Kruger, the building's architect who commissioned the work.

After a hotly controversial hearing today, with artists aligned on one side and ministers on the other, Gov. Thomas J. Mabry left the decision up to Kruger. The governor said he would not undertake to act as a censor of art.

Kruger indicated he probably would announce his decision tomorrow.

With Mabry as referee, Santa Fe artists charged objecting ministers with ignorance of art, which the men of God admitted. The ministers charged the artists not qualified to speak on morality. This the artists stoutly denied.

The ministers asked that "Miss Fertility" be replaced. At times the debate grew heated with the artists, seated along one wall, facing the ministers, across the room. "Miss Fertility" leaned against the wall behind the latter.

The Rev. Robert Brown of the Berean Baptist church, who set off the furore over the terra-cotta gal, led off.

"I'm not an art critic," he said. "The only thing I can interpret is morals. As a minister of God I feel that this thing is repugnant on a public building."

He said he had been assured by the architect, W. C. Kruger, that the governor had given authority for the removal of the offending bas-relief. The governor denied this.

In view of the reclining position of the figure, Mr. Brown called it "extremely suggestive."

Mr. Brown declared "Man is fertile and woman isn't."

Black-bearded William Longley, the sculptor, replied with a word not in good usage among his clerical opponents.

Governor Mabry said he didn't think "Fertility a pretty picture."

John Sloan, artist, said the Sistine chapel in Rome was filled with nudes, done by Michaelangelo. However, he added, the Catholic church has "so degenerated" it probably wouldn't tolerate this kind of art in a church now.

Sloan complained many persons acted as if they were proud of their ignorance of art. "Would they be proud if they couldn't read?" he asked.

"Before you scold me any more," said the governor, "I want to say I like pretty pictures. This thing is not even pretty."

"By God," exclaimed Longley, apparently tense, "pictures were printed in newspapers and magazines, some that are 'completely obnoxious.'"

Sloan said the young sculptor's work was properly termed "Earth". The name "Fertility" was coined by The New Mexican for publicity's sake. "It was a clever idea," he said.

Mentioning Sloan and Will Shuster, also present, Randall Davey, artist, said: "None of us has ever been attacked on the ground of lack of morals."

"How is it possible for Mr. Brown, if he knows nothing about art, to say this is immoral?" queried Davey. He said it was up to the artists to decide. "I think we're making monkeys of ourselves by taking this thing up," he said.

None of the artists was as ignorant of morals as Mr. Brown was of art, said Shuster. He quoted that one: "Evil be to him who evil thinketh." He said Longley's design was beautiful, agreeing with his fellow-artists; there was nothing about it to cause any "sensual excitement."

No jury of artists has suggested that it was in the slightest pornographic, said Sloan.

"There are other people in the state besides artists," retorted Ray Smith, member of the Berean Baptist church.

"It's up to us to educate those people," said Sloan.

"It's up to us to educate you," said Smith.

When the discussion turned to the propriety of fig leaves Sloan said they were the work of somebody else; the artist.

"A Republican campaign sticker could be used just as well," Sloan said. "Or would you prefer a Democratic sticker?"

"Let's keep politics out of this," said the governor.

Sloan told the gentlemen of the cloth "I can show you things in the Bible that would make this look like lemonade."

"I can explain morals and you can't," Mr. Brown told Kruger.

Shuster asked the minister if he got any erotic stimulus out of "Fertility."

"It's repulsive and that's all," said the minister.

The furore over "Miss Fertility" began when one of Mr. Brown's congregation saw her a few days ago on the northwest corner of the new building. A vagrant wind had blown away the heavy paper covering her.

There are other "Fertilities" around the building, which still remain covered. She adorns one of six different figures, all the work of Longley, which have been placed in the other walls just beneath the second story windows. The others are a conquistador, a sun, an Indian, a mountain lion, representing New Mexico, and a priest-builder. Each of the series appears four times.

Governor Mabry ducked the issue by tossing it to the architect. There was not much surprise when he had the spandrels removed. Considering how small was the objecting minority, it was a fine display of lack of courage. Morgan informs me that when one of the spandrels was broken up, as it had to be to get it out of the wall, he got one breast as a souvenir for Harrison, the New Mexican's *editor, and he believes that McNulty got the other. At least one undamaged bas-relief is set up now, in a Santa Fe garden.*

OCTOBER 8, 1950:   MAN'S WORLD, EH?

By John McGuire.

Reports that our Mister McNulty has been standing by night on his rooftop, his eyes fixed longingly on the western horizon and his plaintive voice calling "Calla" instead of "Chloe" are only partially true. But it serves to illustrate the gentleman's realization that it isn't altogether a man's world.

This is not to say that Mister McNulty is not newspaperman enough to hold down any job on the staff, including the woman's page; it only means he's been a total washout as a woman. Calla Hay was never like this, and the place won't be the same until she returns from her California vacation.

By his own admission, McNulty has been in the newspaper business since Richard Harding Davis was writing freshman theses. But he has never learned to regard a pink tea in the same light as a story in which the faithless blonde murders her bookmaker husband with the butt of Junior's "Hopalong Cassidy" revolver. And it gets worse every day.

Two weeks ago, to make a stab at the date upon which we decided it was no longer prudent to refer to the greying man as "Abigail," a bunch of the local girls were whooping it up in one of the downtown flower shows. They had arranged, in their womanly way, to identify each flower arrangement for purposes of judging—and also to squeeze in more entries. The one that transformed Mister McNulty from a grimly determined society editor pro tempore into a sputtering drill sergeant was the little number labelled: Arrangement For A Sick Dollie.

Now McNulty is not a man who goes around trampling out petunias. On the contrary, his artist wife Agnes Tait has a virtual hothouse arrangement which disguises the entrance to their home. But you don't foist off that sick dollie business on this fellow. You could sooner sell him Brooklyn bridge.

Mrs. Hay knows her way around in this business of reporting the activities of women. She broke McNulty into the game by getting him nearly paralyzed at La Cantina. By the time he returned to the city room he was ready to show the P.E.O. a thing or two—and there was something about doing-this-thing-standing-on-my-head. He's been on his ear ever since.

Once long ago our Mister Bailey stepped into the society slot. He had to be billed as the "Only Society Editor In The World Who Chews Tobacco." Now that is a lot of hooey; Mister Bailey smokes a very neat cigaret exclusively. But it was good for his ego, and he did a creditable job.

McNulty had only the ephemeral stimulus of his favorite four fingers of Bellows to guide him into the job of woman's editor. If he has not increased his intake it's not because the A.A.U.W. and the W.C.T.U. haven't given him good reason. And he's thinking about switching over to Johnny Miles' camp after the big blowout by the Republican women. He keeps wishing Norman Thomas would run again.

If Paso Por Aqui seems to have shrivelled in length, or if the item about the bride's illusion veil sounds more like she was carrying an armful of railroad ties it is not because McNulty hasn't tried. We've seen him biting his lip as though he would just about go to pieces. He's tried to be a lady about the whole thing, girls, and you should hoist your creme de menthe in a show of united support.

But heaven help him who tells our McNulty his slip is showing.

OCTOBER 22, 1950: [*Banner headline above masthead, page one.*] HUGE RUSTLIN' DEAL CHARGED BIGGEST SINCE PANCHO VILLA BORDER RAIDS. TODHUNTER'S RANGE RAIDED; NET 101 CALVES.

By Bill Bailey,
New Mexican Staff Reporter.

DEMING, Oct. 21.—Cattle rustling, bigger than anything since Pancho Villa drove herds across the border, has been allegedly uncovered on the Diamond L ranch west of here, owned by the prominent and respected Margaret Todhunter. Bob Compton, 30-year-old foreman of the Diamond L, is in jail here in lieu of $30,000 bond facing trial on four charges and goes to Silver City Tuesday for arraignment on two more rustling charges. Mrs. Todhunter was not involved, officers said. One hundred and one cattle ranging from three to 10 months old were seized on the vast "West Ranch" of the Diamond L in a roundup ordered by Jim Miller, veteran brand inspector for the New Mexico Cattle Sanitary board. Joining him were sheriff's officers, state police, ranchers, cowboys and foremen from neighboring outfits that were victimized by the rustling. Mrs. Todhunter, widow of the widely known stockman Jim Todhunter, and the "Flying Grandmother" of Parade magazine and the motion pictures was completely excused of complicity, District Attorney Tom Foy of Silver City told The New Mexican. "She cooperated fully and her grandson Jimmie Porcher joined the roundup to rid the ranch of the stolen animals," said Foy. "She was in Hawaii, New York and all over the country while this was going on," the district attorney said.

The alleged theft of 101 animals, Foy told The New Mexican, is the biggest rustling activity uncovered in New Mexico of his knowledge since Pancho Villa raided the border ranches.

Compton, a single man, came to the Diamond L as a foreman in 1948. Today, Foy said, the FBI reported that he had been twice convicted of cattle theft in Texas. Details of the Texas cases had not been received.

JANUARY 7, 1951: ANGRY "I AM" MOB LAYS SIEGE TO NEW MEXI-
CAN ON SUIT TALE. Editors Get Faces Slapped by Disputants.

The New Mexican was in a state of siege and riot for five hours Saturday by throngs protesting publication of an article Friday referring to a damage suit filed against Mrs. Edna Ballard, president of the "I Am" activity.

Three employes were assaulted physically.

An antique table was crushed.

Four riotous individuals were evicted by police.

A restraining order against the group was issued by district court.

The newspaper and employees were threatened with—

Death by 5 P. M. by a divine hand.

A boycott by advertisers of the community.

A $10 million libel suit.

The wrath of "the flaming sword of St. Germaine."

Cancelled subscriptions.

Bankruptcy.

Further rioting.

Operation of the newspaper was suspended from 8:15 a.m. until about 1 p.m. as crowds who said they were "I Am" students swarmed through the halls and offices of the building berating all they encountered.

Managing editor John "Mickey" McGuire was slapped by a woman who refused to give her name when he instructed a typist to continue work after a visitor had ordered him to desist.

The same person, a portly woman in a fur-trimmed coat, seized Editor Will Harrison and shook him forcibly and slapped him soundly on the left cheek with a gloved right hand.

A young blonde, another who refused to give her name, encountered Society Editor Calla Hay with wide swings across a counter. Mrs. Hay suffered an injured finger.

An antique table in the office of Publisher Robert McKinney

was crushed, inadvertently, when a large number attempted to crowd into the room for a conference with Harrison.

Police were called shortly before 9 a.m. when a woman who did not identify herself encountered women employees in the circulation and classified advertising departments with a hexing oath. She pointed at them individually and repeated slowly "G—— damn you."

EXPLANATION.

"When I say 'G—— damn you' I mean damn you up inside," she explained as she moved from employee to employee. . . .

Assistant Women's Editor Gay Kaufmann was encountered by one of the crowd in the news room who implored "St. Germaine to stick a fiery sword in your guts." St. Germaine is a patron saint of the I Am activity.

A member of one of the mid-morning groups called down death on McGuire "by 5 p.m." Another set the same time for the death of Harrison.

The crowds, frequently at a riot stage as they surged through the building, came in groups ranging from half a dozen to forty. Harrison estimated that he talked to 240 during the day.

PROTESTED STORY.

They were protesting an article in the Friday paper which related that an I Am student had sued Mrs. Ballard for $25,000. . . .

Mrs. Ballard told Harrison and McKinney that the only statement she would make would be through her lawyers. She said the paper would be sued for libel, boycotted by the merchants of the city and submitted to further riots, unless there was a complete retraction Sunday of all that was published Friday and in equally big type.

Mrs. Ballard told Harrison and McKinney that the boycott, rioting and libel action would be called off if a copy of all material pertaining to the case were submitted to her and approved by her before publication Sunday. . . .

The protesting delegates repeatedly promised that the newspaper would go in bankruptcy and its employes be cast on the streets and selling shoestrings and pins, "and nobody will buy your pins."

While many of the protesters conducted themselves with dignity others were vehement in their denunciation. Reporter William McNulty was called "the biggest Communist in Santa Fe" and "the biggest pimp in New Mexico."

Tom Fleek, security officer at Los Alamos and husband of Jackie Fleek, New Mexican reporter, was in the office at the time of arrival of one of the groups. One of them swung at him, pointed a finger, and shouted: "Look, A Communist". . . .

Police armed with court injunctions and side arms were set up in relays to guard the New Mexican property over the weekend.

Obviously, Mrs. Ballard's legal position was untenable. Shortly after noon the New Mexican *obtained a restraining order against her from Judge David Carmody. In a Sunday editorial it not only rejected her terms but, seizing a fine opportunity, made a production of it.*

On January 12 the paper reported that Mrs. Ballard had apologized, everything was quiet, and it, in turn, had asked that the injunction it had obtained against the group be dismissed.

MAY 13, 1951: SAGE COMMENT.

By William McNulty.

In the arrogance of our youths we called him Cementhead Ryan but looking back over the years I wonder who were the cementheads, he or we. In any case, I think he made the most profound remark about women, sex and marriage I ever heard.

Nothing in Freud, Jung, Havelock Ellis, Sophocles or Lao-tse equals it for wisdom and if Cementhead's philosophy could be enforced, probably one quarter of the world's woes would vanish.

It was in the early prohibition days and Cementhead's was the hangout for the staff of the Lawrence News. The merit, the single merit of Cementhead's homebrew was that it was liquid; strange yeast formations, often in shapes like seashores [*seahorses?*] and other marine fauna used to float up and down in the glass. You simply poked in your beer with your finger and reached them out; to use a spoon would have been sissyish. The News was a rundown newspaper and the few dollars we got were earned the hard way. For one thing, we usually worked under physical difficulties, writing a story while a carpenter, knee on the desk, sawed at a board or hammered at a shelf. On account of a congenital failure to pay rent, the News was forced to move often, each time bringing on an outburst of office alterations.

The News editor was a haggard, harassed, ambulating cluster of stomach ulcers encased in a frail envelope of wrinkled flesh. The newspaper's morgue consisted solely of five cuts which he carried in the pocket of whatever suit he was wearing and which he would take out and riffle whenever one of the five persons was even remotely connected with a story.

These cuts were: (1) Mayor O'Brien, (2) Father O'Reilly, (3) Alderman Tom Bresnahan, (4) Street Superintendent Jack Brent and (5) Giuseppe Malovarde, the 1922 champion barber of Lawrence, Mass., and its suburbs.

Perhaps it should be explained that these barbershop competitions were among the most thrilling municipal events of Lawrence, Mass. They were financed by barber supply houses, the contests were held in the city hall, the barber chair being on the main floor and the contestants, mostly excitable Italians, performing before the crowded, cheering galleries.

The persons barbered were stumblebums who would do anything for a lazy buck and also—Jailer Ned Rafferty was understood to receive an unofficial $10 fee—the entire roster of unfortunates who had landed in the clink overnight; these were marched to the city hall and their ordeal in convict line. Anybody who balked was likely to feel the back of Rafferty's hand not to say the pressure of his foot. So high was the casualty rate at these fast barbering contests that confirmed lushes were known to keep off the stuff for as much as a week before the announced date.

The time each contestant was making was called each five seconds, the place was a bedlam and naturally, a piece of ear or a snip of gullet would fall to the floor, the sight of spurts of blood driving the onlookers to new frenzies.

As I said, Giuseppe Malovarde won the championship in 1922 but the period of Cementhead's place was three years later and the editor was still carrying Malovarde's cut in his pocket.

The most exciting thing about the News was whether you'd get paid on Saturday. The treasurer had a no doubt kindly intentioned method of letting us know he had failed to raise the payroll; he left the doors of the office safe wide open and went home. From then on, it was every man for himself selling classified ads over the counter; with each sale, you'd beat it down to Cementhead's.

Ryan was a morose hulk of a man; his legs were so short and his stomach so big that he seemed pyramid shape.

He sat at one end of the bar and waddled grudgingly to wait on the customers. A teetotaler, he held them in open contempt, but if they had to drink in some place, he felt it might as well be his.

The time I speak of, it was going on dusk and Ned Borland, the neighborhood fancy dan, happened to pass the saloon. Someone remarked that he was "chasing" so-and-so.

For once Cementhead volunteered a comment. He looked up in astonishment and said, "What's he chasing her for? He has a wife hasn't he?"

Let's see you top that out of Plato or Confucius.

On September 8, John Sloan died in Hanover, New Hampshire, at the age of eighty. It was the first summer that he had not spent in Santa Fe since he first arrived there in 1919 with Randall Davey.

SEPTEMBER 9, 1951:   LAST TRIBUTE PAID TO SLOAN BY OLD FRIENDS.

All of Santa Fe—everybody who knew of or heard of John Sloan—was saddened by his death Saturday. From men who knew him well, and loved him, came these final tributes to a long life and a happy one:

Will Shuster, one of Los Cinco Pintores and long-time friend of Sloan—John Sloan, the perpetually inquisitive, humorous, acid and violent child of art is dead.

Our friendship was so deep, his passing stuns me into wordlessness. I can only hope, as an artist's son, to have the courage and ability to build on the liberal and understanding foundations which he has revealed to me in 31 years of association.

Witter Bynner, poet—
FAREWELL, DEAR JOHN
Farewell, Dear John, who led us all with strength,
 With laughter, with indomitable pride:
Which means for us that in the final length
 And breadth of spirit it is we who died
Unless we feel goodbye with more than tears,
 Feel life, not death, from you, and use our years.
Witter Bynner.

Oliver La Farge, Pulitzer Prize novelist—I met Sloan when we collaborated on the book for the Misses White's remarkable Inter-Tribal Exposition of Indian Art. I was young and green; he received me as if he, too, were young. He was; he was a man who never grew old.

He whipped young men's minds with his extreme statements, his humor, his theories, his paradoxes, and his novelties. He was Irish, combative, never dull, pugnacious, sincere. His company was always electric and always fun. He had unlimited warmth to give—and I should hate to have had him for an enemy.

If a full dress biography of Sloan's eighty years is ever written, its proper title should be "Portrait of an Artist as a Young Man."

AUGUST 31, 1952: AN INSIGHT INTO CUSTOMS IN SANTA FE, A CAPITAL CITY OF THE UNITED STATES.

By Oliver La Farge.

This piece is being written in the calm before Zozobra, but it will appear in mid-Fiesta. This is the season of the maximum influx of visitors to Santa Fe, and also the season when the inhabitants of the Ancient City and environs let down their hair and act completely natural (i.e. slightly loony), just like the

City Council. For the benefit of those visitors who, on Sunday, may still be able to read fairly fine print, we shall explain a few things about Santa Fe and New Mexico that may have been puzzling them.

The name "Santa Fe" is pronounced "Santa Fay," and not "Santerfee." It is not correct to put an accent on the "e." It is a Spanish, not a French name.

Santa Fe is the capital of New Mexico, and New Mexico, many of our visitors will be disappointed to hear, is one of the 48 states of the Union. United States money is accepted here at face value —in fact, it is accepted avidly. You will not have to submit to a customs inspection or pay duty on the things you may buy here, unless possibly if you enter the Republic of Texas.

New Mexico is part of the United States, but it is not part of Texas. Texas is much longer and wider than New Mexico, but the latter state is a great deal thicker. Rhode Island is smaller, wetter, and has clams, while New Mexico is high and dry, and has tamales, hence the atomic bomb.

Santa Fe is very old and hence the streets are very tired. It is an old Spanish custom to apologize to a street when you bump over a rut. That rut may well have been started by one of De Vargas' men trailing his pike as he walked along. Treat it with respect. If you don't, it will bust your springs for you.

The Spanish-speaking people of Santa Fe are not Mexicans. They differ from Mexicans physically, in manner of speech, and in customs. They have fought for the United States in every war since, and including, the Civil War.

The Indians you see peddling their wares are not subsidized by the Chamber of Commerce or Fred Harvey. They are independent entrepreneurs and exemplify the rugged individualism and personal enterprise so valued by all good Republicans.

The government of this city is strictly nonpartisan, a curious fact since all members of the City Council are staunch adherents of either the Republican or the Democratic party. Regardless of party affiliation, the majority party always defends the status quo and is particularly quick to fight off any attempt to meddle with the police force, while the minority party always battles vainly for a long list of reforms. This has been going on for 250 years, and is another old Spanish custom.

The state Republican party has a habit of nominating ex-mayors of Santa Fe for governor or lieutenant governor, or both. This is because any man optimistic enough to accept the position of mayor of this madhouse will be game for almost anything. The Democrats then snow the candidate under, especially on the East Side. This is an old Texas custom.

The "Mexican" food that you may eat while you are here is not Mexican. It is local. Along the border, you find some similar dishes, but they are not identical. As you get well into Mexico the cuisine changes radically. A few dishes do remain pretty well constant; among these are chocolate and tamales, the consumption of which on festive occasions is an old Aztec custom. The Aztecs learned it from the Toltecs, the Toltecs learned it from the Mayas, and the Mayas learned it from the Old Santa Fe Association.

The first person to put a marshmallow in Mexican-style chocolate was Doña Encarnación Cantando y Bailando de Paniagua in 1884. She did it with the simple and reasonable intention of poisoning a deputy sheriff, instead of which she nourished and delighted him (thus achieving much the same ultimate end) and established a new Spanish custom.

All visitors are very welcome to Fiesta. We hope they will enjoy themselves as much as we enjoy watching their picturesque costumes and their interesting customs. The idea is for everyone to have a good time and feel at home. This is also an old Spanish custom.

In his first campaign for the presidency, General Eisenhower, speaking at Gallup, made history when he promised the Indians that they would be consulted in regard to the appointment of officials directly dealing with their affairs. The effect of this promise upon the Indians of the United States was electrifying. It produced, among other phenomena, the following advertisement by the Navajo Tribe in support of Glenn L. Emmons of Gallup, who was the man finally appointed commissioner of Indian affairs.

The tribe that had this advertisement published had come a long way from the marauding villains of the early 1860's or the unfortunate victims of the concentration camp at Bosque Redondo later in that decade, a little less than ninety years earlier.

DECEMBER 31, 1952: [*Full-page ad with headlines; page divided into three columns of text.*] A STATEMENT BY THE NAVAJO TRIBE ON THE APPOINTMENT OF A COMMISSIONER OF INDIAN AFFAIRS. A MESSAGE TO: ALL INDIAN TRIBES; ALL INDIAN WELFARE ORGANIZATIONS; GOVERNORS INTERSTATE INDIAN COUNCIL; AND PEOPLE OF THE UNITED STATES.

This letter is being written primarily to make known, publicly or otherwise, the wishes of the Navajo Nation in regard to who should be considered and appointed as the next Commissioner of Indian Affairs.

Since the national election, November 4, 1952, the newspapers have published many stories, and the mail of many Indian Tribes has been besieged with literature, urging the appointment of certain persons to the high office of Commissioner of Indian Affairs.

The Navajo Tribe, the largest in the Nation and living in three states, has reserved its appraisal of this situation until its leaders could make a thorough study of the qualifications of all persons who are being mentioned for this appointment.

THE NAVAJOS FEEL IT'S TIME TO SPEAK.

We have not been hasty in making our feelings known, for the decision President Eisenhower will make in the appointment of our leader is to us the most important decision he will make. With our very lives at stake, the Navajos chose to watch and wait and then to go minutely into the background of each person who has been mentioned for the appointment.

WHY THE NAVAJOS ARE SO CONCERNED.

Navajo life is an intense drama. The striving of the will of our people is the moving force in this drama. The Navajos must be turned from anticipated death, from fatalism to action, from inferiority to healthful pride; but under leadership of the past and present in Washington, that goal is not yet reached. We cry out for a leader who will truly give us physical and spiritual life. If this does not occur under Republican leadership, we must be ready to meet the long Indian Night—perhaps the last.

Democracy today is locked with anti-democratic forces in a world-wide struggle. The Navajos, and in a large measure every other Tribe, have waged a comparable struggle for many lifetimes. Their victory is important to our own country and to the world. The emerging Navajos and their brothers should play a decisive role in the struggle for the maintenance of democratic institutions.

NEW HOPE FOR THE INDIANS.

Ninety-five per cent of the Navajos voted the Republican ticket straight! This united front was crystalized with the visit of General Eisenhower to our Gallup, New Mexico ceremonials when he promised that the Navajos would play an important part in the naming of a new Commissioner. General Eisenhower turned the beam of public opinion on a shameful chapter in the nation's history.

During most of its 127 years of operation, the Bureau of Indian Affairs has pursued a shoddy course of costly mismanagement and political maneuvering under administrations of both parties. At times it seemed that the Bureau was going far out of its way to force many American Indians to the status of second-class citizens, under political, economic and social handicaps.

The Congress itself has not been without blame, for budget dollars for Indian reservation development has come grudgingly and in stingy amounts.

The Navajos of Arizona and New Mexico are long-suffering testimonials of the Bureau's bad faith. Americans are rightfully proud of their treaties made and kept with other nations. Yet, not once in the 84-year period since the signing has the Bureau, or the Congress, lived up to the full terms of the Treaty of 1868 between the United States and the Navajo Indians. . . . [*Continues with ringing endorsement of Glenn L. Emmons for Commissioner.*]

Advisory Committee of the Navajo Tribal Council
Sam Ahkeah, Chairman

On June 15, 1865, the New Mexican *announced the arrival of four Sisters of Charity who intended to establish a hospital. Shortly thereafter, it noted that the Sisters would be going about soliciting funds and urged that everyone contribute. The change that had occurred between then and 1953 in the situation of these nuns and their hospital is in its way as dramatic as that which occurred to the Navajos, who in 1865 were suffering and starving at Bosque Redondo.*

JANUARY 4, 1953:   THE SISTERS OF CHARITY.

Northern New Mexico owes a great debt of gratitude to the Sisters of Charity and the hundreds of persons who helped them, for the magnificent new St. Vincent hospital which is open for public inspection today for the first time. Accumulating the necessary $3,500,000 for this great institution of mercy was a staggering task. But many willing hands made it possible. Contractors, builders and suppliers helped, too, holding their costs to bare minimums, and in some cases taking no profit at all.

The handsome new hospital replaces the venerable old structure in which many medical miracles were performed, but which had become outmoded and a fire hazard throughout the long years of service to Santa Fe and northern New Mexico. It is safe to say that nowhere in a city of comparable size is there a better equipped, more modern hospital offering anything more to its patients in the way of facilities, care or comfort.

It has been a long, hard road for the Sisters of Charity since they first began caring for the sick in an adobe hut here in 1865. Those angels of mercy who first came here from Cincinnati probably never dreamed of a building so large, so perfect, for the carrying on of the work they started.

The Sisters of Charity have invited the public to inspect the new building today (Sunday) from 1 to 5 p.m. You will be thrilled by what you see.

In 1952, General Patrick J. Hurley ran against Senator Dennis Chavez, losing by a shade over 5,000 votes. General Hurley was

411

not helped in his campaign by an Oklahoma newspaper which published a hot editorial pleading with the people of New Mexico to elect a real "American" in place of the "Mexican" incumbent.

The loser contested the election, which led to an unusually careful study of election procedures in the state, under supervision of a Senate committee. Editorials, commentaries, and news stories ran all through 1953. We give two items here, because of the picture they give of what can go on in an election in New Mexico. In this instance, unlike earlier ones, the New Mexican's *coverage was factual and impartial.*

FEBRUARY 8, 1953:   BALLOTS SAID MISSING IN PAT-DENNIS CONTEST.

Forces of Republican Patrick J. Hurley, who is contesting the election of Sen. Dennis Chavez (D-NM), said Saturday more records of the November election are missing. Hurley spokesman Steve Alex, who earlier said all ballots had been burned in Dona Ana, Otero and Lincoln Counties, said investigators have found a number of pollbooks missing in San Miguel and Mora Counties. He said at least one book was burned and soaked so as to be illegible. These records were supposed to have been impounded in a Las Vegas bank, Alex said.

At Mora, Miss Peggy Cassidy, who took over as county clerk the first of the year, said ballot boxes, ballots and registration books of that county are impounded in the Las Vegas bank.

She said one registration book had been damaged—"I guess it might have been rained on. Some of the pages are torn, too. But the damage is old."

"I believe the pollbooks are locked in my office closet—all but one," she added. "I believe that book was sent to the secretary of state by mistake."

Manuel Galindre, San Miguel County clerk at Las Vegas said, "all the books are intact" in that county. "I have them in my office." He said other San Miguel election records are still impounded in the Las Vegas bank. . . .

"I have just verified that additional records have either been destroyed or are missing," Alex said. "Following our disclosure of yesterday that ballots were burned in three southern counties, we have discovered that pollbooks are missing in San Miguel and Mora Counties.

"Our investigators have been in Las Vegas and are unable to find six pollbooks in San Miguel County. Two and possibly others are missing in Mora County.

"As soon as our investigators began checking the Mora County books some additional books were brought in immediately, from where we don't know. One of them, from Precinct 26, had been immersed in water and the cover was burned. The inside pages were almost completely obliterated. Books for precincts 12-b and 22 were also brought in from some place unknown to us. All of those books, including those of Mora County, were supposed to have been impounded in the Las Vegas Savings Bank."

FEBRUARY 9, 1953:   DIG DEEPLY.

The senatorial investigators who come here to check up on Patrick Hurley's allegations of election irregularities may be forgiven if they arrive at the conclusion that New Mexico balloting practices are loose, to say the least. They will find that in three counties the ballots have been burned at the direction of a district judge, although notice of a contest had been served and the minimum time for destroying ballots after an election had not yet expired. They apparently also will find that poll books are missing in at least two counties where, if the books are not located, it will be almost impossible to check on the eligibility of voters.

In the light of these revelations it is hardly surprising that national commentators say New Mexico is noted for crooked elections.

Probably it would be a good thing for the Senate investigators to probe deeply into the last election and make public every instance of skullduggery they find. A few good, stiff jail raps hung on some of those who despoil our right of franchise would be a healthy thing.

Will Harrison, who, after he left the New Mexican, *became a highly successful political commentator, noted in his February 11 column that if all the eighteen thousand ballots included in the burned boxes were thrown out, Hurley would experience a net loss of fifty-three votes.*

The investigation dragged on through much of 1953, and the findings were not made public until after the close of the period covered in this book. The wild irregularities were a disgrace; they were also anciently familiar to New Mexicans, and they did not decisively favor anyone. The Senate committee could have ruled that no valid election had been held—and there were many in the state who hoped it would—but that step must have seemed too drastic. The irregularities were reported and condemned; the election of Chavez was upheld.

FEBRUARY 17, 1953: MORTUARY OPPOSES 'ENCHANTMENT' PLATE.

By Will Harrison.

The operator of a New Mexico funeral home has addressed a plea to the state Bureau of Revenue for special license plates for his hearses which do not have the state slogan, "Land of Enchantment" printed across the plates.

The firm's drivers, the letter said, are sometimes chided and embarrassed when transporting "clients" to such less enchanting places as Texas and California.

When the New Mexican *was first being published, three groups of Indians living within, or partly within, the state dominated the news—the Navajos, the Apaches, and the "Utahs." Above, at the end of 1952, we heard from the Navajos. Now the Apaches reappear, also in a new role.*

FEBRUARY 18, 1953: 'RED HATS' BIG HELP IN FORESTS.

By Mrs. Tom Charles and Steve Lowell.

Mescalero (AP)—"Apaches!" Hearts beat fast and frontiersmen in the Old West grabbed their rifles when they heard that cry.

414

Nowadays, to a rancher, a lumberman, or the people of a tiny mountain village threatened by a raging forest fire, the word the once-fierce tribesmen are coming brings new hope.

From the Mescalero Apaches, the Forest Service has wrought the nucleus of a band of expert timber fire battlers.

It was in 1948 that A. B. Shields, forest ranger on the Mescalero reservation, asked for volunteers to form a crack fire-fighting outfit.

Just back from World War II, 19 descendants of Apache chieftains, Cochise, Naiche, Victorio and Geronimo responded to form the "Red Hats."

The Forest Service had a hunch the Apaches with their background of rigorous life, personal ruggedness and knowledge of woods lore would make good fire crews. The government agency was right.

Out of the training came the core of an organization which has grown to 100 men and has earned compliments all over the West....

After their job in Trinity Forest, Ranger Ralph W. White wrote the Mescalero officials:

"Your crews were far and above all other crews on the fire.... As for fire line construction, I personally would prefer one 25-man Indian crew to any other three 25-man crews to which we have access"....

The Mescaleros have won so much acclaim that the Indian Service is spreading training to other reservations over the Southwest—to the Hopis of Arizona; to the Santa Clara, Isleta, Zuñi and Santo Domingo pueblos of New Mexico; to the White River Apache Reservation of Arizona; and to the Jicarilla Apaches of New Mexico.

Since the publication of this report, the tribes named and some others have distinguished themselves as fire fighters all over the West, with the Red Hats still in the lead. That organization grew up quite naturally from the recruitment of Mescaleros to protect their own timber, which is their reservation's principal asset.

It is too bad that during these last years the Utes failed to break

*into print. It was not until later that they won their famous, $30,-
000,000 damage suit against the United States and set up remarkable programs of community development and progress. One Ute
tribe, after seeking medical advice on certain problems, is now
having itself psychiatrized en masse. For the sake of contrast, we
refer the reader to the second item for November 28, 1849.*

*Under the date of January 21, 1922, we reported the official
recognition of the volunteer fire department by the city. Since
then it has continued as one of the marvels of Santa Fe—a volunteer outfit governed by rigorous rules, that gives the city first-class,
professional-level protection. It is highly fitting, as this record
draws to a close, to include another mention of that remarkable body.*

OCTOBER 22, 1953:   THE DEBT GROWS.

Once again Santa Fe doffs its hat to its volunteer firemen—the
men who walked into the teeth of yesterday's roaring Colwes
Pontiac fire and fought it to a standstill, preventing it from
spreading to an adjoining structure. Reports up to this moment
indicate that Chief Ellis Bauer and his men did a magnificent job.

The New Mexican account of the fire told an eyewitness story
of how one of the firemen—one of the two badly cut by flying
glass—risked his life to pour water on the seething mass of flames
despite the flying glass and the gagging smoke. The story also
mentioned that the Colwes fire was probably the worst here in a
decade or so—another tribute to the promptness of the fire-fighting force and the fire-prevention work it carries on.

When one considers that these men are "amateurs" who devote many hours of their time without pay to learn the intricate
craft of protecting the city against fire, the debt owed by the rest
of us becomes more obvious.

Santa Fe is most fortunate to have a million-dollar fire department at a nickel's cost.

Remorselessly, New Mexico is changing. Our concluding three items record important aspects of that change, in regard to the political positions of the once dominant Spanish-Americans, of the Roman Catholic church, and, once again, of the Indians. The "Dixon Case," summarized in the second story, was initiated on March 10, 1948, by a number of Protestants resident in or near the mountain town of Dixon.

NOVEMBER 2, 1953: SPANISH-ANGLO POLITICAL BALANCE SHOWS SIGNS OF BEING WASHED OUT.

By Will Harrison.

New Mexico's historical division of public offices among those of Spanish and Anglo names is in danger of being entirely washed out next year.

It is a natural consequence of the great influx of Anglo voters but leaders of both parties are worried about the consequences. They hope to restore some semblance of balance in next February's state nominating conventions but their prospects are dim.

When these characters get the running fever they are not easily deterred by appeals for harmony and fairness.

Presently there are only two of 15 elective officials in the statehouse with Spanish names. This is the lowest number in all the history of the state.

The most significant break in the custom of balancing the tickets on this basis came in 1950 when the office of secretary of state went to Beatrice Roach, the first in the history of the state with a non-Spanish background to hold the office.

In recent elections both parties have paired Anglo and Spanish names in the governor and lieutenant governor positions but even this gesture is imperilled according to the talk that is going on now about prospective candidates for those places.

NOVEMBER 11, 1953: FAMED 'DIXON CASE' NOW A CLOSED ISSUE.

By Robert Zimmerman.

A long battle over separation of church and state in the New Mexico public school system came to a quiet end last week. At-

417

torneys in the historic legal proceedings called the "Dixon Case" announced there would be no further appeals. . . .

The 28 persons who joined to become plaintiffs in the Dixon suit charged that members of religious orders had failed to make adequate separation of religion and education in the public schools where they taught.

The suit, filed by Santa Fe attorney Harry Bigbee, charged that the teachers deliberately "introduced the teaching of Catholicism" into public schools. . . .

Six months later the case came to trial before District Judge E. T. Hensley, Jr., of Portales, who was appointed to hear the case after District Judge David Carmody withdrew.

In the seven days of the trial, 95 witnesses took the stand and 178 exhibits were introduced as evidence. The black and brown habits of nuns and brothers were seen frequently in the courtroom, and dozens of members of religious orders took their turn in the witness chair.

Witnesses testified that crucifixes were displayed in classrooms, prayers were recited, and, in some instances, Catholic students were dismissed to visit a priest for confession during school hours.

Catholic teachers did not dispute many of the allegations, but emphasized that prayers were said only "before" and "after" regular school classes, and that religious instruction was not a part of the curriculum for non-Catholic students. . . .

Five months later [*Judge*] Hensley filed his full, written decision and judgment in the case. It had an earthquake effect on the school systems of northern New Mexico.

He specifically banned 124 nuns and brothers from future teaching in New Mexico public schools, ordered that tax-supported classes no longer be held in church-owned buildings, and ruled that free textbooks and free bus transportation could not be extended to private and parochial schools.

On the other hand, Hensley found nothing wrong with the practice itself of employing nuns and brothers in public schools, provided that religious doctrine was not injected into their teaching.

The next round of the famous case took place in the supreme

court. While legal aspects were still being argued . . . Archbishop Edwin V. Byrne announced that members of the Catholic orders would no longer take teaching jobs in the public schools. . . .

Defense attorneys sought to have the case dismissed because of Archbishop Byrne's announcement, but the supreme court held that the case should be pursued to a conclusion in a legal sense. . . . [*The supreme court opinion was written by Justice James Mc-Ghee. It upheld the principal points of the district court's decision. Fifty new classrooms had to be built to replace those formerly in church-owned buildings.*]

One northern county school supervisor said he hoped the state would not forget the debt owed to Catholic nuns who pioneered as teachers in backward areas of New Mexico and who, in many cases, maintained schools in circumstances which would have discouraged many a lay teacher.

"I think it can only be regarded as a good thing we have eliminated constitutional violations from our school systems," he added, "but it is indeed regrettable that we had to lose so many good teachers at the same time."

DECEMBER 2, 1953: CHARGE MOCKERY. ZUNIS PROTEST DANCES BY SCOUTS.

La Junta, Colo. (AP)—The leader of the Koshares Boy Scouts vigorously denies his youngsters ridicule dances of the Zuni Pueblo Indians of New Mexico.

Yesterday, the Zunis, angered by what they consider a mockery of their sacred religious dances, said they plan to appeal to U. S. Indian Commissioner Glenn Emmons and consult attorneys.

Pueblo Gov. Conrad Lesarlley displayed a picture story from the Denver Post showing La Junta Scouts imitating the sacred Shalako and Mudhead dances.

"These are sacred dances," Lesarlley said. "These boys are not Indians. They are mocking us."

Lesarlley said tribal leaders are considering barring non-Indian spectators from the annual Shalako feast of dedication and thanksgiving. Hundreds of guests witnessed ceremonies Monday night.

J. F. Burshears, La Junta scoutmaster, said, "We are not trying to ridicule or make fun of the dances in any way. We have attempted to interpret the sacred dances because we think they are beautiful."

He praised his troop for having "interested more people in Indian dancing" than could otherwise have been possible. The troop has performed such dances numerous times through the West.

Burshears said the annual winter ceremonial of the Koshares is scheduled Dec. 26–27 and the boys expect to invite Zuni and other Indian groups to attend.

It seems often to be difficult for white men to believe that Indians who retain their old religions have no more desire to have their sacred forms of worship publicized as entertainments than would white Christians wish to have the more sacred parts of their services similarly exploited. The Governor of Zuñi was able to get his point across, however, and the Boy Scouts since then have performed only those dances that the Indians approve. In exchange, the Zuñis have given them some extra coaching.

New Mexico changes, and so does Santa Fe, but neither the state nor its capital has yet entirely lost its old qualities. There was the case of the ballot box from one of the western counties, the keys of which had been put inside the box before it was locked. To get it open took a tricky legal procedure before proper witnesses, and when opened, in addition to votes and keys, the box was found to contain a ristra, *or string of red chili.*

I am happy to be able to report that in 1956, on the Camino del Monte Sol, *a sculptor with a pickax forced a large out-of-state paving company to realign its entire curb, which had been laid out and poured so as to encroach on private property. Further, during the Fiestas of 1958, three young ladies rode their ponies into the lobby of La Fonda, passing over the spot where, ninety-one years earlier, Chief Justice Slough fell with his derringer in his hand, and one took her animal without incident on through the bar and into the outdoor dining space behind. The horses behaved admirably and the visitation was well received.*

INDEX

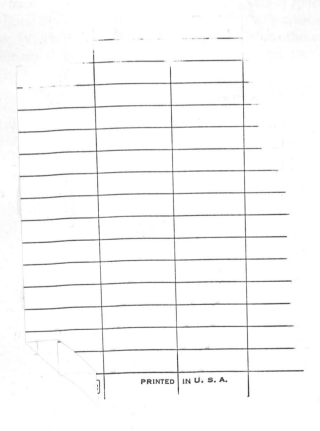

PRINTED IN U. S. A.

SANTA FE

Has been set in 11-point Electra with 2 points of spacing between the lines. Electra was designed by the American artist and typographer, W. A. Dwiggins. The serifs are flat, but otherwise old-style traditions are observed. Electra was chosen for this book for its legibility and sharpness of design.

UNIVERSITY OF OKLAHOMA PRESS : NORMAN